Distributed Relational Database
Cross-Platform Connectivity and Applications

Silvio Podcameni
Manfred Mittelmeir
Michele Chilanti

International Technical Support Organization
San Jose, California 95120

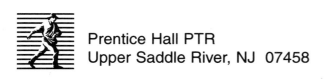

Prentice Hall PTR
Upper Saddle River, NJ 07458

Editorial/Production Supervision: Craig Little
Acquisitions Editor: Michael Meehan
Manufacturing Manager: Alexis R. Heydt
Cover Design: Design Source
Cover Design Director: Jerry Votta
Valuable production assistance provided by Gail Wojton of the ITSO Raleigh Center

Published by Prentice Hall PTR
Prentice-Hall Inc.
A Simon & Schuster Company
Upper Saddle River, NJ 07458

The publisher offers discounts on this book when ordered in bulk quantities.
For more information, contact: Corporate Sales Department, Prentice Hall PTR,
One Lake Street, Upper Saddle River, NJ 07458; Phone: 800-382-3419; fax: 201-236-7141;
email: corpsales@prenhall.com

Printed in the United States of America

10 9 8 7 6 5 4 3 2 1

ISBN 0-13-570797-8

Third Edition (June 1996)

This edition applies to current versions and releases of IBM distributed relational database products
(DB2 for MVS/ESA, SQL/DS for VM, SQL/DS for VSE, DB2 for OS/400, DB2 for AIX, DB2 for OS/2).
Consult the latest edition of the applicable IBM bibliography for current information on the product.

Comments may be addressed to: IBM Corporation, International Technical Support Organization,
Dept. 471, Building 80-E2, 650 Harry Road, San Jose, CA 95120-6099

When you send information to IBM, you grant IBM a nonexclusive right to use or distribute the
information in any way it believes appropriate without incurring any obligation to you.

Prentice-Hall International (UK) Limited, *London*
Prentice-Hall of Australia Pty. Limited, *Sydney*
Prentice-Hall Canada Inc., *Toronto*
Prentice-Hall Hispanoamericana, S.A., *Mexico*
Prentice-Hall of India Private Limited, *New Delhi*
Prentice-Hall of Japan, Inc., *Tokyo*
Simon & Schuster Asia Pte. Ltd., *Singapore*
Editora Prentice-Hall do Brasil, Ltda., *Rio de Janeiro*

Contents

Figures

Tables

Preface

This book is the result of a project run at the IBM International Technical Support Organization (ITSO) Centers in Boeblingen, Poughkeepsie, Rochester, and San Jose to set up DRDA connectivity between DB2 for OS/2, DB2 for AIX, DB2 for OS/400, SQL/DS for VM and VSE, and DB2 for MVS/ESA across networks and run applications accessing all platforms. It is based on an actual DRDA network linking the ITSO Centers in Europe and the United States. Network connectivity issues are addressed, and guidelines are presented to establish DRDA communications across networks. Information is provided to guide the reader through the steps required to set up the communications and database connectivity. The material is based on the actual installations performed and experience gained during the project. Sample applications that query and update databases in the network from any of the participating centers are also provided.

Audience

This book is written for technical personnel responsible for setting up Distributed Relational Database Architecture (DRDA) connectivity among IBM relational database products. A background in Systems Network Architecture (SNA) communications is assumed, as well as a basic knowledge of the IBM relational database products and their associated operating systems.

How This Book Is Organized

This book is organized as follows:

- Chapter 1, "Introduction"

  In this chapter we summarize what we achieved during the residency. We also position the Distributed Relational Database Architecture (DRDA) in the marketplace and provide some hints and tips on distributed project management.

- Chapter 2, "What's New?"

  In this chapter we describe the new functions provided by the products we used to build our distributed database environment.

- Chapter 3, "DRDA Concepts and DB2 Products"

  In this chapter we describe the basic principles and concepts of using DRDA to connect IBM relational database management systems (RDBMSs) on different operating systems.

- Chapter 4, "ITSO System Scenario"

  In this chapter we describe the network and systems setup for the IBM ITSO centers where the DRDA connectivity project was conducted. We also describe the software and hardware used for this project in each ITSO center.

- Chapter 5, "OS/2 Platform"

  In this chapter we describe the different connectivity options for DB2 for OS/2 and explain how to set up a configuration to have an OS/2 workstation act as a DRDA application requester (AR) and application server (AS).

- Chapter 6, "AIX Platform"

  In this chapter we describe the different connectivity options for DB2 for AIX and explain how to set up a configuration to have an AIX workstation act as a DRDA AR and AS.

- Chapter 7, "DB2 common server Client Connectivity"

  In this chapter we present some factors to consider when you implement DB2 common server client connectivity using the RDS private protocol. We describe connectivity considerations for both the server and the client workstations.

- Chapter 8, "DB2 for OS/400 Platform"

  In this chapter we discuss the tasks involved to enable DB2 for OS/400 to perform the DRDA AS and AR functions. All of the tasks completed for the OS/400 platform were carried out on systems located in Rochester and San Jose.

- Chapter 9, "VM and VSE Platforms"

  In this chapter we discuss the tasks involved to enable SQL/DS for VM and SQL/DS for VSE to perform the DRDA AS functions. We describe how to implement the DRDA AR functions in SQL/DS for VM. All of the tasks completed for the VM and VSE platforms were carried out on the system located in Boeblingen.

- Chapter 10, "MVS Platform"

  In this chapter we discuss the tasks involved to enable DB2 for MVS/ESA to perform the DRDA AS and AR functions. All of the tasks completed for the MVS platform were carried out on the system located in Poughkeepsie.

- Chapter 11, "Application Development Considerations"

  This chapter contains some considerations on migrating DRDA level 1 applications to DRDA level 2 and porting DRDA applications across different DB2 products. With DRDA level 2, applications can keep multiple connections active at the same time. You may need to redesign part of your applications to take full advantage of this feature. However, in many cases you can migrate to the new functions in a rather smooth way and still achieve performance advantages.

- Chapter 12, "Application Structure"

  In this chapter we provide several application examples using DRDA across the various DB2 product platforms. The purpose of this chapter is to provide application developers with a set of simple code samples highlighting the characteristics of the various DB2 product platforms as ASs and ARs.

- Chapter 13, "Program Preparation: DB2 common server"

  In this chapter we describe the steps required to prepare a DB2 common server program designed to access data in different DB2 database servers. The style of program preparation described refers to programs developed using static and dynamic embedded SQL statements. This chapter does not provide information about call level interface which does not require a program to be precompiled or bound.

- Chapter 14, "Program Preparation: DB2 for OS/400"

  In this chapter we provide information about preparing and running our applications on DB2 for OS/400. The programs were developed on the AS/400 platform but can run with very minor changes on other platforms.

- Chapter 15, "Program Preparation: SQL/DS"

  In this chapter we present guidelines for application implementation and migration for applications coded in other platforms and designed to access SQL/DS (that is, SQL/DS as a DRDA AS) and those "home-grown" applications in SQL/DS that have to interact with the RDBMs of other platforms.

- Chapter 16, "Program Preparation: DB2 for MVS/ESA"

  In this chapter we describe the steps required to prepare a DB2 for MVS/ESA application designed to access data in different database servers.

- Chapter 17, "Code Page Translation"

  Different systems represent data in different ways. When data is moved from one system to another, data conversion is performed when required. DRDA products support such conversion. In this chapter we discuss some data conversion considerations for the SQL/DS and DB2 common server platforms.

- Appendix A, "SNA Definitions and Connectivity Parameters"

  In this appendix we present some SNA definitions and explain their relationship to the DRDA connectivity parameters.

- Appendix B, "Problem Determination for DB2 common server"

  In this appendix we explain how to tackle problems experienced with DB2 or DDCS common server by using the facilities provided by the underlying operating environment, the products themselves, and additional products.

*   Appendix C, "Bibliography"

    In this appendix we list related publications where you may find more information on this subject.

Special Notices

This publication describes how you can use the IBM Distributed Relational Database Architecture (DRDA) to integrate IBM relational database products into a network. It is written primarily for customer personnel and IBM technical professionals with networking responsibilities in heterogeneous environments.

The information in this publication is not intended as the specification of any programming interfaces that are provided by DRDA or the products supporting it. See the PUBLICATIONS section of the IBM Programming Announcement for the current level of the products listed below for more information on the formal product documentation:

*   ACF/VTAM
*   AIX
*   AIX/6000
*   CICS/VSE
*   DB2 for MVS/ESA
*   DB2 for OS/2
*   DB2 for OS/400
*   DB2 for AIX
*   DDCS for OS/2
*   DDCS for AIX
*   MVS/ESA
*   OS/400
*   SQL/DS
*   VM/ESA
*   VSE/ES

References in this publication to IBM products, programs or services do not imply that IBM intends to make these available in all countries in which IBM operates. Any reference to an IBM product, program, or service is not intended to state or imply that only IBM's product, program, or service may be used. Any functionally equivalent program that does not infringe any of IBM's intellectual property rights may be used instead of the IBM product, program or service.

Information in this book was developed in conjunction with use of the equipment specified, and is limited in application to those specific hardware and software products and levels.

IBM may have patents or pending patent applications covering subject matter in this document. The furnishing of this document does not give you any license to these patents. You can send license inquiries, in writing, to the IBM Director of Licensing, IBM Corporation, 500 Columbus Avenue, Thornwood, NY 10594 USA.

The information contained in this document has not been submitted to any formal IBM test and is distributed AS IS. The information about non-IBM (VENDOR) products in this manual has been supplied by the vendor and IBM assumes no responsibility for its accuracy or completeness. The use of this information or the implementation of any of these techniques is a customer responsibility and depends on the customer's ability to evaluate and integrate them into the customer's operational environment. While each item may have been reviewed by IBM for accuracy in a specific situation, there is no guarantee that the same or similar results will be obtained elsewhere. Customers attempting to adapt these techniques to their own environments do so at their own risk.

The following terms are trademarks of the International Business Machines Corporation in the United States and/or other countries:

ACF/VTAM	Advanced Peer-to-Peer Networking
AIX	AIX/6000
AnyNet	APPN
AS/400	AT
BookManager	BookMaster
C Set ++	C/MVS
C/VM	C/2
C/400	CICS
CICS OS/2	CICS/ESA
CICS/MVS	CICS/VSE
CICS/VM	CICS/6000
COBOL/2	COBOL/370
COBOL/400	Current
DATABASE 2	DATABASE 2 OS/400
DataHub	DataJoiner
DataRefresher	DB2
DB2/2	DB2/400
DB2/6000	Distributed Relational Database Architecture
Distributed Application Environment	Distributed Database Connection Services/2
DRDA	ES/3090
FFST	FFST/2
First Failure Support Technology	IBM
ILS/400	IMS
IMS/ESA	InfoWindow
Integrated Language Environment	Language Environment
MVS/ESA	NetView
Operating System/2	Operating System/400
OS/2	OS/400
PC/XT	Personal System/2

PROFS	PS/2
RACF	RETAIN
RISC System/6000	S/370
S/390	SAA
ServicePac	SP
SQL/DS	SQL/400
System/370	Systems Application Architecture
Virtual Machine/Enterprise Systems Architecture	VisualAge
VisualGen	VM/ESA
VM/XA	VSE/ESA
VTAM	WIN-OS/2
3090	400

The following terms are trademarks of other companies:

ENCINA is a trademark of Transarc Corporation.

C-bus is a trademark of Corollary, Inc.

PC Direct is a trademark of Ziff Communications Company and is used by IBM Corporation under license.

UNIX is a registered trademark in the United States and other countries licensed exclusively through X/Open Company Limited.

Microsoft, Windows, and the Windows 95 logo are trademarks or registered trademarks of Microsoft Corporation.

C++	American Telephone and Telegraph Company, Incorporated
CompuServe	CompuServe, Incorporated and H&R Block, Incorporated
DCE	The Open Software Foundation
DEC	Digital Equipment Corporation
Hewlett-Packard, HP	Hewlett-Packard Company
Intel	Intel Corporation
IPX, NetWare, Novell	Novell, Incorporated
Microsoft C, MS	Microsoft Corporation
Network File System, NFS	Sun Microsystems, Incorporated
Solaris, Sun, SunOS	Sun Microsystems, Incorporated
Sun Microsystems	Sun Microsystems, Incorporated
X/Open	X/Open Company Limited

Other trademarks are trademarks of their respective companies.

Acknowledgments

The advisors for this project were:

Manfred Mittelmeier
ITSO Boeblingen

Michele Chilanti
ITSO Rochester

Silvio Podcameni
ITSO San Jose

The authors of this book were:

Amy Poon
ISSC Australia

Ana Paula Bueno
IBM Brazil

Gonzalo Quesada
IBM Puerto Rico

Karlheinz Scheible
IBM Germany

Ludwig Wilfert
IBM Germany

Luigi Walter Sartori
IBM Italy

Marcela Toledo
IBM Mexico

Pierre Bernier
IBM Belgium

Rosa Aurora Martinez Salinas
IBM Mexico

Thanks to the following people for the invaluable advice and guidance provided in the production of this book:

IBM Rochester Development Laboratory—USA

Carla Sadtler
ITSO Raleigh

Dave Bennin
ITSO Poughkeepsie

Miguel Crisanto
ITSO Austin

Guido De Simoni
ITSO San Jose

Peter Shum
IBM Toronto Laboratory—Canada

Steve Ritland
IBM Rochester Laboratory—USA

James Pickel
IBM Santa Teresa Laboratory—USA

Cathie Dwyer
DM Strategy and Architecture—USA

Mel Zimowski
DM Strategy and Architecture—USA

Michael J. Swift
Marketing Center—USA

Art Cuellar
Management Technical Marketing Support—USA

Rene Thomine
IBM France

Chapter 1. Introduction

In this chapter we summarize what we achieved during the residencies conducted at the IBM International Technical Support Organization (ITSO) centers in Boeblingen, Germany, Rochester, Minnesota, and San Jose, California. We also position the Distributed Database Architecture (DRDA) in the marketplace and provide some hints on managing distributed projects.

1.1 Results: What We Have

As a result of the work done during the residencies, we established a fully operational Distributed Relational Database Architecture (DRDA) environment linking SQL-speaking relational databases running C language applications against each other's data. This basic framework will also serve as a basis for future ITSO activities in the DRDA and client/server field.

The configuration described in this document includes all currently available DRDA database platforms:

- DB2 for MVS/ESA
- DB2 for OS/2
- DB2 for OS/400
- DB2 for AIX
- SQL/DS for VM/ESA
- SQL/DS for VSE/ESA

To achieve a realistic environment we set up the relational database platforms connecting four IBM ITSOs in different locations and on both sides of the Atlantic.

The decision to place the platforms as far apart as ITSO geography permitted was driven by our desire to get a better "feel" of real-life arenas instead of controlled laboratory-like environments.

This truly distributed setup gave us the means to illustrate the benefits and capabilities of DRDA support for client/server computing. We also accumulated valuable experience with the communications and setup issues in a complex real-world environment with which businesses are expected to interact when developing global applications.

In Figure 1 on page 2 we show the main elements of the network setup for the joint DRDA project among four ITSOs. This project is based on the DRDA connectivity and application exploitation residency.

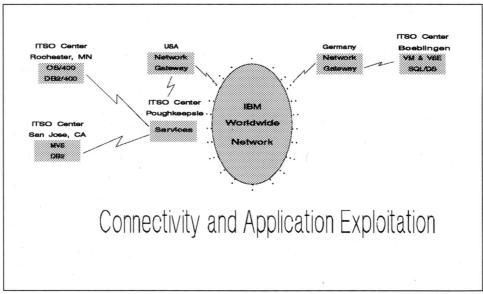

Connectivity and Application Exploitation

Figure 1. *The ITSO DRDA Network:.* Overview of the ITSO Setup for DRDA Cross-Connectivity

1.2 Benefits: What You Get from DRDA

The experiences we document in this book will help you make the most of DRDA and its client/server features to achieve

- Information availability when and where you need it

- Data collection and validation at the source

- Simplified application development across platforms and networks

- Optimum availability and shorter access time with local data

- Access to data on remote platforms as needed

- Location and platform-transparent application coding

- Transparent platform migration

- Application development simplicity: C code on all platforms (COBOL is another alternative)
- Decision support: Queries to remote SQL databases with no code
- Cross-platform mobility for programmers and end users

1.3 DRDA: An All-Around Performer

DRDA provides more than just client/server capabilities. Globalization of your database structure enhances your response capabilities in the marketplace.

DRDA helps you make the most of business opportunities:

- Tactical advantage with local database capabilities
  - Short order turnaround time
  - Data delegation to those directly involved
  - Data entry at the source in real time
  - Data validation at the source, also in real time
  - Fast response to market shifts
  - Host-league security functions
  - Enhanced backout, backup, and recovery features.
- Strategic advantage with global database capabilities
  - Updated enterprise-wide statistics, accounting, forecasting
  - Accurate managerial view of the enterprise
  - Consistent data across your enterprise
  - Decreased amount of redundant data
  - Enhanced backup and recovery of enterprise-critical data
  - Access to remote relational data from user-friendly workstation applications
  - Easy access to mainframe databases
  - Portable code with portable SQL database access
- Locations teamwork—DRDA helps you pool skills and harness the talent across your enterprise's structure.
  - Common language across locations
  - Ownership for each location's data
  - Security delegation

- Data consistency
- Common view of opportunities and issues
- Personnel redeployment without retraining

1.4 Technical Skills: Knowing Your Turf

A unified DRDA information picture across your enterprise enables you to pool your costly information technology personnel resources and share valuable knowledge at every level.

- Networking experts get a unified enterprise view.
- Workstation database users benefit from host database specialists.
- Host database specialists can relate to the workstation users' problems to better understand them.
- Users can get data requirements across to host database specialists in the same language.
- Workstation programmers and host programmers share code and specifications.
- Support expenses are lower than they are with multiple architectures.

1.5 Distributed Project Management

As your information technology projects grow in scope and span wider geographical areas, it is important to keep the workgroups synchronized. For our distributed project we found the following techniques useful:

- Regular conference calls among the participating groups to
    - Report on project progress from each side
    - Agree on format issues to synchronize documentation
    - Brainstorm ideas from different platforms' viewpoints
    - Exchange connectivity and system programming tips
    - Discuss general problems and suggest strategies to tackle them
- E-mail exchange, often as a result of conference calls, to document resulting ideas and directives. For example, OfficeVision's support for distribution lists was a timesaving feature.
- Fax was available but seldom necessary thanks to the previous two tools.
- BookManager and BookMaster publishing helped merge the separate documents of each residency into this joint document.

Additional issues inherent to distribution over a wide geographical area inevitably crop up when considering distributed databases. Their timely consideration will help minimize their impact on the enterprise's performance. Some examples:

- Time zone differences have an impact on
  - Key personnel availability
  - System workload at remote site
  - System downtime at remote site
  - Backup windows
- Character translation among platforms
- Communication delays

1.6 A Case Study: ITSO Customer Scenario

The IBM ITSOs are striving to model global customer scenarios to better understand customer requirements and needs. The setup described in this book linking ITSO locations in Europe and the United States brings together IBM's various relational database manager products configured in deliberately unlike platforms to explore the possibilities of DRDA and demonstrate its application support capabilities.

This project aimed at gathering technical know-how from all of IBM's support centers and was the first in a series of similar and related activities with a strong emphasis on multiple-platform support and cross-environment connectivity. It was also in itself an experiment in distributing work across different countries and languages. As you can see in Figure 1 on page 2 we had two ITSOs linking to the central Poughkeepsie ITSO in the United States. The Poughkeepsie ITSO, in turn, gained access through a gateway to the IBM world network, to which the Germany ITSO was also connected by a separate gateway.

1.7 Focal System Management

Besides distributing your data and applications, IBM tools can help enterprises manage their information technology issues on a global scale, both now and tomorrow, in areas such as

- Multiple network administration: NetView
- Multiple database administration and operation: DataHub
- DRDA level 2: Distributed unit of work (DUW)
- Performance and tuning: Common database concepts across platforms

- Applications development: VisualGen

1.8 Trends and Directions: Toward Interenterprise Networks

In the near future, you will not only face the task of interconnection within your own enterprise but will also have to talk to other corporations as well. There is a bounty of information waiting to be tapped. Some examples are:

- Banks merging information with overseas affiliates
- Transactions involving several financial institutions
- Corporations linking with taxation agencies
- Manufacturers requesting standards from agencies (ISO, ANSI)
- International catalog sales companies linking up with overseas partners
- Hospitals trading disease statistics and organ transplant rosters
- Public libraries and information banks accessing outside documents

DRDA, an *open* standard for SQL database communications pioneered by IBM, is built on solid foundations and standards and is up to the challenge of global communications. It offers

- Rich variety of database functions
- Robust support for ongoing improvements and extensions
- Third-party availability
- Incorporability by leading software vendors
- Potential to integrate
  - IBM platforms
  - Non-IBM platforms
  - Across multiple networks
  - Across multiple corporations
  - Support for current and future application development

IBM is commited to DRDA development with its ongoing work to extend the power and capability of DRDA to all participating platforms, ensuring growth and migration paths for SQL products in AIX, MVS/ESA, OS/2, OS/400, VM/ESA, and VSE/ESA.

Access to non-IBM products and protection for your investment in those products are guaranteed as the non-IBM suppliers adhering to the DRDA standard gradually make it available.

1.9 DRDA Implementation Status

Table 1 on page 8 shows the DRDA implementation status for non-IBM vendors who have licensed the DRDA architecture. Table 2 on page 9 shows the DRDA implementation status for IBM products.

Table 1. *DRDA Implementation Status of Non-IBM Vendors*

Vendor	Status 1	Status 2	Status 3	Status 4	Status 5	Status 6	Status 7	Status 8
Attachmate	x	x						
Borland International, Inc.								
Cincom Systems, Inc.								
Computer Associates Intl., Inc.								
Cross Access Corporation								
FileTek, Inc.			X	X				
Grandview DB/DC Systems	X		X		X		X	
Information Builders Inc. (IBI)								
Informix Software, Inc.	X	X						
Novell								
Object Technology Intl., Inc. (OTI)	X	X						
Oracle Corporation	X	X						
Progress Software Corporation								
Rocket Software, Inc.	X	X						
StarWare, Inc.	X	X						
Sybase MicroDecisionware Inc. (MDI)	X	X						
Wall Data, Inc.	X	X						
XDB Systems, Inc.	X	X	X	X	X			

Notes:

Status 1 Have announced a DRDA remote unit of work (RUW) application requester (AR) implementation.

Status 2 Have shipped a DRDA RUW AR implementation.

Status 3 Have announced a DRDA RUW application server (AS) implementation.

Status 4 Have shipped a DRDA RUW AS implementation.

Status 5 Have announced a DRDA DUW AS and AR implementation.

Status 6 Have shipped a DRDA DUW AS and AR implementation.

Status 7 Have announced DRDA stored procedure AS and AR implementation.

Status 8 Have shipped DRDA stored procedure.

The values are:

X Yes

Blank No

R Yes, for AR

S Yes, for AS

Table 2. *DRDA Implementation Status of IBM Products*

IBM Product	Status 1	Status 2	Status 3	Status 4	Status 5	Status 6	Status 7	Status 8
DataJoiner	X	X						X
DB2 and DDCS for OS/2	X	X	X	X	R	R	X	X
DB2 and DDCS for AIX	X	X	X	X	R	R	X	X
DB2 Parallel Edition for AIX	X	X						
DB2 and DDCS for HP-UX	X	X	X		R		X	
DB2 and DDCS for NT	X	X	X	X			X	X
DB2 and DDCS for Sinix	X		X		R		X	
DB2 and DDCS for Sun Solaris	X	X	X		R		X	
DB2 for OS/400	X	X	X	X	X	X	X	X
SQL/DS for VSE/ESA			X	X	S			
SQL/DS for VM/ESA	X	X	X	X	S			
DB2 for MVS/ESA	X	X	X	X	X	X	X	X
Transaction Processing Facility	X	X						

Notes:

Status 1 Have announced a DRDA RUW AR implementation.

Status 2 Have shipped a DRDA RUW AR implementation.

Status 3 Have announced a DRDA RUW AS implementation.

Status 4 Have shipped a DRDA RUW AS implementation.

Status 5 Have announced a DRDA DUW AS and AR implementation.

Status 6 Have shipped a DRDA DUW AS and AR implementation.

Status 7 Have announced DRDA stored procedure AS or requester implementation.

Status 8 Have shipped DRDA stored procedure.

The values are:

X Yes

Blank No

R Yes, for AR

S Yes, for AS

For more information about the implementation status of DRDA, contact Mike Swift at IBM Santa Teresa Laboratory, San Jose, CA, USA, (408) 463-4105, mswift@vnet.ibm.com, IBMMAIL(USIB2V64).

Chapter 2. What's New?

A distributed database solution is integrated by a relational database management system (RDBMS), a gateway, and communication products. In this chapter we describe the new functions provided by the products we used to build our distributed database environment.

2.1 DB2 common server

DB2 common server is the generic name for DB2 products running on Intel- or UNIX-based platforms. The functional components of DB2 common server are

- DB2 common server Relational Database Engine
- DB2 common server Single-User
- DB2 common server Database Server
- DB2 common server Client Application Enabler
- DB2 common server Software Developer's Kits
- Administrator's Toolkit
- Distributed Database Connection Services for DB2 common server.

In this section we describe the major functional enhancements of DB2 common server, except for Distributed Database Connection Services (DDCS), which we describe in 2.1.7, "Distributed Database Connection Services for DB2 common server" on page 18.

2.1.1 Relational Database Engine Functional Enhancements

The relational database engine for DB2 common server provides a full-function RDBMS, a cost-based optimizer, and a robust mechanism to ensure data integrity through declarative referential integrity, forward recovery, and multilevel concurrency control. The major functional enhancements for the DB2 common server relational database engine are described below.

2.1.1.1 SQL

SQL capabilities include alignment with SQL92 entry level standards and implementation of large objects support, user-defined functions, user-data types, and triggers among other SQL extensions.

2.1.1.2 SQL Optimizer

The SQL optimizer enhancements are

- More statistics information

  The SQL optimizer can now recognize the speed of CPU and I/O devices where databases are located, thus improving its ability to select the best access paths available.

- Query Rewrite

  The SQL optimizer can transform a user query into a best performer, functionally equivalent query, by applying tuning techniques such as adding logically implied predicates or changing a subselect into a join.

There is a trade-off between the resources consumed by query optimization and query performance improvements, but you have the option to define variable optimization levels to balance resource consumption.

2.1.1.3 Database Performance

In addition to the SQL optimizer enhancements described in 2.1.1.1, "SQL" on page 11, the major database performance enhancements are as follows:

- Multithreaded database engine requires less working set memory.

- The load utility can build indexes, validate primary keys, and generate statistics with a single data scan.

- Backup and recovery operations can be run in parallel against multiple devices.

- Prefetch I/O operations can read several disk pages, and, depending on the setting of the prefetch servers parameter, parallel I/O operations can be done on behalf of a single query.

- Database partitioning allows data to be split across devices, so prefetch operations run more efficiently.

2.1.1.4 Systems Management Support

The *database director* tool is a graphical interface that provides you with a central point of operation to configure database manager instances and databases, back up and recover databases or table spaces, and keep track of nodes, databases, and related parameters required to access local and remote databases.

The relational database engine provides the ability to perform backup operations while users and/or applications are still connected and implements a faster load utility, recovery history files, and database partitioning to ensure systems availability.

The database engine also provides a Simple Network Management Protocol (SNMP) agent to interface with hardware and software central management tools such as IBM NetView for AIX and IBM NetView for OS/2.

2.1.1.5 Compatibility with DB2 for MVS/ESA

Application portability is one of the main goals of compatibility. Therefore the following functions are now supported:

- Scalar functions such as DIGITS and HEX

- TIMEZONE special register

- Ability to refer to a table or view through an alias

- COMMENTS ON extensions for indexes, packages, aliases, and other SQL objects

- Option to update catalog statistics to influence the SQL optimizer

- Ability to recreate a package through the REBIND command.

2.1.1.6 Integrity and Data Protection

Concurrent access to data and data being managed by various data management systems might compromise data integrity. To ensure the integrity of your data, the following functions are supported:

- *DUW*, which is the ability to update or read tables in multiple database servers, within a single unit of work, ensuring data integrity. This topic is covered in 3.1.3, "Degrees of Distribution" on page 47.

- *Read stability support*, which is an isolation level that keeps locks only on qualifying rows accessed by the application program until the unit of work is committed.

2.1.1.7 Object Relational Capabilities

Enhancements to object relational capabilities include large object support, user-defined types, user-defined functions, and triggers, all of which enable you to create more flexible applications.

2.1.2 DB2 common server Single-User

DB2 common server Single-User provides an isolated user with the power of the relational database engine, plus the following set of functions:

2.1.2.1 Local Client Application Enabler

The local Client Application Enabler is a set of functions that enable a DB2 local client. Refer to 2.1.4, "DB2 common server Client Application Enabler" on page 15 for more information.

2.1.2.2 Application Development Environment

DB2 common server Single-User provides an environment in which to develop database application programs through the use of such interfaces as embedded SQL, DB2 call level interface (DB2 CLI), and DB2 application programming interfaces (DB2 APIs). It also provides a prototyped environment using the command line processor (CLP) interactive SQL. Refer to 2.1.5, "Software Developer's Kit" on page 16 for additional details.

2.1.2.3 Database Director

The database director is the central point for cataloging and controlling local databases and instances and performing visual explain functions.

2.1.2.4 Visual Explain

Visual explain provides a visual explanation of your SQL statement access path. Refer to 2.1.5, "Software Developer's Kit" on page 16 for more information.

2.1.3 DB2 common server Database Server

In addition to the relational database engine enhancements, DB2 common server provides *DRDA application server support* and *client access support*.

2.1.3.1 DRDA Application Server Support

DB2 common server's DRDA application server enables application requesters such as DB2 for MVS/ESA, SQL/DS for VM, and DB2 for OS/400 to access DB2 common server databases.

2.1.3.2 Client Access Support

DB2 common server client access support provides local and remote clients with transparent access to local as well as remote databases. Supported remote client platforms are OS/2, DOS, Windows, Macintosh, AIX, HP-UX, and Solaris.

DB2 common server and DDCS for common server can be accessed from multiple platforms by using current or even previous versions of the client database products.

Transport Control Protocol/Internet Protocol (TCP/IP) is now supported for Intel-based servers and clients, Macintosh clients, and UNIX-based servers and clients. Table 3 on page 15 lists the client, server, and protocol combinations supported.

Table 3. *Clients, Servers, and Protocols Supported by DB2 common server*

Client	DB2 for OS/2 1.2	DB2 for OS/2 2.1	DB2 for AIX 1.1, 1.2	DB2 for AIX 2.1	DB2 for HP-UX 1.1, 1.2	DB2 for Solaris 1.2
CAE for AIX 1.1, 2.1	N/A	APPC, TCP/IP	APPC, TCP/IP	APPC, TCP/IP	TCP/IP	TCP/IP
CAE for OS/2 1.2, 2.1	APPC, NetBIOS, IPX/SPX	APPC, NetBIOS, IPX/SPX, TCP/IP	APPC, TCP/IP	APPC, TCP/IP, IPX/SPX	TCP/IP	TCP/IP
CAE/DOS 1.2	NetBIOS, IPX/SPX	NetBIOS, IPX/SPX, TCP/IP	TCP/IP, IPX/SPX	TCP/IP, IPX/SPX	TCP/IP, IPX/SPX	TCP/IP, IPX/SPX
CAE for Windows 1.2, 2.0	NetBIOS, IPX/SPX	NetBIOS, IPX/SPX, TCP/IP	TCP/IP, IPX/SPX	TCP/IP, IPX/SPX	TCP/IP, IPX/SPX	TCP/IP, IPX/SPX
CAE for HP-UX 1.1, 1.2	N/A	APPC, TCP/IP	APPC, TCP/IP	APPC, TCP/IP	TCP/IP	TCP/IP
CAE for Solaris 1.1, 1.2	N/A	APPC, TCP/IP	APPC, TCP/IP	APPC, TCP/IP	TCP/IP	TCP/IP
CAE for Macintosh 1.1	N/A	TCP/IP	TCP/IP	TCP/IP	TCP/IP	TCP/IP

2.1.4 DB2 common server Client Application Enabler

The DB2 common server Client Application Enabler is a run-time environment for applications accessing remote database servers. The environment is built on every DB2 common server product to provide DB2 client functions by means of the features discussed below.

2.1.4.1 DB2 Client Setup

Through the DB2 client setup tool, you can catalog the databases and nodes that your DB2 client will access, BIND your DB2 client applications and tools, and gather and format data for problem determination.

2.1.4.2 Remote Administration Capabilities

If installed with the DB2 common server Software Developer's Kit or Administrator's Toolkit, remote administration capabilities enable a remote DB2 client to perform database administrative tasks such as database monitoring, backup, and recovery.

2.1.4.3 Directory Caching

Directory caching is a database manager configuration option that reduces DB2 client connection cost by means of caching the DDCS (DCS), database, and node directories into memory.

2.1.4.4 DRDA Stored Procedures

DB2 clients use DRDA stored procedures to invoke an application program to be run at the DRDA application server. Stored procedures reduce network traffic, so you can expect performance improvements and increased data integrity. For additional details on DB2 stored procedures refer, to 2.3, "Stored Procedures" on page 24.

2.1.5 Software Developer's Kit

The DB2 common server Software Developer's Kit is a product designed to provide an application development environment for database application programmers. It includes all required development tools, except the compilers. It is an integrated component of DB2 common server Single-User and an additional supplement for DB2 common server database server.

The major enhancements for this product are described below.

2.1.5.1 DB2 Call Level Interface Extensions

The DB2 CLI is a callable SQL interface to DB2 database servers, compatible with Open Database Connectivity (ODBC) specifications. CLI is a C and C++ application programming interface. It is based on the use of function calls to pass dynamic SQL statements as function arguments.

Because DB2 common server CLI applications use a standard set of functions to execute SQL statements at run time, there is no need to precompile or bind. Applications developed with the DB2 CLI are independent of any database vendor programming interface, so they can be easily ported from one database management system to another.

Following are the enhancements to the DB2 CLI:

- DB2 CLI supports ODBC Level 1 functions and all but three ODBC Level 2 functions.
- The DB2 features available for both DB2 CLI and ODBC applications are
  - Double-byte data types
  - Stored procedures

- Two-phase commit connections
- User-defined types
- User-defined functions
- Compound SQL statements (see 2.1.7.4, "Compound SQL Statement" on page 19)
- The features available for CLI applications are
  - Large objects support
  - SQLCA data
  - Null termination of output strings

2.1.5.2 Programming Language Support
The Software Developer's Kit products provide C, C++, COBOL, and Fortran precompilers to support the development of embedded SQL applications. The kit supports a number of key development tools in each DB2 platform and provides a documented API for development tool providers, so that they can directly support precompiling capabilities within their tools.

2.1.5.3 Visual Explain
Visual explain is a graphical tool that can be used to represent an SQL statement access path, tune SQL statements, assess the need for database changes, determine the source of problems for SQL statements, and even model how a database change is going to impact access paths.

2.1.5.4 BIND Options
The Software Developer's Kit enables you to gain access to the full set of bind options supported by the server to which your application binds.

2.1.5.5 Flagger Option
The flagger option is a PREP command option used to flag SQL statements that DB2 for MVS/ESA does not support.

2.1.6 Administrator's Toolkit
The administrator's toolkit is a graphical database administration tool that can be installed on either the database server workstation or a remote client workstation.

The functions that the toolkit provides are described below.

2.1.6.1 Database Director

The database director is the central point for cataloging and controlling local databases and instances.

2.1.6.2 Visual Explain

The visual explain function provides a visual explanation of your SQL statement access path. See 2.1.5, "Software Developer's Kit" on page 16 for details.

2.1.6.3 Performance Monitor

The performance monitor helps you monitor and tune the performance of your DB2 system. By using this tool, you can

- Define your own statistics
- Detect and analyze performance problems in the database manager or database applications
- Tune SQL statements
- Identify exception conditions according to user-defined thresholds

2.1.7 Distributed Database Connection Services for DB2 common server

Distributed Database Connection Services for DB2 common server is the common name used to address DDCS for OS/2 and UNIX-based platforms.

DDCS for DB2 common server enables DOS, Windows, OS/2, and UNIX applications to access and update data stored in relational databases such as DB2 for MVS/ESA, DB2 for VM, DB2 for VSE, and DB2 for OS/400, as well as for non-IBM DRDA-compliant database managers. The database manager product does not have to be installed on the workstation.

The single-user version of DDCS for DB2 common server enables a local client to access DRDA-compliant database managers. This version is available only for the OS/2 platform.

The multiuser gateway version of DDCS for DB2 common server can receive concurrent requests from multiple local and remote clients and reroute the requests to the appropriate DRDA server.

Below we describe the major enhancements to DDCS for DB2 common server Version 2.3.

2.1.7.1 DRDA BIND Options

DRDA BIND options are fully supported in the DB2 PREP and DB2 BIND commands. Thus a DDCS user can fully exploit the available BIND options of the database server where the package is being created.

2.1.7.2 Stored Procedures Support

Through DDCS for DB2 common server, DB2 client applications can invoke DB2 for OS/400 and DB2 for MVS/ESA stored procedures, improving performance by reducing network traffic. For more information about stored procedures refer to 2.3, "Stored Procedures" on page 24.

2.1.7.3 DUW

An application program can now access one database and then switch to a second database before committing the data. In other words an application progran can access multiple databases in the same unit of work.

DDCS for DB2 common server allows an application program to read multiple databases in the same unit of work. The ability to update multiple databases in the same unit of work depends on the products you use.

2.1.7.4 Compound SQL Statement

Compound SQL enables multiple SQL statements to be grouped together, sent as a compact, continuous stream of SQL statements, and executed as a single block. Because this function reduces network overhead, response time improvements can be expected.

Compound SQL can include only static SQL statements.

There are two types of compound SQL: *ATOMIC compound SQL* and *NOT ATOMIC compound SQL*. Even though DDCS for DB2 common server supports only NOT ATOMIC compound SQL, we explain both types of compound SQL below.

ATOMIC Compound SQL: ATOMIC compound SQL creates a save point at the beginning of a group of compound SQL statements. This save point is the commit or rollback scope. Thus every SQL statement in the block must complete successfully for the database changes to be committed, and it takes only one failing SQL statement to roll back all of the database changes made by the SQL statements in the block.

NOT ATOMIC Compound SQL: With NOT ATOMIC compound SQL, individual SQL statements are a part of the unit of work initiating the compound SQL request. Thus the database changes, promoted by each SQL statement in the group, are committed regardless of the results of the preceding SQL statement. Changes are rolled back only if the unit of work initiating the compound SQL request is rolled back.: The *import utility* benefits from NOT ATOMIC compound SQL. You can use the new COMPOUND=n import utility option to specify that *n* number of INSERT statements be performed at one time as part of a compound SQL statement.

The NOT ATOMIC compound SQL statement can be used with any DRDA AS to which DDCS for DB2 common server V2.3 can connect, for example, DB2 for MVS/ESA V2.3.

2.1.7.5 Prefetch

Prefetch improves the response times for queries that return large result sets. This function combines the blocking technique used in previous versions of DDCS, with the DDCS's ability to fetch rows of data for an open cursor before the application actually requests the data.

Prefetch is performed automatically and transparently every time you issue an SQL OPEN or FETCH statement. Basically, when you issue an SQL OPEN statement, DDCS gets a block of data. If the query has more data on the server side, DDCS asynchronously issues another DRDA FETCH to get the next block of data. The first block is processed by subsequent SQL FETCH. The only difference is that the next time DDCS has to send out another DRDA FETCH request for the next block, chances are the next block is already in the workstation. At this time DDCS issues another asynchronous DRDA FETCH to get a subsequent block. This process improves performance for queries that have a large answer set.

Prefetch is different from DB2 for MVS/ESA continuous block fetching in that DDCS does not need a separate LU6.2 session and does not tie up extra VTAM buffers along the way. Continuous block fetching keeps pumping the data from the AS to the AR that is buffered and paused by VTAM. DDCS requests only one extra block at a time. In practice an extra block at a time is sufficient for most machines and uses. Any more than that could tie up the machine cycle and buffers because the application is too slow to fetch all of the data.

2.1.7.6 SQLCODE Mapping

As IBM relational database products do not always produce the same SQLCODEs and tokens for similar errors, DDCS for DB2 common server maps SQLCODEs and tokens from each IBM DRDA server to the OS/2 and UNIX-based systems. You can turn this function ON and OFF as needed. If you are accessing a non-IBM DRDA server, you can tailor mapping files to address your non-IBM DRDA server messages.

2.1.7.7 Accounting String Support

Accounting string support provides the ability to send accounting strings from DDCS for DB2 common server to the DRDA server. Accounting strings are integrated with system-generated data and user-supplied data. They are provided to help system administrators keep track of resource utilization associated with each user's access.

2.2 DB2 for OS/400

DB2 for OS/400, the OS/400 integrated RDBMS, plays a key role as a DRDA AS in the distributed database environment arena. Below we describe the major enhancements to the DB2 for OS/400 V3.1 advanced functions and distributed database functions.

2.2.1 Advanced Functions

DB2 for OS/400 provides new database functions that address both traditional application and distributed computing requirements without affecting the maturity and stability it has always provided. DB2 for OS/400 delivers a set of advanced functions that enhance its compatibility with the rest of the DB2 family products and its performance.

2.2.1.1 Referential Integrity

Referential integrity support has been implemented for other database management systems such as DB2 for MVS/ESA and DB2 common server. This support is now enabled in DB2 for OS/400, increasing its maturity and reliability.

Referential integrity is the ability to automatically enforce the relationships that data in different tables must have. These relationships, so-called business rules, used to be enforced by writing some extra code in application programs, but accidental updates could still be performed through other interfaces.

Referential integrity enables you to delegate to the system the enforcement of the business rules. In this way, application programmers have to define only referential constraints, which are always checked, regardless of how and when a database change takes place. Application maintenance is easier and business rules enforcement quicker because referential integrity constraint is performed at the system level.

Referential integrity can be set through either the OS/400 native interface or the SQL interface.

2.2.1.2 Triggers

Complex business rules can be enforced through the use of triggers, which are user-written programs activated when a data change is performed in the database. Triggers are automatically activated, regardless of how the changes take place. Triggers are supported in a DRDA environment. Refer to 2.4, "Triggers" on page 39 for more information.

2.2.1.3 SQL Standard Conformance

SQL standard conformance supports the industry standard database access language for consistent data access across heterogeneous platforms. Conformance is to the IBM SQL

Version 1, ANSI X3.135.1992, ISO 9075-1992, and FIPS 127-2 standards. Support is provided for embedded static, dynamic, and extended dynamic SQL.

2.2.1.4 Systemwide Database Catalog

The systemwide database catalog enables you to query all objects on a system, through the use of a single system catalog, which has been enhanced to provide referential integrity support.

2.2.1.5 Advanced SQL Optimizer

The advanced SQL optimizer has a multifrogger capability and an automatic rebind feature. With the multifrogger capability, all of the key fields in a multiple selection predicate can be analyzed, thus narrowing the range of records to be retrieved.

The automatic rebind feature is used to determine access methods based on changes to database objects and statistics.

2.2.1.6 EXPLAIN

The EXPLAIN function provides you with a report of the access method used by individual queries. Access method information is very useful when you want to enhance query performance by implementing query and/or database changes.

2.2.1.7 Multiple Isolation Levels

Four record locking options are provided:

- **Read stability (*ALL)**

  Locks only rows read during a transaction and keeps rows locked until the transaction commits.

- **Cursor stability (*CS)**

  Maintains locks on the current and previously changed rows only.

- **Uncommitted read (*UR)**

  Neither acquires nor examines database locks for read-only operations.

- **No Commit (*NONE)**

  Does not acquire locks and disables transaction management.

2.2.1.8 Block INSERT and FETCH Statement

The block INSERT and FETCH statement provides applications with the ability to write and read arrays of rows directly, rather than one row at a time.

2.2.1.9 Automatic Record Blocking

Automatic record blocking provides the ability to return blocks of records to client applications rather than one row after another. Individual records in the current block can then be read locally with no need to access the server.

2.2.1.10 Parallel Data Access

The parallel data access feature enables the activation of multiple internal DB2 for OS/400 tasks for each physical device. As data is often spread over multiple devices, this feature enables DB2 for OS/400 to transmit data from disk to memory faster than with the previous single task I/O architecture.

2.2.1.11 Query Governor

The query governor enables you to set a timeout value for a query, thus preventing a long-running query from consuming large amounts of resources and negatively affecting the performance of other queries. Query governor, in conjunction with stored procedures, is supported in a DRDA environment.

2.2.2 Distributed Database Functions

DB2 for OS/400 is a DRDA level 2 compliant database management system; therefore it supports DUW as well as two-phase commit. It also supports stored procedures.

2.2.2.1 Distributed Unit of Work

DB2 for OS/400 provides DUW support. Thus you can access multiple database servers in a single unit of work, easily bringing your enterprise data together in a report or a program.

DB2 for OS/400 can act as a DRDA AR for the following IBM DRDA ASs:

- DB2 for MVS/ESA
- SQL/DS for VM
- SQL/DS for VSE
- DB2 common server

DB2 for OS/400 can act as a DRDA AS for the following DRDA ARs:

- DB2 for MVS/ESA
- DB2 for VM
- DB2 common server
- Non-IBM DRDA requesters

DB2 for OS/400 supports multiple-site update in a single unit of work, through the implementation of two-phase commit process, along with a function called synchronization point manager (SPM).

When DB2 for OS/400 acts as an AR, the following conditions should be met to support DRDA level 2 DUW:

- When preparing the SQL program you must set the connection method parameter (RDBCNNMTH) to (*DUW).

- To support multiple-site update in a unit of work, the participating database management systems must be at DRDA level 2 or the first DRDA connection must be to a DRDA level 2 AS. In this case all connections to a DRDA level 1 AS are read-only. If the first connection is to a DRDA level 1 AS, updates are allowed only at that AS.

See 11.1.1, "DRDA Level 2: Introduction" on page 319.

2.2.2.2 Stored Procedures

Stored procedures provide an easy way of invoking AS/400 programs from a client application. By using stored procedures, you reduce network traffic, so you can expect performance improvements. See the next section, 2.3, "Stored Procedures," for more details.

2.3 Stored Procedures

Stored procedures are user-written programs typically with embedded SQL statements. The programs are compiled and stored in a local or remote database server.

The server procedure executes and accesses the database locally and returns information to the client application. Applications that use stored procedures consist of two components: the calling component and the server component. The calling component is part of the client application and executes on the client. The server component executes the stored procedure at the database server.

Before stored procedures were available for DRDA applications, network send and receive operations were required for most SQL statements; for example, SELECT, UPDATE, and INSERT require network I/O operations. Other SQL statements might not require a network operation; for example, the FETCH statement requires only one network send and receive operation for each block of rows returned by the server. Figure 2 on page 25 illustrates the processing of SQL statements in relation to the network send and receive operation for an application that runs on a DDCS workstation and accesses data in a DB2 for MVS/ESA V3 server. In this scenario, each DRDA request or reply represents one network I/O operation.

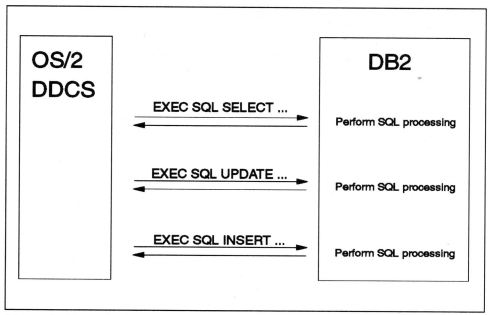

Figure 2. *Network Flows for Remote SQLs*

Although the elapsed time of the network I/O operation might not be long, it can become a concern if your application issues a large number of SQL statements. This concern is magnified if you are using relatively slow network connections.

With the availability of stored procedures for DRDA applications, the client application issues a single network send and receive operation to run the stored procedure, which typically consists of multiple SQL statements. See Figure 3 on page 26.

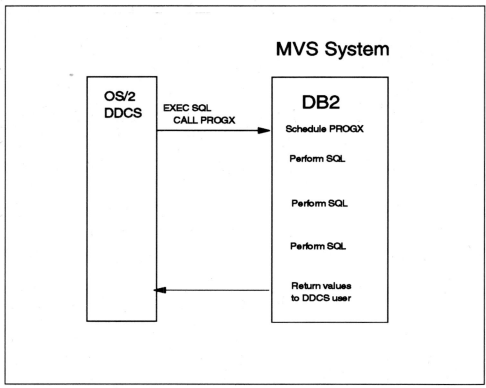

Figure 3. Minimum Network Flows with Stored Procedure

The stored procedure contains a series of SQL statements, but only the initial request and the final result flow across the network. Therefore network traffic is significantly reduced.

2.3.1 Benefits

Stored procedures offer the following benefits for applications that operate in a client/server environment:

- Reduced network send and receive operations

  The number of network send and receive operations is reduced, which improves application elapsed time and CPU time. In addiiton, the SQL statements issued by the stored procedure run locally, so there is no added "distributed" overhead on those statements. For applications that issue many SQL statements, the saving can be significant.

- Application protection

The stored procedure code is not installed in the client location. Thus sensitive parts of an application can be encapsulated and protected from unauthorized access.

- Design flexibility

  Without stored procedure support, the business logic of DRDA applications is limited to the client's location. Now application designers can split the logic between the client and server, and the client and server code can be written in different programming languages.

- Simplified application development and maintenance

  Programmers for the client do not have to understand the server database design. Stored procedures can be maintained at a central server location; application logic changes are transparent to the client.

- Improved development productivity

  Programs can be used by many local or remote clients.

- Access to features that exist only on the database server

  Some functions and features are not available in a client database but are supported by some database servers. Through the use of stored procedures, database clients can access these special functions or features. For example, an OS/2 client can execute the DB2 for MVS/ESA DISPLAY DATABASE command in an instrumentation facility interface format by encapsulating the command in a stored procedure on the DB2 for MVS/ESA server.

Except for SQL/DS for VM and VSE, all IBM DB2 database managers support stored procedures. Any DRDA AR, including those of vendor platforms, can invoke these procedures.

2.3.2 DB2 for MVS/ESA

DB2 for MVS/ESA V4 stored procedures broaden your client/server implementation choices. In this section we discuss some implementation aspects of stored procedures that are specific to DB2 for MVS/ESA. In this section we refer to DB2 for MVS/ESA as *DB2*.

2.3.2.1 Client Implementation

Local DB2 applications or remote DRDA applications can issue the new SQL CALL statement to invoke a stored procedure. The statement is part of the ISO/ANSI proposal for SQL3, that is, the statement will be an OPEN solution for invoking stored procedures among RDBMS vendors that support the SQL ISO/ANSI standard.

The SQL CALL statement is implemented as static SQL, but each of its input parameters can be supplied at execution time. For example, the procedure name to be invoked can be determined dynamically. The syntax of the statement is as follows:

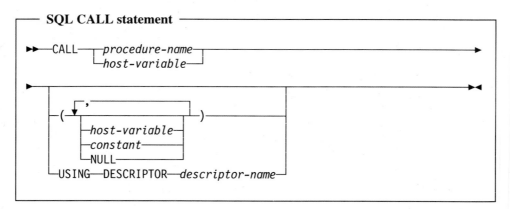

Note: If the stored procedure is located on a DB2 common server, all parameters must be supplied through host variables; constant and NULL values are not supported.

Each parameter of the stored procedure can be specified by using a host variable, a constant, or NULL value. When the CALL statement is executed, the value of each parameter of the statement is assigned to the corresponding parameter of the stored procedure.

Alternatively, you can use an SQLDA name in the USING DESCRIPTOR clause to specify the parameters for the stored procedure. Each host variable described by the identified SQLDA is a parameter of the CALL statement. The SQLDA must contain the following fields:

- SQLN to indicate the number of SQLVAR occurrences provided in the SQLDA.

- SQLDABC to indicate the number of bytes of storage allocated for the SQLDA.

- SQLD to indicate the number of variables used in SQLDA when processing the statement. This number is equal to the number of parameters of the stored procedure.

- SQLVAR occurrences to indicate the attributes of the variables.

For more details on the statement syntax and parameter assignment rules, refer to the *DB2 for MVS/ESA Application Programming and SQL Guide*.

Much of the anticipated use of stored procedures is through the distributed data facility (DDF); however, DB2 for MVS/ESA stored procedures can also be invoked from local

SQL CALL statements. Local applications using stored procedures can be processed even when DDF has not been started.

If the stored procedures contain dynamic SQL statements, users must have the privileges required to execute those statements, unless the *DYNAMICRULES* BIND package option of the stored procedure has specified otherwise. We discuss authorization in more detail in " Authorization" on page 35.

2.3.2.2 SQL Support

A DB2 stored procedure can perform most of the DB2 operations that are supported for local DB2 applications. It can issue static or dynamic SQL statements of the following types:

- Data definition language (DDL) statements such as CREATE and DROP
- Data control language (DCL) statements such as GRANT and REVOKE
- Data manipulation language (DML) statements such as SELECT, UPDATE, and DELETE

The SQL statements are not limited to local processing. The stored procedure can contain references to tables using three-part names or aliases to access data in another DB2 server location through DB2 private protocols.

A stored procedure can also issue DB2 commands. A workstation application on a local area network (LAN) can use a stored procedure to issue a DB2 -DISPLAY THREAD command and have the output returned to the workstation through an output host variable. This capability was not available to DRDA ARs previously.

There are a few restrictions on the SQL run in a stored procedure. When a stored procedure executes any of the following statements, DB2 returns an SQL error code and places the DB2 thread in a "must roll back" state:

- CALL

  A stored procedure cannot call another stored procedure. However, a stored procedure can invoke other programs. For example, a stored procedure written in C can issue function calls and subroutine calls to other programs.

- COMMIT

  The client application program is responsible for issuing the COMMIT statement.

- CONNECT

- RELEASE

- ROLLBACK

- SET CONNECTION

- SET CURRENT SQLID

When the client application program regains control under the "must roll back" state, it must either execute a ROLLBACK statement or terminate, which causes an automatic rollback of the unit of work. Therefore a ROLLBACK statement within a stored procedure can be used as a device to force a rollback when an error is detected, such as when the caller program provides input that violates a business rule.

Note: A stored procedure uses call attachment facility (CAF) calls implicitly. Thus DB2 rejects any explicit CAF calls.

2.3.2.3 Server Implementation

DB2 for MVS/ESA V4 supports static and dynamic SQL in stored procedures. You can develop stored procedures in the following languages:

- COBOL
- C
- PL/I
- Assembler

You can also use VisualGen, one of the IBM's visual programming products, to develop, test, and generate stored procedures that run on DB2 for MVS/ESA. VisualGen fully supports DRDA for the DB2 family.

Stored procedures are designed to run in the LE/370 environment. Thus whatever language you choose, ensure that the compiler for the language and the LE/370 run-time library are available. The stored procedures are executed in a separate address space called the *stored procedure address space* (SPAS).

Stored Procedure Address Space: The SPAS, a new DB2 for MVS/ESA address space, has the naming convention of *XXXXSPAS*, where *XXXX* is the DB2 for MVS/ESA subsystem name. It is used to run DB2 stored procedures.

The SPAS is started when you issue the DB2 for MVS/ESA -START command. It is a normal DB2 for MVS/ESA application address space, so it can be canceled or stopped without bringing DB2 down.

The SPAS contains multiple MVS task control blocks (TCBs), which are used to run multiple stored procedures in parallel. The implication is that your application throughput can be improved. The number of TCBs is specified at installation time but can be changed later.

When a DRDA client application connects to DB2 for MVS/ESA, an MVS TCB and a DB2 thread are created for this requester. When the stored procedure is called, the TCB of the requester is put in a wait state, and one of the available, idle SPAS TCBs is selected to run the stored procedure. The thread is passed from the requester TCB to the SPAS TCB together with information about the stored procedure from the DB2 for MVS/ESA catalog. On successful completion of the stored procedure, the thread is passed back to the requester TCB. The next section describes the steps involved in processing a stored procedure.

Processing Flow: A client program can call one or more stored procedures. To help you understand the steps involved in executing a stored procedure, we discuss a simple case in which one stored procedure is called by a remote client. Figure 4 on page 32 shows a client application using a stored procedure to manipulate the data in the remote DB2 for MVS/ESA server. The stored procedure is denoted as *procedure X*.

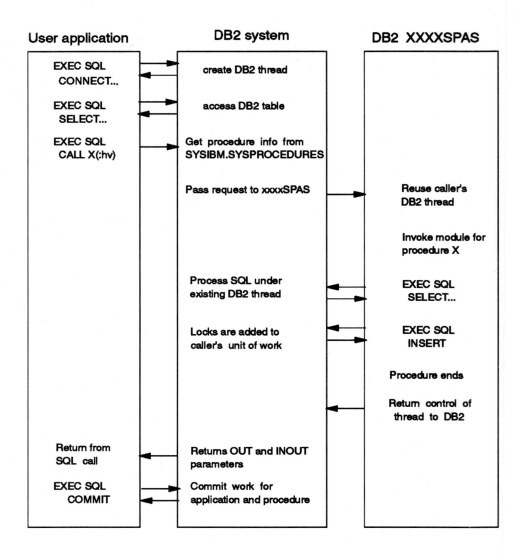

Figure 4. *Stored Procedure Processing Flow*

Procedure X is invoked by the SPAS through CAF. The processing sequence is as follows:

1. The user application running at the client database creates a DB2 for MVS/ESA thread. The client in this example is a DRDA requester; hence the SQL CONNECT statement initiates the creation of the DB2 for MVS/ESA thread.

2. The client issues an SQL SELECT statement to the DB2 for MVS/ESA server.

3. The client issues an SQL CALL statement to invoke procedure X. One parameter is provided through a host variable.

4. DB2 for MVS/ESA searches the SYSIBM.SYSPROCEDURES catalog table for the rows associated with procedure X. Information retrieved from the catalog is cached so that future references to procedure X do not require I/O to the catalog.

5. DB2 for MVS/ESA finds an MVS TCB in the SPAS that is available for use. DB2 for MVS/ESA notifies the SPAS to run procedure X.

6. The SPAS uses LE/370 product libraries to load and run the MVS load module associated with procedure X, which has access to a parameter list containing the input and output parameters provided by the SQL CALL statement. Procedure X uses the parameters to issue SQL statements.

7. Procedure X executes its SQL statements. DB2 for MVS/ESA reuses the thread of the user that issued the SQL CALL statement to run the procedure. It verifies that the owner of the package containing the SQL CALL statement has EXECUTE authority for the package associated with procedure X.

8. Before terminating, procedure X assigns values to the output parameters specified in the SQL CALL statement. After procedure X terminates, DB2 for MVS/ESA copies the output parameters into the client application's parameter area.

9. Control returns to the client program. DB2 for MVS/ESA closes all cursors opened by procedure X.

10. The client program issues a COMMIT request. The COMMIT operation covers all SQL operations, whether executed by the application or the stored procedure, for that unit of work.

Note: DB2 for MVS/ESA does not commit or roll back any changes from the SQL in a stored procedure until the client program executes a COMMIT or ROLLBACK statement outside the procedure.

The fact that the execution of a stored procedure reuses the DB2 for MVS/ESA thread of the client application brings about the following benefits:

- The client's SQL authorities are used for the stored procedure SQL processing. This is important if the stored procedure contains dynamic SQL statements.

- Locks obtained by the stored procedure become part of the client's unit of work. Thus the SQL operations of the stored procedure can be committed or rolled back within the caller's unit of work. Hence the client application maintains explicit control over the span of each unit of work.

- The reuse of a thread saves CPU cost, so DB2 for MVS/ESA can process stored procedure requests efficiently.

DB2 for MVS/ESA Catalog Table: To use a stored procedure, you must define the stored procedure to the *SYSIBM.SYSPROCEDURES* catalog table. This table is different from most other catalog tables in that the data in the table can be directly manipulated through SQL statements. Therefore you can simply use an SQL INSERT statement to define the stored procedure. The definition of the procedure must include the following information:

- Procedure's collection, program, and language

  The COLLECTION column idenfities the name of the package collection to be used when the procedure is executed. The LANGUAGE column identifies the programming language used to create the procedure. In addition, each procedure must be uniquely identified by the combination of the following columns:

  PROCEDURE Contains the name of the procedure

  LUNAME VTAM LUNAME name from which the SQL CALL statement can be made. If this column is blank, programs at any location can call this procedure.

  AUTHID Authorization ID that can execute the CALL statement. If this column is blank, any user can invoke this procedure.

- Attributes of input/output parameters

  These values are stored in the PARMLIST column. DB2 for MVS/ESA determines the attributes of the parameters according to the list type (LINKAGE).

- Other information

  Other information would include processing time limit and run-time options. Because you can have several rows of definitions for a given procedure name, you can vary the procedure attributes according to the AUTHID and LUNAME values. For example, you can specify a LUNAME value to define a different processing time limit (in the AUSTIME column) for a group of database clients originating from that LU.

For a complete description of the SYSPROCEDURES table refer to the *DB2 for MVS/ESA SQL Reference*.

Note: The specification in the AUTHID column does not automatically give users all privileges to execute the procedure. The normal database authorization rules apply.

Authorization: To use stored procedures, the client authorization ID must be given at least one of the following privileges in DB2 for MVS/ESA:

- EXECUTE privilege on the stored procedure package
- Ownership of the stored procedure package
- PACKADM authority for the package's collection
- SYSADM authority

If the stored procedure contains dynamic SQL, the authorization ID used by DB2 for MVS/ESA to execute the statements depends on the *DYNAMICRULES* BIND PACKAGE option for the stored procedure. If DYNAMICRULES is set to:

- *RUN*, DB2 for MVS/ESA uses the SQL authorization ID of the client for authorization checking of dynamic SQL statements. This is the default setting.
- *BIND*, DB2 for MVS/ESA uses the authorization ID of the package owner for authorization checking of dynamic SQL statements.

A typical stored procedure contains multiple SQL statements, as well as some programming logic that you cannot include in an SQL statement. Moreover, a stored procedure can access non-SQL resources that are available to the DB2 for MVS/ESA SPAS. For example, you can access

- VSAM files
- Flat files
- APPC/MVS conversations
- CICS/MVS or IMS transactions through the use of the Message Queue Interface (MQI) or CICS EXCI

When a DB2 for MVS/ESA stored procedure accesses a non-SQL resource, MVS does not discern that the DB2 for MVS/ESA SPAS is performing work for a DB2 for MVS/ESA client. The MVS user ID (userid) for the stored procedure is the RACF userid associated with the MVS started task running the DB2 for MVS/ESA stored procedures. It is important to note that the RACF protected resources are accessed through this RACF userid, not the userid of the DB2 for MVS/ESA client. Figure 5 on page 36 shows the various userids that are used to access SQL and non-SQL resources.

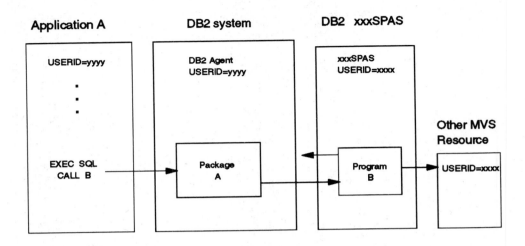

Figure 5. Userids for Accessing SQL and Non-SQL Resources

Non-SQL Resource Considerations: The DB2 for MVS/ESA SPAS is treated as a normal address space by MVS. If you access recoverable resources, such as CICS transactions, DB2 for MVS/ESA is unaware of this activity and thus does not perform commit coordination. Any changes made in these recoverable resources are in a separate unit of work; the commit or abort is independent of the commit or abort action taken by the DB2 for MVS/ESA thread.

The SPAS contains multiple MVS TCBs, which are used to run multiple stored procedures in parallel. If you access non-SQL resources, you must ensure that they can accommodate concurrent access by multiple applications, or TCBs, in the same address space. If parallel processing is not possible, you must serialize the access within your application, for example, by using MVS ENQUEUE services.

2.3.3 DB2 common server

DB2 common server V2 also provides stored procedures to broaden your client/server implementation choices. In this section we discuss some implementation aspects of stored procedures that are specific to DB2 common server.

2.3.3.1 Client Implementation

Local DB2 common server applications can issue an SQL CALL statement to invoke a stored procedure at a remote database server. The database server can be any type of

RDBMS that supports the CALL statement, for example, DB2 for MVS/ESA, or DB2 common server. The client application and the stored procedure are on the same RDBMS; the stored procedure is executed locally.

The SQL CALL statement can be embedded in an application program, and it can only be run statically. However, the procedure name and the input parameters can be determined at execution time by using host variables. The syntax of the statement is as follows:

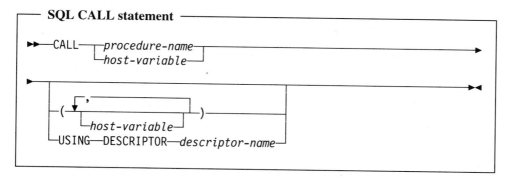

There are two ways of specifying the procedure name in your CALL statement: a *host variable* or a *procedure name*. If you use a host variable, the value is not converted to uppercase. If you use a *procedure name*, the value is converted to uppercase.

A procedure name can be up to 254 bytes and take several forms, depending on the server at which the procedure is stored; for example, DB2 common server supports library and function names, wherea DB2 for MVS/ESA supports three-part names. For portability, the procedure name should be specified as a character string of no longer than 8 bytes. For more information about the naming conventions for procedure names for each server, refer to *DB2 SQL Reference for common servers*.

The method of assigning variables to parameters of the procedure is similar to that for DB2 for MVS/ESA. See 2.3.2.1, "Client Implementation" on page 27.

Depending on the server where the stored procedure is located, your client program parameters might or might not have to match exactly those of the stored procedure. If the server is a DB2 common server, the parameters must have matching data types. If the server is DB2 for MVS/ESA or DB2 for OS/400, conversion between compatible data types is carried out by the server. For example, the INTEGER data type in your client program is converted to match with the FLOAT data type of the stored procedure.

2.3.3.2 Call Level Interface

CLI programs can invoke stored procedures by passing a CALL statement to an *SQLExecDirect()* function or to an *SQLPrepare()* function followed by an *SQLExecute()* function. Although CALL statements cannot be prepared dynamically, CLI accepts the statements as if they could be dynamically prepared. For details on using the CLI refer to the *DB2 Call Level Interface Guide and Reference for common servers.*

You can use the *SQLProcedures()* function to obtain a list of stored procedures available at the database server and the *SQLProcedureColumns()* function to determine the type of parameters for the stored procedure. These functions can be used for the DB2 common server and DB2 for MVS/ESA.

2.3.3.3 Server Implementation

DB2 common server supports static and dynamic SQL in stored procedures. You can develop stored procedures in the following languages:

- COBOL
- C, C++
- REXX
- Fortran

The stored procedure cannot issue COMMIT or ROLLBACK statements, either statically or dynamically, if the client application has the CONNECT TYPE 2 parameter in effect.

To build a stored procedure you must

1. Precompile it
2. Compile it
3. Link it to produce a library
4. Bind it to the database server

Note that, for all of these steps, the procedure must use the same code page as the database. In addition, if you execute the client program and the procedure on the same node (same machine), this node must be configured as a client/server.

Stored Procedure and Fencing: A stored procedure can run outside the firewall, that is, isolated from the database manager, or inside the firewall, that is, together with the database manager. The latter is called a *not-fenced stored procedure*. You can indicate that a stored procedure is fenced or not-fenced by placing it in a special directory. For an OS/2 example, assuming that DB2 is installed in the D: drive, place a stored procedure in

---

1 For AIX to support REXX, you have to install IBM AIX REXX/6000.

the *D:\SQLLIB\function* path for a fenced stored procedure and in the *D:\SQLLIB\function\unfenced* path for a not-fenced stored procedure.

Not-fenced stored procedures provide a performance gain: however, they could damage your database. Thus you should use a not-fenced stored procedure only when you have to maximize the performance benefits and only after you have thoroughly tested the stored procedure before you run it as a not-fenced stored procedure.

OS/2 supports programs to run in multiple threads. If you run not-fenced stored procedures in OS/2, ensure that the program is reentrant, or that the access to the static variables of the program is serialized.

DB2 common server Catalog Table: To support client applications to use the *SQLProcedures()* and *SQLProcedureColumn()* functions, you must define the stored procedure in the *pseudo catalog table for stored procedure registration*, which is a table with the name DB2CLI.PROCEDURES.   DB2 common server supplies a sample command line processor input file, STORPROC.DDL, which you can use to create the table. The pseudo catalog table is basically a derivation and an extension of the DB2 for MVS/ESA SYSIBM.SYSPROCEDURES table. For more information about the pseudo catalog table refer to the *DB2 Call Level Interface Guide and Reference for common servers*.

Authorization: To use stored procedures, the client authorization ID must be given at least one of the following privileges in DB2 common server:

- EXECUTE privilege on the stored procedure package
- CONTROL privilege on the stored procedure package
- SYSADM or DBADM authority

2.4 Triggers

Triggers represent one of the most powerful new features of DB2 for OS/400 and DB2 common server. We describe several techniques to show how you can take advantage of triggers in your application environment.

Triggers are *application independent.* They are user-written programs that are activated by the database manager when some data change is performed in the database. Triggers are mainly intended for monitoring database changes and taking appropriate actions. The main advantage of using triggers instead of calling the program from within an application is that triggers are activated automatically, no matter which interface generated the data change.

In addition, once a trigger has been put in place, application programmers and end users will not be able to circumvent it. When a trigger gets activated, the control shifts from the application program to the database manager, and the operating system executes the specifications you coded in the trigger program to perform the actions you designed. The application waits until the trigger ends and then gets control again.

It is important to identify which database files have to be monitored and which events should call the triggers, keeping in mind that a trigger is called every time the event occurs. We recommend that you think of triggers as part of your database design rather than as a function related to a specific application.

You can use a trigger program for the following purposes:

- Enforce business rules, no matter how complex they are

  You might want to ensure, for instance, that whenever you enter an order in your database, the customer you are dealing does not have a bad credit history. A trigger associated with the order file can perform this checking consistently and take the appropriate actions.

- Data validation and audit trail

  You might need to ensure that whenever a sales representative enters an order, he or she is actually assigned to that particular customer. You also want to keep track of the violation attempts. Again, a trigger could be activated on the order file to perform the validation and track the violators in a separate file.

- Integrating existing applications and advanced technologies

  Your company sends a confirmation fax to customers after they have accepted an order from you. Triggers can be the ideal solution to integrate your existing order entry application with your new facsimile support on AS/400.

- Preserve data consistency across different files

  In this case, triggers can complement the referential integrity support, because they provide a powerful range of data validation and business actions to be performed when data changes in your database.

Triggers ensure that your database always complies with your business needs, providing consistent checking and taking the appropriate actions every time data is changed.

Triggers provide the following benefits:

- Application independence

  DB2 for OS/400 and DB2 common server activate the trigger program no matter which interface you are using to access the data. Rules implemented by triggers are enforced consistently by the system rather than a single application.

- Easy maintenance

  If you must change the business rules in your database environment, you simply have to update or rewrite the triggers. You do not have to change the applications; they will transparently comply with the new rules.

- Code reusability

  Functions implemented at the database level are automatically available to all applications using that database. You do not have to replicate those functions throughout the different applications.

- Easy client/server application development

  Client/server applications take advantage of triggers. In a client/server environment triggers provide a way of splitting the application logic between the client and the server system. In Figure 6 on page 42, you can see how client applications need not implement the functions performed by the triggers on the server side. In addition, client applications do not need specific code to activate the logic on the server side. Application performance might also benefit from this implementation by reducing data traffic across communication lines.

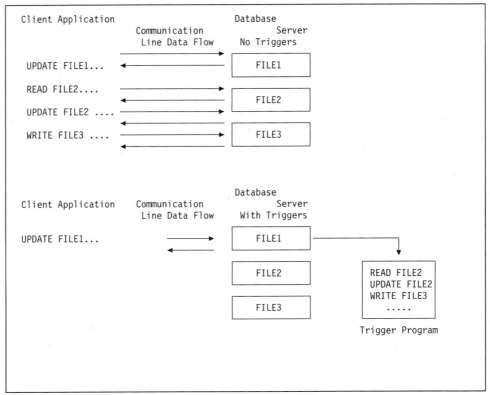

Figure 6. Using Triggers in Client/Server Application Development

2.4.1 Trigggers and DRDA

Consider the following DRDA level 2 AR design with triggers for DB2 for OS/400:

1. If you have to access and modify data located at a remote site from within a trigger, you can open Distribued Data Management Architecture (DDM) files or start an Advanced Program-to-Program Communication (APPC) session with a remote partner program. When accessing remote data in those ways, you can take advantage of the two-phase commit offered by DB2 for OS/400. If the trigger fails after a remote access and an exception is sent back to the originating application, the whole transaction will be put into a rollback required state. In these cases, it is absolutely necessary that an escape message is sent back to the calling interface, by either the system or the trigger, to ensure that all changes are rolled back consistently.

2. The following SQL and command language (CL) statements are never allowed on trigger programs:

- SQL CONNECT statement
- SQL SET CONNECTION statement
- CRTSQLPKG

3. As Figure 7 shows, triggers can be activated remotely by a DRDA change. Data changes performed by the trigger program can be commited or rolled back by the AR, if the trigger program is compiled with ACTGRP(*CALLER).

If you have to access multiple locations in the same logical unit of work, the AR has to control the connection switching.

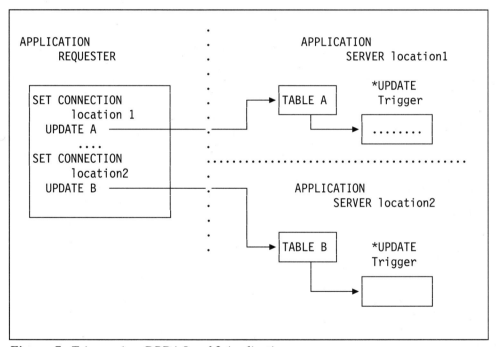

Figure 7. *Triggers in a DRDA Level 2 Application*

For more information about the design and implementation of triggers refer to *DB2/400 Advanced Database Functions*.

Chapter 3. DRDA Concepts and DB2 Products

Today many companies and organizations use personal computers and UNIX-based workstations to run graphical user interface (GUI) applications. To enforce access control, data security, data integrity, and daily backups, many of those companies and organizations have decided to keep their vital data on mainframes. Connecting that data on different platforms has been a problem for a long time. The use of DRDA overcomes this problem.

In this chapter we describe the basic principles and concepts of using DRDA to connect IBM RDBMSs on different operating systems.

3.1 DRDA Concepts

The foundation of IBM's distributed database solution, DRDA, is a robust software architecture that protects data integrity and security. The DB2 family of products implements DRDA. DRDA enables you to keep your existing security, backup, accounting, and other data management procedures while allowing you to access your data with applications through the GUI on your workstation.

DRDA is a set of protocols that allow transparent connectivity between RDBMSs on different platforms, whether they are in different rooms or on different continents. DRDA coordinates communication between systems by defining what must be exchanged and how it must be exchanged.

At this time, DRDA describes two levels of distribution: *RUW* and *DUW*. All DRDA products support RUW where an application can access one database server with multiple requests within one unit of work. DUW allows an application to access more than one database server within a unit of work; that is, the application can switch between database servers before committing the data. This gives an application programmer the ability to create an application involving multiple database servers, local and remote, at the same time.

Any combination of RDBMSs that supports DRDA can be connected within one unit of work, with the exception of SQL/DS for VSE, which can only be an AS. Your ability to update multiple databases by using DUW depends on the products you are using.

DDCS for OS/2 and DDCS for AIX allow client application enablers (CAEs) on OS/2, DOS, Windows, and AIX database platforms to transparently access and update database objects on DRDA servers. The DB2 common server products have also implemented the

DRDA AS function, which enables applications on MVS/ESA, VM, and OS/400 to access data in DB2 common servers without having DDCS for OS/2 or DDCS for AIX installed.

3.1.1 Architectures Used to Access Distributed Data

To implement the connections between a DRDA database server and a DRDA requester the following IBM architectures are used:

- System Network Architecture (SNA)

  Describes the rules that products agree on when exchanging data.

- Distributed Data Management Architecture (DDM)

  Describes the model of the database environment. It provides commands, parameters, data objects, and reply messages that work as an intermediate language that all systems understand.

- SNA Management Architecture (MSA)

  Transfers and manages alerts. It defines a consistent method of sending and recording error messages.

- Formatted Data Object Content Architecture (FD:OCA)

  Provides a description of the data with information about data types and representation.

- Character Data Representation Architecture (CDRA)

  Provides character data integrity when data is transmitted between systems with different code pages and character representation.

3.1.2 Roles of DRDA Databases

In a DRDA environment every database platform can play a different role for different applications at the same time. So it may well be that DB2 for MVS/ESA is acting as an AS for an OS/2 application and, at the same time, as an AR for an MVS application connecting through DRDA to an OS/400.

3.1.2.1 Clients

A database client is the component that runs the application program which issues SQL statements to request the data. Typical database clients are the CAE components that are available for OS/2, DOS, Windows, and AIX on IBM platforms.

3.1.2.2 Application Requesters

In DRDA terminology, an AR is the code that handles the application end of a distributed connection; it is the application that is requesting data or services from the AS. In a workstation environment, the DDCS product functions as an AR on behalf of application programs. As DRDA does not require any local database functions, DDCS can be installed without having the support for local databases. DDCS provides access to host database servers for applications executing in the DDCS workstation or acting as a gateway for applications executing on a client workstation. For example, on an AIX workstation you need only DDCS for AIX to connect to the host databases. DB2 for AIX is not required unless there is a requirement to process a local database on the workstation. The DDCS for OS/2 gateway supports NetBIOS, TCP/IP, Novell IPX/SPX, and APPC for client communications. The DDCS for AIX gateway supports TCP/IP, Novell IPX/SPX, and APPC for client communications.

A request is routed to the correct destination by using database directories that contain the communication information and the name of the target database server.

3.1.2.3 Application Servers

In DRDA terminology, an AS is the code that handles the database end of the connection. It performs database operations for the client and sends the results back to the requesting client. The AS code is part of the database management system on which the requested data resides.

3.1.3 Degrees of Distribution

There are several degrees of distribution of database management. This section explains the degree of distribution you need to satisfy different DRDA requirements. Table 4 summarizes the main characteristics of each distribution type.

Table 4. *Types of Access to Distributed Database*

Distribution Type	Requests in a Unit of Work	RDBMS in a Unit of Work	RDBMS in a Request	Commitment Control
				Number of RDBMSs
RUW	Many	One	One	Single Phase
				Single RDBMS
DUW	Many	Many	One	Two Phase
				Coordinated across multiple RDBMSs
Database Directed DUW	Many	Many	One	Two Phase
				Coordinated across multiple RDBMSs
Distributed Request	Many	Many	Many	Two Phase
				Coordinated across multiple RDBMSs

A unit of work is a single logical transaction of one or more SQL statements in which either all of the statements commit successfully or, if one statement fails to commit, the whole sequence is considered unsuccessful. As a consequence, if the transaction is successful, the changes requested are applied to the database, and the transaction is committed. If any part of the transaction is unsuccessful, the requested changes are not applied, and the RDBMS rolls back the transaction; that is, the database is in the same condition as it was before the transaction was started.

3.1.3.1 RUW

RUW is implemented in DRDA level 1. RUW allows an application program to read or update data at one remote location in a unit of work. Each RUW can contain multiple SQL statements that must access the same database management system. An application program can update several remote databases, but it can access only one database within a unit of work. When the application is ready to commit the work, the commit is initiated at the database management system where the unit of work was executed. The next unit of work can then access either the same database management system or another one. Figure 8 summarizes RUW.

- DRDA level 1
- One RDBMS in a unit of work
- Multiple requests in a unit of work
- Multiple cursors in a unit of work
- One RDBMS in a request
- Application program initiates the commit or rollback.
- Commitment at a single RDBMS

Figure 8. RUW Summary

3.1.3.2 DUW

DUW is implemented in DRDA level 2. It allows an application program to access more than one database within a unit of work, that is, the application can switch between different databases before committing the data. It is possible to have an application program working with multiple databases within the same unit of work, regardless of whether the database servers are remote or local.

DUW supports two-phase commit. Commit and rollback are coordinated at all database server locations so that, if a failure occurs anywhere in the system, data integrity is preserved. Commitment coordination is provided by an SPM.

With DUW capability, you can connect to multiple database servers without disconnecting from the previously established connections. Opened cursors are kept open until the application disconnects from the database server.

Your ability to update multiple databases within a unit of work involving two-phase commit depends on the DRDA level supported by the participants. Figure 9 on page 49 summarizes DUW.

- DRDA level 2
- Several RDBMS in a unit of work
- Application directs the distribution of work
- Multiple requests in a unit of work
- Multiple cursors in a unit of work
- One RDBMS in a request
- Application program initiates the commit or rollback.
- Commitment coordination across multiple RDBMS

Figure 9. DUW Summary

3.1.3.3 Database-Directed DUW

In database-directed DUW, within one unit of work, an application connects to a database management system that can execute one or more requests locally or route some or all of the SQL requests to other database management systems. The database management system determines which system manages the data referenced by the SQL request and automatically directs the request to that system. Within a single unit of work, SQL statements can be directed to multiple database management systems, but all objects of a single SQL statement are constrained to be at a single database management system.

When the application commits the unit of work, it initiates the commit, and commitment coordination is provided by an SPM. Figure 10 summarizes database-directed DUW.

- Architecture not yet defined
- Several RDBMS in a unit of work
- Database directs the distribution of work
- Multiple requests in a unit of work
- Multiple cursors in a unit of work
- One RDBMS in a request
- Application program initiates the commit or rollback.
- Commitment coordination across multiple RDBMS

Figure 10. Database-Directed DUW Summary

3.1.3.4 Distributed Request

The distributed request (DR) is significantly more sophisticated than RUW and DUW. It removes all data location restrictions. Although DR has not yet been fully described in DRDA, it will eventually enable you to access data at multiple locations within a single SQL statement.

With DR, you can have several SQL statements within a unit of work, and you can access more than one RDBMS with each SQL statement. It allows, for instance, joining of database tables residing on different platforms. Commit and rollback will also be coordinated for DR. Figure 11 summarizes DR.

- Architecture not yet defined
- Several RDBMS in a unit of work
- Database directs the distribution of work
- Multiple requests in a unit of work
- Multiple cursors in a unit of work
- Several RDBMS in a request
- Application program initiates the commit or rollback.
- Commitment coordination across multiple RDBMS

Figure 11. Distributed Request Summary

3.2 The DB2 Family of Products

In this section we cover the products that are available today to manage your enterprise data so that you can access it as easily as if it were on your local workstation.

IBM RDBMS products are available on many different operating systems, including MVS, VM, VSE, OS/400, OS/2, AIX, HP-UX, and Solaris. These products are collectively known as the DB2 family of products. They are available for the mainframe and for Intel- and UNIX-based platforms.

All members of the DB2 family have the same basic architecture as the original MVS/ESA version and use many of the same key algorithms. It is important to understand, however, that the later products are not just a port from DB2 for MVS/ESA to other operating systems. Their internal components have been optimized to exploit the specific features of each platform.

The following products are available:

- DB2 for MVS/ESA

- SQL/DS for VM

- SQL/DS for VSE
- DB2 for OS/400
- DB2 Parallel Edition for AIX
- DB2 common server
  - for OS/2
  - for AIX
  - for Sun Solaris
  - for HP-UX
  - for Windows NT
  - for Sinix
  - DB2 Software Developer's Kit (SDK) Version 2.

Although DB2 for MVS/ESA is known as a robust database with very high availability, performance, and usability, the new Version 4 provides a better platform than ever for application development and data management in an open client/server environment. Version 4 improves DB2's foundation for data integrity and security in a distributed enterprise. Up to 25,000 distributed users can connect to a DB2 for MVS/ESA subsystem. A total of 2,000 threads can be active simultaneously, which enables 200,000 concurrent connections with 16,000 active threads in an eight-way data-sharing configuration.

SQL/DS is a vital component in IBM's Information Warehouse strategy. It is a key member of the DB2 family of products and represents the strategic relational database product for VSE and VM operating environments. SQL/DS provides database solutions across operating systems and ever-increasing levels of integration among all members of the DB2 family.

Note: SQL/DS is the DB2 equivalent for the VSE and VM operating system environments. Its name will be changed to DB2 for VSE and DB2 for VM in the next release.

DB2 for OS/400 provides the stability and compatibility of previous releases of the AS/400 database (database management systems) with the standards-based technology required for an unlike computing environment. DB2 for OS/400 gives you standards conformance, advanced functions, distributed capabilities, and high performance. The DB2 for OS/400 product is integrated directly into OS/400. It includes the support necessary for new and existing database applications for AS/400.

DB2 Parallel Edition is an extension of the DB2 for AIX relational database for RISC System/6000 systems. It is an industrial strength database management system for use in decision support, online transaction processing, and line-of-business applications. DB2 Parallel Edition specializes in speeding up complex queries by splitting them into many parts that can then be run on many processor nodes in parallel. Queries that once took hours or even days to run on conventional systems can now be executed in minutes. DB2 Parallel Edition is implemented using a "shared nothing" architecture. Such an architecture allows nodes to be added to the system easily, providing near-linear performance scale-up as nodes are added to your parallel system. All access plans are automatically created for parallel execution, with standard SQL and no additional programming.

DB2 products running on a workstation are collectively known as DB2 common server. They run on similar platforms and share the same code base. For each platform—OS/2, AIX, HP-UX, Windows NT, Sinix, and Sun Solaris—a set of products and components are available and can include the following:

- DB2, the relational database engine
- DDCS, used to access DRDA ASs
- Administrator's Toolkit, used at the client or server workstation to perform database administration tasks
- Client application enablers, used at the client workstation
- Software Developer's Kit, used at the client or server workstation to develop database applications

Figure 12 on page 53 shows the conceptual relationship among the components of DB2 common server. More information on valid configurations and environments is presented throughout this book and in the *Information and Concepts Guide for common servers*.

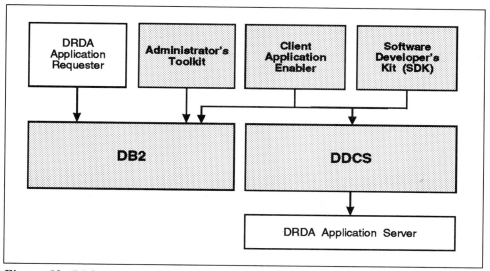

Figure 12. DB2 common server Components

3.2.1 DB2 common server Connectivity Concepts

DB2 common server products offer two major options when it comes to connecting to other DB2 relational database engines:

- Remote data services (RDS) - also known as DB2 common server private protocol
- DRDA.

You have no option but DRDA when you have to connect a DB2 common server to DB2 running on a mainframe platform like MVS, VM, VSE or OS/400. You can choose between RDS and DRDA when you have to establish connections between DB2 common servers. In this particular case, however, the recommended option is RDS, for at least four reasons:

- RDS gives better performance than DRDA in a workstation environment.
- RDS provides more connectivity options for network protocols.
- You do not need DDCS (a separately priced product)
- At the time of writing, RDS provides more in terms of distributed features, allowing DUW with two-phase-commit support. The DRDA level currently implemented by DB2 common server products provides DUW capability but without two-phase commit protocol support, unless there is a suitable transaction manager like ENCINA. Note that generally this is true for DB2 common servers only. You can

exploit DUW with two-phase commit support, for example, between DB2 for MVS and DB2 for OS/400.

Needless to say, in your network you can have both DRDA and RDS connections and that is even true for a single workstation. For example, you can have a DB2 common server connected through DRDA to some DB2s on mainframes, connected through RDS to some DB2 common servers, and connected through DRDA (although not recommended) to other DB2 common servers as well.

Although there are two different options when connecting DB2 common servers, the option you choose does not in any way affect your environment and the way you develop applications (apart from what we previously stated about the temporarily different support offered in terms of distributed features). Both DRDA and RDS have the common goal of making it possible to develop applications that can transparently access databases located over a network, providing the features that you normally expect from more traditional, single database oriented applications (concurrency control, transaction integrity, access control).

The difference between RDS and DRDA is that DRDA broadens the scope to make it all possible also outside the workstation-like environment and, since it is a published architecture, to any non-IBM product that complies with it. This redbook focuses on DRDA connectivity options. However, in Chapter 7, "DB2 common server Client Connectivity" on page 201 you can find information about RDS connectivity.

Whichever you choose, RDS or DRDA, to establish connections you must:

- Configure the network
- Configure the database product installed on the workstation.

Note that DB2 common server, as well as any other product of the DB2 family, does not come with specific software for network communications. It relies on one of the communications software products available in the marketplace.

3.2.2 Product Levels Required

This section provides you technical information about the prerequisite product levels you need to implement a DRDA environment similar to the environment we implemented during the residencies. However, the software market changes quickly, so contact your software dealer or your IBM Representative or consult the appropriate forum on CompuServe or the Internet to obtain the latest information.

3.2.2.1 DRDA Workstation Products

DDCS for OS/2 Version 2.3 prerequisites:

- One of the following operating systems:

- IBM OS/2 Version 2.11 or later
- IBM OS/2 Warp
- IBM OS/2 Warp Connect

- IBM Communications Manager/2 Version 1.1 or later

- IBM DB2 common server Version 2.1 or later if you want to install local databases on your DDCS gateway

You can connect to the following IBM relational database products:

- DB2 for MVS/ESA Version 2 Release 3 or later
- SQL/DS Version 3 Release 3 for VM/SP R6 or VM/ESA R1 or later
- SQL/DS Version 3 Release 4 for VSE/ESA V1.3 or later
- DB2 for OS/400 Version 2 Release 2 or later

DDCS for AIX Version 2.3 prerequisites:

- One of the following operating systems:

  - IBM AIX Version 3.2.4
  - IBM AIX Version 3.2.5
  - IBM AIX Version 4.1 or later

- If you have IBM AIX 3.3.4 or 3.2.5 installed, you need one of the following products:

  - IBM AIX Server/6000 Version 2.1.1 with PTFs U435033 and U435034
  - IBM AIX Services/6000 Version 1.2 with PTFs U417689

- If you have IBM AIX 4.1 you need one of the following products:

  - IBM SNA Server/6000 Version 2.2
  - IBM Desktop SNA Version 1.1

You can connect to the following IBM relational database products:

- DB2 for MVS/ESA Version 2 Release 3 or later
- SQL/DS Version 3 Release 3 for VM/SP R6 or VM/ESA R1 or later
- SQL/DS Version 3 Release 4 for VSE/ESA V1.3 or later
- DB2 for OS/400 Version 2 Release 2 or later

3.2.2.2 DRDA Host Products
DB2 for MVS Version 2 Release 3 prerequisites:

The following fixes are required:

- APAR PN60988 to use DB2 for MVS/ESA as an AR to DB2 common server products
- PTF UN54600 to connect to AIX

- PTF UN56735 for correction of DRDA protocol errors

DB2 for MVS/ESA Version 3 Release 1 prerequisites:

The following fixes are required:

- APAR PN60988 to use DB2 for MVS/ESA as an AR
- PTF UN54601 to connect to AIX
- PTF UN56736 for correction of DRDA protocol errors
- PTF UN73393 to use two-phase commit with CICS/6000

DB2 for MVS/ESA Version 4 Release 1 prerequisites:

The following fixes are required:

- APAR PN69689 to use DRDA stored procedures with COBOL or PL/I
- APAR PN69748 to use DRDA stored procedures with C

SQL/DS Version 3 Release 3 for VM and VSE prerequisites:

The following fixes are required:

- PTF UN43497 to connect to AIX
- APAR PN69073 to use SQL/DS on VM as an AR
- PTF UN47865 to use SQL/DS on VM as an AR from AIX

DB2 for OS/400 Version 2 Release 2 prerequisites:

The following fixes are required:

- PTF SF13747 to connect to AIX
- PTF SF13748 to connect to AIX

3.3 DRDA Network Connection

DRDA uses the LU 6.2 protocol for communication between the AR and the AS in an SNA network. The LU 6.2 protocol is also known as APPC. For more information on APPC, see the chapter entitled "LU 6.2 and APPC" in the *DRDA Connectivity Guide*.

For LU 6.2 communications between different platforms you can also use the IBM AnyNet family of products. The AnyNet products use features of VTAM to use APPC over a TCP/IP network. Thus two APPC application programs can communicate without any change through TCP/IP.

With DB2 common server Version 2.1, workstation database products are capable of DRDA AS functions. Application programs on MVS, VM, and OS/400 can directly access all DRDA server platforms, whereas application programs on AIX, OS/2, Windows, and DOS platforms need the DDCS product.

Figure 13 on page 58 shows a typical DRDA environment. Remote clients are included in the example. If you do not need remote clients, there is no need to install remote client support. You can also use a single-user DDCS system, which supports only one user at a time and no remote clients.

Depending on the operating system of the DDCS workstation and of the remote client, different communication protocols are available.

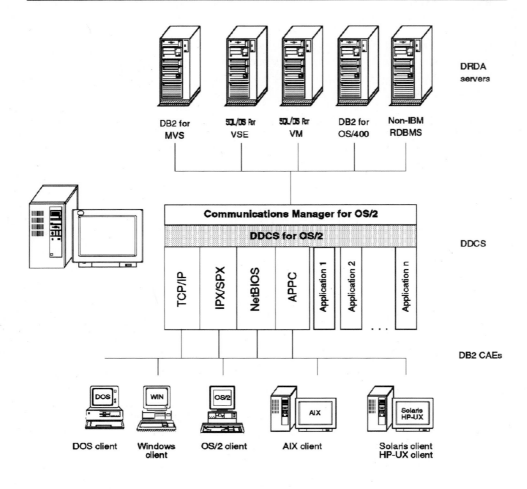

Figure 13. DDCS Connections (OS/2 Example)

Detailed information about communication protocol support is given in the *Information and Concepts Guide for common servers*.

You do not have to have the DB2 relational database engine installed on the DDCS workstation. If you want a complete RDBMS on the DDCS workstation, you can order DB2 separately.

3.3.1.1 APPC and APPN

Before you can establish a connection between two nodes you must consider the differences between APPC and Advanced Peer-to-Peer Networking (APPN).

In an APPC environment an application in one node can communicate on a peer basis with an application in another node. Communication is possible only if one node has explicit definitions for the other node.

In an APPN environment there is no need for one node to have explicit definitions for the other node. A node can initiate a session to any partner by using dynamic resource definition. APPN network nodes provide intermediate session routing, enabling a session to pass through another node so that each APPN network node acts as a system services control point (SSCP). Figure 14 shows an example of an APPN network.

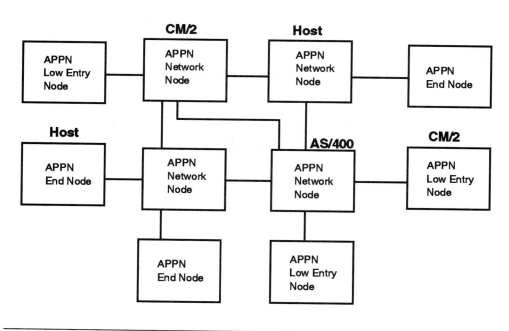

Figure 14. APPN Network

There are two types of APPN nodes:

- Network node (NN)

  An NN provides such APPN services as session routing and directory service to other APPN nodes attached to it.

- End node (EN)

  An EN must be connected to an NN to take advantage of the APPN routing services. Only one NN can be designated as the preferred NN server.

  An EN without a node server is referred to as a low entry network (LEN) node. An LEN cannot use APPN routing services; therefore you must define all resources it wants to use.

Figure 15 shows the difference between APPC and APPN. Let us assume that node C is a network node; if you use APPC verbs, you can connect from node A, node B, node D, and node E to node C. To connect from node A to node E, however, you have to go through node C, so you have to use APPN verbs.

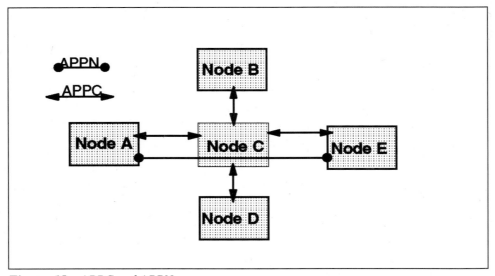

Figure 15. APPC and APPN

3.3.1.2 Establishing a Conversation

To establish a conversation, several events have to occur before the data can be transferred between the two nodes. When the workstation node dials in to the network node it sends a frame called XID. This XID contains the node ID (IDBLK/IDNUM in VTAM terminology) of the calling workstation. If VTAM finds a matching physical unit (PU) definition, it activates the resources belonging to that PU. Refer to Appendix A, "SNA Definitions and Connectivity Parameters" on page 517.

To activate an LU to LU session, a BIND request must be sent from one LU to the other. The BIND request sent by the originating LU is negotiable, that is, the receiving LU can return a BIND response indicating that it wants to change certain characteristics. In this way the relationship between the two LUs for this session is negotiated, and a single session is started as shown in Figure 16 on page 61.

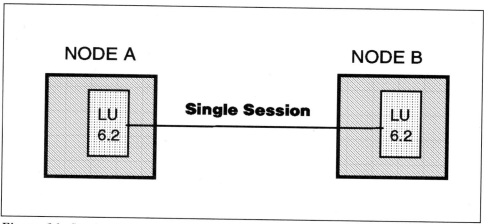

Figure 16. *Single Session*

The single session manages the movement of data. You can also initiate parallel sessions between the same LU pair or multiple sessions with more than one partner LU as shown in Figure 17 on page 62.

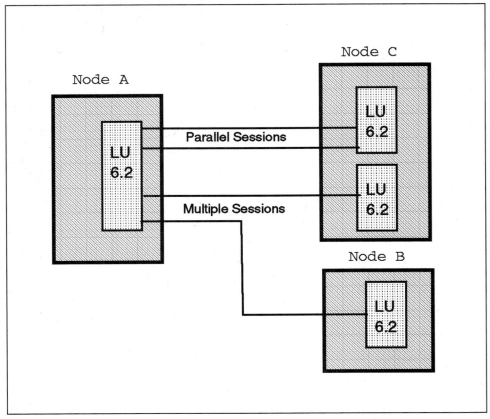

Figure 17. Session Types

After the session is successfully started, an ALLOCATE verb issued by one of the transaction programs (TPs) can start the conversation. A TP is an application program that issues APPC commands and communicates with the other TP application at the remote side. The TP requester program must specify the following information to establish an APPC conversation:

1. Local LU to identify the LU to be used on this node

2. Partner LU to identify the LU on the remote node

3. The mode used for the LU to LU session

4. The transaction program name (TPN) of the application to start on the remote node.

A conversation is a send and receive relationship between two TPs using APPC verbs as shown in Figure 18 on page 63. There can never be more than one conversation in a session. If multiple conversations are needed, you must use parallel sessions.

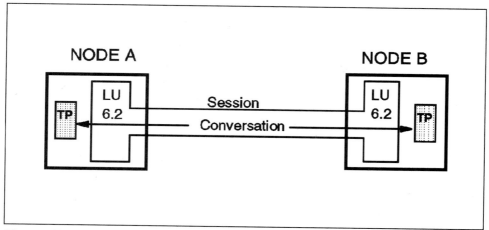

Figure 18. *Conversation*

Figure 19 on page 64 summarizes the process to establish a conversation between a server and a requester.

1. Establish the link

   This is shown as an SSCP to SSCP session. It could also be a control point (CP) to CP session.

2. Start the session

   This is shown as an LU to LU session.

3. Initiate the conversation

   This is the establishment of the conversation between the two TPs (APPL).

Whenever a requester allocates a conversation, such information as the partner LU name, the TPN (APPL) that should be invoked on the server, and the log mode name must be provided. In the workstation environment you specify this information in the LU 6.2 side information profile.

When a request to invoke a TP is received on a server workstation, you must configure a TP profile with information about where to find the executable for the TPN and its characteristics.

If a workstation is both a requester and a server, both profiles (TP and LU 6.2 side information) must be configured.

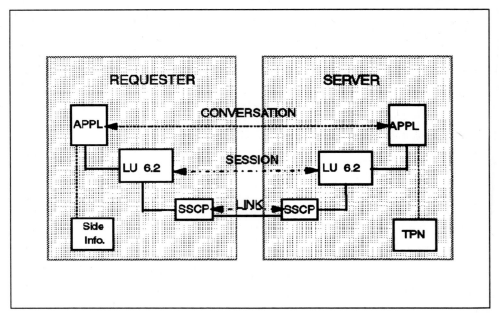

Figure 19. Connection

Chapter 4. ITSO System Scenario

In this chapter we describe the network and systems setup for the IBM ITSO centers where the DRDA connectivity project was conducted. We also describe the software and hardware that were used for the project.

Four ITSO centers participated in this project: San Jose, California, Rochester, Minnesota, and Poughkeepsie, New York, in the United States, and Boeblingen, Germany.

The objectives of our project were to

- Set up DRDA connections among the ITSO centers
- Develop some sample applications
- Demonstrate DRDA AR and AS functions using the sample applications

The four centers are linked by several networking systems because they are "remote" from each other. Figure 20 illustrates the approximate geographical distances among the four centers.

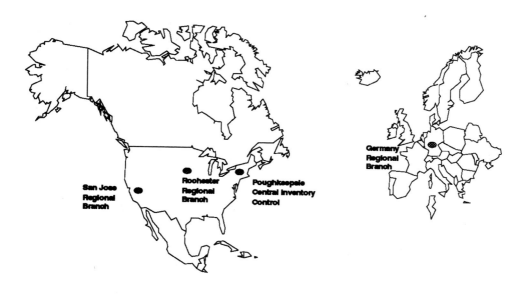

Figure 20. *ITSO System Scenario*

Our sample application scenario involves an international product distribution company that processes its inventory control on a central system located in Poughkeepsie. The company also has regional branches in Europe and in the eastern and western United States. One of the company's policies is that each regional branch can purchase the hardware equipment that meets its needs. We discuss the application design that supports this policy in Chapter 12, "Application Structure" on page 351.

4.1 Network Connectivity

The sample application chosen for our project is based on a well-known scenario used in other DRDA publications. We modified it to fit our environment in order to illustrate some important DRDA features, such as DUW and two-phase commit.

Our ITSO network environment includes resources from two networks: USIBMSC (United States) and DEIBMIPF (Germany). The two networks are linked by the IBM worldwide network, which consists of a series of components such as the network control program (NCP) connected to each other. Figure 21 on page 67 shows an overview of the network connections.

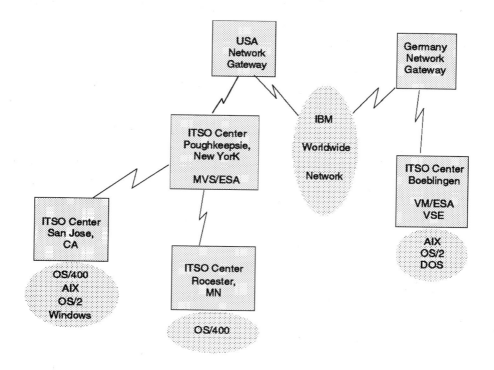

Figure 21. ITSO Network

Figure 21 also shows the operating systems for each ITSO center. The USIBMSC network for the United States consists of

- OS/400 at the ITSO-San Jose Center
- AIX at the ITSO-San Jose Center
- OS/2 at the ITSO-San Jose Center
- Windows at the ITSO-San Jose Center
- MVS/ESA at the ITSO-Poughkeepsie Center
- OS/400 at the ITSO-Rochester Center

The DEIBMIPF network for Germany consists of

- VM

- VSE
- AIX
- OS/2
- DOS

Several network components—token ring, split bridge, leased line, and backbone—make up the connections among the ITSO centers. Figure 22 shows the network connections with these components, the operating systems for each RDBMS, and the associated LU names.

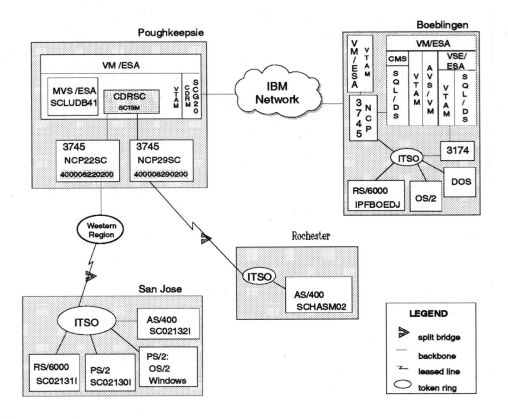

Figure 22. ITSO Network Configurations

The ITSO-San Jose Center systems and the ITSO-Rochester Center systems are connected to the token-ring segment in the corresponding centers. Each segment is bridged through one or more split bridges to a token-ring segment that is connected to the NCP (NCP22SC for the San Jose Center, NCP29SC for the Rochester Center) in Poughkeepsie. The systems use the NCPs as gateways, which are defined as switched major nodes in the USIBMSC network. Refer to 4.1.2.1, "San Jose" on page 71 and 4.1.2.3, "Rochester" on page 74 for the details of the connectivity setup for the two centers.

At the ITSO-Poughkeepsie Center, the MVS/ESA system is defined as part of the USIBMSC network.

The VM and VSE systems at ITSO-Boeblingen Center are connected through the IBM backbone network to the VTAM system at the ITSO-Poughkeepsie Center. The backbone network is illustrated by the *IBM Worldwide Network* in Figure 21 on page 67. Refer to 4.1.2.4, "Boeblingen" on page 76 for more details of the connectivity setup for the Boeblingen Center.

The USIBMSC network supports APPN, so we had the option of using APPN for communications among the United States centers. Some NCPs in the IBM network do not fully support APPN, so we used APPC for communications between Germany and the United States.

4.1.1 Connectivity Parameters

Before setting up the communications between any two systems, we recommend that you first collect the SNA and DRDA parameters for the local and partner systems. To obtain the SNA connectivity parameters, contact your network support personnel. To obtain the DRDA connectivity parameters, contact your database administrators.

The subsequent chapters in this book describe for each system platform the definitions and profiles from which you can obtain the SNA and DRDA parameter values. Table 5 and Table 6 on page 70 summarize the parameter values we used.

Table 5 (Page 1 of 2). SNA and DRDA Connectivity Parameter Values for USIBMSC					
Parameter	**MVS**	**OS/400 (San Jose)**	**OS/400 (Rochester)**	**AIX**	**OS/2**
3745 LAN address	n/a	400008220200	400008290200	400008220200	400008220200
Local LAN adapter address	n/a	400052047158	400052006000	4000520471C5	4000520471C7

Table 5 (Page 2 of 2). *SNA and DRDA Connectivity Parameter Values for USIBMSC*

Parameter	MVS	OS/400 (San Jose)	OS/400 (Rochester)	AIX	OS/2
TCP/IP address	n/a	n/a	n/a	9.113.36.198	9.113.36.232
IDBLK	n/a	056	056	071	05D
IDNUM	n/a	02132	06000	02131	02130
Control point	SC19M	SC02132I	SCHASM02	SC02131	SILVIO[2]
LU name	SCLUDB41	SC02132I	SCHASM02	SC02131I	SC02130I
RDB_NAME	CENTDB2	SJAS400	RCAS400	SJ6SMPL	SJ2SMPL
Transaction program prefix	X'07'	X'07'	X'07'	n/a	n/a
Transaction program name	6DB	6DB	6DB	DB26TPN	DB22TPN

Table 6. *SNA and DRDA Connectivity Parameter Values for DEIBMIPF*

Parameter	VM/ESA	VSE	AIX	OS/2
3174 LAN address	n/a	n/a	400020201001	400020201001
Local LAN adapter address	n/a	n/a	40001010101B	40001010100E
TCP/IP address	n/a	n/a	9.164.188.10	9.164.188.14
IDBLK	n/a	n/a		05D
IDNUM	n/a	n/a	*3	E00E
Control point	IPFV2	IPFV2A	IPFP221B	IPFCP20E
LU name	IPFA2GL4	IPFA21CD	IPFBOEDJ	IPFCL0E0
RDB_NAME	S34VMDB0	S34VSDB1	BO6SMPL	DBSRV4D
Transaction program name	S34VMDB0	TPN1	DB26KTP	DB2DUMMY

---

[2] The CP for OS/2 is the node name defined in the CM/2. We used APPN, so we could set the CP name to any character string of up to 8 bytes; we set the string to "SILVIO."

[3] The IDBLK and IDNUM for AIX is an XID node ID, which is set to "*" for peer connections.

For specific information on how to define each parameter, refer to the corresponding chapter for each platform.

It is not within the scope of this book to explain how to implement a VTAM network. You should work in collaboration with your network specialist to understand the existing VTAM environment in your enterprise. Discuss with your network specialist the modifications and extensions that your DRDA will require in the VTAM environment. Refer to Appendix A, "SNA Definitions and Connectivity Parameters" on page 517, for more information about connectivity parameters.

4.1.2 Hardware and Software Configurations

In this project we used IBM RDBMSs to illustrate their connectivity in a DRDA environment. We also focused on the development considerations for applications that access distributed data.

Each ITSO center has one or more RDBMSs installed. Some of the systems are connected to SNA through a token ring; others are defined as VTAM applications; it depends on the operating systems to which the RDBMSs belong. In this section we describe the hardware and software we used for the RDBMSs for each center.

4.1.2.1 San Jose

We installed the following RDBMSs in the ITSO-San Jose Center:

- DB2 for OS/400

- DB2 for AIX

- DB2 for OS/2

In addition we installed the Software Developer's Kit (SDK) for OS/2 and SDK for Windows in two separate PS/2s. Figure 23 on page 72 illustrates the machines, the RDBMSs, and the connectivity.

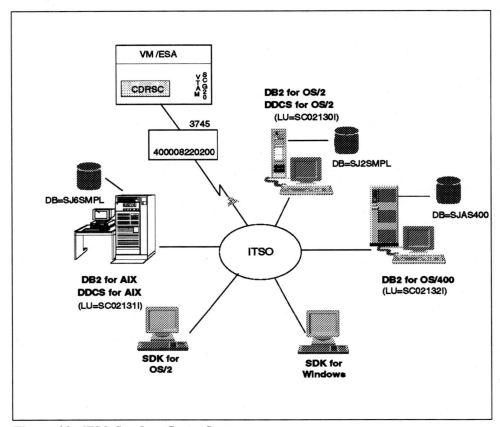

Figure 23. ITSO-San Jose Center Systems

The DB2 for AIX, OS/2, and OS/400 are AR and AS systems. They can establish connections to remote servers, for example, to the DB2 for MVS/ESA system, through the 3745, using APPN. The three machines can communicate with each other using *peer-to-peer* connections.

The SDK for OS/2 and SDK for Windows are clients. They can connect to any local and remote servers, for example, to the DB2 for OS/400 in Rochester, the SQL/DS for VM in Boeblingen, through DDCS for OS/2 or DDCS for AIX.

The token ring supports three communication protocols: NetBIOS, APPC, and TCP/IP. All systems in the token ring can use any one of the protocols, except for the Windows clients, which only support NetBIOS and TCP/IP.[4]

Table 7 summarizes the hardware we used for each operating system at the ITSO-San Jose Center.

Table 7. ITSO-San Jose Center Hardware	
Operating System	**Hardware**
OS/400	• AS/400 9404 E06 • 40 MB Memory • 4 GB DASD • 16/4 Token-Ring Adapter
AIX	• RISC System/6000 Model 4 • 128 MB Memory • 3 GB Hard Drive • 16/4 Token-Ring Adapter
OS/2, SDK/2, Windows	• PS/2 Model 9595 • 24 MB Memory • 1 GB Hard Drive • 16/4 Token-Ring Adapter

Table 8 summarizes the software we used for each machine.

Table 8 (Page 1 of 2). ITSO-San Jose Center Software	
Operating System	**Software**
OS/400	• OS/400 V3.1
AIX	• AIX/6000 V4.1.3 • SNA Server V2.2 for AIX/6000 • DB2 for AIX V2.1 • DDCS for AIX V2.3 • SDK for AIX V2.1

---

[4]   Windows clients also support IPX/SPX. However, we did not use IPX/SPX in our project, so we do not include it in our discussion.

Table 8 (Page 2 of 2). ITSO-San Jose Center Software	
Operating System	**Software**
OS/2	• OS/2 V3 • CM/2 V1.11 • TCP/IP for OS/2 V2.0 • DB2 for OS/2 Server V2.1 • DDCS for OS/2 MultiUser Gateway V2.3
OS/2	• OS/2 V3 • CM/2 V1.11 • TCP/IP for OS/2 V2.0 • SDK for OS/2 V2.1
Windows	• IBM DOS V6.3 • Microsoft Windows V3.1 • TCP/IP for DOS V2.1.1 • SDK for Windows V2.1 • Microsoft Visual C++ V1.50

4.1.2.2 Poughkeepsie

The hardware was a 9021 machine. We used DB2 for MVS/ESA V4.1, which ran on MVS/ESA V5.1.0. MVS/ESA was installed as a guest system under the VM/ESA system.

4.1.2.3 Rochester

We installed DB2 for OS/400 at the ITSO-Rochester Center. Figure 24 on page 75 illustrates the machine, the RDBMS, and the connectivity.

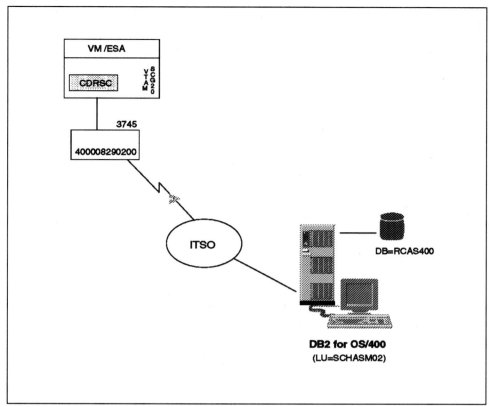

Figure 24. ITSO-Rochester Center System

The DB2 for OS/400 is an AR and AS system. It can establish connections to remote servers, for example, to the DB2 for MVS/ESA system through the 3745, using APPN.

Table 9 summarizes the hardware we used for the OS/400.

Table 9. ITSO-Rochester Center Hardware	
Operating System	**Hardware**
OS/400	• AS/400 9404 E06 • 40 MB Memory • 4 GB DASD • 16/4 Token-Ring Adapter

Table 10 on page 76 summarizes the software we used for the machine.

Table 10. ITSO-Rochester Center Software	
Operating System	**Software**
OS/400	• OS/400 V3.1

4.1.2.4 Boeblingen

We installed the following RDBMSs at the ITSO-Boeblingen Center:

- SQL/DS for VM
- SQL/DS for VSE
- DB2 for AIX
- DB2 for OS/2

In addition we installed the Software Developer's Kit (SDK) for DOS in a PS/2.

The VM and VSE systems were installed as guest systems under a VM/ESA system. There were two VTAM systems: one installed in the VSE system and the other in the VM/ESA system. Figure 25 on page 77 illustrates the machines, the RDBMSs, and the connectivity.

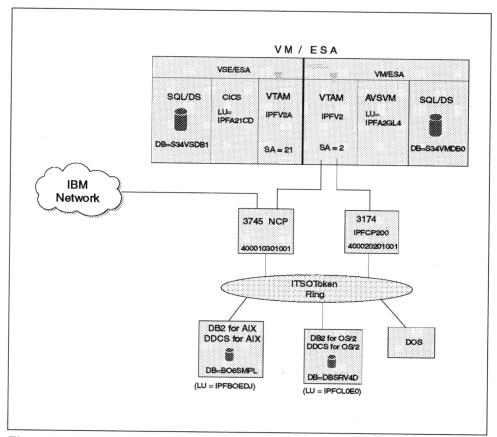

Figure 25. ITSO-Boeblingen Center Systems

The VTAM system in VM/ESA is connected to the 3745 NCP, which is linked to the IBM network that connects to Poughkeepsie. It is also connected to the other VTAM system through a virtual channel-to-channel adapter (VCTCA).

All systems in the token ring communicate with systems outside the token ring through the 3174 controller. Because the IBM network had not implemented full APPN support, APPN was not used in Boeblingen.

The SQL/DS systems communications are set up differently for the VM/ESA and the VSE environments. The S34VMDB0 uses the APPC/VM VTAM support (AVS) machine to handle APPC communications, and the S34VSDB1 uses CICS.

DB2 for AIX and DB2 for OS/2 are AS and AR systems. They can establish connections to remote servers, for example, to the DB2 for MVS/ESA system, through the 3174, using APPC. These two systems can communicate with each other using *peer-to-peer* connections.

The SDK/DOS is a client. It can connect to any local and remote servers, for example, to the DB2 for OS/400 in Rochester, to the DB2 for MVS/ESA in Poughkeepsie, through the DDCS for AIX or DDCS for OS/2 systems.

The token ring supports three communication protocols: NetBIOS, APPC, and TCP/IP. For communications between DB2 for OS/2 and DB2 for AIX, APPC or TCP/IP can be used. The DOS client can use NetBIOS or TCP/IP to connect to DB2 for OS/2 or DB2 for AIX.

Table 11 summarizes the hardware we used for each operating system.

Table 11. ITSO-Boeblingen Center Hardware	
Operating System	**Hardware**
VM/ESA VSE	• IBM 9221
AIX	• RISC System/6000 Model 520 • 64 MB Memory • 1 GB Hard Drive • 16/4 Token-Ring Adapter
OS/2	• PS/2 Model 9595 • 16 MB Memory • 1 GB Hard Drive • 16/4 Token-Ring Adapter
DOS	• PS/2 Model 8570 • 4 MB Memory • 120 MB Hard Drive

Table 12 summarizes the software we used for the machines.

Table 12 (Page 1 of 2). ITSO-Boeblingen Center Software	
Operating System	**Software**
VM/ESA	• VM/ESA V2.1 • SQL/DS V3.4

Operating System	Software
VSE	• VSE V1.3.4 • SQL/DS V3.4
AIX	• AIX/6000 V3.2.5 • SNA Server V2.1 for AIX/6000 • DB2 for AIX V2.1 • DDCS for AIX V2.3.
OS/2	• OS/2 V3 • CM/2 V1.11 • TCP/IP for OS/2 V2.0 • DB2 for OS/2 Server V2.1 • DDCS for OS/2 MultiUser Gateway V2.3.
DOS	• IBM DOS V6.3 • MS Windows V3.1 • TCP/IP for DOS V2.1.1 • SDK for Windows V2.1 • CAE/DOS V1.2.1.

Table 12 (Page 2 of 2). ITSO-Boeblingen Center Software

Chapter 5. OS/2 Platform

In this chapter we describe the different connectivity options for DB2 for OS/2 and explain how to configure an OS/2 workstation to act as a DRDA AR and AS.

The example we use in this chapter is the OS/2 platform at the ITSO-San Jose Center. A similar example was implemented at the ITSO-Boeblingen Center. We point out the differences where relevant.

5.1 DB2 for OS/2 Connectivity Options

Table 13 on page 82 summarizes the connectivity options for DB2 for OS/2 and DDCS for OS/2 from both the DRDA and RDS points of view. Refer to 3.2.1, "DB2 common server Connectivity Concepts" on page 53 to understand how to position RDS and DRDA. We followed the current terminology, which differs slightly between the two connectivity options, although the two basic roles (requiring and providing services) are, of course, conceptually the same regardless of the architecture.

Note that the DB2 for OS/2 server and DDCS for OS/2 server enable a single workstation to play the four roles indicated in Table 13 on page 82: RDS client, RDS server, DRDA AR, and DRDA AS.

Below we explain the entries in Table 13 on page 82.

Products implementing function
> One basic function can be found in more than one product. This is the case with the RDS client function (the core function of CAE for OS/2), which is also part of SDK, DB2, and DDCS for OS/2.

Network protocol
> Different network protocols are available to implement connectivity options.

Update system database directory
> The system database directory lists the databases available to applications. RDS and DRDA both require this directory to be updated on the client side.

Update node directory
> The node directory lists the network nodes holding databases. RDS and DRDA both require this directory to be updated on the client side.

Update DCS directory
> The DCS directory lists remote DRDA databases.

Update DB2COMM (environment variable)

When serving remote clients, DB2COMM must be set according to the network protocol used.

Update TPNAME (database manager configuration file parameter)

The TPNAME is required for APPC communications. It must be set according to the TPN in CM/2.

Update SVCENAME (database manager configuration file parameter)

The SVCENAME is required for TCP/IP communications. It must be set according to the TCP/IP port in the \etc\services file.

Update NNAME (database manager configuration file parameter)

The NNAME is required for NetBIOS communications. NNAME does not have to match other configuration parameters.

Update IPX_SOCKET FILESERVER OBJECTNAME (database manager configuration parameters)

The IPX_SOCKET FILESERVER OBJECTNAME is required for IPX/SPX communications, depending on the IPX/SPX type of addressing used (direct addressing or file server addressing).

Update TM_DATABASE (database manager configuration file parameter)

TM_DATABASE must be set when using DUW with two-phase commit protocol support in DB2 common server. It must be set to a DB2 common server database, or to 1ST_CONN, that is, the first database to which the application connects will play the role of transaction manager database.

Table 13 (Page 1 of 2). *DB2 for OS/2 Connectivity Options*

	RDS Client	**RDS Server**	**DRDA AR**	**DRDA AS**
Products implementing function	CAE, SDK, DB2, DDCS	DB2 (1)	DDCS (2)	DB2 (1)
Network protocol	TCP/IP, NetBIOS, APPC, IPX/SPX	TCP/IP, NetBIOS, APPC, IPX/SPX	APPC	APPC
Update system database directory	Y	N (3)	Y	N (3)
Update node directory	Y	N	Y	N
Update DCS directory	N	N	Y	N

Table 13 (Page 2 of 2). DB2 for OS/2 Connectivity Options				
	RDS Client	**RDS Server**	**DRDA AR**	**DRDA AS**
Update DB2COMM	N	Y	Y	Y
Update TPNAME	N	Y	Y	Y
Update SVCENAME	N	Y	Y	N
Update NNAME	Y	Y	Y	N
Update IPX_SOCKET FILESERVER OBJECTNAME	N	Y (4)	Y (4)	N
Update TM_DATABASE	Y	N	N	N

Notes:

1. DB2 multiuser required; DB2 single-user only handles local clients (applications running on the workstation where DB2 is installed).
2. DDCS gateway can serve remote clients to route their requests to DRDA ASs but does not provide DBMS functios.
3. System database directory is automatically updated when the database is created.
4. If all clients use direct addressing, FILESERVER and OBJECTNAME can be set to '*'. Otherwise, the parameters must be set to proper values and the DB2 server must be registered at the NetWare File Server.

5.2 Our Scenario

In our scenario we installed both DB2 and DDCS on the OS/2 workstation and activated the DRDA AR and AS functions. Both functions require that you set up CM/2 profiles. Some of the profiles are common to both functions, and some are specific to an AR or an AS function.

5.3 OS/2 Products

In our scenario we used the following products:

```
IBM OS/2 Base Operating System
Version 3.00     Component ID 562274700
Type 0
Current CSD level: XR03001
```

```
IBM Communications Manager/2
Version 1.11      Component ID 2207800
Current CSD level: WR0615

IBM DB2 for OS/2 Server
Version 2.10      Component ID 562204401
Type 32-bit
Current CSD level: WR08000

IBM DDCS for OS/2 MultiUser Gateway
Version 2.30      Component ID 562205700
Type 32-bit
Current CSD level: WR08000
```

To check the products and versions installed on your machine, run the OS/2 SYSLEVEL command.

5.4 PU 2.1 and Host Hardware Connection Options

PU 2.1 support is generally required to operate a multiuser DDCS for OS/2 workstation environment. It is a prerequisite if you want to use DB2 for OS/2 as an AS. PU 2.1 can initiate contact with another node without being predefined in that node. It can exchange identification and negotiate capabilities with other nodes. Because it acts independently, you can think of a PU 2.1 as a mini SSCP because it has CP capabilities.

All configuration examples we refer to are based on a PU 2.1, but it is possible to run DDCS for OS/2 in a PU 2.0 configuration. In a PU 2.0 configuration the local LU is defined as a dependent LU, so it cannot issue BIND by itself to start a session; it has to wait for the SSCP (VTAM) to establish a session. Also, concurrent requests to the remote database are single-threaded through DDCS for OS/2 on their way to DRDA servers. This method may be adequate during initial testing and development work. It may also be necessary until the intervening network components between the DDCS for OS/2 workstation and the DRDA server have been upgraded to support PU 2.1 operations. Sooner or later, however, you will find that the limitation of only one DRDA connection is not sufficient and will prevent other applications and users from accessing remote databases.

Customers will be using a wide variety of workstation-host connection software and hardware, so it is important to understand which types of existing host network components can support DRDA operations. The hardware and software components listed below exemplify the host connectivity options that can be considered when configuring workstation-host connections, at the time of writing. The list is not intended to be definitive or necessarily complete. The available options and specific hardware and software product levels will continue to evolve. For exact information you should contact your IBM networking specialist.

- PS/2 SNA gateway machine (needs OS/2 EE 1.3 plus NS/2 , or above)
- 3172 local (an optional interconnect channel extender is available)
- 3174 local/remote

  - PU 2.0
  - PU 2.1 passthru support with RPQ
  - PU 2.1 full function support with configuration support C

- 3725/3745 (full PU 2.1)
- 3174 token gate

  - PU 2.0 support
  - Leased and/or dialed connection
  - Up to eight client workstations per 3174, one 3174 session to host

- PS/2 with SDLC card
- PS/2 with DFT (3174 plus RPQ gives PU 2.1 passthru level support)

5.4.1 Connections Using a 3174

At the ITSO-Boeblingen Center our token-ring LAN was connected to the network through a 3174, in addition to a 3745. In this configuration, we chose the 3174 to connect to the DRDA hosts in Poughkeepsie, Rochester, and San Jose.

In this configuration, the steps you have to perform and the information that you have to provide are conceptually the same as for the San Jose environment when using APPC connections.

5.5 Required Connection Information

Before you start the implementation of the connections, be sure to have all necessary information available. Request the following information from your network or VTAM coordinator and DRDA AS database administrator.

If you are connecting to an MVS, VM, or VSE DRDA AS, have available the information listed in Table 14 on page 86.

Table 14. *Parameters Required for OS/2 to MVS, VM, or VSE Connection*

MVS/ESA	Our Value	VM/ESA and VSE/ESA	Our Value	OS/2
NETID	USIBMSC	NETID	USIBMSC	Network ID
LOCADD (NCP)	400008220200	LOCADD (NCP)	400008220200	Token-ring address
MODEENT	IBMRDB	MODEENT	IBMRDB	Mode name
SSCP	USIBM.SC19M	SSCP	USIBM.SC19M	Partner node name
APPL	USIBMSC.SCLUDB41	APPL	DEIBMIPF.IPFA2GL4	Partner LU
PU	Silvio	PU	Silvio	Local node name
RDB_NAME	CENTDB2	RESID/DBDIR	S34VSDB1	Target database name.

If you are connecting to an OS/400 AS, have available the information listed in Table 15.

Table 15. *Parameters Required for OS/2 to OS/400 Connection*

OS/400	OS/2	OS/400 Command	Our Value
LCLNETID	Network ID	DSPNETA	USIBMSC
ADPTRADT	Token-Ring address	WRKLIND (*TRLAN)	400008220200
MODE	Mode name	WRKMODD	IBMRDB
Local control point (LCLNETID)	Partner node name	DSPNETA	SC02132I
Remote transaction program	Transaction program name		X'07'6DB
RDB_NAME	Target database name	WRKRDBDIRE	SJAS400

For a description of the SNA parameters, see Appendix A, "SNA Definitions and Connectivity Parameters" on page 517.

The configuration we describe does not include any of the steps required to establish a 3270 emulation session, which may also be quite useful. For our link to the DRDA hosts in Poughkeepsie, Rochester, and Boeblingen, we attached to an IBM 3745 controller connected to our token-ring network, and from there on through VTAM to all partner LUs.

5.6 OS/2 Application Requester

Here are the steps to follow to configure a DDCS workstation for a DRDA connection:

1. Set up the CM/2 profiles to establish the network connection between your machines.

2. Update the database directories with the appropriate information so that an application can connect to the remote database, finding its way through the system database directory, node directory, and DCS directory.

3. If you intend to use CLP or any other utility when connecting to the DRDA server, bind the utilities packages to the DRDA server.

In the sections that follow we present the definitions required to configure an OS/2 workstation as a DRDA AR.

Unlike previous versions, DB2 for OS/2 is not a prerequisite for DDCS for OS/2 unless you want to have local databases on your workstation. DDCS version 2.3 can work stand-alone (single-user) or as a gateway (multiuser).

5.6.1 DDCS for OS/2 Communications Planning Information

Before configuring a multiuser DDCS for OS/2-to-DB2 host connection, you must gather information from several sources to enable the following components to be configured:

- Remote client workstation definitions

- DDCS for OS/2 workstation definitions

- Host DB2 server definitions

Appendix A, "Worksheets," in the *DDCS for OS/2 Installation and Configuration Guide* includes the following checklists which are very useful during configuration planning:

- MVS, VSE, and VM Server Worksheet
- OS/400 Server Worksheet
- OS/2 Configuration Worksheet
- OS/2 Connection to Server Worksheet
- OS/2 Configuration for Remote Clients Worksheet

If you are unfamiliar with SNA networking concepts, the introductory material in the *DRDA Connectivity Guide* is an excellent source of information. However, the CM/2 and MVS VTAM/NCP product reference libraries are the definitive source of network configuration information; refer to them for specific information.

5.6.2 CM/2 Files

During the interactive configuration process, CM/2 creates some files to store the information you enter. The names of these files are always the same as your configuration name. You can find the following files on your system:

- CFGNAME.CFG
  This file contains binary information about your DLC, 3270, 5250, x.25, ACDI, and SRPI profiles and cannot be altered.
- CFGNAME.NDF
  This file contains all SNA-, APPC-, and APPN-related definitions in ASCII format so they can be read and manually updated. Information about the format of the .NDF

file can be found in the CMVERIFY.TXT file in CMLIB. If you manually change change the configuration in the .NDF file, you must verify the changes using the CMVERIFY command.

- CFGNAME.SEC
  This binary file contains security information such as session security passwords.
- CFGNAME.CF2
  This binary file is the result of the verify process, which must be run after each change in the CM/2 configuration. The CF2 file together with the .CFG file will be used when CM/2 is started.

In the sections that follow, we describe how to configure the CM/2 profiles required by DDCS for OS/2.

5.6.3 Configuring APPC APIs through the Token Ring

To configure APPC APIs through the token ring, perform the following steps:

1. Double-click on the Communications Manager Setup icon.

2. Click on the Setup push button.

3. On the Open Configuration panel, specify a configuration name. If you already have a configuration file, you can use the existing name. In our case we used APPN (see Figure 26 on page 89).

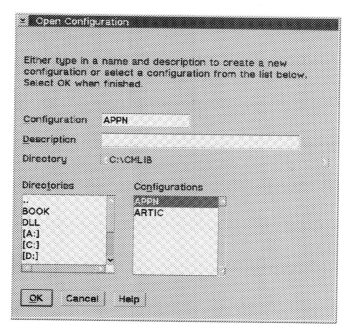

Figure 26. *Open Configuration Window*

4. Click on the OK push button.

5. On the Communications Manager Configuration Definition window, check Commonly used definitions and select APPC API's through Token-ring as shown in Figure 27 on page 90

6. Click on the Configure... push button.

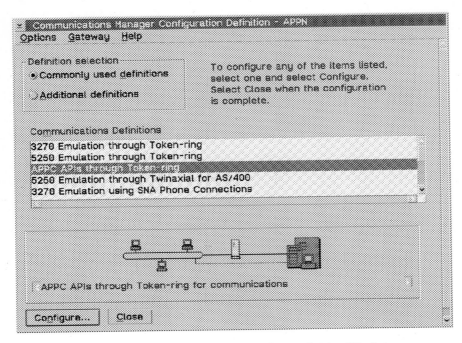

Figure 27. Communications Manager Configuration Definition Window

On the APPC API's through Token-ring window (see Figure 28 on page 91), you have to define the identification and type of your workstation and where it is connected to the outside network. If you modify an existing configuration, these parameters may already be defined.

The setting of the node type defines how your workstation is connected within the network. If you select:

- End node - to a network node server

  Your workstation is an EN and participates in an APPN network by using a network node server. A network node server provides directory and routing services for your workstation. It can establish a special session, called a CP-to-CP session, with the NN to obtain service from this NN. You must enter the token-ring address value of your network node server in the network node server address (hex) field.

  In San Jose we used APPN to connect to DB2 for MVS/ESA in Poughkeepsie and to the OS/400 in Rochester, so we chose the node type "End Node - to a network server" and specified the token-ring address of the 3745 to the Poughkeepsie network node.

- End node - no network node server

  Your workstation does not have access to a network node server. This type of node can participate in SNA communications and use APPC routing. However, it cannot use APPN routing and directory services, so it cannot establish a CP-to-CP session with the NN. This kind of node is also called a low entry node (LEN). You may also select this option if you do not know the address of your network node server.

  Since we used APPC in Boeblingen, this is the option we chose for Boeblingen.

- Network node

  Your workstation serves as an APPN NN server. A network node server provides intermediate session routing and directory services for workstations in its node.

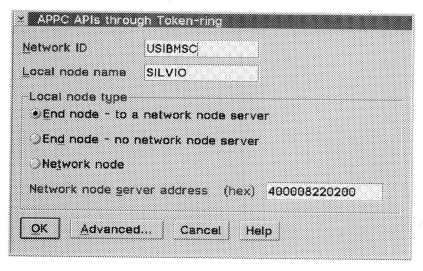

Figure 28. *APPC APIs through Token Ring*

7. Click on the Advanced.. push button to display the Communications Manager Profile List window as shown in Figure 29 on page 92.

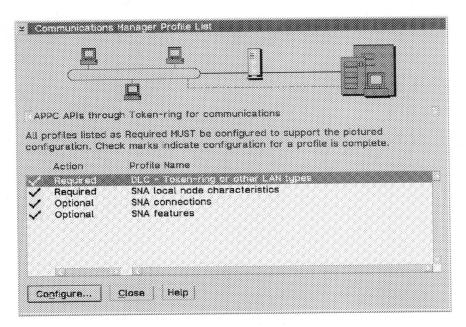

Figure 29. Communications Manager Profile List

The Communications Manager Profile List window is the starting point for configuring all other profiles in CM/2.

5.6.4 Data Link Control Profile

The data link control (DLC) profile describes the DLC layer that is responsible for the exchange of protocols between the two nodes. It ensures reliable delivery of messages. Protocols are provided for sequencing, acknowledgment, error recovery, and the establishment and maintenance of synchronization between the paired stations.

To configure this profile, select DLC - Token-ring or other LAN types in the window shown in Figure 29 and click on the Configure... push button. A window similar to that shown in Figure 30 on page 93 is displayed.

For our configuration we used the defaults shown in Figure 30 on page 93, which are normally sufficient. If your workstation is also defined as DRDA server, do not forget that CM/2 has implicit link capabilities that allow it to create link definitions for nodes that dial into CM/2, because a link station is required for every one of these links. If you increase the maximum link stations, be sure to set your link station parameter, in LAN Adapter and Protocol Support (LAPS), or Network Transport Services/2 (NTS/2), accordingly.

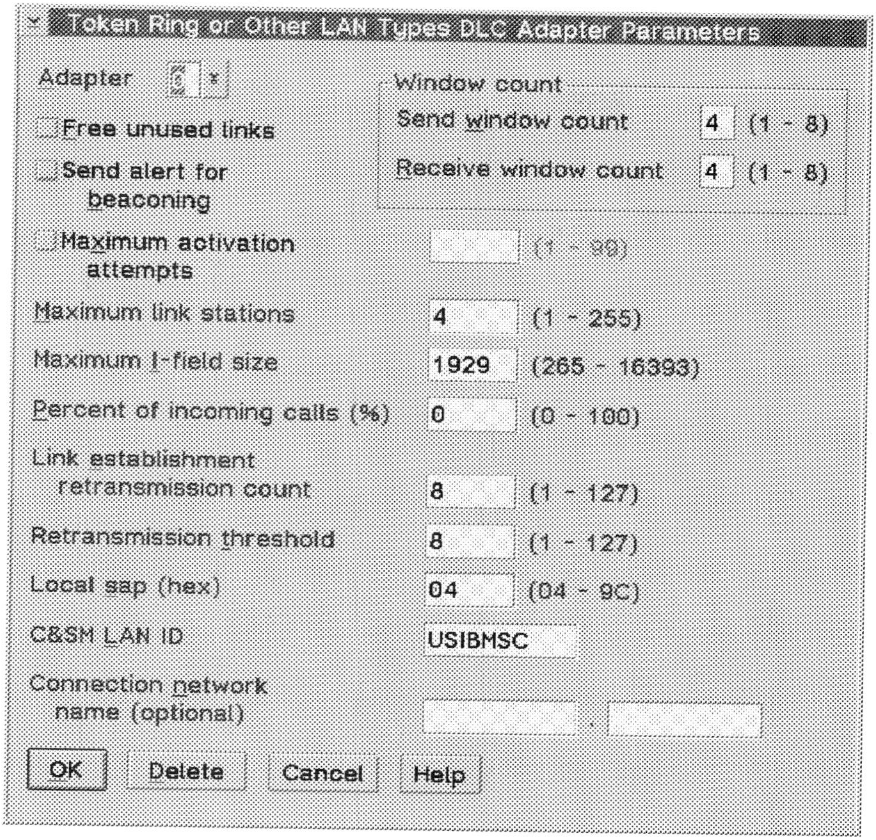

Figure 30. DLC Adapter Parameters

5.6.5 SNA Local Node Characteristics

To configure the SNA local node characteristics profile, select SNA local node characteristics on the Communications Manager Profile List window (Figure 29 on page 92) and click on the Configure... push button. A window similar to that displayed in Figure 31 on page 94 is displayed.

The local node name must always be defined. The local node name is also the default local LU. It is the CP name and is an LU 6.2 type. All APPC applications can use this LU, and there is no need to define any additional local LUs. When you configure the SNA local node characteristics, your local node name is automatically defined as your local node alias name. You can alter this alias name if you want. You can give it a more meaningful name than the name provided by your network administrator. Note that we defined most of the parameters for the Local Node Characteristics window on the APPC APIs through Token-ring window (Figure 28 on page 91). The parameter not defined is the Local node ID. This ID must be the same as the IDBLK/IDNUM specified in your PU definition in VTAM (see Figure 256 on page 521).

If you want to change your local node alias name, click on the Options... pushbutton and overwrite the default local node alias name. For the remaining definitions in Figure 32, use the defaults.

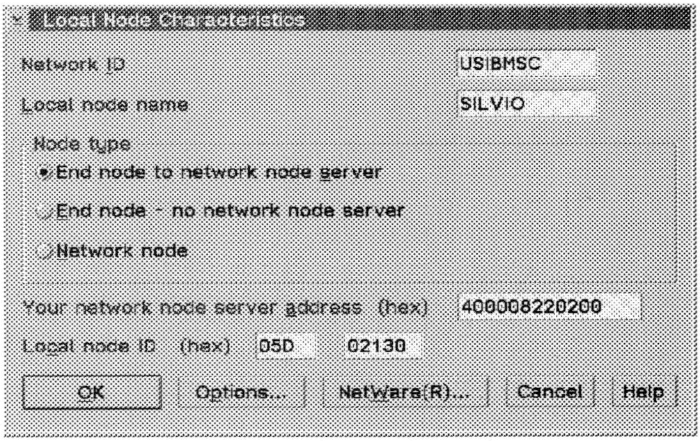

Figure 31. *Local Node Characteristics*

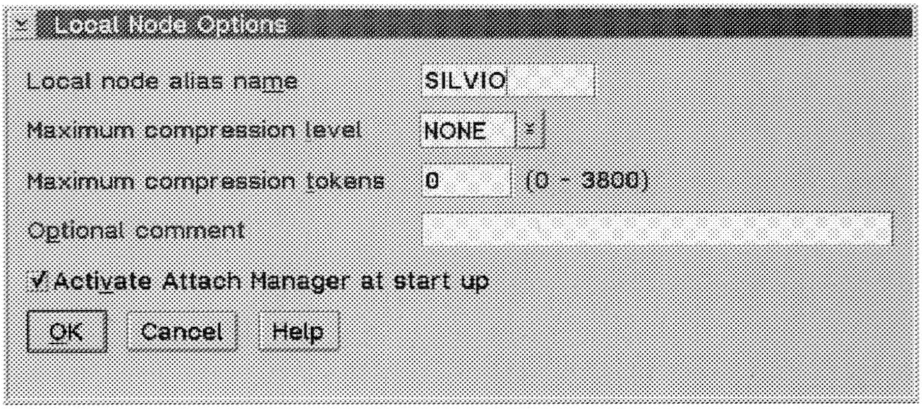

Figure 32. *Local Node Options*

The following statements are generated in your .NDF file as a result of the above definitions:

```
DEFINE_LOCAL_CP  FQ_CP_NAME(USIBMSC.SILVIO   )
                 CP_ALIAS(SILVIO  )
                 NAU_ADDRESS(INDEPENDENT_LU)
                 NODE_TYPE(EN)
                 NODE_ID(X'05D02130')
                 NW_FP_SUPPORT(NONE)
                 HOST_FP_SUPPORT(NO)
                 MAX_COMP_LEVEL(NONE)
                 MAX_COMP_TOKENS(0);
START_ATTACH_MANAGER;
```

5.6.6 SNA Connections

The next step is to define your DRDA server connection. A connection is a logical link between your workstation and another node. The SNA connection profile contains information about the partner node type associated with this connection and the related partner LUs. We required two connection profiles: one that enables access to the IBM network, and one that enables access to the DB2 for OS/400 in San Jose, which was located in the same token-ring LAN as our PS/2 workstation.

For the workstation in San Jose, the connection that enabled access to the IBM network was already configured because our network server was used for this purpose. The connection was automatically created when we configured APPC APIs through the token ring described in 5.6.3, "Configuring APPC APIs through the Token Ring" on page 88.

We still had to configure the connection to the AS/400 in San Jose, which was an APPN connection. To configure the connection perform the following steps:

1. On the Communications Manager Profile List window shown in Figure 29 on page 92, select SNA connections and click on the Configure... push button.
2. The window shown in Figure 33 on page 96 is displayed. Select To peer node.

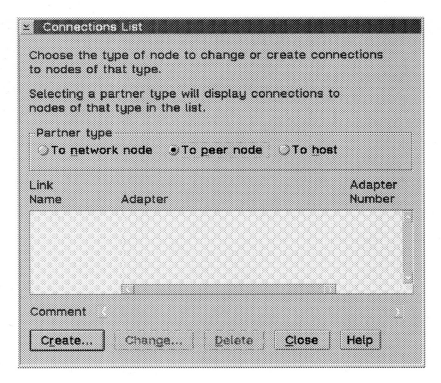

Figure 33. SNA Connections List

3. Click on the Create.. push button to display the Adapter List window shown in Figure 34 on page 97.

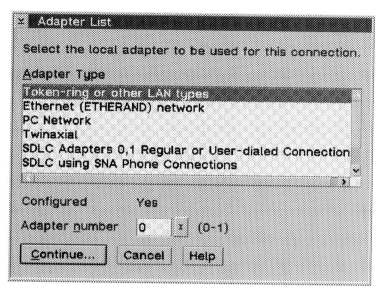

Figure 34. Adapter List: OS/400

4. For Adapter Type, select Token-ring or other LAN types (or the adapter you are using) and enter the adapter number that you have specified in the DLC profile. Click on the Continue... push button to display the Connection to a Peer Node window shown Figure 35 on page 98.

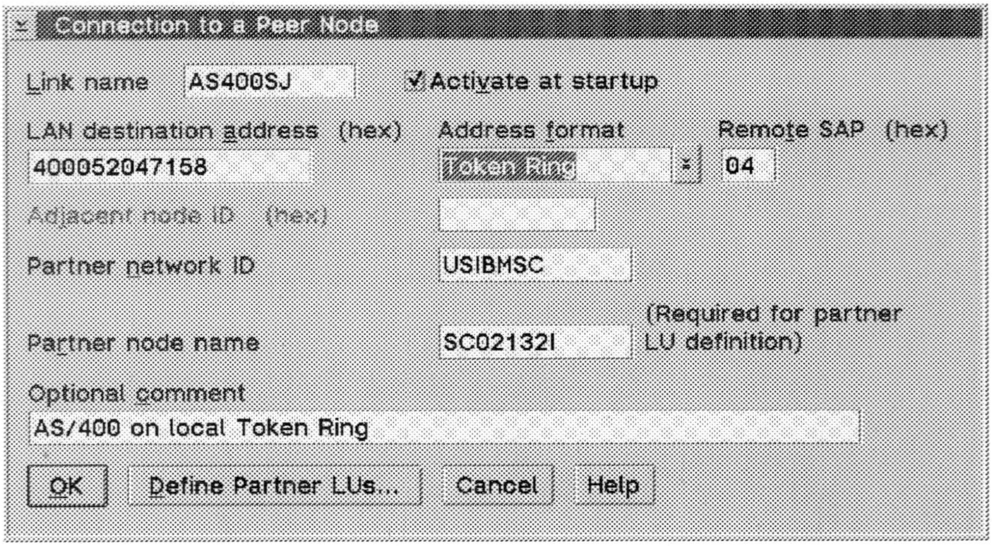

Figure 35. Connection to a Peer Node

On this window,

- Enter a name for the Link name.

- Verify that the Activate at startup button is checked.

- In the LAN destination address field, enter the LAN adapter address specified in the AS/400 system.

- If you enter a value in the Adjacent node ID field, you cannot enter a value in the LAN destination address field. If you enter a value in the Adjacent node ID field instead of specifying a value in the destination information field, the link can be activated only by the partner node, so this definition cannot be used for APPN connections.

- Enter the partner network ID of the AS/400. In our configuration this ID was the same as our network ID. To get the network ID information for the OS/400, use the OS/400 DSPNETA command.

- Enter the partner node name, which corresponds to the default CP information, which you also obtain through the OS/400 DSPNETA command.

- Click on the OK push button to complete this connection definition.

You do not have to specify a partner LU for this connection because the connection to the AS/400 is an APPN connection.

5.6.7 Configuring APPC Partner LUs

Because the connections from OS/2 at San Jose to the SQL/DS for VM and SQL/DS for VSE systems do not use APPN, we must configure a connection profile and define all partner LUs in this connection. When you define a connection using the SNA connections profile, you can also define partner LUs to be associated with this specific connection.

The connection we used to reach the systems in Boeblingen was the same as our network server, so we had to update it with the information about the partner LUs.

Perform the following steps to update the connection:

1. On the Communications Manager Profile List window shown in Figure 29 on page 92, select SNA connections and click on the Configure... push button.

2. The Connections List window shown in Figure 36 on page 100 is displayed. Check the To network node radio button, select the link that is already configured, and click on the Change... push button.

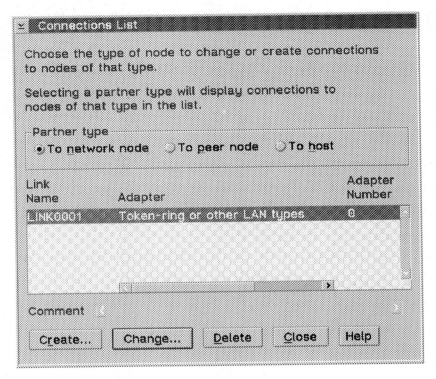

Figure 36. SNA Connections List: Network Node

3. The Adapter List window shown in Figure 37 on page 101 is displayed.

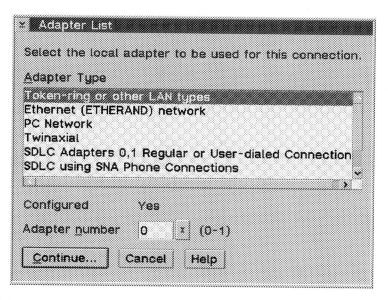

Figure 37. *Adapter List: Network Node*

4. Click on the Continue... push button to display the Connection to a Network Node window shown in Figure 38 on page 102.

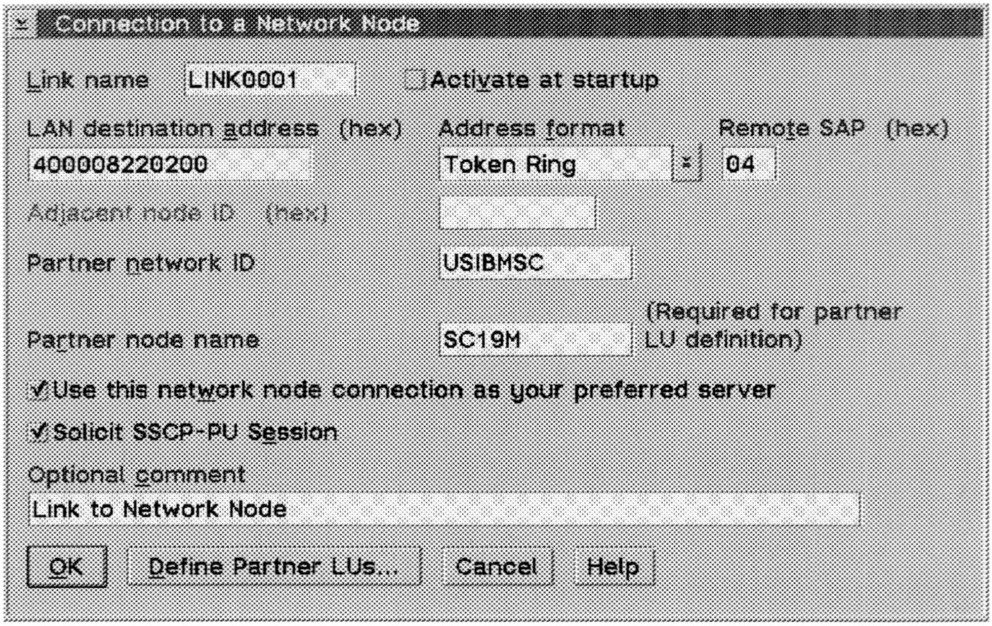

Figure 38. *Connection to a Network Node.*

Verify and complete the information on the Connection to a Network Node window (Figure 38) as follows:

- Since you want to define partner LUs for your connection, make sure that the `Activate at startup` radio button is not checked. If you do not select `Activate at startup`, you can still activate the link by using one of the following methods:

  - The partner node can activate the link; this means that the link will be activated by an incoming connection.
  - You can use subsystem management to activate the link manually.

  Check that the partner network ID specified is the VTAM network ID that provides access to your network. For the partner node name, enter the SSCP of the adjacent VTAM.

  Once you have entered the partner network ID and the partner node name in this window, select the `Define Partner LUs....` push button to display the Partner LUs window shown in Figure 39 on page 103.

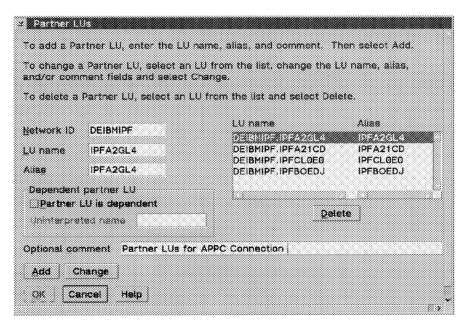

Figure 39. Partner LUs Window: Link Definition

In the Partner LUs window, you can enter the network ID, LU name, and alias for the partner LU that you are defining. Click on the ADD push button to add an entry to the LU name list. The network ID does not have to be the same as the network ID of the local node on which you are defining this partner LU. Use this method whenever your node does not have a connection to an APPN Network Node Server. By using this method, you are identifying the link that should be used by CM/2 to reach this LU when sending the BIND request. In all cases, if you are not sure about the capabilities of your partner node, use this method of defining your partner LU. The defined partner LU is also transferred to the partner LU definition in the SNA features profile. For our configuration, our network node enabled APPN and APPC connections.

Figure 40 on page 104 shows the .NDF file entry when you configure a partner LU using the connections profile. Both the DEFINE_PARTNER_LU and the DEFINE_PARTNER_LU_LOCATION statements are generated. CM/2 can then determine the link with which this partner LU should be associated.

```
DEFINE_PARTNER_LU    FQ_PARTNER_LU_NAME(DEIBMIPF.IPFA24GL)
                     PARTNER_LU_ALIAS(IPFA21CD)
                     PARTNER_LU_UNINTERPRETED_NAME(IPFA24GL)
                     MAX_MC_LL_SEND_SIZE(32767)
                     CONV_SECURITY_VERIFICATION(NO)
                     PARALLEL_SESSION_SUPPORT(YES);

DEFINE_PARTNER_LU_LOCATION FQ_PARTNER_LU_NAME(DEIBMIPF.IPFA24GL)
                     WILDCARD_ENTRY(NO)
                     FQ_OWNING_CP_NAME(USIBMSC.SC19M)
                     LOCAL_NODE_NN_SERVER(NO);
```

Figure 40. NDF Statements for Partner LU (from Connections Profile)

5.6.8 SNA Features Profiles

The SNA features describe information about communication sessions in an SNA environment and the TPs that use those sessions. SNA features information includes LU definitions, TP definitions, session security requirements, and side information for Common Programming Interface Communications (CPIC). To configure SNA features, select SNA features in the Communications Manager Profile List window (Figure 29 on page 92) and click on the Configure... push button. The SNA Features List window shown in Figure 41 on page 105 is displayed.

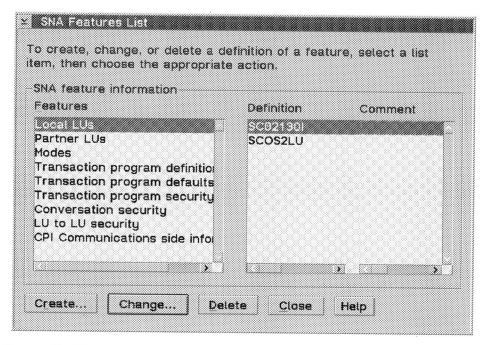

Figure 41. *SNA Features List*

5.6.8.1 Local LU

Normally you do not have to define a local LU because as stated previously your local node name is your default LU. If you have a requirement to configure a local LU, select Local LUs in the SNA Features List window (Figure 41) and click on the Create... push button. The Local LU window shown in Figure 42 on page 106 is displayed.

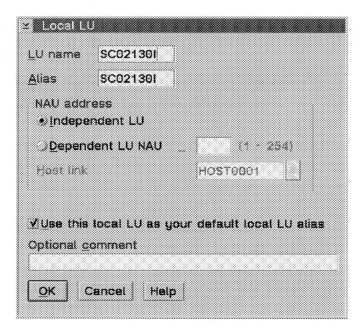

Figure 42. *Local LU*

When you define your local LU (Figure 42) for your DDCS workstation, be sure to select Independent LU for the network accessible unit (NAU) address. To ensure that your workstation uses this local LU when DDCS starts the APPC connection you have two options:

- Set the OS/2 APPCLLU environment variable to the local LU alias before the APPC connection is started. For example,

  SET APPCLLU=SC0231I

  When the APPC connection is started, the specified local LU is used.

- On the Local LU window, check the box that says "Use this local LU as your default local LU alias." If your CM/2 is earlier that CM/2 V1.11, you can directly add an entry to the CM/2 configuration file (.NDF) specifying the default local LU alias. The DEFAULT_LOCAL_LU_ALIAS entry is located in the DEFINE_DEFAULTS section of the configuration file (.NDF) as in the following example:

  DEFINE_DEFAULTS   DEFAULT_LOCAL_LU_ALIAS(SC0231I)

  If you update the .NDF file manually, you must verify the .NDF file by using the CMVERIFY command.

The APPCLLU environment variable value overrides the .NDF file specification.

If you are not using the VTAM dynamic independent LU definition facility, the
independent LU must be defined in the VTAM definition for this PU. Figure 43 on
page 107 shows how an independent LU is defined in VTAM. The LOCADDR=0
indicates that this LU is an independent LU.

```
SC02130 PU   ADDR=01,                                    +
        IDBLK=05D,IDNUM=02130,                         +
        ANS=CONT,DISCNT=NO,                            +
        IRETRY=NO,ISTATUS=ACTIVE,                         +
        MAXDATA=265,MAXOUT=7,                            +
        MAXPATH=1,                               +
        PUTYPE=2,SECNET=NO,                          +
        MODETAB=VMXAMODE,DLOGMOD=DYNRMT,                      +
        USSTAB=USSRDYN,                        +
        PACING=1,VPACING=2
*
SC02130A LU   LOCADDR=002
SC02130B LU   LOCADDR=003
SC02130C LU   LOCADDR=004
SC02130D LU   LOCADDR=005
SC02130I LU   LOCADDR=0,DLOGMOD=LU62APPB
SC02130J LU   LOCADDR=0,DLOGMOD=LU62APPB
SC02130K LU   LOCADDR=0,DLOGMOD=LU62APPA
SC02130L LU   LOCADDR=0,DLOGMOD=LU62APPA
```

Figure 43. Sample LU Definition in VTAM

5.6.8.2 Partner LU

Partner LU information includes the fully qualified name and the alias name of the
remote LU. You have to configure a partner LU for every partner you want to refer to by
an alias name. You have two options in CM/2 for defining partner LUs and partner LU
aliases:

- Use the SNA connections profile

  If your workstation is a LEN, use this method. To configure a partner LU using this
  method, refer to 5.6.6, "SNA Connections" on page 95.

- Use the SNA Features Profile

  On the SNA Features List shown in Figure 41 on page 105, select Partner LUs
  and click on the Create... push button. The Partner LU window (Figure 44 on
  page 108) is displayed.

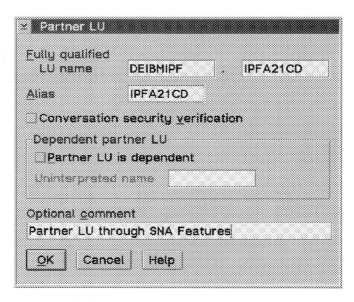

Figure 44. *Partner LU Window*

Enter the fully qualified name of the partner LU. The fully qualified name consists of the network ID of the partner LU and the LU name. You also have to enter the alias, which is a local name for the partner LU. This creates an entry telling CM/2 the fully qualified name of the LU when you use this alias. However, this method of defining a partner LU does not tell CM/2 on which link to send the BIND when you refer to this LU.

Use this method when your node has an active connection to an APPN network node server. When you refer to this LU, CM/2 does not know which link to use to send the BIND, so it issues a LOCATE request to its network node server to find the location of the LU.

If you use an APPN connection, you do not have to define a partner LU. When an EN (APPN) is connected to a serving NN and the resource is not found in the local directory, CM/2 directs the request to the serving NN, and a search request takes place in the network node. When a LEN (APPC) is connected to a serving NN and the resource is not found in the local directory, no further search is done by CM/2.

5.6.8.3 Modes

When establishing a session between two LUs, you must specify a mode. The mode contains information about the characteristics of the session. The mode name is the unique name you assign to the set of session capabilities that you specify on the Mode Definition window (Figure 45 on page 109). The mode name is a shorthand way of referring to a particular set of capabilities. To establish a connection, the same mode name must exist on both sides of the link. Create your mode with specifications similar to those shown in Figure 45 on page 109. This mode name must also be defined in VTAM.

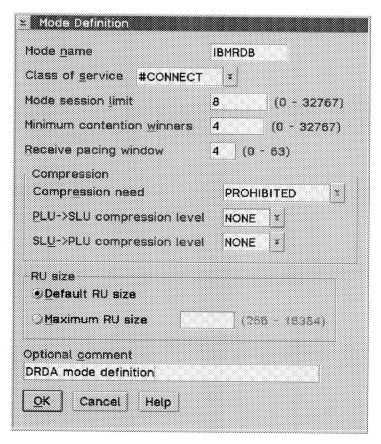

Figure 45. *Mode Definition*

5.6.8.4 CPIC Side Information

The CPIC side information is a new profile used by DDCS for OS/2 Version 2.3. CPIC is an SAA-compliant API that provides a platform-independent interface. An application using the CPIC interface can run without changes on any SAA platform.

The CPIC side information provides information required to establish a conversation with a partner program. The information that is provided includes the name of the partner program and the name of the LU supporting the session used by the partner program.

You have to create a CPIC side information profile for each DRDA AS to which you intend to connect.

To create CPIC side information, follow these steps:

1. From the SNA Features List, select CPI Communications side information as shown in Figure 46 and click on the Create... push button to add new CPIC side information.

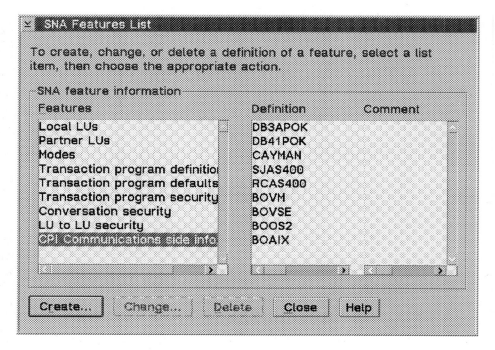

Figure 46. SNA Features List: CPI Communications Side Information Window

2. The CPI Communications Side Information window shown in Figure 47 on page 111 is displayed.

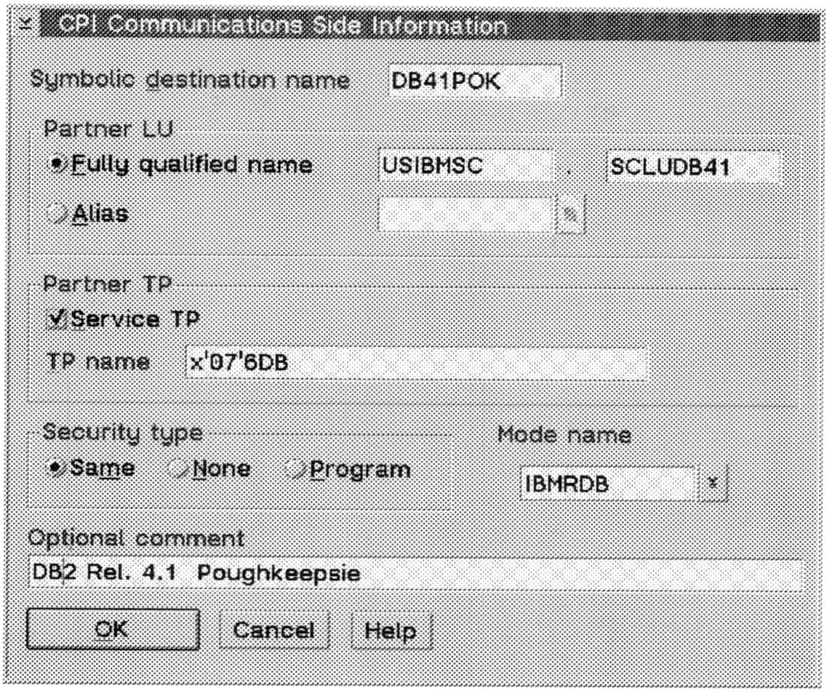

CPI Communications Side Information

Symbolic destination name DB41POK

Partner LU
- ● Fully qualified name   USIBMSC   . SCLUDB41
- ○ Alias   %

Partner TP
- ☑ Service TP
- TP name x'07'6DB

Security type   Mode name
- ● Same ○ None ○ Program   IBMRDB   ×

Optional comment
DB2 Rel. 4.1 Poughkeepsie

OK   Cancel   Help

Figure 47. CPI Communications Side Information

On the CPI Communications Side Information window you provide information
about the server you want to define. Figure 47 shows an example of our connection
to DB2 for MVS/ESA. We had to configure other CPIC side information profiles to
connect to the DB2 for OS/400 in San Jose, DB2 for OS/400 in Rochester, and
SQL/DS for VM and SQL/DS for VSE in Boeblingen. We also created profiles to
connect to the OS/2 and AIX machines in Boeblingen, using APPC. A DRDA
connection is not recommended between DB2 common server products. The
recommended method of connecting DB2 common server products is the RDS
private protocol.

- The Symbolic destination name defines the name of the CPIC side
  information. You can choose any name you like. You will use this name when
  you catalog the node directory for this AS.

- For Partner LU you can use the fully qualified name if you want to
  communicate with a partner LU that you have not yet defined. This may be the
  case when you use APPN. A fully qualified name consists of both the network
  name and the LU name of the partner LU. You can also use the alias if you

want to communicate with a partner LU that you have previously defined. If you specify an alias, you cannot specify the fully qualified name.

- For `Partner TP`, specify the remote TPN. This information is case sensitive. You must specify a value because there is no default value in CM/2. The value that you must specify for a DB2 for MVS/ESA or DB2 for OS/400 DRDA AS is X'07'6DB. The value that you must specify for SQL/DS for VSE or VM/ESA is defined during the installation and customization of these products. If the value contains hexadecimal data (such as X'07'6DB), you must also check `Service TP`.

- You can choose any security type because the security type specified when you catalog an entry in the node directory overrides this specification.

- For the `Mode` name, select the name you have defined for your DRDA connections, such as IBMRDBM.

5.7 Database Directories and Definitions

To connect to a DRDA database server, DDCS requires information in the database directories. If you want to add, change, or delete entries in the database directories, you must have either SYSADM or SYSCTRL authority.

In this section we outline the tools and techniques that you can use to maintain the various directories and describe the key parameters that are recorded in the directories. Although we provide examples for the OS/2 platform, with minor modification the examples are also valid for the AIX platform.

You must specify entries in the following directories to enable the DDCS workstation to connect to a DRDA AS:

- Node directory
- System database directory
- Database connection services (DCS) directory

Parameters related to information such as the DRDA service heap size and directory caching in the database manager configuration file may also need to be adjusted using one of the tools or techniques described in the following section.

5.7.1 Tools and Techniques

You can use several tools and techniques to create and maintain the directories:

- The *database director*, a new tool for DB2 common server, provides a GUI to DB2 objects and enables you to perform such tasks as
  - Configuring databases and database manager instances

- Managing the directories required to access local and remote databases and instances

- Backing up and recovering databases or tablespaces

• The DB2DD. command can alternatively be issued from the OS/2 command line to start up the database director, on the OS/2 platform.

For the AIX platform, you invoke the database director by issuing the *db2dd* command from the AIX command line.

• CLP

• An API that provides callable routines that can be used to maintain the directories.

Refer to the *DB2 Application Programming Guide for common servers* for more information about the API.

When you open the database director you get a window with a tree structure of defined nodes for your active instance.

For DB2 common server you can create multiple instances on a single workstation and have them run concurrently on one physical machine. There are separate database directories for each instance. If you have multiple instances defined on your workstation, be sure to select the right instance when you catalog your DRDA AS databases. The instance is set by the DB2INSTANCE environment variable (default DB2). It becomes active when you issue a DB2START command.

For OS/2 the DB2INSTANCE environment variable is defined in the CONFIG.SYS file or can be set by issuing

```
SET DB2INSTANCE=DB2
```

from the OS/2 command line.

For AIX the DB2INSTANCE environment variable is defined in the .profile file of the user that issues the *db2start* command or can be set by issuing

```
export DB2INSTANCE=DB2
```

from the AIX command line.

For more information about instances refer to the *DB2 Administrator Guide for common servers*.

5.7.2 Cataloging in the Node Directory

To catalog a node for the DRDA AS to which you want to connect follow these steps:

1. Open the IBM Database 2 Folder (OS/2 platform).

2. Start the database director by double-clicking on the Database Director icon in the IBM DATABASE 2 icon view (OS/2 platform).

   For the AIX platform, issue the *db2dd* command.

3. Select the active instance and click on the + sign next to the appropriate icon (in our case DB2). Click on the + sign next to the Directories icon. This activates the Database Director - Tree View shown in Figure 48.

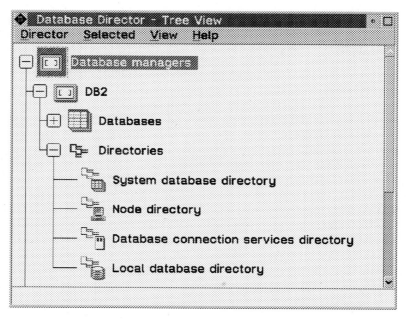

Figure 48. *Database Director - Tree View: OS/2 Platform*

4. Click on the Node directory icon to display a list of all defined nodes (if any) for this instance as shown in Figure 49 on page 115.

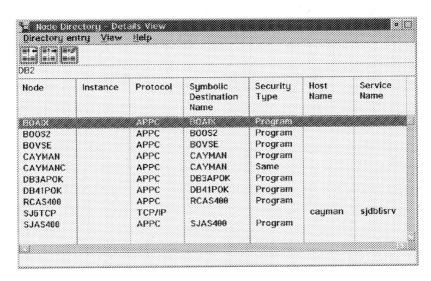

Figure 49. *Node Directory - Details View*

5. Click on `Directory entry` and then on `Catalog...` to display the Node Directory Entry - Catalog notebook as shown in Figure 50 on page 116.

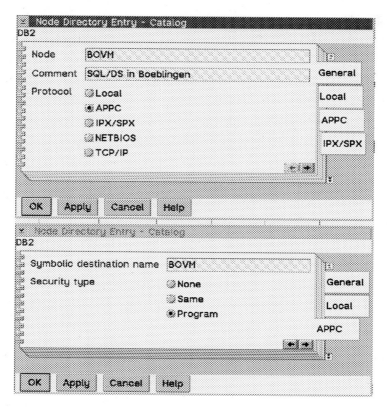

Figure 50. *Node Directory Entry - Catalog*

Provide the following information:

- Node

  This is an alias that identifies the remote node. It should be a meaningful name to make it easier to remember.

- Protocol

  As we use DRDA, the protocol must be APPC.

- Symbolic destination name

  This name must correspond to an entry in the CPIC side information (OS/2 platform) and the LU 6.2 CPIC side information profile name. It contains the necessary information to set up an APPC connection to the server (partner LU name, mode name, partner TPN). This name is case sensitive. Refer to 5.6.8.4, "CPIC Side Information" on page 109 for OS/2 and 6.4.2.9, "LU 6.2 Side Information Profile" on page 181 for AIX.

- Security type

  - None

    Specifies that no security information is sent to the partner LU. This option is not supported by DRDA.

  - Same

    Specifies a userid together with an indicator that the user has been already verified. Only the userid is sent to the partner LU. The password is not sent to the partner LU. This implementation requires that the partner LU at the AS be configured to accept already verified security.

  - Program

    Specifies that a userid and a password must be included in the allocation request sent to the partner LU for authentication.

You can also use CLP to catalog an entry in the node directory by issuing the following command:

```
DB2 catalog appc node boevm remote BOVM security program
```

You can also use CLP to list all entries in the node directory by issuing the following command:

```
DB2 list node directory
```

You have to catalog one entry in the node directory for each AS to which you intend to connect.

5.7.3 Cataloging in the System Database Directory

The system database directory contains an entry for each database that can be accessed from a workstation. The directory contains information about whether a database is local or remote, the authentication type, the database name, and the database alias. To get a list of all databases in the system database directory, click on the System database directory icon on the Database Director - Tree View (Figure 48 on page 114). The System Database Directory - Details View window (Figure 51 on page 118) is displayed.

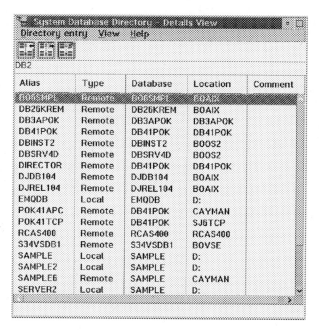

Figure 51. *System Database Directory - Details View*

To catalog a database in the system database directory, click on the Directory entry and then on Catalog... to display the System Database Directory - Catalog window (Figure 52 on page 119).

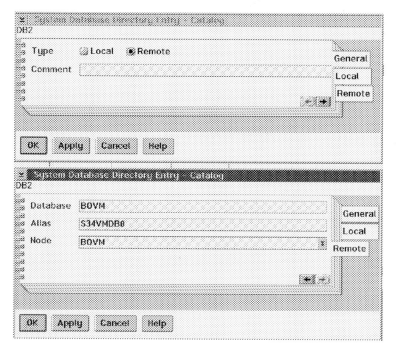

Figure 52. *System Database Directory - Catalog Window*

Enter the following information:

- Select the Remote radio button because you want to catalog a remote database. Enter an optional comment.

- Click on the remote tab. The window in the lower part of Figure 52 is displayed, where you have to enter the required information.

- Database name: BOVM. For the DRDA AS, this is a pointer to the DCS directory where the real name (RDB_NAME) of the AS database can be found.

- Alias: S34VMDB0. This is the name by which the database is known at the workstation. It is referenced by applications and CLP when you issue the CONNECT statement. If you do not specify an alias, the database manager uses the database name as the alias.

- Node: BOVM. This is the name of the node where the database is located. This name must match a name of an entry in the node directory. Click on the OK push button when you are done.

The cataloged database now appears in the System Database Directory - Details View list as shown in Figure 53 on page 120.

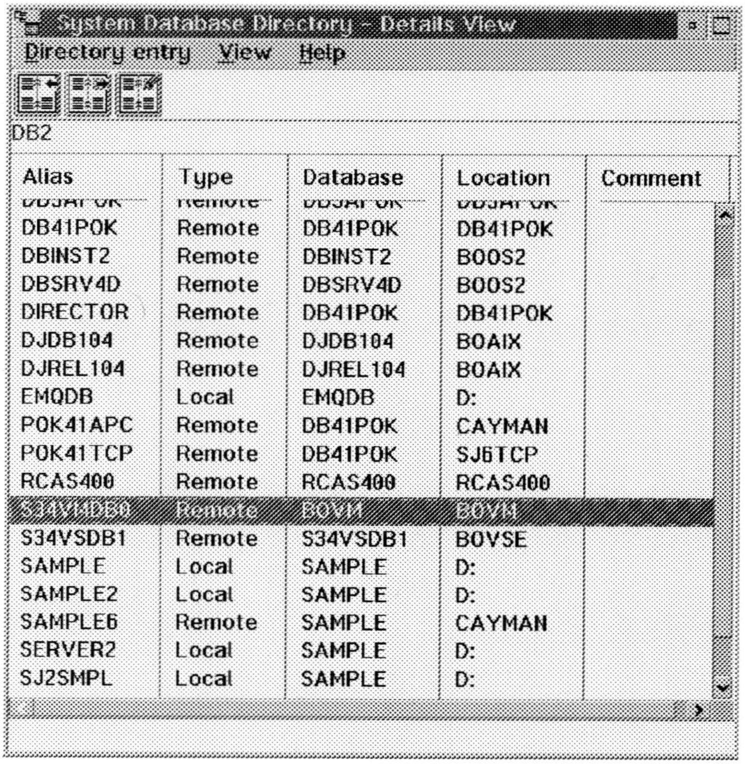

Figure 53. System Database Directory - Details View: Cataloged Database

The AUTHENTICATION parameter defines where the authentication should take place. Here are the AUTHENTICATION parameter value options:

- SERVER

  Specifies that authentication takes place at the server.

- CLIENT

  Specifies that authentication takes place on the node where the application is invoked.

- DCS

  Specifies that authentication takes place at the DRDA AS.

With the level of the product we used in our project, the database director did not support the AUTHENTICATION parameter when cataloging a database. Therefore the default authentication when using the database director is the authentication specified at the instance level. The authentication level of an instance is defined in the database manager configuration file. To obtain the authentication specified at the instance level, issue the following command:

```
DB2 get database manager configuration
```

To change the authentication specified at the instance level, you can issue the following command:

```
DB2 update database manager configuration using authentication server
```

If you do not want to change the authentication at the instance level but want to catalog a database with an authentication different from the instance level, you have to use CLP and issue a command similar to this:

```
DB2 catalog database BOVM as S34VMDBO at node boevm authentication DCS
```

To get a list of all databases cataloged in the system database directory using CLP, issue the following command:

```
DB2 list database directory
```

Figure 54 on page 122 shows the output of this command.

```
System Database Directory


Number of entries in the directory  = 9


Database 2 entry:

    Database alias            = SJ6SMPL
    Database name             = SAMPLE
    Node name                 = CAYMAN
    Database release level    = 6.00
    Comment                   =
    Directory entry type      = Remote
    Authentication            = CLIENT


Database 3 entry:

    Database alias            = DIRECTOR
    Database name             = DB41POK
    Node name                 = DB41POK
    Database release level    = 6.00
    Comment                   =
    Directory entry type      = Remote
    Authentication            = SERVER


Database 6 entry:

    Database alias            = BOVM
    Database name             = S34VMDB0
    Node name                 = BOVM
    Database release level    = 6.00
    Comment                   =
    Directory entry type      = Remote
    Authentication            = DCS


Database 9 entry:

    Database alias            = SAMPLE2
    Database name             = SAMPLE
    Database drive            = D:
    Database release level    = 6.00
    Comment                   =
    Directory entry type      = Indirect
```

Figure 54. *System Database Directory: Database Entries*

5.7.4 Cataloging in the DCS Directory

The DCS directory contains an entry for each DRDA AS that can be accessed from the workstation. When the application issues a CONNECT statement specifying a remote database using APPC protocol, the database manager searches the DCS directory for a matching database name entry. If it finds a matching entry, it uses the DRDA protocol for the connection. If it does not find a matching entry, it uses the private protocol. To catalog a DCS database do the following:

1. Click on the Database connection services directory icon on the Database Director - Tree view window (Figure 48 on page 114). The Database Connection Services Directory - Details View is displayed (Figure 55), listing the DCS databases (if any) for this instance.

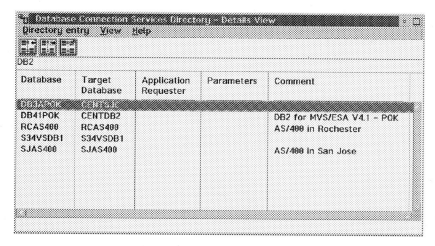

Figure 55. *Database Connection Services Directory - Details View*

2. Click on Directory entry, then on Catalog... to display the Database Connection Services Directory Entry - Catalog notebook as shown in Figure 56 on page 124.

Figure 56. *Database Connection Services Directory Entry - Catalog*

Provide the following information:

- Database

  Specifies the DCS database name to catalog. This name must match the database name you entered when you cataloged this database in the system database directory.

- Target database

  Specifies the real name (RDB_NAME) of the target host database to catalog.

- Application requester

  If using the DDCS AR code, you do not have to specify a value for this parameter. The default value causes DDCS to be invoked.

- Parameters

  You can specify a parameter string defining SQLCODE mapping, interrupt handling, and disconnect events. For further explanation of this string, refer to the *DDCS User's Guide for common servers.*

You can also use CLP to catalog an entry in the DCS directory by issuing the following command:

```
DB2 catalog dcs database bovm as s34vmdb0
```

You can also use CLP to list all entries in the DCS directory by issuing the following command:

```
DB2 list DCS directory
```

5.7.5 Binding the DDCS Utilities

Before you can use the database utilities and tools like CLP, CLI, REXX interface, import, and export on your remote DRDA AS, you first have to bind them against each DRDA server. You have to bind only the utilities and tools you want to use.

All application programs (utilities can also be considered application programs) developed by using embedded SQL must be bound to each database where you want to use them. During the bind process, database access plans are stored for each SQL statement that will be executed. These access plans are contained in bind files created during precompilation. After the bind files are bound to the AS, they are contained in the remote package.

During installation of DDCS, all of the required bind files are copied into the SQLLIB\BND directory. For each platform there is a file containing a list (xxx.lst) of all the necessary bind files for that platform. Instead of binding all of the bind files one after the other, you can use the list of bind files to execute the bind in one step. The list of bind files required for the DDCS utilities can be found in the following files:

- **ddcsmvs.lst**   for MVS
- **ddcsvse.lst**   for VSE
- **ddcsvm.lst**   for VM
- **ddcs400.lst**   for OS/400

When you bind one of these list files to a database, the BIND command binds each individual utility to that database. You can bind each of the files separately to each of your DRDA servers.

The DDCS utilities must be bound to each DRDA AS once from **each type** of client platform (CAE/2, Windows, CAE/AIX) before they can be used with that DRDA AS. You need to bind each type of client once. All subsequent connections from the same type of client can use the utilities without getting an SQL0805N error, which indicates that there is no package available for the application.

5.7.5.1 Privileges

To execute the bind, you must have sufficient authority on the DRDA AS to which you bind. No special authority is required for the DDCS workstation.

- For DB2 for MVS/ESA

  - SYSADM authority

    or
  - SYSCTRL authority

    or
  - BINDADD and CREATE IN COLLECTION NULLID authority

  Note: BINDADD and CREATE IN COLLECTION NULLID privileges are sufficient to bind DDCS, unless the original bind was done by someone else and you want to bind the package a second time. NULLID is the collection where the packages are created.

- For VSE or VM

  - DBA authority

  Note: If you want to use the GRANT option on the BIND command (to avoid granting access to each DDCS package individually), the NULLID user ID must have the authority to grant authority to other users on some system tables.

- For OS/400

  - CHANGE authority or higher on the NULLID collection.

- For AIX or OS/2

  You need to bind to AIX or OS/2 only if your client workstation is of a different type from your DDCS workstation.

  - SYSADM authority

    or
  - DBADM authority

    or
  - BINDADD privilege if a package does not exist

    or
  - BIND privilege on the package if it exists

5.7.5.2 Binding

To bind your DDCS utilities against a DRDA AS (in our example DB2 for MVS/ESA), use CLP. Issue commands similar to the following:

```
db2 connect to DATABASE user USERID using PASSWORD
db2 bind path\@ddcsmvs.1st blocking all
    sqlerror continue messages ddcsmvs.msg grant public
db2 connect reset
```

where DATABASE is the alias name of the DRDA AS. USERID and PASSWORD apply to the DRDA AS (be sure to have the appropriate privileges). ddcsmvs.lst is the bind list file for MVS. path is the location of the bind list file, for example, drive:\sqllib\bnd\.

┌─ **Bind execution time** ──┐
│   │
│ The bind process might require up to 15 minutes to complete. Be patient. Even if │
│ there is no hard disk activity and your session seems to be "dead," this process is │
│ time consuming.   │
│   │
└──┘

Use the GRANT option of the BIND command to grant EXECUTE privilege to PUBLIC or to a specified user name or group ID.

Note: If you do not use the grant option, you must GRANT EXECUTE (RUN) individually to each user or group ID.

Table 16 lists all of the bind files and package names that are used by different components of DDCS.

Table 16 (Page 1 of 2). Bind Files and Packages Used by DDCS					
Component	**Bind File**	**Package**	**MVS**	**VM/VSE**	**OS/400**
Binder (used by the Grant bind option)	db2ajgrt	sqlabxxx	yes	yes	yes
DB2 Call Level Interface (CLI)					
Isolation Level CS	db2clics	sqll1xxx	yes	yes	yes
Isolation Level RR	db2clirr	sqll2xxx	yes	yes	yes
Isolation Level UR	db2cliur	sqll3xxx	yes	yes	yes
Isolation Level RS	db2clirs	sqll4xxx	yes	yes	yes
Isolation Level NC	db2clinc	sqll5xxx	no	no	yes
Using MVS table	db2clims	sqll7xxx	yes	no	no
Using OS/400 table names (rel 3.1 or later)	db2clias	sqllaxxx	no	no	yes
Using VSE/VM table names	db2clivm	sqll8xxx	no	yes	no

Component	Bind File	Package	MVS	VM/VSE	OS/400
Table 16 (Page 2 of 2). Bind Files and Packages Used by DDCS					
Command Line Processor (CLP)					
Isolation Level CS	db2clpcs	sqlc2xxx	yes	yes	yes
Isolation Level RR	db2clprr	sqlc3xxx	yes	yes	yes
Isolation Level UR	db2clpur	sqlc4xxx	yes	yes	yes
Isolation Level RS	db2clprs	sqlc5xxx	yes	yes	yes
Isolation Level NC	db2clpnc	sqlc6xxx	no	no	yes
REXX					
Isolation Level CS	db2arxcs	sqla1xxx	yes	yes	yes
Isolation Level RR	db2arxrr	sqla2xxx	yes	yes	yes
Isolation Level UR	db2arxur	sqla3xxx	yes	yes	yes
Isolation Level RS	db2arxrs	sqla4xxx	yes	yes	yes
Isolation Level NC	db2arxnc	sqla5xxx	no	no	yes
Utilities					
Export	db2uexpm	sqlubxxx	yes	yes	yes
Import	db2uimpm	sqlufxxx	yes	yes	yes

The xxx in the Package column in Table 16 on page 127 depends on the type of the client platform. The xxx values are

- For DB2 CAE for Windows Version 2.1 = 4W0
- For DB2 CAE for OS/2 Version 2.1 = 4D0
- For DB2 CAE for AIX Version 2.1 = 4C0.

If you want to bind a specific utility, you can also bind the .bnd file that corresponds to the utility. You do not have to bind the complete .lst file. Here is an example of how to bind a specific file by using CLP:

```
db2 connect to DATABASE user USERID using PASSWORD
db2 bind path\db2clpcs.bnd blocking all
    sqlerror continue messages vmclics.msg grant public
db2 connect reset
```

5.7.5.3 Binding Back-level Clients

If a back-level client did not use DDCS or is defining a new connection to a DRDA AS, do the following:

- For DB2 for OS/2 Version 1.0 or 1.2 clients, create a bind list file (for example, db22cli.lst) with the following lines:

```
sqlabind.bnd+
sqlueiwi.bnd+
sqluigsi.bnd+
sqluiici.bnd+
sqluiict.bnd+
sqluexpm.bnd+
sqluimpm.bnd+
sqlurexp.bnd+
sqlarxcs.bnd+
sqlarxrr.bnd+
sqlarxur.bnd
```

and bind the list file.

- For DB2 CAE/2 Version 1.0 or 1.2, create a bind list file (for example, db2cae.lst) with the following lines:

```
db2ajgrt.bnd+
db2clics.bnd+
db2clpcs.bnd+
db2clprr.bnd+
db2clpur.bnd+
db2ueiwi.bnd+
db2uigsi.bnd+
db2uiici.bnd+
db2uiict.bnd+
db2uexpm.bnd+
db2uimpm.bnd+
db2urexp.bnd
```

and bind the list file.

For detailed information about the BIND command refer to 13.1.3, "Creating a Package through the BIND Command" on page 405 or the *DDCS User's Guide for common servers*.

5.8 DB2 for OS/2 As an AS

With DB2 common server you can also use your DB2 as an AS, so that applications residing on other platforms can transparently access DB2 for OS/2 resources by using DRDA AR requests. In this section we review the steps to configure your workstation to function as an AS. Basically you have to configure CM/2 profiles and update the database manager configuration file to support APPC clients. You must also verify that the DB2 at the requester platform is configured correctly.

5.8.1 CM/2 Profiles

Configuring CM/2 to enable the AS function is basically the same as configuring it to accept APPC non-DRDA clients.

If your workstation is already defined as a DRDA AR, there is not much you have to define in CM/2 to enable it to receive requests from a DRDA AR. If you have not configured your workstation as a DRDA AR, configure the following profiles:

- DLC profile

  To configure the DLC pofile, refer to 5.6.4, "Data Link Control Profile" on page 92.

- Local node characteristics

  To configure the local node characteristics profile, refer to 5.6.5, "SNA Local Node Characteristics" on page 93 and make sure that you have checked the Activate Attach Manager at start up box on the Local Node Options window (see Figure 32 on page 94). The attach manager handles the incoming APPC connection requests and passes them to the appropriate TP.

- Local LU profile

  You have to configure the local LU profile if the partner LU name specified in the DRDA AR does not match the local node name you have configured in the local node characteristics profile. To configure the local LU profile, refer to 5.6.8.1, "Local LU" on page 105.

- Partner LU profile

  You have to configure the partner LU profile if the DRDA AR or the APPC client sends the userid with an indication that it was already verified. In this case you should check the Conversation security verification box on the Partner LU window (Figure 44 on page 108). For this environment, you must also set the database manager configuration AUTHENTICATION parameter to CLIENT. To configure the partner LU profile, refer to 5.6.8.2, "Partner LU" on page 107.

- Connection profile

  If the DRDA AR is APPN capable and your workstation is configured as an EN, you do not have to configure the connection profile. If the DRDA AR is not APPN capable, you have to configure this profile. To configure the connection profile refer to 5.6.6, "SNA Connections" on page 95.

- Mode

  To configure the mode profile refer to 5.6.8.3, "Modes" on page 108.

- Conversation security profile

If the DRDA AR or the APPC client sends a userid with a password, you must configure the conversation security profile. To configure the conversation security profile refer to 5.8.2.2, "Conversation Security" on page 135.

- TP profile

  For incoming requests, you must also define a TP profile. DDCS uses the same TPN as DB2 for OS/2. You can set up your TPs as described in 5.8.2.1, "TP Profiles."

5.8.2 Configuring Additional Profiles

For the version of the products we used, there are some changes concerning the TP and the existence of an environment variable called DB2COMM.

When a client wants to connect to a DB2 for OS/2 workstation, the inbound request has to go through CM/2. The sections that follow describe how to set up the TP profile and the related security definitions.

You can now use TCP/IP to connect from an OS/2, DOS, or Windows Client to a DB2 for OS/2 server or a DDCS for OS/2 multiuser gateway. Refer to 7.1.3.1, "Configuring the Server Workstation for TCP/IP" on page 204 for information about how to configure the server workstation to support TCP/IP clients.

5.8.2.1 TP Profiles

With the version of the products we used, the TP is operator preloaded, *not* Attach Manager started as in previous versions. As a result, an OS/2 TP executable file specification is of no relevance. The previous TP programs, sqlciaa.exe (for database connections) and sqlcnsm.exe (for interrupts), are no longer required and are not provided. If you have existing TP definitions for the X'07'6DB and X'07'6SN service TPs, ensure that the operation type in the TP definition is changed to queued, operator preloaded. Because the TP is operator preloaded, the specification of the OS/2 program path and file name field is of no relevance. However, the OS/2 program path and file name field is a mandatory input field, so you must still enter some information when you configure the TP (see Figure 57 on page 132).

To configure the required TPs to support remote DRDA and APPC clients follow these steps:

1. On the Communications Manager Profile List window (Figure 29 on page 92), select SNA features and click on the Configure... push button. The SNA Features List window (Figure 41 on page 105) is displayed.
2. On the SNA Features List window select Transaction program definitions and click on the Create... push button. The Transaction Program Definition window shown in Figure 57 on page 132 is displayed.
3. Enter your TPN (in our case DB22TPN) and any information in the OS/2 program path and file name field. Remember that you have to specify something in this

field because it is not an optional field (see Figure 57 on page 132). This profile is used for database connections and database interrupts from Version 2 clients.

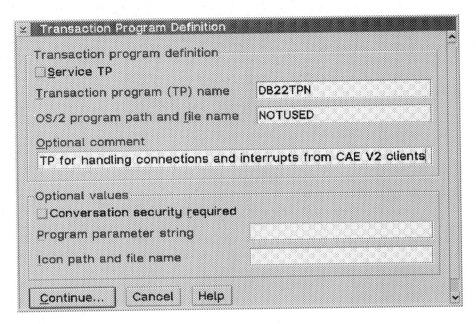

Figure 57. Transaction Program Definition

4. Click on the Continue... push button. The Additional TP Parameters window is displayed. Specify the parameters as shown in Figure 58.

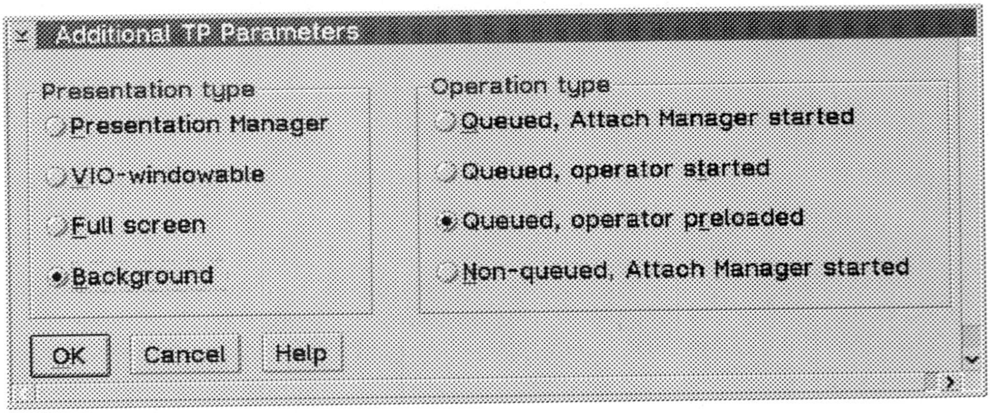

Figure 58. Additional TP Parameters

Presentation type defines the presentation type of the local TP you are defining. Presentation type is the method attach manager uses to display the TP on the screen.

Operation type is the method used to start and load the TP. It also determines whether several copies of a remotely started TP can run at the same time. You must select Queued, operator preloaded, which indicates that one version of the program is run at a time. If an attach request arrives and the program has not been started, the attach request is rejected. Subsequent attach requests that arrive while the program is active are queued.

5. If you have to support connections from CAE Version 1 clients, add the DB2INTERRUPT profile as shown in Figure 59. The DB2INTERRUPT profile is used for database interrupts from CAE/2 Version 1 clients. Enter any information in the OS/2 program path and file name field.

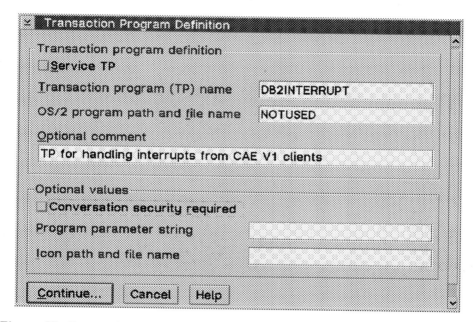

Figure 59. Transaction Program Definition: CAE/2 Version 1 Clients

6. If you have to support connections from DB2 for OS/2 Version 1 clients, you have to add two profiles. One profile (Figure 60 on page 134) is used to handle connections, and the other (Figure 61 on page 135) is used to handle interrupts. You must use the TPN shown in the profile. You must also specify the additional parameters shown previously in Figure 58 on page 132.

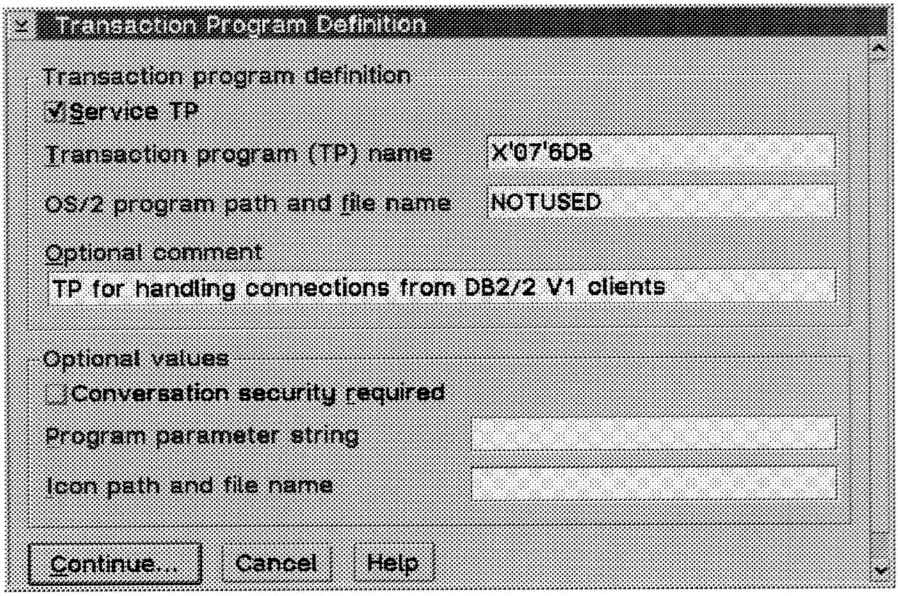

Figure 60. *TP Parameters for Down-Level Clients: Handling Connections*

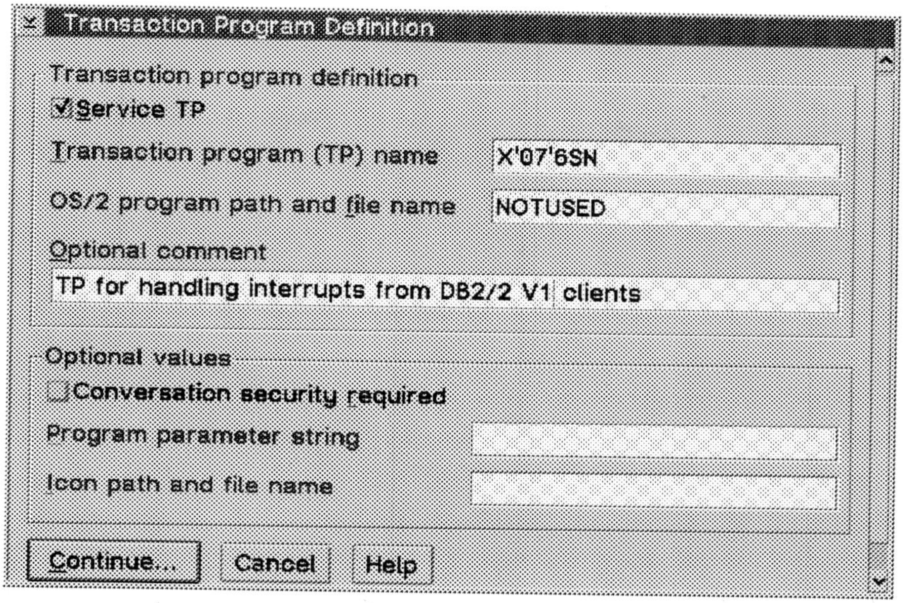

Figure 61. TP Parameters for Down-Level Clients: Handling Interrupts

Only one instance of DB2 can support down-level DB2/2 Version 1 clients. These clients use the hardcoded service TPN, X'07'6DB. Specify the instance by setting the DB2INSTANCE environment variable to the instance name that should be used.

5.8.2.2 Conversation Security

You must configure at least one conversation security profile if the DRDA AR or the APPC client sends a userid and a password. Conversation security profile information can include userids and passwords for all individuals who have access to protected nodes. For all inbound requests the attach manager compares the userid and password sent with the userid and password pairs that you have defined in the conversation security profile.

To configure conversation security profiles follows these steps:

1. On the Communications Manager Profile List window (Figure 29 on page 92), select SNA features and click on the Configure... push button. The SNA Features List window (Figure 41 on page 105) is displayed.
2. On the SNA Features List window, select Conversation security and click on the Create push button. The Conversation Security window shown in Figure 62 on page 136 is displayed.
3. Enter the user ID and password, or, if you want to use the OS/2 User Profile Management (UPM) to authenticate the userid for incoming allocation requests,

check the `Utilize User Profile Management` box. We recommend that you use the OS/2 UPM to secure database resources.

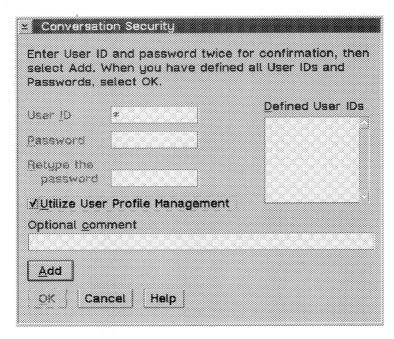

Figure 62. *Conversation Security*

5.8.3 Updating the DB2COMM Environment Variable

When your workstation is a database server and one or more of your clients has APPC connections defined such as DRDA AR, you have to add APPC to the DB2COMM environment variable, usually in the CONFIG.SYS file , or on the command line. You must specify in the DB2COMM environment variable all protocols that the server workstation should support. Here is an example of the DB2COMM environment variable supporting requests from APPC (DRDA or non-DRDA), NetBIOS, and TCP/IP clients:

```
DB2COMM=appc,netbios,tcpip
```

5.8.4 Updating the TPNAME Parameter

You must update the TPNAME parameter of your database manager configuration file with the value you specified when you configured the TPN, as explained in 5.8.2.1, "TP Profiles" on page 131. Here is an example of how to update the TPNAME parameter using CLP:

`DB2 update database manager configuration using TPNAME DB22TPN`

To update the TPNAME with the database director, do the following:

1. Open the IBM `Database 2 Folder`.

2. Start the database director by double-clicking on the `Database Director` icon in the IBM DATABASE 2 icon view.

3. Select the active instance and click on the appropriate icon (in our case DB2). This icon should be highlighted as shown in Figure 63.

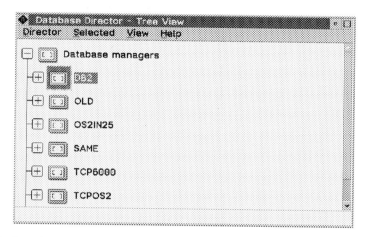

Figure 63. *Database Director - Tree View: Setting the TPNAME Parameter*

4. Click on `Selected` and choose `Configure...` The DB2 Configure window appears.

5. Click on the `Protocols` tab and in the DB2 - Configure window enter your TPN, in our case, DB22TPN, as shown in Figure 64 on page 138.

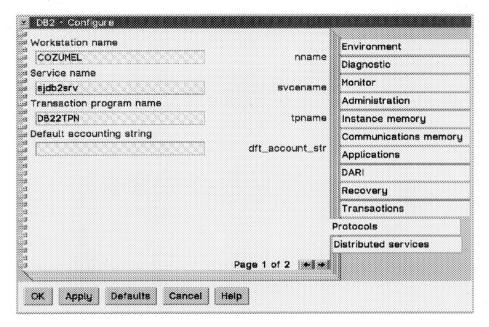

Figure 64. *DB2 - Configure Window: Protocols*

5.9 CM/2 Configuration Summary

When you have finished your configuration, CM/2 automatically runs a verify procedure to check for errors. If it detects any problems, it suggests that you look in the VERIFY.LOG file, where you can find the cause of your problem and probably some hints on how to solve it.

Figure 65 on page 139 summarizes the CM/2 profiles you have to define when using either an APPC or APPN connection for a DRDA AS or DRDA AR.

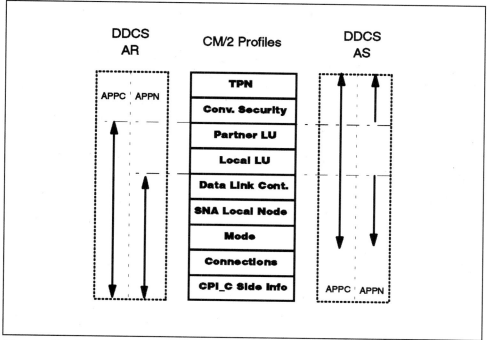

Figure 65. *Configuration of CM/2 Profiles*

5.10 Testing LU-to-LU Sessions

CM/2 also gives you tools and utilities to test your defined SNA links and view the parameters for your active configuration.

1. To use the subsystem management tool, select the Subsystem Management icon from the Communications Manager icon view. The Subsystem Management window shown in Figure 66 on page 140 is displayed.

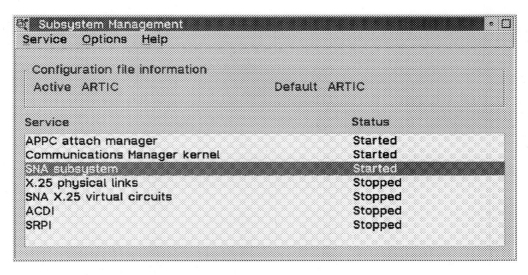

Figure 66. Subsystem Management

2. On this window you can see the status of all CM/2 subsystems.

3. Select SNA subsystem. The SNA Subsystem window displays a list of available resources as shown in Figure 67.

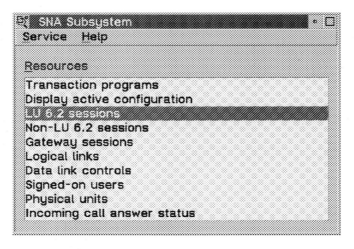

Figure 67. SNA Subsystem: Available Resources

4. Select LU 6.2 sessions to show all active sessions (Figure 68 on page 141).

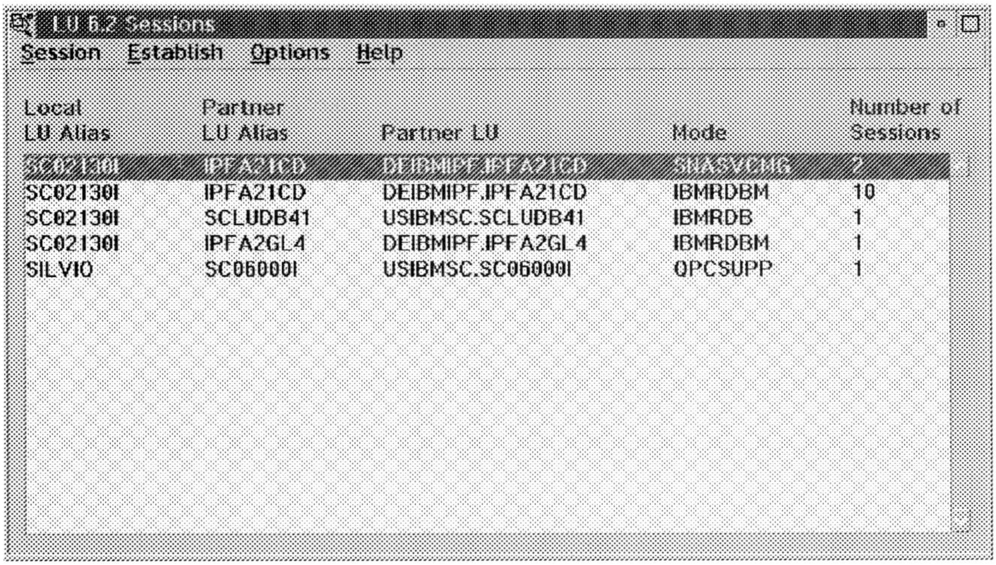

Figure 68. LU 6.2 Sessions

5. In Figure 68 select Establish to display the Establish LU 6.2 Session window shown in Figure 69 on page 142. Using this window, you can establish a session by specifying either the fully qualified name of your partner LU or its alias. You also have to select the appropriate mode from the pull-down menu.

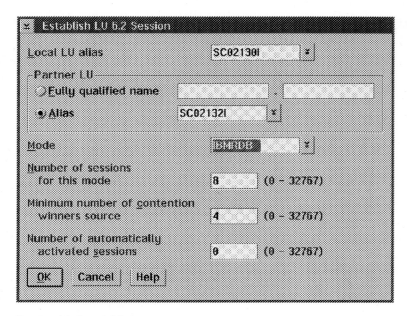

Figure 69. *Establish LU 6.2 Session*

For more information about CM/2 subsystem management and other options, refer to the CM/2 documentation.

5.11 Security

In this section we describe the networking security, authentication process, and database security considerations for the OS/2 platform. Networking security is closely related to the authentication process, so we present the two topics together. Network security is implemented through the underlying communications products.

The authentication process validates a userid against a password. For the OS/2 platform, the authentication process can take place in different locations, depending on your specification.

UPM performs authentication in the OS/2 platform. UPM enables you to manage the user data required for user authentication.

5.11.1 DDCS for OS/2

First we discuss the security considerations for a DDCS stand-alone workstation. The considerations are also valid if the DDCS workstation is a gateway workstation used by a local user.

Whether your configuration is stand-alone or client/server, the security type that you specified when you configured the CPIC side information profile is ignored. Also, the AUTHENTICATION parameter in the database manager configuration file applies only for local databases. When cataloging a remote database, the value you specify for the AUTHENTICATION parameter overrides the value specified in the database manager configuration file.

5.11.1.1 Stand-Alone or Local Users

When you catalog a database in the system database directory you have three options for the AUTHENTICATION parameter value:

- AUTHENTICATION=CLIENT

  Essentially the authentication takes place in the client workstation. For a local user or a stand-alone configuration, authentication takes place locally.

- AUTHENTICATION=SERVER

  This value is conceptually the same as AUTHENTICATION=CLIENT; the user is authenticated locally. In addition, the authentication process can take place in the DRDA AS. We describe these implementations below when we explain the SECURITY parameter.

- AUTHENTICATION=DCS

  Authentication takes place on the DRDA AS.

When you catalog the APPC node for the DRDA connection, you have two options for the SECURITY parameter value:

- SECURITY=SAME

  A password is not sent to the DRDA AS.

- SECURITY=PROGRAM

  A password is sent to the DRDA AS.

If you specify AUTHENTICATION=CLIENT, you have to specify SECURITY=SAME. In this case the userid is authenticated locally, and only the userid is sent to the DRDA AS. If the DRDA AS uses VTAM, the APPL statement for the RDBMS must specify SECACPT=ALREADYV. If the DRDA AS is DB2 for OS/400, the SEC parameter in the remote configuration list must be set to *YES for the LU that represents this DDCS workstation. Refer to the DRDA AS security sections for the platform specifics.

If you specify AUTHENTICATION=SERVER and SECURITY=SAME, the userid is authenticated locally, and only the userid is sent to the DRDA AS.

If you specify AUTHENTICATION=SERVER and SECURITY=PROGRAM, the userid is first authenticated locally. If the authentication process is successful, the userid and the password are sent to the DRDA AS, where the user is authenticated again. For this combination of parameters, the userids must be maintained on both the DDCS workstation and the DRDA AS.

If you specify AUTHENTICATION=DCS, the only option you have is SECURITY=PROGRAM. The userid is not authenticated locally; the userid and the password combination are sent to the DRDA AS, where the user is authenticated.

The userid or the userid and password are always folded to uppercase before being sent to the DRDA AS.

Table 17 summarizes the authentication scheme for a DDCS workstation without remote clients.

Table 17. *Security Matrix: DDCS without Remote Clients—OS/2 Platform*			
DDCS Workstation			**DRDA AS**
Authentication	**Security**		
CLIENT	SAME	`userid/pwd`	userid
SERVER	SAME	`userid/pwd`	userid
SERVER	PROGRAM	`userid/pwd`	`userid/pwd`
DCS	PROGRAM	userid/pwd	`userid/pwd`

The reverse highlighted userid/pwd shows the userid and password combination that is verified and where authentication takes place.

5.11.1.2 Clients

When you catalog a database in the client workstation, you also have three options for the AUTHENTICATION parameter value:

- AUTHENTICATION=CLIENT

   Authentication takes place on the client workstation. You can only specify AUTHENTICATION=CLIENT if the DDCS gateway also has AUTHENTICATION=CLIENT. Although the userid is not authenticated on the DDCS gateway workstation, a userid with the same, different, or no password at all must also be defined to UPM at the DDCS gateway workstation. For this specification only the userid is sent.

   The same considerations apply for DDCS for OS/2 client workstations as for DDCS stand-alone workstations concerning VTAM or AS/400. Also, if APPC is the communication protocol being used to connect to the DDCS gateway workstation, you must configure a partner LU profile and check the Conversation security verification box (Figure 44 on page 108).

- AUTHENTICATION=SERVER or DCS

  There is no difference between AUTHENTICATION=SERVER or AUTHENTICATION=DCS at the client workstation. The userid and password are always sent to the DDCS gateway workstation. If you are using APPC as the communications protocol, you have to configure the conversation security verification profile as described in 5.8.2.2, "Conversation Security" on page 135.

  Below we describe we describe what happens when AUTHENTICATION=SERVER or DCS specified on the client workstation is combined with various AUTHENTICATION parameter values in the DDCS gateway workstation:

  - If AUTHENTICATION=CLIENT is specified at the DDCS gateway workstation, this is not a valid combination.

    If you are accessing a local database on the DDCS server workstation (not a DRDA remote database), the userid and password are sent to the DDCS gateway workstation but are not authenticated there. The userid and password are sent back to the client workstation to be authenticated at the client. Only the userid, with an indication that it was already verified, is sent to the DRDA AS.

  - If AUTHENTICATION=SERVER and SECURITY=SAME are specified at the DDCS gateway workstation, the userid and password are sent to the DDCS gateway workstation and are authenticated there. Only the userid, with an indication that it was already verified, is sent to the DRDA AS.

  - If AUTHENTICATION=SERVER and SECURITY=PROGRAM are specified at the DDCS gateway workstation, the userid and password are sent to the DDCS gateway workstation and are authenticated there. If the authentication process is successful, the userid and password are sent to the DRDA AS to be authenticated there.

  - If AUTHENTICATION=DCS and SECURITY=PROGRAM are specified at the DDCS gateway workstation, the userid and password are sent to the DDCS gateway workstation but are not authenticated there unless you are using APPC for the connection. The userid and password are sent to the DRDA AS to be authenticated there.

If you are using APPC to connect from the client to the DDCS gateway workstation, it makes no difference which value you specify for the SECURITY parameter in the client workstation. In general the communications protocol being used to communicate from the client to the DDCS gateway workstation is also transparent. The exception is when you use APPC; whenever a password is sent, the user is authenticated at the DDCS gateway workstation regardless of whether authentication also takes place at other locations. Also, if a password is sent, the conversation security profile must be configured as described in 5.8.2.2, "Conversation Security" on page 135. If a password is not sent, the partner LU for the client must be configured at the DDCS gateway workstation with the Conversation security verification box checked (Figure 44 on page 108).

Table 18 summarizes the authentication scheme for a DDCS workstation serving remote clients. Note how we have essentially nested Table 17 on page 144 in a broader scenario to account for the clients.

Table 18. *Security Matrix: DDCS with Remote Clients*

Client Workstation		DDCS Workstation			DRDA AS
Auth		Auth	Sec		
CLIENT	`userid/pwd`	CLIENT	SAME	`userid`	userid
SERVER or DCS	userid/pwd	SERVER	SAME	`userid/pwd`	userid
SERVER or DCS	userid/pwd	SERVER	PROGRAM	`userid/pwd`	`userid/pwd`
SERVER or DCS	userid/pwd	DCS	PROGRAM	userid/pwd	`userid/pwd`

Authentication takes place wherever userid/pwd is reverse highlighted.

5.11.2 User Profile Management

DB2 uses UPM to control access to databases by having users log on to the database manager. Users log on to UPM before connecting to the database or by specifying a userid and password in the CONNECT statement. You can use UPM to create, manage, and view individual and group user IDs as well as set authority levels.

In this section we briefly review the main elements of UPM; refer to Appendix H of the *DB2 for OS/2 Installation and Operation Guide* for more information.

5.11.2.1 Logging On to UPM with Multiple IDs

You can log on to UPM with multiple user IDs. Use this feature to start several application programs under different user IDs. There are two ways to enable multiple logons at your workstation (and control selective logoffs). Use either of these methods:

- Type LOGON /O=MULTI at the OS/2 prompt and press Enter. As each application starts, the UPM logon window appears.
- Embed UPM logon and logoff commands in each application program you want to start with its own user ID. UPM provides two APIs, one for logon and one for logoff.

5.11.2.2 User Profiles, User Logon Profiles, and Node Logons

The UPM *user profile* is primarily used to record information about users who will log on and access resources that are owned by the local workstation. The UPM *user logon profile* records information that can be used when the local workstation user has to access remote server resources. When a local logon occurs, the user logon profile is also made available. UPM, behind the scenes, uses the information in the user logon profile to pass user ID and password information to a given remote server. Different remote server user IDs (and passwords) can thus be associated with a given local user ID through the user logon profile. These profiles can be manipulated with UPM services (see Figure 70).

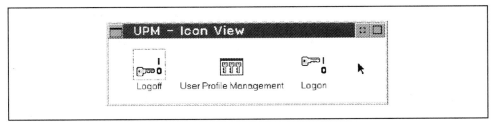

Figure 70. *UPM Services Window*

Logon status information is recorded in an internal OS/2 table that is maintained in the workstation's memory. The table includes information such as

```
user ID
password
remotename (if applicable)
nametype (local, remote LU6.2 node, or domain)
session id
process id
validated indicator    /* logon has been authenticated */
```

5.11.2.3 Logon Considerations

UPM recognizes the following workstation logon types:

- **Local**

  Userid and password are checked at logon time.

- **Node**

  The userid and password are stored and can be used later when the user attempts to access the specific remote server. The user can have multiple node logons.

- **Domain**

  The userid and password are stored and then used at logon time at the domain controller.

A UPM LOGON command can be issued manually at the OS/2 command line or through a program by issuing a call to the UPMGLGN routine. This routine enables you to log on and log off from UPM within an application program. Figure 71 on page 148 shows examples of the LOGON command issued at the OS/2 command line.

```
LOGON BOEISC /P=DRDA1A /L              /* local logon */

LOGON BOEISC /P=DRDA1A /N=NODEDDCS     /* node logon   */

LOGON BOEISC /P=DRDA1A /D=ITSCPOUK     /* domain logon */
```

Figure 71. LOGON Command Examples Using the OS/2 Command Line

UPM user logon profile records are used by UPM. When local logon occurs, all the user logon profile records are made available. When you access a remote server and do not specify a userid and password in the CONNECT statement, UPM selects the user and password (if required) to be used as follows:

- If there is a logon profile that represents the remote DDCS server workstation (or the DRDA AS), the userid and password that is contained in the profile are used.

- If there is a node logon for the connection, UPM uses this userid and password.

- If no matching entry is found for the logged on user, but there is an active local logon, this userid and password are used.

- If none of the above is true, and depending on the DB2UPMPR environment variable setting, the OS/2 user is prompted to enter a userid and password in the UPM node logon window.

In summary here are the security considerations when you connect to a database and do not specify a userid and password. For remote databases the system searches for a node-specific userid and password in the active profiles of the user. If the system does not find a node-specific userid and password, it checks to see whether the user is logged on locally. If the user is not logged on locally, depending on the DB2UPMPR environment variable setting, the system invokes UPM, which displays the logon window where the user can enter the userid and password.

The DB2UPMPR environment variable can be used to specify whether the user is prompted for a userid and password (DB2UPMPR=ON) or not (DB2UPMPR=OFF). Environment variables are set either from the OS/2 command line or in the CONFIG.SYS file by using the SET function as follows:

```
SET DB2UPMPR=ON  (default)
```

You get an SQL error if DB2UPMPR=OFF, and you are not logged on to UPM, and you do not specify a userid and password in the CONNECT statement,

If UPM prompts you to log on, the logon is persistent, that is, you remain logged on in UPM.

When you connect to a database you can explicitly provide a userid and password as follows:

```
CONNECT TO database USER userid USING password
```

If you specify a userid and password in the CONNECT statement, the logon is not persistent. Also, if you have a previous node logon, the userid and password specified in the CONNECT statement are used instead of the node logon.

5.11.2.4 Database Considerations

Below we describe the considerations for DDCS for OS/2 as an AR.

Access to database objects is controlled by the AS. A userid is required by the database manager at the AS. After authentication by the security facilities of the operating system, the database manager checks the privileges of the userid. The minimum requirement is that the user be allowed to connect to the database. After connection is established, the privileges for the required database object are checked. Although UPM permits users to be members of security groups, UPM group identifiers are not sent to DRDA ASs.

As described in Chapter 13, "Program Preparation: DB2 common server" on page 395, in order to execute SQL statements on the DB2 for OS/2 AS, you have to bind a package at the AS. You do not need any local authorization to bind or execute a remote package. The required authorization is dependent on the AS platform.

Note that when binding to a remote AS, you can specify a GRANT option. Using the GRANT option of the BIND command, you can GRANT EXECUTE and BIND privileges to a userid. You can also use the GRANT statement to grant execute and bind privileges to a userid.

5.11.3 AS Security

In this section we describe the security considerations when an AR accesses data at the DB2 for OS/2 AS.

5.11.3.1 AUTHENTICATION Parameter

For DB2 for OS/2 V2.1 local databases, authentication is specified at the instance level as the AUTHENTICATION parameter of the database manager configuration file. The AUTHENTICATION parameter specified applies to all databases of that instance. The

AUTHENTICATION parameter defines where authentication is performed. For local databases the parameter can be CLIENT or SERVER.

The AUTHENTICATION parameter for local databases is defined when you

- Create the instance
- Create the first database of the instance, when not already defined for the instance
- Use the default (AUTHENTICATION=SERVER)

Because for the current level of CM/2 there is no way of extracting the password, if your DB2 for OS/2 acts as an AS, you must specify the AUTHENTICATION parameter value as CLIENT in the database manager configuration file. This specification accepts that a userid and password or a userid and an indication that the user was already verified at the AR be sent from the AR to the DB2 for OS/2 AS workstation.

5.11.3.2 CM/2 Profiles

If the AR sends the userid and password, you must configure the conversation security profile as described in 5.8.2.2, "Conversation Security" on page 135.

If the AR sends the userid with an indication that the userid was already verified at the AR, you must configure a partner LU and check the Conversation security verification box in the Partner LU window (Figure 44 on page 108).

Note that checking of the Conversation security verification box is irrelevant when you configure the TP.

Userids may be sent in uppercase or lowercase; however, passwords must be sent in uppercase.

5.11.3.3 DB2 for OS/2 Privileges

After authentication is done by the security facilities of the operating systems, the database manager checks the privileges of the userid. The minimum requirement is that the user be allowed to connect to the database. After connection is established, the privileges for the required database object are checked.

The userid is known as the authorization ID by the database manager. UPM also permits users to be members of security groups. Note that UPM group identifiers are not valid userid specifications when the AR connects to DB2 for OS/2 AS. The userid and user group cannot have the same name. An individual user can also belong to one or more user groups, which are authorization IDs as well. The authorization IDs and the related privileges are stored in the database's system catalog.

Authorization is controlled in three ways:

- Explicit authorization, controlled with the GRANT and REVOKE statements

- Implicit authorization, controlled by creating and dropping database objects like tables, plans, or views.

- Indirect privileges, associated with packages

As described in Chapter 13, "Program Preparation: DB2 common server" on page 395, in order to execute SQL statements on DB2 for OS/2, you have to bind a package from the AR. When the package is created, the creator of the package is assigned the EXECUTE and CONTROL privileges. This userid needs privileges for all tables and SQL objects used in the application program. The privileges must be explicitly defined (not granted to groups or public).

Note: For DRDA ARs, this means that the bind userid (the user who does the bind), the OWNER, and the QUALIFIER must have the same value. The collection ID can be different.

The system administrator and the database administrator have the CONTROL privilege for any created package.

To execute the application from a remote AR, the user must have EXECUTE privilege to execute the package locally.

Use the GRANT to PUBLIC statement to allow all users to run the package.

A package can contain

- Static SQL statements

  Users granted EXECUTE privilege for a package are automatically granted EXECUTE privilege for each statement of the related application program. Thus the end users do not need any table privileges if the package contains static SQL statements only.

- Dynamic SQL statements

  The contents of a dynamic SQL statement are not known before execution. The application program builds the dynamic SQL statement, and DB2 dynamically preprocesses the statement, using SQL PREPARE or EXECUTE IMMEDIATE.

  For execution of the statement, users need table privileges for all tables and SQL objects used in the statement.

SQL objects are, for example, tables, views, indexes, and databases. Users can get privileges granted to create delete, update, insert, or read individual SQL objects. For dynamic SQL statements this authority is required.

5.11.4 Types of UPM Users

UPM recognizes three types of users:

- A **user** can perform logon and logoff, change the password, and run applications.

- A **local administrator** has, in addition to the user type, system administrator authority (SYSADM) for any local database.

- An **administrator** has, in addition to the local administrator type, permission to maintain UPM definitions.

5.11.5 Session Level Security

The AS can request session level security. To implement session level security on the OS/2 platform, you have to configure the LU-to-LU security in the SNA features of CM/2. To implement session level security in VTAM, specify VERIFY=REQUIRED in the APPL statement and set up some RACF definitions.

5.11.6 Selecting UPM Userids

The userid is a one- to eight-character string that must be unique in a particular operating system. The restrictions for userid names are documented in the *DB2 Administration Guide for common servers*.

Userids and passwords are registered in uppercase.

For the OS/2 platform, the userid and password as well as other UPM profile data are stored on the workstation in the C:\MUGLIB\ACCOUNTS\NET.ACC file.

5.11.7 CICS for OS/2 Considerations

CICS for OS/2 enables you to run transactions from many users under one userid. When CICS for OS/2 is started, it is associated with the OS/2 user name with which it is defined. This name is used as the userid. All CICS processes use this userid when communicating with the database manager. Therefore all privileges must be granted to the userid that is assigned to CICS. Individual CICS users do not need any database manager privilege.

CICS for OS/2 also has an interface to a security subsystem to verify individual userids and passwords. Using this information CICS can define which users can run specific CICS programs. This information is not used, however, when communicating with the database manager.

5.12 DDCS for OS/2 Migration

DDCS for OS/2 includes all necessary migration steps in the installation program. When migrating from a down-level version of DDCS to Version 2.3, minimum user action is involved. In this section we describe how to migrate to a DDCS for OS/2 gateway. If you are also installing DB2 for OS/2 Version 2.1, the installation process migrates your local databases from previous versions. If you do not have a backup of your database before you attempt migration, and the migration fails, there is no way of restoring your database by using DB2 Version 2 or the previous Version of the database manager. Refer to the following DB/2 for OS/2 documentation:

- *DB2 for OS/2 Installation and Operation Guide*
- *Information and Concepts Guide for common servers*
- *DB2 Administration Guide for common servers.*

5.12.1 Installation

You can install DDCS for OS/2 in the same directory as it was installed before. The installation procedure detects previous Versions of DB2/2 and DDCS/2 and removes them. You cannnot install or run different releases of the products on the same workstation. For DDCS for OS/2 Version 2.3, DB2 for OS/2 Version 2.1 is the only compatible version. It is no longer a prerequisite for DDCS to have DB2 for OS/2 installed. All necessary files to run DRDA services are contained on the product diskettes or the CD-ROM. Before you start the installation, be sure all database services are stopped. Install the product as instructed.

After installation, perform a shutdown and restart your system to effect the changes in the CONFIG.SYS file. Open the new DATABASE 2 folder (Figure 72).

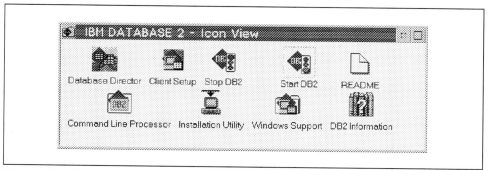

Figure 72. IBM DATABASE 2 Folder

There is not much difference compared with having the DB2 for OS/2 database product installed. The difference is that you cannot have local databases on the workstation, but you still have the database director to maintain your configuration and directory files and the CLP to issue commands.

5.12.2 Restrictions after Migration

After you have rebooted your workstation, you can connect to your AS databases only if the userid specified for the host connection is also defined in the local UPM. During migration the database authentication is set to server, so UPM validates the userid at the workstation.

With the level of the products we used in our project, you should issue a local logon before attempting the connection. If you are not logged on locally, UPM prompts you to log on. In this case, the logon is successful but not the connection, so the CONNECT statement abends. The next time you try to connect, the connection is successful because you are already logged on.

If you catalog a new database using a migrated node and specify the AUTHENTICATION parameter (any value), when you try to connect to the AS, you get an SQL1331N error stating that the CPIC security type is not valid. Therefore if you have to catalog a new database using a migrated node directory structure, do not specify the AUTHENTICATION parameter.

These are known restrictions when migrating with the GA level of the DDCS for OS/2 product. Fixes are under development and will be included in the product when available.

The workaround for these restrictions is to define a CPIC side information in your CM/2 configuration and recatalog your nodes including the CPIC side information. Refer to 5.7.2, "Cataloging in the Node Directory" on page 113

5.12.3 Connecting DB Clients after Migration

Although the DDCS gateway cannnot bear local databases, to support remote clients, you must observe the same settings and parameters as used for the server product; that is, you must

- Set the DB2COMM environment variable to the appropriate protocols
- Issue the DB2START command

When installing DDCS for OS/2 multiuser, the installation procedure adds the following definition to your CONFIG.SYS file:

SET DB2NBSESSIONS=35

DB2NBSESSIONS specifies the number of NetBIOS sessions that should be reserved for DB2 use. This can conflict with the total number of NetBIOS sessions defined for your workstation. Therefore, if you get an error message when issuing the DB2START command, check the DB2DIAG.LOG file for information about the cause of the problem.

Chapter 6. AIX Platform

In this chapter we describe the different connectivity options for DB2 for AIX and explain how to configure an AIX workstation to act as a DRDA AR and AS.

The example we use in this chapter is the AIX system at the ITSO-Boeblingen Center.

6.1 DB2 for AIX Connectivity Options

Table 19 on page 158 summarizes the connectivity options for DB2 for AIX and DDCS for AIX, from both the DRDA and the RDS points of view. Refer to 3.2.1, "DB2 common server Connectivity Concepts" on page 53 to understand how to position RDS and DRDA. We followed the current terminology, which differs slightly between the two connectivity options, although the two basic roles (requiring and providing services) are, of course, conceptually the same regardless of the architecture.

Note that the DB2 for AIX server and DDCS for AIX server enable a single workstation to play the four indicated in Table 19 on page 158: RDS client, RDS server, DRDA AR, and DRDA AS.

The following paragraphs explain the entries in Table 19 on page 158.

Products implementing function
> One basic function can be found in more than one product. This is the case with the RDS client function (the core function of CAE for AIX), which is also part of SDK, DB2, and DDCS for AIX.

Network protocol
> Different network protocols are available to implement connectivity options.

Update system database directory
> The system database directory lists the databases available to applications. RDS and DRDA both require this directory to be updated on the client side.

Update node directory
> The node directory lists the network nodes holding databases. RDS and DRDA both require this directory to be updated on the client side.

Update DCS directory
> The DCS directory lists remote DRDA databases.

Update DB2COMM (environment variable)
When serving remote clients, DB2COMM must be set according to the network protocol used.

Update TPNAME (database manager configuration parameter)
The TPNAME is required for APPC communications. It must be set according to the TPN in SNA Server.

Update SVCENAME (database manager configuration parameter)
The SVCENAME is required for TCP/IP communications. It must be set according to the TCP/IP port in /etc/services.

Update IPX_SOCKET FILESERVER OBJECTNAME (database manager configuration parameters)
The IPX_SOCKET FILESERVER OBJECTNAME is required for IPX/SPX communications, depending on the IPX/SPX type of addressing used (direct addressing or file server addressing).

Update TM_DATABASE (database manager configuration parameter)
TM_DATABASE must be set when using DUW with two-phase commit protocol support in DB2 common server. It must be set to a DB2 common server database, or to 1ST_CONN, that is, the first database to which the application connects will play the role of transaction manager database.

Table 19 (Page 1 of 2). *DB2 for AIX Connectivity Options*

	RDS Client	**RDS Server**	**DRDA AR**	**DRDA AS**
Products implementing function	CAE, SDK, DB2, DDCS	DB2 (1)	DDCS (2)	DB2 (1)
Network protocol	TCP/IP, APPC (3)	TCP/IP, APPC, IPX/SPX (3)	APPC	APPC
Update system database directory	Y (4)	N (5)	Y	N (5)
Update node directory	Y (4)	N	Y (4)	N
Update DCS directory	N	N	Y (4)	N
Update DCE directories	Y (4)	N	Y (4)	N
Update DB2COMM	N	Y	Y	Y

Table 19 (Page 2 of 2). DB2 for AIX Connectivity Options

	RDS Client	RDS Server	DRDA AR	DRDA AS
Update TPNAME	N	Y	Y	Y
Update SVCENAME	N	Y	Y	N
Update IPX_SOCKET FILESERVER OBJECTNAME	N	Y (6)	Y (6)	N
Update TM_DATABASE	Y	N	N	N

Notes:

1. DB2 server required.

2. DDCS gateway can serve remote clients to route their requests to DRDA ASs, but it does not provide DBMS functions.

3. DB2 multiuser and DDCS gateway can serve IPX/SPX clients, but the AIX client component (CAE) cannot be connected through IPX/SPX to any DB2 server. Typical IPX/SPX RDS clients are Windows machines.

4. DCE directories can be used as an alternative to database, node, and DCS directories.

5. Database directory is automatically updated when the database is created.

6. If all clients use direct addressing, FILESERVER and OBJECTNAME can be set to '*'. Otherwise, the parameters must be set to proper values and the DB2 server must be registered at the NetWare File Server.

6.2 Our Scenario

In our scenario we installed both DB2 and DDCS on the AIX workstation and activated the DRDA AR and AS functions. Both functions require that you set up SNA Server profiles. Some of the profiles are common to both functions, and some are specific to an AR or an AS function.

The AIX configuration in Boeblingen has the following hardware and software configuration:

- Hardware
  - RISC System/6000 Model 520
  - 64 MB of Memory
  - 1 GB Hard Drive
  - Token-Ring Adapter

- Software
  - AIX/6000 Version 3.2.5 Enhancement 5
  - SNA Server Version 2.1 for AIX/6000
  - DB2 for AIX Version 2.1
  - DDCS for AIX Version 2.3
  - Software Developer's Kit Version 2.1

6.2.1 RISC System/6000 Definition in VTAM (Boeblingen, Germany)

Figure 73 shows the VTAM definition for the RISC System/6000.

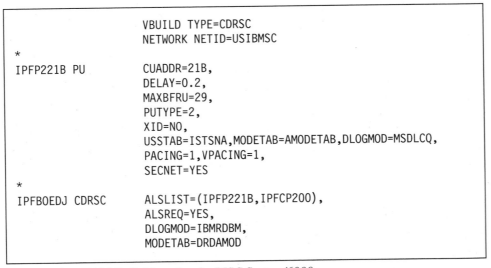

```
                    VBUILD TYPE=CDRSC
                    NETWORK NETID=USIBMSC
*
IPFP221B PU         CUADDR=21B,
                    DELAY=0.2,
                    MAXBFRU=29,
                    PUTYPE=2,
                    XID=NO,
                    USSTAB=ISTSNA,MODETAB=AMODETAB,DLOGMOD=MSDLCQ,
                    PACING=1,VPACING=1,
                    SECNET=YES
*
IPFBOEDJ CDRSC      ALSLIST=(IPFP221B,IPFCP200),
                    ALSREQ=YES,
                    DLOGMOD=IBMRDBM,
                    MODETAB=DRDAMOD
```

Figure 73. VTAM Definitions for the RISC System/6000

6.3 SNA Server/6000 Version 2.1

SNA Server/6000 V2.1 is the successor product to SNA Services/6000 V1.2. Below we describe the major enhancements in SNA Server/6000 V2.1.

6.3.1 Nomenclature Changes

The following changes in nomenclature have been incorporated in SNA Server/6000 V2.1.

- Attachments are now called *link stations*.
- Connections are now called *sessions*.

- Physical and logical link profiles are now combined into a new SNA *DLC profile*.
- Extended Interface is now called *Operating System Subroutine API*

6.3.2 Optional Gateway Support

SNA Server/6000 V2.1 offers optional gateway support on AIX Version 3.2.3 or later. The product, SNA Gateway/6000 V2.1, is available in addition to SNA Server/6000 V2.1. It enables a RISC System/6000 to be used as gateway in place of a 3174 controller and provides a connection between one or more host systems and one or more downstream workstations.

6.3.3 Full APPN Support

SNA Server/6000 V2.1 fully supports IBM SNA APPN. This support enables a RISC System/6000 workstation to function as an NN or an EN in an APPN network using independent LU 6.2.

6.3.4 Link Stations

A link station (called an attachment in SNA Services/6000 V1.2) provides a CP for a single link that connects a local node to an adjacent node in an SNA network. The link station can either call or listen.

6.3.4.1 Calling Link Station

A calling link station initiates the activation of a link. SNA Server/6000 V2.1 uses dynamic calling link stations to support APPN connection networks. The dynamic link station support is set in the SNA DLC profile.

6.3.4.2 Listening Link Station

SNA Server supports selective listening link stations, nonselective listening link stations, and dynamic listening link stations:

- A selective listening link station accepts a link activation request only from a specific remote link station. This function is enabled by specifying the remote link station name or address in the link station profile.

- A nonselective listening link station accepts a link activation from any partner station. This function is enabled by omitting both the remote link name and address in the link station profile.

- A dynamic listening link station is not explicitly configured. SNA Server/6000 V2.1 uses the configuration for the SNA DLC to support link activation. The ability to permit dynamic listening at the station level must be configured in the SNA DLC profile. A dynamic listening link station cannot be used for dependent LU sessions.

6.3.4.3 Link Station Restart

Link stations can be configured to restart automatically with the following link restart capabilities:

- Restart on activation
- Restart on normal deactivation
- Restart on abnormal deactivation

6.3.5 Node Operations

SNA Server/6000 V2.1 enables you to configure a RISC System/6000 workstation as a node in an SNA network. Configuration is a process of specifying the information that enables the RISC System/6000 to operate a node in an SNA network. SNA Server/6000 V2.1 stores this information in SNA profiles which are maintained in two databases:

- Working database, which contains the new or changed profiles
- Committed database, which contains the verified profiles

The profiles can be dynamically updated. Before new or changed profiles can be used, the entire profile database in the working database must be verified with the update option to place the profiles in the committed database.

6.3.6 Migration Routines and Utilities

SNA Server/6000 V2.1 includes migration tools to enable you to migrate the existing SNA Services/6000 V1.2 profiles to the new SNA Server/6000 V2.1.

The *peu* command creates a set of default definitions in SNA Services/6000 V1.2. The *mksnadb* command creates a set of default definitions in SNA Server/6000 V2.1.

The *sna* command is new in SNA Server/6000 V2.1. It is a single command with many flags and options to completely control, display the status of, and trace SNA Server/6000 V2.1. This replaces the *startsrc* command, although some of the compatibility is maintained.

6.4 AIX As a DRDA AR

DDCS for AIX provides applications with transparent access to ASs using DRDA. The workstation on which DDCS is installed is called the DDCS workstation. DRDA ASs can be accessed by local clients on the DDCS workstation and by remote clients. For remote clients, DDCS acts as a gateway between the client workstation and the DRDA server database management system.

6.4.1 SNA Profiles Relationship

For the explanation that follows, refer to Figure 74.

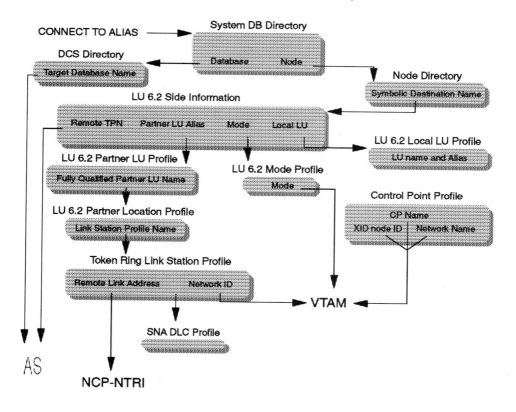

Figure 74. *SNA Profiles Relationship*

For each DRDA AS to which this DDCS workstation can connect, there must be an entry in the system database directory that points to entries in the DCS and node directories, as explained in 6.4.3.2, "Updating the Directories" on page 189. In the node directory you should specify the LU 6.2 Side Information profile name that relates to the communications requirements to connect to the DRDA AS.

The LU 6.2 Side Information profile, known to the DB2 node directory as the Symbolic Destination Name, has information such as

- The local LU name used for the connection

- The partner LU name

- The log mode name profile

- The TPN that should be invoked to establish the conversation

As explained in 6.4.2.5, "LU 6.2 Local LU Profile" on page 172, you might have to configure an LU 6.2 Local LU profile and an LU 6.2 Partner LU profile.

You have to configure an LU 6.2 Partner Location profile indicating how to locate the partner LU. In this profile you specify information such as the partner location method.

If your environment is similar to ours, the location method is through a token-ring link station, so you must configure a Token-Ring Link Station profile.

In the Token-Ring Link Station profile you specify information such as the token-ring address of the communication device that enables connection from the workstation to the network and the Token-Ring DLC profile.

In the Token-Ring DLC profile you specify which DLC should be used when establishing communication. This is where communication messages leave or arrive in the workstation.

Table 20 shows the DRDA parameters, the symbolic destination name that matches information in the LU 6.2 Side Information profile and node directory, and the security type implemented for connections between the AIX and other systems.

Table 20 (Page 1 of 2). Database Definitions and Relationship to SNA Profiles								
Database	DB2 for AIX - San Jose	DB2 for OS/400 - San Jose	DB2 for OS/2 - Boeblingen	DB2 for MVS - Poughkeepsie	DB2 for OS/2 - San Jose	DB2 for OS/400 - Rochester	SQL/DS for VM - Boeblingen	SQL/DS for VSE - Boeblingen
Alias	SJ6SMPL	SJAS400	DBSRV4D	CENTDB2	SJ2SMPL	RCAS400	DB2VM	DB2VSE
Node	AIXSJC	AS4SJC	DBSRV4	MVSESA	OS2SJC	OS4RC	VMESA	VSEESA
Connectivity type	APPC	APPC	APPC	APPC	APPC	APPC	APPC	APPC

Database	DB2 for AIX - San Jose	DB2 for OS/400 - San Jose	DB2 for OS/2 - Boeblingen	DB2 for MVS - Poughkeepsie	DB2 for OS/2 - San Jose	DB2 for OS/400 - Rochester	SQL/DS for VM - Boeblingen	SQL/DS for VSE - Boeblingen
Symbolic destination name	sdaixsj	sdas4sj	DBSRV4	sdpokdb2	sdos2sj	sdos4rc	boevmis2	DBVSETPN
Security type	PGM	PGM	PGM	PGM	PGM	PGM	PGM	PGM
Authentication	DCS	DCS	DCS	DCS	DCS	DCS	DCS	DCS
RDB_NAME	SJ6SMPL	SJAS400	DBSRV4D	CENTDB2	SJ2SMPL	RCAS400	S34VMDB0	S34VSDB1

6.4.2 Configuring SNA Profiles

For our connection in Boeblingen, we used one token-ring adapter attached to a LAN and connected to a 3174 communication controller.

The order we suggest you to follow is *not* the order explained in 6.4.1, "SNA Profiles Relationship" on page 163. When using System Management Interface Tool (SMIT) to configure the profiles, if a profile parameter name value is already configured, you can press F4 and select it.

Use a fast path to get to the SNA profiles by invoking SMIT as follows:

```
smit sna
```

All SNA profiles are configured by using the advanced configuration. To get to the advanced configuration options, invoke SMIT and select the following items:

1. Configure SNA Profiles
2. Advanced Configuration

When we refer to invoking SMIT for the SNA profiles, we assume you are using the above procedure.

To configure SNA profiles, you must have root authority.

6.4.2.1 Configuring the Token-Ring Adapter

Before configuring the SNA profiles, you must to verify that the Token-Ring Adapter is configured correctly. Invoke SMIT and select the following items:

1. Devices

2. Communications

3. Token-Ring Adapter

4. Adapter

5. Change/Show Characteristics of a Token-Ring Adapter

You should get a screen similar to that shown in Figure 75.

```
                Change/Show Characteristics of a Token-Ring Adapter

   Type or select values in entry fields.
   Press  Enter AFTER making all desired changes.

                                            (Entry Fields)
   Token Ring adapter                       tok0
   Description                              Token-Ring High-Perfor>
   Status                                   Available
   Location                                 00-03
   RECEIVE DATA TRANSFER OFFSET             (92)
   TRANSMIT queue size                      (30)
   RECEIVE queue size                       (30)
   STATUS BLOCK queue size                  (10)
   RING speed                                16
   Receive ATTENTION MAC frames             no
   Receive BEACON MAC frames                no
   Enable ALTERNATE TOKEN RING address      no
   ALTERNATE TOKEN RING address             (0x40001010101c)

   F1=Help            F2=Refresh           F3=Cancel          F4=List
   F5=Reset           F6=Command           F7=Edit            F8=Image
   F9=Shell           F10=Exit             Enter=Do
```

Figure 75. *Change/Show Characteristics of a Token-Ring Adapter*

Note: Ensure that the value for Status is *Available* and that the RING speed is in accord with the speed of your LAN.

If you have to change some information in the Token-Ring Adapter and get a message stating that the Token-Ring Adapter cannot be changed because it is busy, do the following before attempting to change it:

1. Make sure that the adapter is not being used by any other subsystem, such as TCP/IP.

2. Place the adapter in defined status by issuing the following command:

   rmdev -l tok0

If, after the changes, the Token-Ring Adapter is still unavailable, issue the following command:

```
mkdev -1 tok0
```

To obtain a list of available adapters issue the following command:

```
lsdev -Ccadapter
```

and check that the token-ring adapter that you want to use is listed.

6.4.2.2 Token-Ring Data Link Control

Data Link Control (DLC) is a set of communications protocols that support orderly exchanges of data over a link. Basically, the DLC manages a communications adapter.

SNA Server/6000 V2.1 requires you to supply information about DLC characteristics in the SNA DLC Profile. Therefore you must have DLC configured and available.

Before the system can use an installed DLC, you must first add the desired DLC manager. In our case the DLC manager is *dlctoken* because we are using a Token-Ring Adapter.

If the system has been previously configured to use DLC, you can check its existence by issuing the *lsdev -Cc dlc* command.

To add DLC to your system, invoke SMIT and select the following items:

1. Devices
2. Communications
3. Token-Ring Adapter
4. Services
5. Data Link Controls
6. Add a Token-Ring Data Link Control

You should get a screen similar to that shown in Figure 76 on page 168.

```
                    COMMAND STATUS

Command: OK              stdout: yes              stderr: no

Before command completion, additional instructions may appear below.

dlctoken Available




F1=Help            F2=Refresh         F3=Cancel            F6=Command
F8=Image           F9=Shell           F10=Exit
```

Figure 76. SMIT Screen after Successful Addition of DLC for Token Ring

6.4.2.3 Token-Ring Link Station

The Token-Ring Link Station profile associates the link station with either the CP for APPN services or a user-specified PU. It also associates the link station with an SNA DLC Profile, which defines the hardware adapter and DLC characteristics of the link.

To configure the Token-Ring Link Station profile, invoke SMIT and select the following items:

1. Links

2. Token Ring

3. Token-Ring Link Station

4. Add a Profile

You should get a screen similar to that shown in Figure 77 on page 169.

```
                      Add Token-Ring Link Station Profile

Type or select values in entry fields.
Press Enter AFTER making all desired changes.

 (TOP)                                          (Entry Fields)
   Profile name                                   DBSRV4
   Use Control Point's XID node ID?               yes
     If no, XID node ID                           (*)
 * SNA DLC Profile name                           (tok0.00001)
   Stop link station on inactivity?               no
     If yes, Inactivity time-out (0-10 minutes)   (0)
   LU address registration?                       no
     If yes
        LU Address Registration Profile name      ()
   Trace link?                                    no
           If yes, Trace size                          long

   Adjacent Node Address Parameters
     Access routing                               link_address
     If link_name, Remote link name               ()
     If link_address,
        Remote link address                       (400020201001)
        Remote SAP address (02-fa)                (04)

   Adjacent Node Identification Parameters
     Verify adjacent node?                        no
     Network ID of adjacent node                  (DEIBMIPF)

   Link Activation Parameters
     Solicit SSCP sessions?                       yes
     Initiate call when link station is activated? yes
     Activate link station at SNA start up?       yes
     Activate on demand?                          no
     CP-CP sessions supported?                    yes
     If yes
        Adjacent network node preferred server?   no
           Partner required to support CP-CP sessions?   no
     Initial TG number (0-20)                     (0)

   Restart Parameters
     Restart on activation?                       no
     Restart on normal deactivation?              no
     Restart on abnormal deactivation?            no

     Transmission Group COS Characteristics
     Effective capacity                           (15974400)
     Cost per connect time                        (0)
     Cost per byte                                (0)
     Security                                     nonsecure
     Propagation delay                            lan
     User-defined 1                               (128)
     User-defined 2                               (128)
     User-defined 3                               (128)

   Comments                                       ()
 (BOTTOM)

 F1=Help          F2=Refresh        F3=Cancel         F4=List
 F5=Reset         F6=Command        F7=Edit           F8=Image
 F9=Shell         F10=Exit          Enter=Do
```

Figure 77. *Add Token-Ring Link Station Profile SMIT Screen*

Following is a brief explanation of the most relevant parameters in Figure 77.

• **Use Control Point's XID node ID?** Select one of the following values:

- **yes.** Associates the link station with the XID node ID of the APPN CP. Selecting this value places the link station under the control of the APPN CP, with full APPN support.

- **no.** Excludes the link station from the control the APPN CP and places it under the control of a PU you designate. If you select this value, you must specify the XID node ID of the PU represented by this link station. Specifying link stations with unique XID node ID values enables SNA Server/6000 V2.1 to support dependent LU traffic with multiple hosts.

- **XID node ID** Enter a hexadecimal value that identifies the PU that controls this link station. The system default value is an asterisk (*), which represents an XID value of 00000000, which indicates that no XID node ID is specified.

- **LU address registration?** If the value you select is **yes**, generic LU addresses are registered to this link station. Select this value only if this link station is used for generic SNA sessions. You also must create a Generic LU Address Registration Profile containing the registered LUs. Enter the name of the registration profile in the LU Address Registration Profile name field for this link station. If you select **no**, you are not using generic LU address registration and do not require a generic LU address registration profile for this link station.

- **Remote link address** For a call or selective listen link station, enter the network address of the remote station. The network address must be unique to the specific adapter card of the remote station. If you enter *link address* in the Access routing field but do not enter a remote link address, the link station is a *nonselective listen link station*, that is, it accepts a link activation request from any remote station, but it can handle only one link at a time.

- **Network ID of adjacent node** Enter the network ID of the adjacent node. If the adjacent node does not supply a CP name in XID exchanges, you must enter a value in this field and define an LU 6.2 Partner Location Profile to define the adjacent node resources.

6.4.2.4 Control Point

The Control Point profile describes the characteristics of the CP on the local RISC System/6000. A RISC System/6000 workstation must have one (and only one) Control Point profile. To configure the Control Point profile, invoke SMIT and select the following items:

1. Control Point

2. Change/Show Control Point Profile

You should get a screen similar to that shown in Figure 78 on page 171.

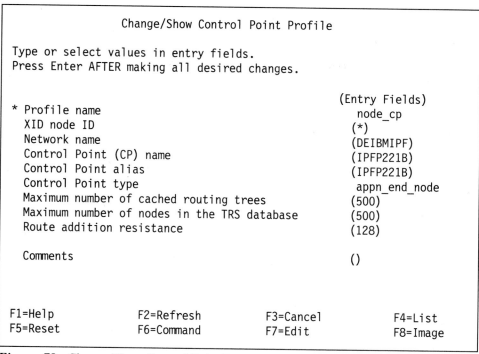

```
              Change/Show Control Point Profile

Type or select values in entry fields.
Press Enter AFTER making all desired changes.

                                                    (Entry Fields)
* Profile name                                          node_cp
  XID node ID                                           (*)
  Network name                                          (DEIBMIPF)
  Control Point (CP) name                               (IPFP221B)
  Control Point alias                                   (IPFP221B)
  Control Point type                                    appn_end_node
  Maximum number of cached routing trees                (500)
  Maximum number of nodes in the TRS database           (500)
  Route addition resistance                             (128)

  Comments                                              ()



F1=Help            F2=Refresh          F3=Cancel          F4=List
F5=Reset           F6=Command          F7=Edit            F8=Image
```

Figure 78. *Change/Show Control Point Profile Screen*

Following is a brief explanation of the most relevant parameters in Figure 78.

- **Profile name** This field displays the name of the Control Point Profile, *node_cp*. The system uses the profile name to refer to the set of characteristics that you describe in the profile. You must have one and only one Control Point Profile in SNA Server/6000 V2.1; you cannot change its name.

- **XID node ID** Enter a value that the CP on the local system can use to identify itself as a PU. This value is used only for switched links (Token Ring, Ethernet, X.25, and switched SDLC). Enter one of the following values:

  - For a peer network using independent LU 6.2, use the default wildcard value, (*).

  - For dependent communication with a host system, specify a unique XID node ID. This value must uniquely identify the local node in the subarea network.

  The XID node ID has two parts:

  Block Number The first three hexadecimal digits provide an identifier, or block number, that is unique to each product on the network. The value of *071* identifies the local node as a RISC System/6000 workstation. If you are connecting to a VTAM host, the block number you specify must match the IDBLK parameter value in the VTAM PU definition macro.

ID number The last five digits distinguish a specific piece of equipment from all other similar pieces of equipment on the network. If you are connecting to a VTAM host, the ID number is the IDNUM parameter value in the VTAM PU definition macro.

- **Network name** Enter the network name of the CP. The network name distinguishes this network from other networks to which it can be connected. The network name, combined with the CP name, forms a unique identifier (the fully qualified name) for this CP.

- **Control Point (CP) name** The Control Point (CP) name distinguishes this CP from other CPs that may be connected to the network. This name, combined with the network name, forms a unique identifier (fully qualified name) for this CP.

- **Control Point alias** Enter an alias that can be used on the local system in place of the CP name. Using an alias for the control point enables you to change the CP name without having to update all LU 6.2 Side Information Profiles that refer to the CP.

- **Control Point type**

  Select one of the following values:

  - *appn_network_node* The CP provides NN services.

  - *appn_end_node* The CP provides APPN EN services. If you do not provide APPN services, choose *appn_end_node* as your CP type.

6.4.2.5 LU 6.2 Local LU Profile

The LU 6.2 Local LU profile describes the characteristics of a local LU 6.2. Local LUs can be independent or dependent.

For an independent LU 6.2 session, the node CP can serve as a local LU, so you do not have to configure a Local LU profile. You must configure an LU 6.2 Local LU profile if other profiles, such as the LU 6.2 Side Information profile, refer to an alias other than the node CP alias. If a Side Information profile does not specify a local LU, the node CP acts as the default local LU.

If you are not using the VTAM dynamic independent LU definition facility, the CP or the local LU name must match an LU name defined for the RISC System/6000 in VTAM.

For dependent LU 6.2 sessions, you must define an LU 6.2 Local LU profile. We used an independent LU with a name different from the CP alias name, so we configured an

LU 6.2 Local LU profile. To configure an LU 6.2 Local LU profile, invoke SMIT and select the following items:

1. Sessions

2. LU 6.2

3. LU 6.2 Local LU

4. Add a Profile

You should get a screen similar to that shown in Figure 79.

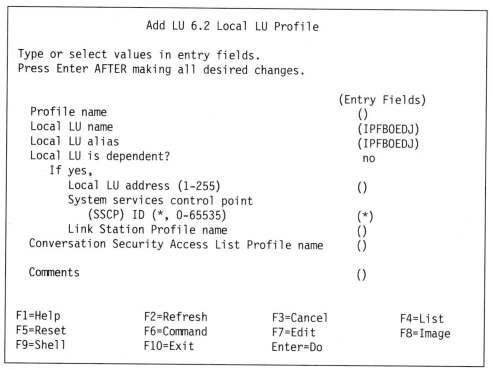

```
                      Add LU 6.2 Local LU Profile

Type or select values in entry fields.
Press Enter AFTER making all desired changes.

                                                 (Entry Fields)
    Profile name                                 ()
    Local LU name                                (IPFBOEDJ)
    Local LU alias                               (IPFBOEDJ)
    Local LU is dependent?                       no
      If yes,
         Local LU address (1-255)                ()
         System services control point
            (SSCP) ID (*, 0-65535)               (*)
         Link Station Profile name               ()
    Conversation Security Access List Profile name  ()

    Comments                                     ()


F1=Help            F2=Refresh        F3=Cancel          F4=List
F5=Reset           F6=Command        F7=Edit            F8=Image
F9=Shell           F10=Exit          Enter=Do
```

Figure 79. *Add LU 6.2 Local LU Profile Screen*

Following is a brief explanation of the most relevant parameters in Figure 79.

- **Profile name** Enter a name for the new LU 6.2 Local LU profile in this field.

- **Local LU name** Enter the name of the local LU in this field. This LU name must be unique with respect to all other local LUs defined on this node, and its fully qualified local LU name must be unique across the network. SNA Server/6000 V2.1

generates the fully qualified LU name by concatenating this LU name to the network name defined in the Control Point profile (DEIBMIPF.IPFBOEDJ).

- **Local LU alias** Enter an alias for the local LU. This alias can be used in an LU 6.2 Side Information Profile or with the *sna* command to refer to this local LU.

- **Local LU is dependent?** Select one of the following values to specify whether the LU 6.2 is dependent or independent:

    - **yes** The local LU 6.2 is dependent and cannot initiate LU-to-LU sessions. A host SSCP controls session activation.

    - **no** The local LU 6.2 is independent, and sessions can be activated without SSCP.

- **Local LU address** If the local LU is dependent, enter the local LU address in this field. The value you enter must match the value specified for the LOCADDR parameter in the VTAM/NCP LU resource definition statement.

- **SSCP ID** This field specifies the ID of the SSCP that controls this dependent LU in the subarea network. This identifier is defined on the host system to which this node is connected and is used for host verification.

- **Link Station Profile name** Select the name of the Link Station Profile shown in Figure 77 on page 169 that describes the characteristics of the link station used for sessions with the remote LU.

- **Conversation Security Access List Profile name** Enter the name of an LU 6.2 Conversation Security Access List profile. This profile specifies a set of user names with permission to remotely allocate a session with this local LU. If the user name is a valid AIX user, you do not have to configure a Conversation Security Access List profile.

6.4.2.6 Partner LU Profile

The Partner LU profile defines parameters for establishing a session with a specific partner LU. You can define an LU 6.2 Partner LU profile to specify nondefault session characteristics.

You must define a Partner LU profile to specify the following characteristics:

- Define a partner LU alias
- Disable (or enable) parallel session support
- Enable (or disable) session level security
- Specify a conversation security level

Note: You should define only one LU 6.2 Partner LU profile for each partner LU. The *veryfysna* command rejects duplicate Partner LU profile definitions.

To configure an LU 6.2 Partner LU profile, invoke SMIT and select the following items:

1. Sessions

2. LU 6.2

3. LU 6.2 Partner LU

4. Add a Profile

You should get a screen similar to that shown in Figure 80.

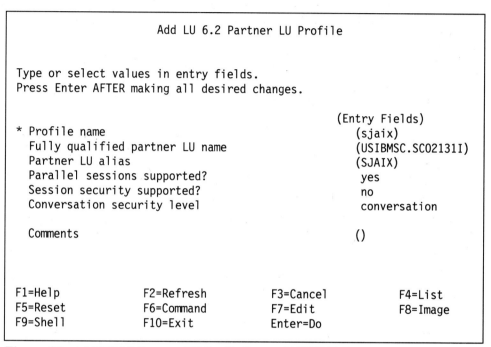

```
                        Add LU 6.2 Partner LU Profile


    Type or select values in entry fields.
    Press Enter AFTER making all desired changes.

                                                    (Entry Fields)
     * Profile name                                    (sjaix)
       Fully qualified partner LU name                 (USIBMSC.SC02131I)
       Partner LU alias                                (SJAIX)
       Parallel sessions supported?                    yes
       Session security supported?                     no
       Conversation security level                     conversation

       Comments                                        ()



    F1=Help            F2=Refresh          F3=Cancel          F4=List
    F5=Reset           F6=Command          F7=Edit            F8=Image
    F9=Shell           F10=Exit            Enter=Do
```

Figure 80. *Add LU 6.2 Partner LU Profile Screen (AIX/6000 San Jose)*

Following is a brief explanation of the most relevant parameters described in Figure 80.

- **Profile name** Enter the name of the new Partner LU profile. The system uses this name to identify the session characteristics specified in the profile.

- **Fully qualified partner LU name** Consists of two parts: *network_name.lu_name*. The network name (first part) entered in this field must match the name of the network where the partner LU resides. The partner LU name entered here must match the name of a local LU on the remote system (second part). The partner LU must also be an LU 6.2, and every fully qualified LU name must be unique (USIBMSC.SC02131I).

- **Partner LU alias** The alias specified in this field is used by the SNA Server/6000 V2.1 node to refer to the name entered in the `Fully qualified partner LU name` field in this profile.

- **Parallel sessions supported?** Select a value to specify whether multiple concurrently active sessions are supported with the partner LU. Dependent LU 6.2 protocol does not support parallel sessions.

  - **yes** Multiple concurrent sessions are supported with the partner LU.

  - **no** Only one session can be active with the partner LU.

- **Session security supported?** Session-level security is used to verify that the partner LU is authorized to establish sessions with the local node. Session security is available only for LU 6.2 sessions.

  Select one of the following values:

  - **yes** Session-level security is required for sessions with the partner LU. In this case you should define an LU 6.2 Session Security profile to specify the session security parameters.

  - **no** Session-level security is not used.

- **Conversation security level** Conversation security information from the partner LU is verified against information in the Conversation Security Access List profile. Only when the conversation security information has been verified can the partner LU allocate a session with the local LU. This parameter is not used when the workstation is being used as an AR. It is only used when the workstation is used as an AS. Following are the available conversation security levels:

  - none

    Inbound allocation requests from the partner LU do not have to contain security information. They are accepted unconditionally by the Local LU. With this setting, neither a user name nor password is passed to the TP for a resource security check.

    This option is not valid when you are configuring an LU 6.2 Partner LU profile for a DRDA AR.

  - conversation

    Inbound allocation requests from the partner LU must contain both a user name and a password. The user name and password are verified against the `Conversation Access Security List` field specified in the Conversation Security Access List profile named in the Local LU profile.

    Also, the user name and password combination must be valid and known in the AIX workstation (/etc/passwd file).

If the user is a valid login user name and sends a valid password, you do not have to configure the Conversation Access Security List profile.

 - already_verified

    Indicates that the local LU on the node that sends the allocation request verified the user name and password. This implies that the partner LU may send only the user name and an indication that the user has already been verified, or the partner LU may send the user name and a password. If the partner LU sends the user name and a password, the user is also authenticated on the AIX server workstation.

6.4.2.7 LU 6.2 Partner Location Profile

The Partner Location profile identifies the owning CP and network node server for a specific remote LU. Define this profile in the following situations:

 - If the partner LU is located on an adjacent LEN node.

 - If the node containing the partner LU is accessed through a local link station that is configured to activate on demand.

 - To predefine the location of a resource on a remote node in order to improve network performance by reducing the number of broadcast searches.

For our definition in Boeblingen we used the Partner LU Location profile because the partner LU is located on an adjacent node and the node that contains the partner LU is accessed through a local link station.

To configure a LU 6.2 Partner LU 6.2 Location profile, invoke SMIT and select the following items:

1. Sessions
2. LU 6.2
3. Partner LU 6.2 Location
4. Add a Profile

You should get a screen similar to that shown in Figure 81 on page 178.

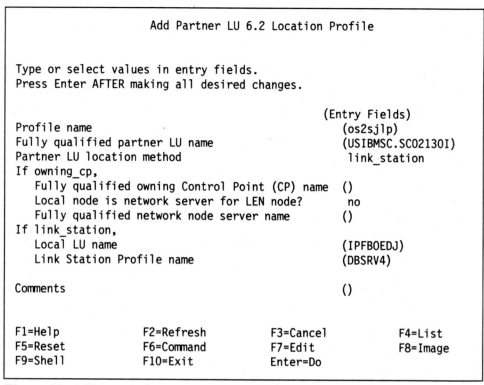

```
                    Add Partner LU 6.2 Location Profile


Type or select values in entry fields.
Press Enter AFTER making all desired changes.


                                                (Entry Fields)
Profile name                                    (os2sjlp)
Fully qualified partner LU name                 (USIBMSC.SC02130I)
Partner LU location method                       link_station
If owning_cp,
   Fully qualified owning Control Point (CP) name  ()
   Local node is network server for LEN node?      no
   Fully qualified network node server name        ()
If link_station,
   Local LU name                                (IPFBOEDJ)
   Link Station Profile name                    (DBSRV4)

Comments                                        ()


F1=Help           F2=Refresh        F3=Cancel          F4=List
F5=Reset          F6=Command        F7=Edit            F8=Image
F9=Shell          F10=Exit          Enter=Do
```

Figure 81. Add Partner LU 6.2 Location Profile Screen (OS/2 San Jose)

Following is an explanation of the most relevant parameters described in Figure 81.

- Partner LU location method

  Two methods are used to support your partner LU 6.2:

  - owning_cp

    Specified when the partner LU is located by first finding the CP in the network specified by the name given in the Fully qualified owning Control Point (CP) name field. APPN directory and routing services first locate the CP in the network. Once the CP is located, the BIND is forwarded to the partner LU on the CP over the link over which it was found.

  - link_station

    Specified when the partner LU is assumed to be located on the other side of the link identified by the Link Station profile name specified in the Link Station Profile name field. In this case, APPN directory and routing services are completely bypassed; the BIND is immediately sent across the specified link in anticipation of the partner LU being available on the opposite side of the link.

Note that the entry in the If link_station field is valid only if the local node type specified in the Control Point profile is *appn_end_node*. APPN network nodes cannot statically associate a partner LU's location with a particular link.

- Local LU name

  Provides the name of the local LU to be matched with the partner LU name specified in the `Fully qualified partner LU name` field to identify which session is to use the link specified in the `Link Station Profile name` field. This value is valid only when the Partner LU location method is *link_station*.

- Link Station Profile name

  Provides the name of the Link Station profile which specifies the link over which the session identified by the `Fully qualified partner LU name` and `Local LU name` fields is to activate. This value is valid only when the Partner LU location method is *link_station*.

6.4.2.8 LU 6.2 Mode Profile

The LU 6.2 Mode profile specifies the parameters that the local LU uses to activate and control sessions with the partner LU. These parameters can be used to tune throughput, availability, and system resource requirements for the sessions associated with the mode. To configure an LU 6.2 Mode profile, invoke SMIT and select the following items:

1. Sessions
2. LU 6.2
3. LU 6.2 Mode
4. Add a Profile

You should get a screen similar to that shown in Figure 82 on page 180.

```
┌─────────────────────────────────────────────────────────────────────┐
│                      Add LU 6.2 Mode Profile                          │
│                                                                       │
│  Type or select values in entry fields.                              │
│  Press Enter AFTER making all desired changes.                       │
│                                                                       │
│                                                    (Entry Fields)     │
│  Profile name                                        (IBMRDBM)        │
│  Mode name                                           (IBMRDBM)        │
│  Maximum number of sessions (1-5000)                 (60)            │
│  Minimum contention winners (0-5000)                 (30)            │
│  Minimum contention losers (0-5000)                  (30)            │
│  Auto activate limit (0-500)                         (0)             │
│  Upper bound for adaptive receive pacing window      (16)            │
│  Receive pacing window (0-63)                        (3)             │
│  Maximum RU size (128,...,32768: multiples of 32)    (4096)          │
│  Minimum RU size (128,...,32768: multiples of 32)    (1024)          │
│  Class of Service (COS) name                         (#CONNECT)      │
│                                                                       │
│  Comments                                            ()              │
│                                                                       │
│                                                                       │
│  F1=Help          F2=Refresh         F3=Cancel          F4=List      │
│  F5=Reset         F6=Command         F7=Edit            F8=Image     │
│  F9=Shell         F10=Exit           Enter=Do                        │
│                                                                       │
└─────────────────────────────────────────────────────────────────────┘
```

Figure 82. Add LU 6.2 Mode Profile Screen

Following is an explanation of the most relevant parameters in Figure 82.

- **Profile name** Enter the name of the new Mode profile. The system uses the profile name to refer to the set of characteristics that you describe in the Mode profile.

- **Mode name** Enter the SNA mode name in this field. The SNA network uses this mode name to identify the set of session parameters associated with the mode.

- **Maximum number of sessions** Enter a value to specify the maximum number of parallel sessions allowed between a local and partner LU using this mode. If the partner LU supports fewer parallel sessions on this mode, the value entered here can be negotiated downward.

- **Minimum contention winners** This field defines the minimum number of contention winner sessions that must be reserved for sessions established by the local LU with a partner LU.

- **Minimum contention losers** This field specifies the minimum number of contention loser sessions that must be reserved for sessions established by the local LU with a partner LU. In conjunction with the `Minimum contention winners` field, this field determines how to resolve contention for a session.

- **Receive pacing window** Enter the number of request units (RUs) that the local LU can receive before it must send a pacing response to the remote LU.

- **Maximum RU size** This field specifies the maximum number of bytes in each request and response unit that are sent and received in sessions using this mode.

- **Minimum RU size** The value in this field defines the minimum size for RUs that can be sent and received in sessions using this mode.

- **Class of Service (COS) name** Enter the class of service (COS) name to specify transmission group characteristics for the mode. You can use an IBM-supplied COS or your own.

  SNA Server/6000 V2.1 includes the following IBM-supplied COS definitions:

  - **#BATCH** Specifies a standard, nonsecure COS with medium transmission priority for batch sessions.

  - **#CONNECT** Specifies a standard, nonsecure COS with medium transmission priority.

  - **#CPSVCMG** Specifies a COS used for establishing CP-to-CP sessions between two NNs, between two ENs, or between an EN and its NN server in an APPN network.

  - **#INTER** Specifies a standard, nonsecure COS with high transmission priority for interactive sessions.

  - **#INTERSC** Specifies a secure COS with high transmission priority for interactive sessions.

  - **SNASVCMG** Specifies a COS used for negotiating session limits for LU 6.2 independent sessions.

6.4.2.9 LU 6.2 Side Information Profile

The LU 6.2 Side Information profile defines information that SNA Server/6000 V2.1 can use when a local TP is allocating a conversation with a remote TP. Together with the LU 6.2 Partner LU profile, the LU 6.2 Side Information profile describes a set of characteristics that are used for sessions between the local LU and a specific partner LU on a remote system.

An LU6.2 Side Information profile must be configured on each APPC node to support the following:

- Dependent LU 6.2 sessions
- Session for a local LU other than the node CP

- TPs that do not specify the partner LU, mode, or remote TPNs in the ALLOCATE APPC verb

The most important DRDA consideration is that the LU 6.2 Side Information profile name also be specified in the node directory. For each DRDA AR to which this DDCS workstation can connect, you must configure a corresponding LU 6.2 Side Information profile.

To configure an LU 6.2 Side Information profile, invoke SMIT and select the following items:

1. Sessions
2. LU 6.2
3. LU 6.2 Side Information
4. Add a Profile

You should get a screen similar to that shown in Figure 83, the LU 6.2 CPIC Side Information profile configured to access the SQL/DS VM AS in Boeblingen.

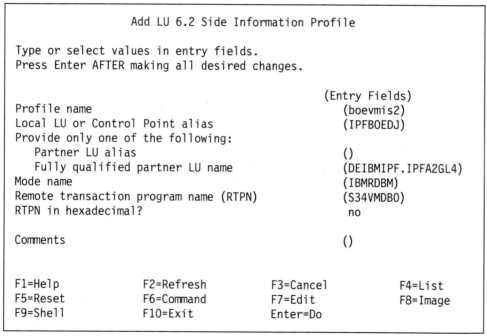

```
              Add LU 6.2 Side Information Profile

Type or select values in entry fields.
Press Enter AFTER making all desired changes.


                                         (Entry Fields)
Profile name                                (boevmis2)
Local LU or Control Point alias             (IPFBOEDJ)
Provide only one of the following:
   Partner LU alias                         ()
   Fully qualified partner LU name          (DEIBMIPF.IPFA2GL4)
Mode name                                   (IBMRDBM)
Remote transaction program name (RTPN)      (S34VMDBO)
RTPN in hexadecimal?                         no

Comments                                    ()


F1=Help           F2=Refresh        F3=Cancel        F4=List
F5=Reset          F6=Command        F7=Edit          F8=Image
F9=Shell          F10=Exit          Enter=Do
```

Figure 83. Add LU 6.2 Side Information Profile Screen (SQL/DS for VM)

Following is an explanation of the most relevant parameters in Figure 83.

- **Profile name** Enter a name for the new Side Information profile. A local TP can specify this name in the OPEN call to identify a set of session parameters. The session parameters include the local LU, partner LU, mode, and remote TP names.

- **Local LU or Control Point alias** Enter the alias of either the local LU or node CP that identifies the local LU for any conversations initiated by TPs using this Side Information profile. If you enter an alias, it must match the alias defined in either the Control Point profile or the LU 6.2 Local LU profile. If you do not enter a value in this field, the node CP serves as the local LU for the Side Information profile.

- **Partner LU alias** Enter or select an alias for the partner LU that specifies the default partner LU for conversations initiated by TPs using this Side Information profile. The TP can override this value. If you enter an alias in this field, you must enter the same alias in the Partner LU alias field of the Partner LU profile.

- **Fully qualified partner LU name** Enter a fully qualified partner LU name similar to that shown in Figure 83 on page 182. It consists of two parts, *network_name.lu_name* (USIBMSC.SCLUDB41).

- **Mode name** Enter or select the name of the mode that specifies the default mode name for conversations initiated by local TPs that use this Side Information profile. Keep in mind that the mode name entered here must correspond to a mode name entered in the LU 6.2 Mode profile. The same mode name must be available to the partner LU.

- **Remote transaction program name (RTPN)** To specify a default TPN for all TPs that use this Side Information profile, enter the TPN to be invoked on the remote system.

- **RTPN in hexadecimal?** Select one of the following values:

  - **yes** The value entered in the Remote transaction program name (RTPN) field is hexadecimal format.

  - **no** The value entered in the Remote transaction program name (RTPN) field is ASCII format.

Figure 84 on page 184 shows the LU 6.2 Side Information profile configured to access the DB2 for MVS/ESA AS in Poughkeepsie.

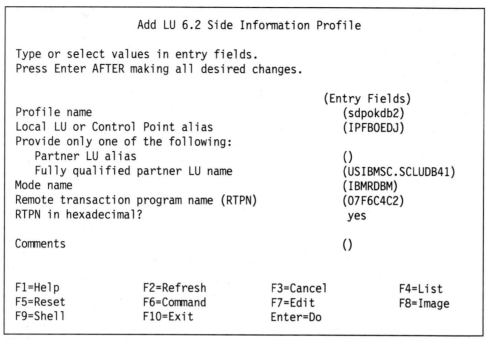

```
                    Add LU 6.2 Side Information Profile

Type or select values in entry fields.
Press Enter AFTER making all desired changes.


                                                  (Entry Fields)
Profile name                                       (sdpokdb2)
Local LU or Control Point alias                    (IPFBOEDJ)
Provide only one of the following:
   Partner LU alias                                ()
   Fully qualified partner LU name                 (USIBMSC.SCLUDB41)
Mode name                                          (IBMRDBM)
Remote transaction program name (RTPN)             (07F6C4C2)
RTPN in hexadecimal?                                yes

Comments                                           ()


F1=Help            F2=Refresh        F3=Cancel          F4=List
F5=Reset           F6=Command        F7=Edit            F8=Image
F9=Shell           F10=Exit          Enter=Do
```

Figure 84. Add LU 6.2 Side Information Profile Screen (DB2 for MVS/ESA AS, Poughkeepsie)

For this connection definition we used the same local LU name and the same mode name we used for the SQL/DS for VM AS at the ITSO-Boeblingen Center (see Figure 83 on page 182). We had to use a different fully qualified partner LU name that matched the LU name defined for DB2 for MVS/ESA in the VTAM APPL statement for DB2 for MVS/ESA.

The Remote transaction program name (RTPN) for SQL/DS for VM uses a specific TPN, S34VMDB0, matching the RESID value specified during SQL/DS for VM installation. DB2 for MVS/ESA uses the service TPN, 076F6C4C2, in hexadecimal.

Figure 85 on page 185 shows the LU 6.2 Side Information profile configured to access the DB2 for OS/400 AS in Rochester.

```
                    Add LU 6.2 Side Information Profile

Type or select values in entry fields.
Press Enter AFTER making all desired changes.


                                               (Entry Fields)
Profile name                                     (sdos4rc)
Local LU or Control Point alias                  (IPFBOEDJ)
Provide only one of the following:
    Partner LU alias                             ()
    Fully qualified partner LU name              (USIBMSC.SCHASMO2)
Mode name                                        (IBMRDBM)
Remote transaction program name (RTPN)           (076F6C4C2)
RTPN in hexadecimal?                             yes

Comments                                         ()


F1=Help          F2=Refresh        F3=Cancel          F4=List
F5=Reset         F6=Command        F7=Edit            F8=Image
F9=Shell         F10=Exit          Enter=Do
```

Figure 85. Add LU 6.2 Side Information Profile Screen (DB2 for OS/400 AS, Rochester)

We used the same local LU name and the same mode name, but the fully qualified partner LU name had to be different and match the LU name defined for DB2 for OS/400 in the default local location of the AS/400 network attributes.

For the Remote transaction program name for DB2 for OS/400, we used the service TPN, 076F6C4C2, in hexadecimal.

We also configured profiles to connect to the OS/400 platform located in San Jose and the VSE platform in Boeblingen.

6.4.3 Verifying the Profiles

After configuring the profiles you must verify them by invoking SMIT and selecting *Verify Configuration Profiles*.

You should get a screen similar to that shown in Figure 86 on page 186.

```
┌─────────────────────────────────────────────────────────────────────┐
│                    Verify Configuration Profiles                      │
│                                                                       │
│  Type or select values in entry fields.                               │
│  Press Enter AFTER making all desired changes.                        │
│                                                                       │
│                                                     (Entry Fields)    │
│  Update action if verification successful              none           │
│  If normal_update or dynamic_update,                                  │
│     Backup file for committed database              ()                │
│     Backup security file for committed database     ()                │
│                                                                       │
│                                                                       │
│                                                                       │
│  F1=Help           F2=Refresh        F3=Cancel          F4=List       │
│  F5=Reset          F6=Command        F7=Edit            F8=Image      │
│  F9=Shell          F10=Exit          Enter=Do                         │
│                                                                       │
└─────────────────────────────────────────────────────────────────────┘
```

Figure 86. *Verify Configuration Profiles Screen*

You have the following options for update actions if the verification is successful:

- none

  Select this option if the verified profiles should remain in the working database. To update the committed database with these profiles, run verification again and select *normal_update* or *dynamic_update* for this field.

- normal_update

  Select this option to update the committed database only if SNA Server/6000 V2.1 is not running. If all profiles are successfully verified, SNA Server/6000 V2.1 promotes them to the committed database. If any errors are found during verification, the new profiles remain in the working database, and you must correct the errors and run verification again to update the committed database.

- dynamic_update

  Select this option to update the committed database while SNA Server/6000 V2.1 is running. If all profiles are successfully verified, SNA Server/6000 V2.1 promotes them to the committed database. If SNA Server/6000 V2.1 is not actually running, this option still updates the committed database if verification is successful. If any errors are found during verification, the new profiles remain in the working database, and you must correct them and run verification again to update the committed database.

6.4.3.1 Testing the Connection

Once verification has successfully completed and the committed database has been updated, proceed to start the SNA Server/6000 V2.1 using SMIT or the command line.

To use SMIT type the following command:

```
smit sna
```

and select the following items:

1. Manage SNA Resources
2. Start SNA Resources
3. Start SNA

From the AIX prompt, issue the following command:

```
/usr/bin/sna -start
```

This command automatically starts SNA Server/6000 V2.1, link stations, and LU 6.2 sessions. You can check that the SNA Server/6000 V2.1 started correctly by issuing the following command:

```
lssrc -ssna
```

Test whether you can establish an LU-to-LU session. Although the session establishment is done automatically when you issue the DB2 CONNECT statement, verify it before issuing the first CONNECT statement. If a session cannot be established, the DB2 CONNECT statement will fail.

To establish an LU-to-LU session, invoke SMIT, issue the following command:

```
smit sna
```

and select the following items:

1. Manage SNA Resources
2. Start SNA Resources
3. Start an SNA Session

You should get a screen similar to that shown in Figure 87 on page 188.

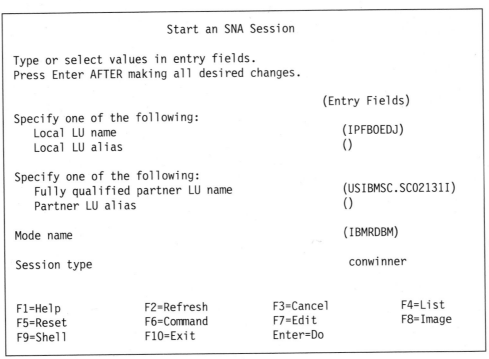

```
                       Start an SNA Session

  Type or select values in entry fields.
  Press Enter AFTER making all desired changes.


                                              (Entry Fields)

  Specify one of the following:
      Local LU name                           (IPFBOEDJ)
      Local LU alias                          ()

  Specify one of the following:
      Fully qualified partner LU name         (USIBMSC.SC02131I)
      Partner LU alias                        ()

  Mode name                                   (IBMRDBM)

  Session type                                conwinner


  F1=Help          F2=Refresh       F3=Cancel         F4=List
  F5=Reset         F6=Command       F7=Edit           F8=Image
  F9=Shell         F10=Exit         Enter=Do
```

Figure 87. Start an SNA Session Screen

On the Start an SNA Session screen, specify the values you specified when configuring the LU 6.2 Side Information profile.

If the establishment of the session is successful, you receive a message similar to the following:

```
                    COMMAND STATUS

Command: OK           stdout: yes         stderr: no

Before command completion, additional instructions may appear below.

Session started: Session ID = EF178F5683653894, Conversation group ID = 3




F1=Help          F2=Refresh       F3=Cancel         F6=Command
F8=Image         F9=Shell         F10=Exit
```

6.4.3.2 Updating the Directories

The tasks you must perform to update the directories for the AIX platform are essentially the same as those documented in 5.7, "Database Directories and Definitions" on page 112. In that section we cover the few differences between the OS/2 and AIX platforms.

Note that the plus (+) and minus (−) signs used on the database director for the OS/2 platform (see Figure 48 on page 114) are replaced by arrows on the database director for the AIX platform as shown in Figure 88.

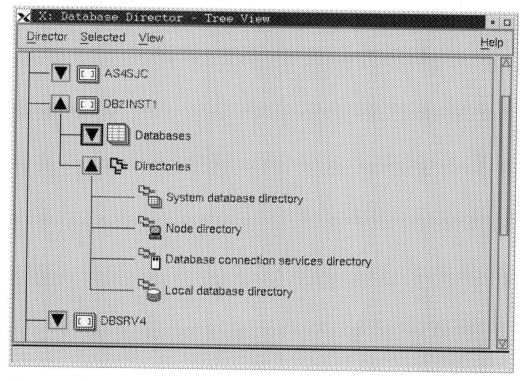

Figure 88. Database Director - Tree View: AIX Platform

6.4.3.3 Binding the Utilities

The tasks you must perform to bind the utilities for the AIX platform are the same as those documented in 5.7.5, "Binding the DDCS Utilities" on page 125.

6.5 DB2 for AIX as an AS

With DB2 common server, you can also use your DB2 as an AS so that applications residing on other platforms can transparently access DB2 for AIX resources by using DRDA AR requests. In this section we review the steps to follow to configure your workstation to function as an AS:

1. Configure SNA Server/6000 profiles.
2. Verify the SNA Server/6000 profiles.
3. Update the database manager configuration file to support APPC clients.
4. Set the DB2COMM environment variable to accept APPC clients.

You also must verify that the DB2 at the requester platform is configured correctly.

6.5.1 SNA Server/6000 Profiles

Configuring   SNA Server/6000 to enable the AS function is basically the same as configuring it to accept APPC non-DRDA clients.

If your workstation is already defined as a DRDA AR, there is not much that you have to define in SNA Server/6000 V2.1 to enable it to receive requests from a DRDA AR. If you have not configured your workstation as a DRDA AR, configure the following SNA Server/6000 V2.1 profiles (in addition to the token-ring adapter, if you are using a token ring, refer to 6.4.2.1, "Configuring the Token-Ring Adapter" on page 165):

- Token-Ring DLC profile

  To configure this profile, refer to 6.4.2.2, "Token-Ring Data Link Control" on page 167.

- Token-Ring Link Station profile

  To configure this profile, refer to 6.4.2.3, "Token-Ring Link Station" on page 168.

- Control Point profile

  To configure this profile, refer to 6.4.2.4, "Control Point" on page 170.

- Local LU profile

  You have to configure the local LU profile if the partner LU name specified in the DRDA AR does not match the CP name you have configured in the Control Point profile. To configure this profile, refer to 6.4.2.5, "LU 6.2 Local LU Profile" on page 172.

- Partner LU profile

  You have to configure this profile if the DRDA AR or the APPC client sends the userid with an indication that it was already verified. To configure a Partner LU profile, refer to 6.4.2.6, "Partner LU Profile" on page 174. Enter *already_verified* for the Conversation Security Level field on the ADD LU 6.2 Partner LU Profile screen (Figure 80 on page 175). You must also set the database manager configuration file AUTHENTICATION parameter to CLIENT.

If the DRDA AR or the APPC client sends the userid and password, you do not have to configure a Partner LU profile, and you can set the AUTHENTICATION parameter of the database manager configuration file to CLIENT or SERVER.

- Mode profile

  To configure this profile, refer to 6.4.2.8, "LU 6.2 Mode Profile" on page 179.

- TPN profiles

  For incoming APPC (DRDA or non-DRDA) requests, you must configure a TPN profile. Remote APPC non-DRDA clients use the TPN configured for the DRDA AR. Once you have configured the TPN to support DRDA AR clients, you do not have to configure a different profile to accept incoming requests from CAE for OS/2 Version 2 or CAE/6000 for AIX Version 2 clients. Also, the TPN profile is common to DB2 for AIX and DDCS for AIX. To configure the TPN profile, refer to 6.5.2.1, "LU 6.2 TPN Profiles."

- SNA Node profile

  You have to update the system defaults in the SNA Node profile as explained in 6.5.2.2, "SNA Node Profile" on page 194.

6.5.2 Configuring Additional Profiles

In this section we explain how to set up the LU 6.2 TPN profile and update the SNA node system defaults profile.

6.5.2.1 LU 6.2 TPN Profiles

To configure the required TPN profile to support remote DRDA and APPC clients, invoke SMIT by following the procedure described in 6.4.2, "Configuring SNA Profiles" on page 165 and select the following items:

1. Sessions

2. LU 6.2

3. LU 6.2 Transaction Program Name (TPN)

4. Add a Profile

You should get a screen similar to that shown in Figure 89 on page 192.

```
                          Add LU 6.2 TPN Profile

Type or select values in entry fields.
Press Enter AFTER making all desired changes.

(TOP)                                                    ·Entry Fields‘
* Profile name                                           (DB26KTP)
  Transaction program name (TPN)                         (DB26KTP)
  Transaction program name (TPN) is in hexadecimal?      no
  PIP data?                                              no
       If yes, Subfields (0-99)                          (0)
  Use Command Line Parameters?                           no
  Command Line Parameters                                ()
  Conversation type                                      basic
  Sync level                                             none/confirm
  Resource security level                                none
       If access, Resource Security Access List Prof.    ()
  Full path to TP executable                             (/home/db2inst1/sqlli
  Multiple instances supported?                          yes
  User ID                                                (2000)
  Server synonym name   no                         +     ()
  Restart action                                         once
  Communication type                                     signals
       If IPC, Communication IPC queue key               (0)
  Timeout Attaches?                                      yes
     If yes, timeout value (0-3600 seconds)              (60)
  Standard input file/device                             (/dev/console)
  Standard output file/device                            (/dev/console)
  Standard error file/device                             (/dev/console)

  Comments   yes                          +              ()
(BOTTOM)

F1=Help           F2=Refresh        F3=Cancel             F4=List
Esc+5=Reset       F6=Command        F7=Edit               F8=Image
F9=Shell          F10=Exit          Enter=Do
```

Figure 89. *Add LU 6.2 TPN Profile Screen*

Enter the following information on the Add LU 6.2 TPN Profile screen:

- Profile name

  The profile name is used to update the TPNAME parameter in the database manager configuration file. Note that this name is case sensitive.

- Transaction program name (TPN)

  For APPC clients, this is the TPN name that is specified in the LU 6.2 Side Information profile. For DRDA ARs, this is the TPN specified in the

  - LINKATTR column of SYSIBM.SYSLOCATIONS in DB2 for MVS/ESA
  - TPN parameter of the COMDIR file in SQL/DS for VM
  - Transaction program of the relational database directory entry in DB2 for OS/400

- Conversation type

  Select *basic* so that SNA Server/6000 can verify that the inbound allocation request specifies a basic conversation before starting the TP.

- Full path to TP executable

  You must specify the full path to the *db2acntp* TPN executable. With this version of the product, one TP executable handles all requests from APPC clients and DRDA ARs. Our complete specification was

  `/home/db2inst1/sqllib/bin/db2acntp`

- Multiple instances supported?

  Specify yes to support multiple instances of this TP executing concurrently.

  If you specify no, only one instance of this TP can execute at a time. Another instance of the TP can be invoked only when the previous instance has completed. Any attempt to invoke the TP while an instance is already running will be rejected.

- User ID

  You have to specify the DB2 for AIX instance owner user ID. To find that user ID, log in as the DB2 for AIX instance owner and issue the *id* command.

- Use the defaults for the other parameters.

If you have to support connections from down-level clients, you need additional TPN profiles. To configure the required additional profiles, modify the Add LU 6.2 TPN Profile screen in Figure 89 on page 192 as follows:

- Set the `Transaction program name (TPN)` to DB2INTERRUPT for down-level SDK and CAE client interrupts.

- Set the `Transaction program name (TPN)` to 07F6C4C2, and specify yes in the `Transaction program name (TPN) is in hexadecimal?` field. This TPN is used for DB2 for OS/2 down-level clients.

- Set the `Transaction program name (TPN)` to 07F6E2D5 and specify yes in the `Transaction program name (TPN) is in hexadecimal?` field. This TPN is used for DB2 for OS/2 down-level client interrupts.

6.5.2.2 SNA Node Profile

The SNA Node profile contains fields that describe the environment and operating characteristics of SNA Server/6000 on the local node.

You must add the trusted group names to this profile, as shown in Figure 90. Determine the group name of your INSTHOME/sqllib/adm/db2sysc for every instance and then use SMIT to update this profile.

To change the defaults, invoke SMIT and select the following items:

1. SNA System Defaults

2. Change a Profile

You should get a screen similar to that shown in Figure 90.

```
                      Change/Show SNA Node Profile

Type or select values in entry fields.
Press Enter AFTER making all desired changes.


                                                  (Entry Fields)
Profile name                                      sna
Maximum number of sessions (1-5000)               (200)
Maximum number of conversations (1-5000)          (200)
Restart action                                    once
Recovery resource manager (RRM) enabled?          no
Dynamic inbound partner LU definitions allowed?   yes
NMVT action when no NMVT process                   reject
Trusted group names                               (db2adm1)
Standard output file/device                       (/dev/console)
Standard error file/device                        (/var/sna/sna.stderr)

Comments                                          ()
```

Figure 90. Change/Show SNA Node Profile Screen

The DRDA-relevant parameter in Figure 90 is the Trusted group names for which you should provide a list of AIX user groups. Enter the DB2 instance owner's primary group. Users in this group are given access to the following SNA functions:

- Allocate with SECUR_SAME

- Use of EXTRACT_FMH5 in the ioctl() or snactl() calls to extract the password from Function Management Header (FMH5) ATTACH REQUEST.

6.5.3 Verifying the SNA Server/6000 Profiles

Follow the steps described in 6.4.3, "Verifying the Profiles" on page 185.

6.5.4 Updating the DB2COMM Environment Variable

When your workstation is a database server and one or more of your clients has APPC connections defined such as DRDA AR, you have to add APPC to the DB2COMM environment variable. This is normally done either in the .profile file or on the command line. You must specify in the DB2COMM environment variable all protocols that this server workstation should support. Following is an example of the DB2COMM environment variable supporting requests from APPC (DRDA or non-DRDA) and TCP/IP clients:

```
DB2COMM=APPC,TCPIP
```

The DB2COMM environment variable should be set for the user that issues the *db2start* command.

6.5.5 Updating the TPNAME Parameter

You must set up the TPNAME parameter of your database manager configuration file with the value you specified when you configured the TPN, as explained in 6.5.2.1, "LU 6.2 TPN Profiles" on page 191. Here is an example of how to update the TPNAME parameter using CLP:

```
DB2 update database manager configuration using TPNAME DB26KTP
```

Updating the TPNAME parameter with the database director is described in 5.8.4, "Updating the TPNAME Parameter" on page 136 for the OS/2 platform. The only difference on the AIX platform is that you have to issue the *db2dd* command to start the database director.

6.6 Security

Security on the AIX platform for DB2 common server products does not conceptually differ in any way from the security on the OS/2 platform as described in 5.11, "Security" on page 142.

Security is implemented by two separate mechanisms:

- Authentication
- Internal security

In a distributed environment, authentication can take place in one or more locations, depending on the configuration of the DBMSs and network products.

The internal security of the DB2 products then rules what the user can do on DB2 resources, after the user has been authenticated.

On the AIX platform userid and password information is managed by the operating system itself, whereas on the OS/2 platform UPM manages userid and password information.

6.6.1 DDCS for AIX: Stand-Alone or Local Users

When the DDCS workstation does not serve any remote client, the authentication mechanism works in exactly the same way as in OS/2 (see Table 17 on page 144).

6.6.2 DDCS for AIX: Clients

For remote clients, security in AIX differs slightly from security in OS/2. The following three options are available when you catalog a database in the client workstation:

- AUTHENTICATION=CLIENT

  Requires that the database be cataloged with AUTHENTICATION=CLIENT on the DDCS gateway as well. However, it is not necessary to define in AIX the same userid used on the client

- AUTHENTICATION=SERVER or DCS

  When one of these options is specified in the client workstation, the userid and password are sent to the DDCS gateway. The security is then managed by the AUTHENTICATION type specified at the DDCS gateway workstation:

  - AUTHENTICATION=CLIENT This specification is incompatible with the type of authentication specified at the client

  - AUTHENTICATION=SERVER and SECURITY=SAME   The userid and password are sent to the DDCS gateway workstation and authenticated there

  - AUTHENTICATION=SERVER and SECURITY=PROGRAM The userid and password are sent to the DDCS gateway workstation where authentication takes place. If successful, the userid and password are routed to the DRDA AS where they are authenticated again.

  - AUTHENTICATION=DCS and SECURITY=PROGRAM   The userid and password are sent to the DDCS gateway workstation and then sent to the DRDA AS. Authentication is performed at the DRDA AS only.

The communications protocol used to connect clients to the DDCS workstation has no impact on the authentication scheme. However, as a general guideline, if the connection is APPC, we recommended that you use SECURITY=NONE on the client (note that SECURITY=NONE cannot be used on the DDCS gateway workstation).

The overall process is not influenced by the AUTHENTICATION parameter set at the DDCS database manager instance level, which would have led to less granularity in the specification of the security policies to access different DRDA ASs.

For a DDCS workstation serving remote clients, the authentication mechanism works in exactly the same way as in OS/2 (see Table 18 on page 146).

6.6.3 Userid and Password Folding

AIX is a case-sensitive environment, and userids and passwords are commonly stored in lowercase format. Before a userid and password can be sent to the DRDA AS, they must be folded to uppercase.

If the SECURITY type specified at the DDCS workstation is SAME, only the userid is sent to the AS. To have the userid folded to uppercase before it is sent:

- For local clients, the login user must belong to the AIX system group. If the login user issues a CONNECT in the form

```
db2 connect to database user another_user using password
```

the user specified in the CONNECT statement does not have to necessarily belong to the AIX system group.

- For remote clients, the DDCS instance owner must belong to AIX system group; otherwise the instance owner userid, which is not folded to uppercase, is sent to the DRDA AS.

Note that these problems can be circumvented when the DRDA AS is DB2 for MVS, because APAR PN70160 provides userid and password folding on the MVS platform before RACF facilities are invoked. Another way to circumvent these problems is to perform inbound translation at the DRDA AS location.

The following redbooks are useful sources of information about security: *DB2 for MVS DRDA Server: Security Consideration* and *DB2 for MVS Connections with AIX and OS/2*.

6.6.4 Database Considerations

A valid userid must be presented to the DRDA AS. Where authentication is performed is of no relevance. Once the DRDA AS has the valid userid, its internal security facility controls any attempts to access its resources (tables, indexes, packages). The minimum requirement is that the userid be granted the privilege to connect to the DRDA AS.

6.6.5 AS Security

As previously stated for the OS/2 platform, as far as DDCS is concerned, the AUTHENTICATION parameter specified at the database manager instance level does not affect how the authentication process is managed.

This is no longer true if you have a DB2 for AIX server engine installed and want to provide remote access to the local databases through the RDS or DRDA protocol.

In particular, DRDA clients (DRDA ARs) link to the DRDA AS facility of DB2 for AIX and to do so they have to communicate by means of APPC.

As with DB2 for OS/2, the AUTHENTICATION parameter is defined on the AIX platform when you

- Create the instance.
- Create the first database within the instance (if not defined during instance creation). If not specified, it defaults to SERVER.

In contrast to DB2 for OS/2, you can use AUTHENTICATION=CLIENT for the database manager instance if you want your DB2 for AIX to play the role of a DRDA AS. In this case, you have to define a specific Partner LU profile, which usually is not required, for the LU representing the incoming DRDA AR. This in order to set Conversation Security Level to *already_verified*.

You also have to add the name of the AIX group of the DB2 instance owner to the list of the trusted group names.

Once again, in an heteregeneous environment there are folding considerations. Figure 91 on page 199 shows how a DB2 for AIX DRDA AS validates the userid and password of an incoming request from a typical DRDA AR such as DB2 for MVS/ESA.

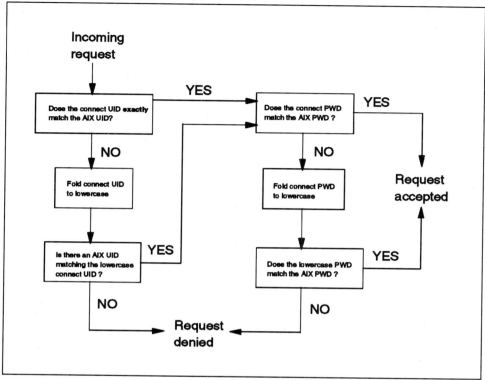

Figure 91. *DB2 for AIX DRDA AS: Userid and Password Validation for Incoming Requests*

To conform to the userid and password management rules on each platform, the system allows the userid and password pair to be kept in uppercase in MVS and in lowercase in AIX, which is the most likely situation.

To configure DB2 for AIX as a DRDA AS, refer to 6.5, "DB2 for AIX as an AS" on page 190.

6.6.6 DB2 for AIX Privileges

With regard to privileges, the considerations for DB2 for OS/2 also apply to DB2 for AIX. Although UPM is not available in AIX, similar facilities are offered by the operating system itself. Individual AIX userids can be assigned to groups, which are valid subject to SQL GRANT and REVOKE statements. Group identifiers are not valid specifications for connections to DB2 for AIX. A userid and a group can share the same name.

The internal process of checking authorizations and the privileges needed to bind and execute packages are the same for both platforms.

6.6.7 Session-Level Security

The DB2 for AIX AS supports the use of session-level security. To implement session-level security with a specific remote LU, select yes in the Session security supported? field in the LU 6.2 Partner LU profile (Figure 80 on page 175) and create a corresponding LU 6.2 Session Security profile.

To implement session-level security in VTAM, specify VERIFY=REQUIRED in the APPL statement.

Chapter 7. DB2 common server Client Connectivity

In this chapter we describe factors to consider when you implement DB2 common server client connectivity using RDS.

We describe connectivity considerations for both the server and client workstations. Note that the connectivity considerations are the same whether the database is located on the server workstation or the server workstation is used as a DDCS gateway to provide access to a DRDA AS.

7.1 Client Communication Setup

DB2 common server RDS supports various communication protocols to allow connected clients to the server workstation:

- NetBIOS
- TCP/IP
- APPC
- IPX/SPX

NetBIOS is not supported in the AIX platform.

In the sections that follow we describe how to set up and initialize the different communication protocols that you can use to access the server workstation from client workstations.

For detailed information about how to set up the client and the server environment, refer to the *DDCS for OS/2 Installation and Configuration Guide*, *DB2 for OS/2 Installation and Operation Guide*, and *DB2 for AIX Installation and Operation Guide*.

7.1.1 Communication Support Initialization

A server workstation supports different communication protocols concurrently. You can decide which communication protocols to start by setting the DB2COMM environment variable. The DB2COMM environment variable is generally specified in the CONFIG.SYS file (OS/2 platform) or in the .profile file of the user that issues the db2start command (AIX platform). Communication protocols are enabled when a db2start command is issued. Any changes in the DB2COMM environment variable are effective on the next db2start command. The DB2COMM environment variable can be also set at the operating system command line. In this case, the db2start command must be issued from this session.

Any combination of the following keywords, separated by commas, is valid for DB2COMM:

```
APPC        initialize APPC support
IPXSPX      initialize IPX/SPX support
NETBIOS     initialize NetBIOS support
NPIPE       initialize named pipe support
TCPIP       initialize TCP/IP support
```

Here is an example of the DB2COMM environment variable setting:

```
SET DB2COMM=APPC,TCPIP
```

Note: If DB2COMM is undefined or set to NULL, communication support is not initialized when the database manager is started.

7.1.2 NetBIOS Configuration

To use NetBIOS support, you must have LAPS installed on both the client and the server workstations. LAPS is available from a number of sources, including

- Communications Manager/2 V1.1 (or later)

- LAN Server 3.0 (or later)

- NTS/2 V1.0 (or later)

- TCP/IP Version 2 (or later)

7.1.2.1 Configuring the Server Workstation for NetBIOS

When using NetBIOS, each workstation on the network must have a unique value specified in the NNAME parameter of the Database Manager Configuration file. You can update the database manager configuration file using

- CLP

    For example,

    ```
    DB2 update database manager configuration using nname COZUMEL
    ```

    where COZUMEL is the workstation name (nname).

- The configuration API, documented in the *DB2 API Reference for common servers*

- The DB2 database director (see Figure 92 on page 203).

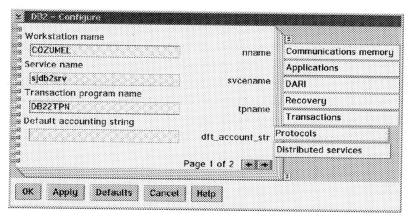

Figure 92. DB2 - Configure Window: NetBIOS

You can control NetBIOS communications with the following DB2 NetBIOS environment variables:

- **DB2NBADAPTERS**

  This environment variable specifies which adapters DB2 uses for NetBIOS LAN communications. You can specify multiple adapters.

- **DB2NBSESSIONS**

  This environment variable specifies the number of NetBIOS sessions that should be reserved for DB2 use.

- **DB2NBINTRLISTENS**

  This environment variable specifies the number of NetBIOS listen commands (ncbs) that will be asynchronously issued. This ensures that the interrupt calls from remote clients can establish connections, even when the server is busy servicing other remote interrupts.

- **DB2NBRECVNCBS**

  This environment variable specifies the number of NetBIOS receive_any commands (ncbs) that the server issues and maintains during operation.

- **DB2NBSENDNCBS**

  This environment variable specifies the number of send commands (ncbs) that the server reserves for use.

- **DB2NBRECVBUFFSIZE**

  This environment variable specifies the size of the DB2 NetBIOS protocol receive buffers.

- DB2NBCHECKUPTIME

  This environment variable specifies the time interval in minutes between each invocation of the NetBIOS protocol checkup procedure.

7.1.2.2 Configuring the Client Workstation for NetBIOS

To configure the client workstation for NetBIOS support, you have to define a workstation name and catalog the server node.

Define Workstation Name: You can use the DB2 Client Setup by double-clicking on the DB2 Client Setup icon in the DB2 folder; select the client menu and follow the instructions.

You can also use the following CLP command:

`update database manager configuration using nname client1`

where `client1` is the workstation name (NNAME).

Catalog Server Node: Cataloging the server node adds an entry in the client's node directory. This entry specifies the remote database server node and the local adapter number that NetBIOS uses.

You can use the DB2 Client Setup by double-clicking on the DB2 Client Setup icon in the DB2 folder; select the node menu and follow the instructions.

You can also use the following CLP command:

`db2 catalog netbios node db2netb1 remote COZUMEL adapter 0`

where

- `db2netb1` is an alias for the actual remote node workstation name (NNAME).

- `COZUMEL` specifies the server_name of the remote server workstation where the target database resides. The server_name must match the NNAME parameter specified in the database manager configuration file of the server.

- The `0` is the logical number of the network adapter at the client workstation.

7.1.3 TCP/IP Configuration

TCP/IP V2.0 or later enables communication support for DB2 clients over TCP/IP.

7.1.3.1 Configuring the Server Workstation for TCP/IP

You must configure the TCP/IP system, define a service name on the server, and record it in the database manager configuration file, as follows;

1. To define a service name on the server, you have to add entries in the TCP/IP `services` file. You can normally find this file in the `tcpip\etc` directory on the drive where TCP/IP is installed. The service name specifications are case sensitive; type each name exactly as the network administrator gave them.

   For example,

   ```
   sjdb2srv      3700/tcp
   sjdb2srvi     3701/tcp
   ```

   The first entry `sjdb2srv` defines the connection service name, followed by the connection port and `/tcp`. The second entry `sjdb2srvi` defines the interrupt service name, followed by the interrupt connection port (connection port + 1), and `/tcp`.

   This defined service name must be specified as the `SVCENAME` parameter value in the database manager configuration file. This information is used to identify the ports on which to listen.

2. You can update the `SVCENAME` parameter in the database manager configuration file using

   - CLP

     For example,

     `DB2 update database manager configuration using svcename sjdb2srv`

     where `sjdb2srv` is the service name specified on the services file.

   - The configuration API, documented in the *DB2 API Reference for common servers*

   - The DB2 database director (see Figure 92 on page 203)

7.1.3.2 Configuring the Client Workstation for TCP/IP

The client workstation must know the address of the host server workstation to which to connect. There are two ways to resolve the address of the host:

- By a name server on your network. This is the recommended approach. See the TCP/IP documentation on how to configure TCP/IP to use a name server.

- By specifying the host address in the local hosts file. The hosts file is typically located in the `\tcpip\etc` directory on the drive where TCP/IP is installed. Here is an example of an entry in the hosts file:

  `9.113.36.232       cozumel`

  where `9.113.36.232` is the IP address of the server workstation and `cozumel` is the host name of the server workstation.

You have to add two entries in the services file on the client for TCP/IP support as follows:

```
sjdb2srv      3700/tcp
sjdb2srvi     3701/tcp
```

If you are connecting to a DB2 Version 2 server, you need only the first entry. The port number entries must match the port number entries in the server's services file. The service name entries can be any name.

Cataloging the TCP/IP Node: Cataloging the TCP/IP node adds an entry in the client's node directory. You must catalog the node, host name, and service name information of the remote server node.

You can use the DB2 Client Setup by double-clicking on the DB2 client setup icon in the DB2 folder; select the node menu and follow the instructions.

You can also use the following CLP command:

```
catalog tcpip node db2tcp1 remote cozumel server sjdb2srv
```

where

- db2tcp1 is a unique name you choose.
- cozumel is the TCP/IP host name of the server.
- sjdb2srv is the service_name defined in the services file.

You can also catalog the TCP/IP node by using the IP address instead of the host name. For example

```
catalog tcpip node db2tcp1 remote  9.113.36.232  server sjdb2srv
```

7.1.4 IPX/SPX Configuration

To enable the IPX/SPX support in a Novell NetWare LAN environment, you must have installed NetWare Requester for OS/2 2.10 or later, which is shipped with the NetWare product.

A clinet can access the server in two ways using the IPX/SPX protocol:

- File server addressing

  The client connects to the DB2 server by retrieving the server's address from a NetWare file server. You need information on the file server, object name, and socket number.

- Direct addressing

  The client connects to the DB2 server by specifying the NetWare internetwork address of the server (bypassing the NetWare file server). No NetWare file server is needed. You need only the socket number.

7.1.4.1 Configuring the Server Workstation for IPX/SPX

You can update the configuration using:

- CLP

  For file server addressing use the following commands:

  ```
  db2 update database manager configuration using fileserver netwsrv
  db2 update database manager configuration using objectname db2inst1
  db2 update database manager configuration using ipx_socket 879F
  ```

  For direct addressing use the following commands:

  ```
  db2 update database manager configuration using fileserver *
  db2 update database manager configuration using objectname *
  ```

- The configuration API

- The DB2 database director (see Figure 93)

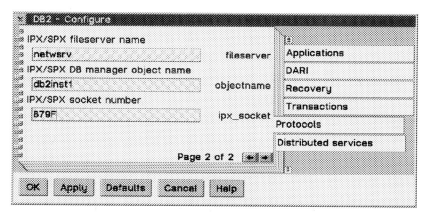

Figure 93. DB2 - Configure Window: IPX/SPX Protocol

When the IPX/SPX parameters have been configured, you must register the DB2 server in the bindery at the NetWare file server before starting DB2 as follows:

```
db2 register db2 server in nwbindery user <userid> password <password    >
```

For this task you have to use your Novell file server login user ID and password, which must have SUPERVISOR or workgroup manager security equivalence.

7.1.4.2 Configuring the Client Workstation for IPX/SPX

You must catalog an entry in the node directory specifying the node name, the NetWare file server name, and the object name information of the remote server node.

You can use the DB2 client setup by double-clicking on the DB2 Client Setup icon in the DB2 folder; select the node menu and follow the instructions.

You can also use the CLP CATALOG IPXSPX NODE command on the client workstation.

File Server Addressing: When using file server addressing, the routing information to your server workstation is retrieved from a NetWare file server. Use the following CLP command:

```
catalog ipxspx node db2ipx1 remote netwsrv server db2inst1
```

where

- db2ipx1 is the name of your server node.
- netwsrv is the name of the NetWare file server on which the database server is registered.
- db2inst1 is the object name that represents the database server.

The values of the object name and file server must match the values of the object name and file server parameters in the database manager configuration file of the server.

Direct Addressing: With direct addressing, the client connects to the server workstation by specifying the NetWare internetwork address of the DB2 server workstation and bypasses the NetWare file server. Use the following CLP command:

```
catalog ipxspx node db2ipx1 remote * server 09212700.400011527745.879E
```

Note: The DB2 server's internetwork address can be retrieved by executing the db2ipxad utility at the DB2 server.

7.1.5 APPC and APPN Configuration

For APPC servers, the requirements are basically the same as the requirements for DB2 common server to act as a DRDA AS. Refer to 5.6, "OS/2 Application Requester" on page 86 for the OS/2 platform, and 6.4, "AIX As a DRDA AR" on page 162 for the AIX platform.

For APPC and APPN clients, the requirements are basically the same as the requirements for DB2 common server to act as a DRDA AR. Refer to 5.8, "DB2 for OS/2 As an AS" on page 129 for the OS/2 platform, and 6.5, "DB2 for AIX as an AS" on page 190 for the AIX platform.

7.1.6 Named Pipe Support

Named pipe support enables local DOS and Windows applications executing under OS/2 to access local DB2 for OS/2 databases without having to use special communications hardware or software. Named pipe support is always installed and initialized automatically if Windows support (DB2 CAE for Windows) is installed.

Named pipe capability is limited to local DB2 CAE/DOS and DB2 CAE for Windows client applications.

With named pipe support DB2 CAE for Windows can now share DB2 configuration and directory files with DB2 common server for OS/2 if both are installed on the same path, so you need to catalog nodes and databases only once for use by both OS/2 and Windows applications without an entry in the node directory. If you use CAE/DOS, you have to maintain separate directories.

7.2 Database Client Connectivity for DOS

In this section we provide information required to establish the connection between a client workstation and a DB2 common server or DDCS workstation. We also describe prerequisite activities involved in configuring CAE/DOS and SDK/DOS.

The CAE/DOS product provides a run-time facility that enables applications running on a client to access a remote database server.

DB2 CAE V1.2.1 is no longer a separate product. It is packaged together with the following DB2 common server products:

- DB2 Single-User for OS/2
- DDCS Single-User
- DB2 Server (OS/2 and AIX)
- DDCS Multiuser Gateway (OS/2 and AIX).

It enables applications to access a remote DB2 for OS/2 or DB2 for AIX server system or a remote DRDA server through a DDCS gateway. Applications can be developed by using embedded SQL, database manager APIs, and DB2 CLI. It also provides ODBC Level 1 driver. DB2 CAE/DOS V1.2.1 includes functions that enable you to connect to remote servers through IPX/SPX, NetBIOS, IBM TCP/IP, FTP TCP/IP, or Novell TCP/IP.

DB2 SDK/DOS provides all DB2 CAE/DOS functions as well as a full application development environment for the client workstation. It includes code examples, precompilers, include files, and other development tools. You need DB2 SDK/DOS to prepare an application for a client workstation.

7.3 Installing CAE/DOS and SDK/DOS

During installation of DB2 CAE/DOS or DB2 SDK/DOS, you are prompted for installation-specific information such as

- Communication protocols
- DB2 environment variables
- Target directory name

Communication Protocols

You can select the following protocols:

- IPX/SPX
- NetBIOS
- IBM TCP/IP
- FTP TCP/IP
- Novell TCP/IP

DB2 Environment Variables

The DB2 environment variables that DB2 CAE/DOS and DB2 SDK/DOS use as default values are defined in the AUTOEXEC.BAT or SETUP.BAT file (see Figure 94).

```
@ECHO OFF
PROMPT $p$g
REM Old PATH statement
REM path=c:\windows;c:\dos
path=c:\crw;c:\windows;c:\dos;c:\tcpdos\bin;c:\windows\system;
C:\SQLLIB\WIN\BIN;C:\CAEDOS\BIN
SET TEMP=C:\DOS
SET DB2USERID=DRDAX5
SET DB2PATH=C:\CAEDOS
SET DB2DBDFT=LOCAL
SET DDCSSETP=-f/NUL -s/e
```

Figure 94. Sample AUTOEXEC.BAT File

You can override some of these default values by specifying the actual values in the SQL statements. You should define a default value for the following DB2 environment variables:

DB2PATH   The path where DB2 CAE/DOS or SDK/DOS is installed. It will be added during the installation process.

DB2DBDFT If an SQL command is issued without being connected to a database, the client initiates the connection to the database alias specified by DB2DBDFT. This value will be added during the installation process if you define one.

DB2USERID The user ID you will be using to connect to a database server. This value will be added during the installation process if you define one. If you do not define a default value, you must enter the user ID in your CONNECT statement.

DDCSSETP The DDCSSETP variable can be used on the client to specify bind options specific to the host environments if you use a DDCS gateway. You can set, for example, the ERROR ALLOWED option, which permits an application to create a package even when some SQL statements are not supported. This might be necessary, for example, when cursors are declared to be FOR FETCH ONLY or WITH HOLD and the application is bound against SQL/DS because the system does not support these cursors.

Target Directory Name

The default installation directory is *c:\sqllib*. You can specify another directory to install DB2 CAE/DOS or DB2 SDK/DOS. In our environment (Boeblingen) we used the *c:\caedos* directory to install the CAE/DOS product.

7.3.1 What's New in DB2 CAE/DOS Version 1.2.1?

The following features have been incorporated in Version 1.2.1 of CAE/DOS:

- Password encryption for better security control. In earlier versions the password is stored in clear text in the DB2PASSWORD environment variable.

- Support for DOS memory extenders.

- No run-time support for Windows applications.

7.3.2 Enabling DOS Client to Access a Database

You must perform the following steps to enable the DOS client workstation to access a database server:

- Update the database manager configuration file
- Catalog the node in the node directory
- Catalog the database in the system database directory

You can use TCP/IP, NetBIOS, or IPX/SPX to enable access to a DB2 for OS/2 server. You can use TCP/IP to enable access to DB2 for AIX. In the sections that follow we show the steps required to enable database access through NetBIOS and TCP/IP.

7.3.2.1 DOS Client Using NetBIOS Support

NetBIOS is the preferred communication protocol for a LAN connection. Follow these steps to establish a NetBIOS connection using CLP:

Update Database Manager Configuration for NetBIOS Support: The workstation *NNAME* parameter of the client must be defined in the database manager configuration file on your DOS client workstation. Here is an example of the command that you can use to update this definition:

```
UPDATE DATABASE MANAGER CONFIGURATION USING NNAME caedos
```

where *caedos* must be a unique workstation name in this NetBIOS network.

Cataloging the Server Node: A node name for the server workstation must be cataloged in the node directory. Here is an example of a command that you can use to catalog a NETBIOS node:

```
CATALOG NETBIOS NODE nodealias REMOTE nnameserver ADAPTER 0
```

where *nodealias* is the node alias that identifies a server for your DOS client workstation, and *nnameserver* is the actual *nname* of the server workstation. It should match the *nname* specified in the database manager configuration file of the server workstation.

To list all cataloged nodes on the client, use the LIST NODE DIRECTORY command. To uncatalog an unused node, use the UNCATALOG NODE command.

Cataloging in the System Database Directory: After cataloging the server node you have to catalog, the databases to which you want access. Here are examples of the CATALOG DATABASE command:

```
CATALOG DATABASE os2db AS os2db AT NODE nodealias AUTHENTICATION server
CATALOG DATABASE vmdb2 AS boebvm AT NODE nodealias AUTHENTICATION server
```

where, for example, *vmdb2* is the alias of the database cataloged on the server workstation, and *boebvm* is the database alias name used in the CONNECT statement from the DOS client workstation. In this example, the AUTHENTICATION *server* is used, so a userid and password must be sent to the server. Note that it is totally transparent to you that the database on the server workstation is a DRDA database.

To list all cataloged databases on the client workstation, use the LIST DATABASE DIRECTORY command. To uncatalog an unused database, use the UNCATALOG DATABASE command.

After you have performed these steps you can connect your DOS client workstation to the server workstation. Use the following command:

```
CONNECT TO dbname
```

where *dbname* is the database alias name that you have cataloged in the system database directory of this workstation.

7.3.2.2 DOS Client Using TCP/IP Support

TCP/IP can be used to access DB2 for OS/2 and DB2 for AIX database servers. To configure TCP/IP for the client, follow these steps:

1. Set the host address (on the client).

2. Set the DB2COMM environment variable (on the server).

3. Update the *services* file (on the server).

4. Update the *services* file (on the client).

5. Update the database manager configuration file (on the server).

6. Catalog the TCP/IP node (on the client).

7. Catalog the database (on the client).

Host Address: The client workstation must know the IP address of the host server to which it is connecting. There are two ways to resolve the address of the host:

- By a name server on your network.

- By specifying the host address in the local *hosts* file.

An entry in the *hosts* file might be:

```
245.256.1.54 hostname
```

where 245.256.1.54 is the IP address of the server and *hostname* is the host name.

If the server resides in the same internet domain as the client, this name can be a flat host name. If the server is not in the same domain, the name must be a fully specified domain name.

Set the DB2COMM Environment Variable (on the server): The DB2COMM environment variable determines which protocols will be enabled when the database manager is started. You can set this variable to multiple values, separated by commas. To enable TCP/IP, set the variable at the server to DB2COMM=TCPIP. Figure 95 on page 214 shows an example of a CONFIG.SYS file that contains the DB2COMM environment variable.

```
SET DB2INSTANCE=DB2
SET DB2PATH=E:\SQLLIB
SET DB2SERVICETPINSTANCE=DB2
SET DB2COMM=TCPIP,NETBIOS,APPC
```

Figure 95. Sample CONFIG.SYS File: DB2COMM Environment Variable

Update the Services File (on the Server):   The TCP/IP *services* file on the server should contain two entries for TCP/IP support for each database manager instance. The first entry is used to handle the connection, and the second entry is used to handle interrupt requests from Version 1 clients and must specify a subsequent port number. For example,

```
db2aix     1300/tcp
db2aixi    1301/tcp
```

where *db2aix* is the value of the *service_name* parameter, *db2aixi* is arbitrary, *1300* and *1301* are the port numbers for the connection and interrupt port, and *tcp* is the protocol.

Update the Services File (on the Client):   You must define two entries in the *services* file on the client. These entries must match the corresponding server entries. The service name, port number, and protocol must be identical. For example, you must define these entries on the client workstation:

```
db2aix     1300/tcp
db2aixi    1301/tcp
```

Update the Database Manager Configuration File (on the Server):   The *service_name* must be updated on the server workstation. Here is an example of the command that you can use to update the service name:

```
UPDATE DATABASE MANAGER CONFIGURATION USING SVCENAME db2aix
```

where *db2aix* is the service name. The service name used must match the service name configured in the *services* file on both the client and the server.

Catalog the TCP/IP Node (on the Client):   You must catalog a TCP/IP node specifying the *hostname* and the *service_name* information of the remote server node. This adds an entry in the client's node directory that points to the remote DB2 server. Here is an example of the command that you can use to catalog a TCP/IP node:

```
CATALOG TCPIP NODE db2node REMOTE hostname SERVER service_name
```

where *db2node* is a name you choose to represent the server node (it must be unique in your node directory list), *hostname* is the TCP/IP host name of the server, and *service_name* is the name defined in the *services* file.

Catalog in the System Database Directory (on the Client): After cataloging the node, you have to catalog the databases to which you want access. Here is an example of the command that you can use to catalog the database:

```
CATALOG DATABASE sj6smpl AS aixdb AT NODE db2node AUTHENTICATION server
```

where *sj6smpl* is the database alias name cataloged on the server workstation, and *aixdb* is the database alias name used in the CONNECT statement from the DOS client workstation. The *db2node* must match the node name you specify when you catalog the TCP/IP node. In this example, the AUTHENTICATION *server* is used, so a userid and password must be sent to the server. Note that it is totally transparent to you that the database on the server workstation is a DRDA database.

7.3.3 Binding the Utilities

If you create a new database on your server, you must create packages for the database utilities by issuing the BIND command from the client workstation. Before issuing the BIND command, you must connect to the database to which you want to bind. For example,

```
CONNECT TO dbname
```

where *dbname* is the alias name of the database to which you want to connect.

Then issue the following command:

```
BIND <path>\@db2ubind.lst BLOCKING ALL
```

where <path> is the drive and full path name of the directory where the bind files are located, and @*db2ubind.lst* is the file containing the list of files to bind to the database. If you have to bind the DOS client to DRDA host environments, issue the same comand as shown above, using the appropriate file name instead of @*db2ubind.lst*

You must issue the BIND command for each database that you want to access.

Chapter 8. DB2 for OS/400 Platform

In this chapter we discuss the tasks to enable DB2 for OS/400 to perform the DRDA AS and AR functions for the OS/400 system located in Rochester.

Similar tasks were performed for the OS/400 system located in San Jose.

8.1 DB2 for OS/400 AR

A DB2 for OS/400 LU 6.2 connection provides the logical interface through which a DRDA AR can access the AS's relational database. This access requires connectivity between relational database managers operating in like or unlike operating environments. For example, access to relational data between two or more DB2 for OS/400s is distribution in a like environment, and access between a DB2 for OS/400 and SQL/DS is distribution in an unlike environment.

When the DB2 for OS/400 acts as an AR, it can connect to any AS that supports DRDA. In this application scenario, the DB2 for OS/400 is a requester to

- DB2 for MVS
- DB2 for VM
- SQL/DS for VSE
- DB2 for OS/400
- DB2 for OS/2
- DB2 for AIX

Refer to 4.1, "Network Connectivity" on page 66 for an overview of the network and connections.

For DB2 for OS/400 to access distributed relational databases, the following must be considered:

- Network configuration
- Relational database directory
- Security requirements
- Problem determination

The following publications provide guidance for implementing an application in an OS/400 DRDA environment:

- *D2/400 Advanced Database Functions*

- *DB2/400 SQL Programming Version 3*

- *DB2/400 SQL Reference Version 3*

- *DB2/400 Query Manager and SQL Development Kit*

- *DB2/400 Query Manager Use* .

8.1.1 Network Configuration

In this section we present an overview of the communication objects required to implement AS/400 DRDA. The DRDA support is based on SNA through APPC communications.

Refer to Figure 24 on page 75 to help you understand the AS/400 configuration discussed below.

The local network ID **1** and control point name **2** in Figure 96 are required for the DRDA network definitions at the AS.

```
Current system name  . . . . . . . . . . . . . . :   SCHASM02
   Pending system name  . . . . . . . . . . . . :
Local network ID . . . . . . . . . . . . . . . :   USIBMSC   1
Local control point name . . . . . . . . . . . :   SCHASM02  2
Default local location . . . . . . . . . . . . :   SCHASM02
Default mode . . . . . . . . . . . . . . . . . :   QPCSUPP
APPN node type . . . . . . . . . . . . . . . . :   *ENDNODE
```

Figure 96. Network Attributes of SCHASM02

Figure 96 shows the token-ring line description to Poughkeepsie.

```
Line description . . . . . . . . . :   POK
Option . . . . . . . . . . . . . . :   *BASIC
Category of line . . . . . . . . . :   *TRLAN

Maximum controllers  . . . . . . . :   40
Line speed . . . . . . . . . . . . :   4M
Maximum frame size . . . . . . . . :   4060
TRLAN manager logging level  . . . :   *OFF
   Current logging level  . . . . . :    *OFF
TRLAN manager mode . . . . . . . . :   *OBSERVING
Local adapter address  . . . . . . :   400052006000
```

Figure 97.   Token-Ring Line Description on SCHASM02

Here is how system SCHASM02 has been set up as an AR in our network. The AR
SCHASM02 is connected through a token ring to all systems in the network.

The values for the RMTNETID **1** and RMTCPNAME **2** in Figure 98 were obtained
from the remote system's network configuration.

```
Controller description . . . . . . :   POK
Option . . . . . . . . . . . . . . :   *BASIC
Category of controller . . . . . . :   *APPC

Link type  . . . . . . . . . . . . :   *LAN
Active switched line . . . . . . . :   ITSCTRN
Character code . . . . . . . . . . :   *EBCDIC
Maximum frame size . . . . . . . . :   16393
Remote network identifier  . . . . :   USIBMSC   1
Remote control point . . . . . . . :   SC19M     2
Initial connection . . . . . . . . :   *DIAL
Dial initiation  . . . . . . . . . :   *LINKTYPE
Switched disconnect  . . . . . . . :   *NO
Data link role . . . . . . . . . . :   *NEG
LAN remote adapter address . . . . :   400008290200
```

Figure 98.   APPC Controller Description on SCHASM02

A control unit description describes the adjacent system in the network. The POK
controller (CRTCTLAPPC) is connected to a VTAM switch major node on a remote
token-ring bridge.

The AS/400 class-of-service description (COS) (Figure 99 on page 220) is used to select the communication routes and transmission priority for sessions using APPN. The mode description (discussed below) points to the COS to use for the LU 6.2 conversation. The COS we used in our environment is the OS/400 default.

```
Class-of-service description . . . :   #CONNECT
Transmission priority  . . . . . . :   *MED
Text . . . . . . . . . . . . . . . :   This COSD is IBM Supplied


----------------------------Line Information----------------------------
                                                    Security
       Line            Link        Cost/   Cost/    for          Propagation
Line   Weight          Speed       Connect Byte     Line            Delay
Row
1      30    MINIMUM   4M          0       0        *NONSECURE   *MIN
             MAXIMUM   *MAX        0       0        *MAX         *LAN
2      60    MINIMUM   56000       0       0        *NONSECURE   *MIN
             MAXIMUM   *MAX        0       0        *MAX         *TELEPHONE
3      90    MINIMUM   19200       0       0        *NONSECURE   *MIN
             MAXIMUM   *MAX        0       0        *MAX         *TELEPHONE
4      120   MINIMUM   9600        0       0        *NONSECURE   *MIN
             MAXIMUM   *MAX        0       0        *MAX         *TELEPHONE
```

Figure 99. COS Description Used on SCHASM02

The mode description (Figure 100 on page 221) provides the session characteristics and number of sessions that are used to negotiate the allowed values between the local and remote location.

```
Mode description . . . . . . . . . :    IBMRDBM

Class-of-service . . . . . . . . . :    #CONNECT
Maximum sessions . . . . . . . . . :    100
Maximum conversations  . . . . . . :    100
Locally controlled sessions  . . . :    10
Pre-established sessions . . . . . :    10
Inbound pacing value . . . . . . . :    7
Outbound pacing value  . . . . . . :    7
Maximum length of request unit . . :    *CALC
Data compression . . . . . . . . . :    *NETATR
Inbound data compression . . . . . :    *NONE
Outbound data compression  . . . . :    *NONE
Text . . . . . . . . . . . . . . . :    DRDA Mode Description
```

Figure 100. Mode Description on SCHASM02

The device descriptions were automatically created on AR SCHASM02 during the initial connection to the remote ASs. In Figure 101 through Figure 106 on page 223, the name of the device corresponds to the LU Name **1** that SNA uses to refer to the remote database because we used *LOC for the device description parameter in the relational database directory entry (see Figure 110 on page 226). *Using *LOC is highly recommended.*

The Remote location (RMTLOCNAME) **2** and Remote network identifier (RMTNETID) **3** parameters on the device descriptions also identify the remote database management system (another DB2 for OS/400, DB2 for MVS/ESA, SQL/DS, DB2 for OS/2, DB2 for AIX).

```
Device description . . . . . . . . :    SC02130I  1
Category of device . . . . . . . . :    *APPC
Remote location  . . . . . . . . . :    SC02130I  2
Local location . . . . . . . . . . :    SCHASM02
Remote network identifier  . . . . :    USIBMSC   3
APPN-capable . . . . . . . . . . . :    *YES
----------------------Mode------------------------
*NETATR
```

Figure 101. APPC Device Description on SCHASM02 for DB2 for MVS Server

```
          Device description . . . . . . . . :  IPFA2GL4  1
          Category of device . . . . . . . . :  *APPC
          Remote location  . . . . . . . . . :  IPFA2GL4  2
          Local location . . . . . . . . . . :  SCHASM02
          Remote network identifier  . . . . :  DEIBMPF   3
          Attached controller  . . . . . . . :  POK
          APPN-capable . . . . . . . . . . . :  *YES
------------------------Mode------------------------
  *NETATR
```

Figure 102. *APPC Device Description on SCHASM02 for DB2 for VM Server*

```
          Device description . . . . . . . . :  IPFA21CD  1
          Category of device . . . . . . . . :  *APPC
          Remote location  . . . . . . . . . :  IPFA21CD  2
          Online at IPL  . . . . . . . . . . :  *NO
          Local location . . . . . . . . . . :  SCHASM02
          Remote network identifier  . . . . :  DEIBMIPF  3
          Attached controller  . . . . . . . :  POK
          APPN-capable . . . . . . . . . . . :  *YES
------------------------Mode------------------------
  *NETATR
```

Figure 103. *APPC Device Description on SCHASM02 for SQL/DS VSE Server*

```
          Device description . . . . . . . . :  SC02132I  1
          Category of device . . . . . . . . :  *APPC
          Remote location  . . . . . . . . . :  SC02132I  2
          Local location . . . . . . . . . . :  SCHASM02
          Remote network identifier  . . . . :  USIBMSC   3
          Attached controller  . . . . . . . :  POK
          APPN-capable . . . . . . . . . . . :  *YES
------------------------Mode------------------------
  *NETATR
```

Figure 104. *APPC Device Description on SCHASM02 for DB2 for OS/400 Server*

```
         Device description . . . . . . . . :   SC02131I  ■1
         Category of device . . . . . . . . :   *APPC
         Remote location  . . . . . . . . . :   SC02131I  ■2
         Local location . . . . . . . . . . :   SCHASM02
         Remote network identifier  . . . . :   USIBMSC   ■3
         Attached controller  . . . . . . . :   POK
         APPN-capable . . . . . . . . . . . :   *YES
    -----------------------Mode----------------------
    *NETATR
```

Figure 105. APPC Device Description on SCHASM02 for DB2 for AIX Server

```
         Device description . . . . . . . . :   SC02130I  ■1
         Category of device . . . . . . . . :   *APPC
         Remote location  . . . . . . . . . :   SC02130I  ■2
         Local location . . . . . . . . . . :   SCHASM02
         Remote network identifier  . . . . :   USIBMSC   ■3
         Attached controller  . . . . . . . :   POK
         APPN-capable . . . . . . . . . . . :   *YES
    -----------------------Mode----------------------
    *NETATR
```

Figure 106. APPC Device Description on SCHASM02 for DB2 for OS/2 Server

Note: Even though these devices were created with the mode name *NETATR, IBMRDBM will be used when a DRDA session is established. The AS/400 will use the mode name defined in the network attributes to automatically create APPC devices. The DRDA conversation will use the mode description defined in the RDB directory entry as shown in Figure 110 on page 226.

If APPN(*YES) is specified when creating the controller description and additional local location or special characteristics of remote locations for APPN are required, APPN configuration lists must be created using the Work with Configuration Lists (WRKCFGL) command. In our scenario, we used an alias, SC06000I, for the local location, SCHASM02, as shown in Figure 107 on page 224. So, we were known to the ITSO Boeblingen network by this alias.

```
Configuration list . . . . . . . . :   QAPPNLCL
Configuration list type . . . . . :   *APPNLCL
-----APPN Local Locations-----
Local
Location   Text
SC06000I alias lu for DRDA
```

Figure 107. APPN Local Location List on SCHASM02

In addition to the local location list, we had to define all remote locations in the remote location list (see Figure 108).

```
Configuration list . . . . . . . . :   QAPPNRMT
Configuration list type . . . . . :   *APPNRMT
----------------APPN Remote Locations------------------
           Remote     Local      Remote    Control
Remote     Network    Location   Control   Point     Secure  Text
Location   ID         SCHASM02   Point     Net ID    Loc
IPFA2GL4   DEIBMIPF   SC06000I   SC19M     USIBMSC   *YES    Boeblingen VM
IPFA21CD   DEIBMIPF   SC06000I   SC19M     USIBMSC   *YES    Boeblingen VSE
SCLUDB41   USIBMSC    SCHASM02   SC19M     USIBMSC   *YES    San Jose MVS
SC02130I   USIBMSC    SCHASM02   SC19M     USIBMSC   *YES    San Jose AIX
SC02131I   USIBMSC    SCHASM02   SC19M     USIBMSC   *YES    San Jose OS/2
SC02132I   USIBMSC    SCHASM02   SC19M     USIBMSC   *NO     San Jose OS/400
```

Figure 108. APPN Remote Location List on SCHASM02

Note that the Secure Loc parameter is set to *YES to indicate that we were using conversation security level SAME. Refer to 8.1.3, "Security Requirements" on page 228 for a detailed discussion.

8.1.2 Relational Database Directory

Each DB2 for OS/400 AR in a distributed relational database network must have a relational database directory. There is only one relational database directory on an AS/400 system. Each AR in the database network must have an entry for its *local* database and one for each *remote* relational database it accesses (see Figure 109 on page 225). The local entry **1** is required for identification to the servers. The names assigned to each remote database must match the name the ASs use to identify their local database. The relational database directory allows DB2 for OS/400 to accept a relational database name from the application and translates it to an SNA NETID.LUNAME value for communication processing. The RDB directory can be maintained by using the Work with RDB Directory Entries (WRKRDBDIRE) control language command.

```
Relational              Remote
Database                Location  Text

RCAS400      ∎1         *LOCAL    Rochester DB2 for OS/400
S34VMDB0                IPFA2GL4  Boeblingen DB2 for VM
S34VSDB1                IPFA21CD  Boeblingen SQL/DS for VSE
B06SMPL                 IPFBOEDJ  Boeblingen DB2 for AIX
DBINST2                 IPFCLOE0  Boeblingen DB2 for OS/2
DBSRV4D                 IPFCLOE0  Boeblingen DB2 for OS/2
CENTDB2                 SCLUDB41  San Jose DB2 for MVS/ESA
SJAS400                 SC02132I  San Jose DB2 for OS/400
SJ2SMPL                 SC02130I  San Jose DB2 for OS/2
SJ6SMPL                 SC02131I  San Jose DB2 for AIX
```

Figure 109. Relational Database Directory on SCHASM02

Figure 110 on page 226 through Figure 115 on page 227 show the directory entries for each relational database that SCHASM02 accessed.

The information you can specify when adding or changing a database directory entry includes

1 Relational database name

2 Remote location name of the database

3 Name of the device used for communications

4 Local location name

5 Remote network identifier

6 Mode name used to establish the communications

7 Transaction program name of the remote database

Note that SQL/DS for VM and SQL/DS VSE did not use the default TPN, *DRDA.

```
Relational database . . . . . . . . . . . . . . . :    CENTDB2     1
Remote location:
   Remote location . . . . . . . . . . . . . . . :     SCLUDB41    2
   Device description . . . . . . . . . . . . . :      *LOC        3
   Local location . . . . . . . . . . . . . . . :      SCHASM02    4
   Remote network identifier . . . . . . . . . :       USIBMSC     5
   Mode . . . . . . . . . . . . . . . . . . . . :       IBMRDBM     6
Transaction program . . . . . . . . . . . . . . :      *DRDA       7
Text . . . . . . . . . . . . . . . . . . . . . . :      San Jose DB2 for MVS/ESA
```

Figure 110. Relational Database Directory Entry for Poughkeepsie DB2 for MVS/ESA

```
Relational database . . . . . . . . . . . . . :     S34VMDB0    1
Remote location:
   Remote location . . . . . . . . . . . . . . :     IPFA2GL4    2
   Device description . . . . . . . . . . . . . :    *LOC        3
   Local location . . . . . . . . . . . . . . . :    SCHASM02    4
   Remote network identifier . . . . . . . . . :     DEIBMIPF    5
   Mode . . . . . . . . . . . . . . . . . . . . :     IBMRDBM     6
Transaction program . . . . . . . . . . . . . :     'S23VMDB0'   7
Text . . . . . . . . . . . . . . . . . . . . . :     DB2 for VM
```

Figure 111. Relational Database Directory Entry for Boeblingen SQL/DS for VM

```
Relational database . . . . . . . . . . . . . :     S34VSDB1    1
Remote location:
   Remote location . . . . . . . . . . . . . . :     IPFA21CD    2
   Device description . . . . . . . . . . . . . :    *LOC        3
   Local location . . . . . . . . . . . . . . . :    SCHASM02    4
   Remote network identifier . . . . . . . . . :     DEIBMIPF    5
   Mode . . . . . . . . . . . . . . . . . . . . :     IBMRDBM     6
Transaction program . . . . . . . . . . . . . :     'TPN1    '   7
Text . . . . . . . . . . . . . . . . . . . . . :     SQL/DS VSE
```

Figure 112. Relational Database Directory Entry for Boeblingen SQL/DS VSE

```
Relational database  . . . . . . . . . . . . . . :   RCAS400      ▌1▐
Remote location:
   Remote location  . . . . . . . . . . . . . . :   *LOCAL       ▌2▐
   Device description . . . . . . . . . . . . . :   *LOC         ▌3▐
   Local location . . . . . . . . . . . . . . . :   SCHASM02     ▌4▐
   Remote network identifier  . . . . . . . . . :   USIBMSC      ▌5▐
   Mode . . . . . . . . . . . . . . . . . . . . :   IBMRDBM      ▌6▐
Transaction program  . . . . . . . . . . . . . :   *DRDA        ▌7▐
Text . . . . . . . . . . . . . . . . . . . . . :   DB2 for OS/400
```

Figure 113. Relational Database Directory Entry for Rochester DB2 for OS/400

```
Relational database  . . . . . . . . . . . . . :   SJ2SMPL      ▌1▐
Remote location:
   Remote location  . . . . . . . . . . . . . . :   SC02130I     ▌2▐
   Device description . . . . . . . . . . . . . :   *LOC         ▌3▐
   Local location . . . . . . . . . . . . . . . :   SCHASM02     ▌4▐
   Remote network identifier  . . . . . . . . . :   USIBMSC      ▌5▐
   Mode . . . . . . . . . . . . . . . . . . . . :   IBMRDBM      ▌6▐
Transaction program  . . . . . . . . . . . . . :   'DB22TPN'    ▌7▐
Text . . . . . . . . . . . . . . . . . . . . . :   DB2 for OS/2
```

Figure 114. Relational Database Directory Entry for San Jose DB2 for OS/2

```
Relational database  . . . . . . . . . . . . . :   SJ6SMPL      ▌1▐
Remote location:
   Remote location  . . . . . . . . . . . . . . :   SC02131I     ▌2▐
   Device description . . . . . . . . . . . . . :   *LOC         ▌3▐
   Local location . . . . . . . . . . . . . . . :   SCHASM02     ▌4▐
   Remote network identifier  . . . . . . . . . :   USIBMSC      ▌5▐
   Mode . . . . . . . . . . . . . . . . . . . . :   IBMRDBM      ▌6▐
Transaction program  . . . . . . . . . . . . . :   'DB26TPN'    ▌7▐
Text . . . . . . . . . . . . . . . . . . . . . :   DB2 for AIX
```

Figure 115. Relational Database Directory Entry for San Jose DB2 for AIX

8.1.3 Security Requirements

In a distributed relational database, the AS controls access to its objects, but the security requirements of the AR and the network connecting them must also be satisfied before distributed database processing can be performed on behalf of an SQL application. The AR selects the end-user name (AS/400 user profile) that is passed to the server when the connection is being established. The user profile name specified in the USER parameter of the SQL CONNECT statement (since OS/400 V2R2) or the user's user profile name (if USER was not specified on the SQL CONNECT) is sent to the AS.

After the AR selects the user name to send to the remote application, it must provide the LU 6.2 network security information dictated by the server. LU 6.2 provides three major network security features:

- Session level

- Conversation level

- Encryption

    Note: Please refer to the publication *Common Cryptographic Architecture Services/400* or the redbook *An Implementation Guide for AS/400 Security and Auditing* for the supported level of encryption on AS/400.

Session-level security is provided through LU-to-LU verification. Each LU has a password that must match the password at the remote LU. This password is specified with the LOCPWD on the CRTDEVAPPC command (APPN *NO) or a location password on the APPN remote location list (APPN *YES). Notice that distributed relational database support now exploits a DDM function that was already implemented there in the past.

The SNA LU 6.2 architecture identifies three conversation security levels that various types of systems in an SNA network can use to provide consistent conversation security across a network of unlike systems. The SNA security levels are

- Security(NONE)

    No user ID or password is sent to establish a connection. This option is not supported by DRDA, but it is the only level supported by the systems network architecture distribution services (SNADS).

- Security(SAME)

    A user ID is required, but no password is sent to the server.

- Security(PGM)

    Both a user ID and password are sent to the server for validation.

DB2 for OS/400 (since OS/400 V2R2) supports all three levels of conversation security. The server controls the SNA conversation levels used for the conversation. In our network, the ASs implemented SECURITY(SAME) as the SNA conversation level. SECURITY(SAME) is implemented on the DB2 for OS/400 AR by defining the AS as a secure location either in its device description (APPC) or in the remote configuration list if APPN is used. DRDA support implicitly sends the user ID when a CONNECT statement is executed even if it is not specified on the CONNECT. In an SQL program the user of the package is taken. Figure 107 on page 224 shows how the requester, SCHASM02, defined the ASs for SECURITY(SAME).

8.1.4 Problem Determination

Figure 116 shows the major components of the OS/400 operating system involved with distributed database when DB2 for OS/400 is an AR.

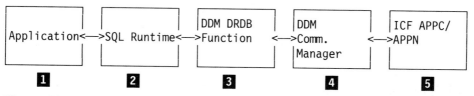

Figure 116. Components of DB2 for OS/400 Support

1 Application is the distributed SQL program.

2 SQL Runtime support on the AR is called from the application to execute SQL statements.

3 DDM Distributed Relational Database Function on the AR converts the SQL operation into the corresponding DDM commands and objects to be sent to the AS for execution.

4 DDM Communications Manager is used to send and receive DDM commands to and from the AR. This manager is also responsible for starting and ending conversations and ensuring that conversations are shared when possible.

5 ICF is the interface between the DDM communications manager and APPC. Problem determination must address issues in all of the above components. Generally speaking, these components can be categorized into three major areas:

- DRDA connect

- Application execution

- Application recovery and cleanup

8.1.4.1 DRDA Connect

There are two ways for a DB2 for OS/400 application to connect to a remote database. Without an SQL CONNECT statement, the application connects to the remote database named during precompilation and/or package creation. In fact, the package contained in the program determines to which AS it is to connect.

- The program runs just as if the database were on the local system. This is an *implicit* connection.

- If there is a need to work with several databases, it is necessary to put the SQL CONNECT in the application. This is an *explicit* connection.

An AR application can connect, implicitly or explicitly, to an AS when it is in the connectable state. Refer to 11.1.3.1, "Connection States" on page 323 for a discussion of connection states in the DRDA level 2 environment.

If the application is not in the connectable state (COMMIT not yet issued), the SQL CONNECT statement will fail. If the AR application is in a connectable state, failure to connect often shows up as failed program start requests on the AS. When DB2 for OS/400 is the AR, error messages are logged in the JOBLOG of the requester job or the QSYSOPR message queue. In the case of security problems, some useful messages might also show up in the history log (QHST) and message queue (QSYSMSG). The reason codes associated with errors are listed in the *AS/400 ICF Programmer's Guide* or *SNA Formats*. If the communication network is configured correctly, the likely causes of failed program start requests to remote ASs are

- RDB directory entries missing or incorrect.

- User ID, password, or authorities are wrong.

- Incompatibility between the AR and AS. For example, CCSID or date formats of the requester job are not supported on the server. (In this case a DDM error X'2121' is issued.)

8.1.4.2 Application Execution

SQLSTATE: The DB2 for OS/400 requester job executes SQL statements at the AS. SQLCODEs and their corresponding SQLSTATEs are returned in the SQL communication area (SQLCA) structure.

Note: SQLCODEs are platform specific as they were developed independently in the past. SQLSTATEs are common to all IBM platforms. Only these should be used for new applications. The SQLCA is updated constantly with information about the SQL statement that ran most recently. SQLSTATE has been designed so that application programs can test for specific error conditions or classes of errors regardless of whether the program is connected to another DB2 for OS/400, DB2 for MVS/ESA, SQL/DS AS, DB2 for OS/2, or DB2 for AIX. The *SAA SQL/400 Programmers Guide* and the *DB2/400 SQL Programming Version 3* manual contain each SQLCODE and the associated message identifier. The complete message can be viewed online by using the Display Message Description (DSPMSGD) command. For example, the message identifier for SQLSTATE 57043 is SQL7021. By keying *DSPMSGD SQL7021 MSGF(QSQLMSG)*, you can see the complete message text for this SQLSTATE (see Figure 117). Remember that the same error condition does not produce the same SQLCODE on different IBM relational database products, but it does produce the same SQLSTATE.

```
Message ID . . . . . . . . . :    SQL7021
Message file . . . . . . . . :    QSQLMSG
   Library  . . . . . . . . . :      QSYS

Message . . .: Local program attempting to run on application server.
Cause . . . .: An attempt was made to run an SQL program in a process
               that is an application server.
Recovery  . .: Initiate another job and run the SQL program in that job.
```

Figure 117. Message Text for SQL7021

Debug: When a DB2 for OS/400 AR job that contains SQL statements is run in debug mode, the database manager puts messages in the joblog about each SQL statement run. References to high-level language statement numbers in debug mode must be taken from the compile listing.

Alerts: For full support in handling distributed relational database problems, alerts and alert logging should be enabled by using the Change Network Attributes (CHGNETA) command. DB2 for OS/400 enables a subset of the DRDB system messages (messages in the CPF3E80 through CPF3E89 range) to trigger alerts for distributed relational database support. If an error is detected at the AS, a DDM message is sent to the AR. The AS/400 AR creates an alert based on that DDM message. When alerts are sent from some modules that support distributed relational databases, a spool file (QPSRVDMP) that contains extensive diagnostic information is also created. This data is called first-failure data capture (FFDC) information. This spool file is created only if the QSFWERRLOG system value is set to *LOG.

Call Stack: You can determine whether the AR job is in a wait or loop condition by displaying the job and monitoring the call stack. If a loop exists in the application, contact the application programmer. If a loop exists in an OS/400 module, report the problem. If the program stack is changing without a loop, the problem is performance. If the stack is not changing, and the QCNSRCV and QAPDEQUE modules are in the stack, the AR is waiting on a reply from the AS.

8.1.4.3 Application Recovery and Cleanup

If an error situation occurs, conversations must be ended, and database changes either confirmed or canceled. The following procedures might be followed to clean up sessions and uncommitted database changes:

- SQL WHENEVER

  SQL/400: A Guide for Implementation OS/400 Version 2 Release 2.0 contains an excellent discussion on using the WHENEVER statement in an SQL program.

  - WHENEVER SQLERROR is very useful in a commitment control environment (remember, if the AS is not a DB2 for OS/400, COMMIT(*NONE) is not allowed) where a number of statements must be processed together. If one statement fails, the logic can be transferred to an error routine that can notify the user, before rolling back to the transaction boundary.

  - When you want to test SQLSTATEs in your program (for example, testing for package existence), you need a way in the error routine to return to the SQL statement which failed. In COBOL you could set a condition for the error routine before the SQL statement is executed. Another method is not to use SQLERROR and test the SQLSTATE immediately after the statement. This approach was chosen for program DRDASU2, which is described in Chapter 12, "Application Structure" on page 351.

  - WHENEVER NOTFOUND provides a structured way to exit from the processing loop if records are not found.

- ROLLBACK/COMMIT

  The current RUW must be confirmed or canceled before the application can decide to continue working with the remote database or return to the local system. ROLLBACK/COMMIT gets the application to a connectable state after an error condition. Keep in mind that a ROLLBACK is automatically done if an application process ends without a final COMMIT being issued (for example, power and communication failures).

- RELEASE ALL

  RELEASE ALL must be used to put the application process in an unconnected state regarding remote databases. The process enters this state when an SQL statement is unsuccessful because of a failure that causes a ROLLBACK operation at the AS and the loss of the connection. In this state the process is still connected to the local database.

8.1.4.4 Common DRDA Network Problems

1. **Problem:** Sense Code 08050000

   Cause: Sessions not available.

Resolution: Vary off and on the APPC device associated with the remote database or dynamically change the number of sessions the local location allows to a mode with the CHGSSNMAX command.

2. **Problem:** Sense Code 080F6051

   Cause: Security parameters do not match.

   Resolution: Change conversation level security parameters so that the AR and the AS are the same.

This sense code (carried in message CPF4734) normally comes up when

- The user ID is missing on the server.

- The user ID does not have proper authority on the server.

- The password is incorrect when you are running under SECURITY(PGM).

3. **Problem:** Sense codes 087D0001, 08570003, and 80030004

   Cause: Network resource not available.

   Resolution: Check with the remote system administrator to verify that the LU (= device on AS/400) associated with the remote database name is active or that the database management subsystem is active.
   Where DB2 for OS/400 is a server, it may also mean that the remote controller and devices are not active (varied off).

8.1.4.5 Helpful Tools

When trying to resolve network or DRDA errors that fail at program start request, two common AS/400 commands are helpful:

- Start Communication Trace (STRCMNTRC)

  Records communication line traffic that can be printed. Specify *YES to the Format SNA Data parameter.

- Display Joblog (DSPJOBLOG)

  DRDA jobs will typically show up in communications subsystem QCMN. The user name associated with the job should be the name of the AR user. The joblog will contain sense code data for failed program start requests.

- Display Message Queue (QSYSMSG)

  Communication errors caused by protocol violations can be viewed by displaying the messages logged in QSYSMSG. Usually these messages are more descriptive than the messages logged in QSYSOPR or the JOBLOG.

The *SNA Formats* manual has more information about the sense codes that you may encounter and a detailed description of the FMH5 and FMH7 headers. LU 6.2 uses

FMH5 to carry a request for a DRDA conversation. It uses FMH7 after a negative response to a bind or application start request to carry information that relates to the error.

Further Reading

- *DRDA Problem Determination Guide*

- *AS/400 Distributed Relational Database Guide*

- *DRDA Problem Determination Guide*

8.2 DB2 for OS/400 AS

AS support on DB2 for OS/400 enables it to act as a database server connected to any one of the following ARs:

- DB2 for AS400

- DB2 for VM

- SQL/DS for VSE

- DB2 for MVS

- DB2 for AIX

- DB2 for OS2

In our application scenario, the AS/400 is an AS to all of these requesters.

8.2.1 Network Configuration

To process distributed database requests on the DB2 for OS/400 database server, you have to define the server system to the network and name the AS database. Defining DB2 for OS/400 AS (RCAS400 and SJAS400) to the network is identical to defining the DB2 for OS/400 AR to the network. See 8.1, "DB2 for OS/400 AR" on page 217 for more information on how to define the AS/400 as an AR to the network.

8.2.2 Database

Define the DB2 for OS/400 AS database the same way that you identify the DB2 for OS/400 AR database. Use the Add RDB Directory Entry command (ADDRDBDIRE) and specify *LOCAL **1** as the remote location (see Figure 118 on page 235 and Figure 119 on page 235). The AS/400 supports only one *LOCAL entry in its relational database directory because the whole system represents a single database.

```
Relational database  . . . . . . . . . . . . . . :   RCAS400
Remote location:
   Remote location  . . . . . . . . . . . . . . :   *LOCAL  1
   Device description . . . . . . . . . . . . . :
   Local location . . . . . . . . . . . . . . . :
   Remote network identifier  . . . . . . . . . :
   Mode . . . . . . . . . . . . . . . . . . . . :   IBMRDBM
Transaction program  . . . . . . . . . . . . . :   *DRDA
Text . . . . . . . . . . . . . . . . . . . . . :   Local Database
```

Figure 118. Local Database Directory Entry on SCHASM02 Rochester

```
Relational database  . . . . . . . . . . . . . . :   SJAS400
Remote location:
   Remote location  . . . . . . . . . . . . . . :   *LOCAL  1
   Device description . . . . . . . . . . . . . :
   Local location . . . . . . . . . . . . . . . :
   Remote network identifier  . . . . . . . . . :
   Mode . . . . . . . . . . . . . . . . . . . . :   IBMRDBM
Transaction program  . . . . . . . . . . . . . :   *DRDA
Text . . . . . . . . . . . . . . . . . . . . . :   Local Database
```

Figure 119. Local Database Directory Entry on SJAS400A San Jose

8.2.3 Commitment Control and Journaling

In DB2 for MVS/ESA or SQL/DS AR environments, it is mandatory to use isolation levels (commitment control on the AS/400) of *cursor stability* or *repeatable read*. DB2 for OS/2 and DB2 for AIX, in addition, support *uncommitted read*. Only DB2 for OS/400 supports the isolation level *no commit*. Refer to *Formal Register of Extensions and Differences in SQL* for more information about isolation level support on the various platforms.

Note: Non-DB2 for OS/400 databases cannot work without commitment control. A distributed relational database application from an unlike AR requires the DB2 for OS/400 server to implement journaling, which is a prerequisite to commitment control. When implementing journaling to support commitment control in the SQL environment, you must consider the following:

• Commitment control on the DB2 for OS/400 AS requires that you journal all activity to a single journal. The DB2 for OS/400 AS user is responsible for ensuring that both SQL and high-level language (HLL) applications satisfy the single journal requirement. This could involve modifying the journal to which changes are directed for either the SQL tables or the physical files.

Journaling is the OS/400 component providing logging facilities for commitment control.

- With versions earlier than DB2 for OS/400 Version 3, tables or files that are to be updated in a unit of work must be journaled in the same journal. If the AR application is only reading (SELECT, FETCH) tables or files, they can be in any journal or no journal at all. This *single journal* limitation has been lifted in OS/400 Version 3. Please refer to the publication *Backup and Recovery—Advanced* for details.

- Local SQL tables and physical files accessed by HLL I/O statements for update must be journaled . HLL I/O statements do not automatically start commitment control. Use the Start Commitment Control command (STRCMTCTL) to activate commitment before running these applications.

- When compiling AR programs with commitment control, the tables referred to in the application program by DML statements must be journaled.

8.2.4 DB2 for OS/400 Catalog

For versions earlier than DB2 for OS/400 Version 3, the scope of the SQL catalog is restricted to a single collection. With Version 3 this limitation has been lifted, and you can find information about all tables, packages, views, indexes, and constraints on the AS/400 system. The catalog tables include the following files in the QSYS2 library:

- QADBXREF
- QADBPKG
- QADBFDEP
- QADBXRDBD
- QADBFCST
- QADBCCST
- QADBIFLD
- QADBKFLD

The database manager provides additional views over the catalog tables. The views provide more consistency with the catalog views of other IBM SQL products and with the catalog views of the ANSI and ISO standard (called *Information Schema* in the standard). The following views are included in the QSYS2 library:

- SYSCOLUMNS
- SYSCST

- SYSCSTCOL
- SYSCSTDEP
- SYSINDEXES
- SYSKEYCST
- SYSPACKAGE
- SYSREFCST
- SYSTABLES
- SYSVIEWDEP
- SYSVIEWS.

Note: The system catalog views in QSYS2 are system objects. Thus any user views created over the catalog views in QSYS2 must be deleted on the install of the operating system. The delete and re-create of the system objects in QSYS2 require that dependents be deleted. A circumvention is to save the user views before the install and restore them after the install. Views can be built over the tables in QSYS over which the catalog views are built. These cross-reference files in QSYS are not deleted during install. Therefore any views built over them are maintained throughout the install.

8.2.5 Security Requirements

When the AS/400 acts as an AS, there are several security issues to resolve:

- Network or location security to verify the identity of other systems in the network

- Conversation level or user-related security to verify the identity and rights of users on local and remote systems

- Object-related security to control user access to particular resources such as tables, programs, and packages

Network, conversation level, and object-related security are applicable only if the security level of the AS/400 is 30 or above. During our project, QSECLVL was 30.

Network Security: We did not specify network security explicitly in our scenario.

Conversation Level Security: The AR sends a user ID to the AS for security processing. The SECURELOC parameter on the APPC device description or the SECURE LOCATION value on the APPN remote configuration list determines what is accepted from the requester for the conversation. See 8.1.3, "Security Requirements" on page 228 for a discussion of SNA levels of conversation security.

- For the SECURITY(NONE) level, DB2 for OS/400 does not expect a user ID or password. Although not supported by DRDA, the conversation is allowed when a default user profile is specified in the communication entry of the communication subsystem where the DRDA AR job is running.

- For the SECURITY(SAME) level, the DB2 for OS/400 expects a user ID and an *already verified indicator* from the AR. Thus the AS allows the AR to verify user security information. In our network environment, we used SECURITY(SAME) on each AS. To use this level of conversation security on DB2 for OS/400, specify SECURELOC(*YES) in the remote configuration list or the APPC device description for the remote location accessing the AS/400. The DB2 for OS/400 requester will send the user ID and an indication that the user has already been verified when the server is defined as a secure location on the requester. In our project, we set up separate communication entries (CMNE) for each AR device with default user *NONE.

Notes:

1. Using the communication entry *ALL with default user *NONE affects other IBM communication jobs (SNADS, Display-Station Passthru) that run in the subsystem. For example, SNADS will not work without a default user profile. Refer to the *AS/400 APPC Programmer's Guide*, for more information.

2. Specifying default user *SYS on the communication entry for a requester location will allow a DRDA conversation even if the requester user ID does not have a corresponding user profile defined on the AS/400. The requester's job will use the default profile, QUSER.

- For the SECURITY(PGM) level, DB2 for OS/400 expects both a user ID and password from the requester for the conversation. To allow a conversation only if both a user ID and password are sent, DB2 for OS/400 must be set up with SECURELOC(*NO) and a default user profile must not be specified for the communication subsystem. The password is validated when the conversation is established and is ignored for any subsequent uses of that conversation.

Note: DB2 for OS/400 accepts only passwords whose alphabetic characters are in uppercase.

Object-Related Security: A DB2 for OS/400 AS must secure its SQL objects and relational database to ensure proper authorization when users access the AS's distributed relational database programs. This is done by using normal AS/400 commands to identify users and specify what each user is allowed to do with an object. You can use either the CL Grant and Revoke Object Authority commands (GRTOBJAUT and RVKOBJAUT) or the SQL GRANT and REVOKE statements to grant and revoke a user's authority to relational database objects. The SQL GRANT and REVOKE statements operate only on packages, tables, and views. In some cases, it is necessary to use GRTOBJAUT or RVKOBJAUT to authorize users to other objects, such as collections and programs. Table 21 on page 239 summarizes the various SQL objects and their default security values after creation by AR users.

Table 21. *Default Security Values for SQL Created Objects*

Object	Object Authority for Owner	Object Authority *Public
Collection	*ALL	*CHANGE
Journal	*ALL	*CHANGE
Journal Receiver	*ALL	*CHANGE
Dictionary Objects (LFs)	*OBJOPR, *OBJMGT, *OBJEXIST	*EXCLUDE
Dictionary Objects (PFs)	*OBJOPR, *OBJMGT, *OBJEXIST	*READ
Catalog LFs and Views	*OBJOPR, *OBJMGT, *OBJEXIST	*OPER
Data Dictionary	*ALL	*CHANGE
User Tables	*ALL	*CHANGE
User Views	*OBJOPR, *OBJMGT, *OBJEXIST	*OPER
User Indexes	*OBJOPR, *OBJMGT, *OBJEXIST	*OPER

Notes:

- This information applies to versions earlier than OS/400 Version 3.
- Public Authority assumes QCRTAUT = *CHANGE.

In a production environment, the end user executing the SQL statements should not have default access to any of the objects on the AS. However, an AR programmer would require a higher level of security access to the AS. In the next section we discuss security considerations in a production environment for the AR programmer and end user.

Note: The reader should be familiar with object authority (*OBJMGT, *OBJOPR, *OBJEXIST and so on) and data authority (*READ, *UPDATE, *ADD, DELETE) concepts. For complete security information, refer to the *AS/400: Security Reference* or the upcoming security redbook, *An Implementation Guide for AS/400 Security and Auditing* .

8.2.5.1 User Authority

Authority to the Collection: The end user must have *USE authority to perform all functions on objects in the collection to which the user is authorized. *USE authority does not allow the user to create objects in a collection.

Creating Objects: Typically, the AR's end user would not need authority to create objects in a collection. Refer to 8.2.5.3, "Programmer Authority" on page 241 for additional details.

Creating Views: The same considerations apply as for creating objects.

Tables: The end user needs specific data rights for each of the functions (SELECT, INSERT, DELETE, UPDATE) in addition to operational rights (*OBJOPR) to the table. *We recommend that users be granted authority to tables only through views.* This would require removal of operational rights to the table for user *PUBLIC. This should be performed before any views are created; otherwise public access for all previously created views will be lost. Further, we recommend that *PUBLIC *have only select capability* to any view.

Views: In versions earlier than DB2 for OS/400 Version 3, data rights for SELECT, INSERT, UPDATE, and DELETE on a view are stored with the table not the view. Data rights for a view are assigned by providing only *OBJOPR on the view itself. For example, if a user is given the data right to read from a table, that user will automatically have the same authorities for all of the defined views if the views have object operational rights for that user. For the OS/400 Version 3 implementation of data rights on views, please refer to the publication *DB2/400 SQL Programming Version 3*.

Note: Authorities for a table and its defined views cannot conflict.

8.2.5.2 SQL Applications

The authority access granted to the AR user that is executing the SQL statements depends on whether the SQL statement is static or dynamic. *Static* SQL statements are embedded in the application. *Dynamic* SQL statements are constructed at program run time. Interactive SQL is an example of a dynamic SQL program.

- For static statements, authority is checked against the profile of the owner of the program (package) containing the SQL statement when running in the *SQL naming mode, or against the profile of the person running the program when running in the *SYS naming mode. See 14.3.1, "Compile/Binding" on page 443 for more information about how to specify *SYS or *SQL naming modes when creating SQL packages on the DB2 for OS/400.

  Note: *SYS can only be used against a DB2 for OS/400 server.

- For dynamic or interactive statements, authority is checked against the profile of the person running the program or processing the statement.

  Note: The DYNUSRPRF(*OWNER) option on the AS/400 Version 2 Release 3 CRTSQLxxx command allows the user to adopt the package owner's authority for all dynamic SQL statements in the package as well. Currently, this option is not supported by DB2 for MVS/ESA, SQL/DS, DB2 for OS/2, DB2 for AIX, or DB2 for OS/400 before Version 2 Release 3.

An end user will need to access distributed databases using static SQL (package) and dynamic/interactive SQL (end user tools). This access requires a flexible security scheme that varies with the type of activity performed. SQL packages created on the AS/400 with *SQL naming mode provide the end user with the authority rights of the package owner during the application process. When the user exits the program, however, access to the same data using interactive SQL or user tools that generate remote SQL statements is limited to the private authorities granted the user by the AS/400 security administrator.

8.2.5.3 Programmer Authority

Application development in a DRDA environment requires that the programmer have the necessary security access to create objects in collections on the AS. For versions earlier than DB2 for OS/400 Version 3 and in an unlike environment, we recommend that SQL objects be created in AS/400 collections, not standard libraries. A library created with the Create Library command (CRTLIB) does not have the catalog tables that a programmer might have to access. With DB2 for OS/400 Version 3, a systemwide catalog is provided in the QSYS2 library.

Programmers also need access to objects to test and debug their applications requiring the same security privileges as the end users. In this section we discuss the appropriate level of security for SQL objects that the programmer needs to create and delete (drop) SQL packages, tables, indexes, and views on the DB2 for OS/400 AS.

Creating Objects: To enable a programmer to add and remove objects in a collection, *CHANGE authority must be granted to

- The data dictionary (*DTADCT) object in the collection with the same name as the collection.
- The collection itself.

Creating Indexes: The programmer must have operational and management rights (*OBJOPR and *OBJMGT) to the table upon which the index will be created in addition to the privileges mentioned previously.

Creating Views: The programmer must have *OBJOPR rights to the table upon which the view will be created in addition to the privileges mentioned previously.

Authority on an SQL Catalog: An SQL catalog consists of a set of views and logical files that contain information about tables, views, packages, and indexes in a collection. If an object is deleted, created, or moved in or out of the collection or if ownership changes, the catalog is updated. For more information about the names of the views contained in an SQL catalog, refer to the *SAA SQL/400 Reference* or *DB2/400 SQL Reference Version 3*. This information is very important to the programmer and will assist with SQL object management in remote collections.

A programmer requires *OBJOPR authority to the views and logical files in the catalog. *READ authority also has to be granted to the underlying physical files that reside in the collection that are part of the catalog facility. There are 17 of these files, named QIDCTxxx (where xxx varies). Only the Grant and Revoke Object Authority commands (GRTOBJAUT and RVKOBJAUT) can be used to change authority for a programmer to perform SELECT statements on system catalog tables.

8.2.6 DB2 for OS/400 Application Environment

In our scenario the DB2 for OS/400 AS, RCAS400, on system SCHASM02 represents the Minnesota regional office, and San Jose SJAS400 on system SJAS400A represents the San Jose regional office. Both are servers for all other platforms. In this section, we discuss creating our application environment when DB2 for OS/400 is a server. To set up the environment the following areas must be addressed:

1. User profiles

2. Collections

3. Authorities on the collections and packages (to avoid a security exposure and data corruption)

8.2.6.1 Considerations

First we have to take into account these major differences between DB2 for OS/400 and the other platforms:

- SQL statements with unqualified table names use the name of the package owner to address the collection where the SQL objects exist. For instance, a SELECT * FROM PART_MAST staement in package DRDASU2 owned by DRDAX5 would require table PART_MAST in collection DRDAX5.

  Note: Collection is also called *qualifier* or *authorization ID* on other platforms.

- For DB2 for OS/2 and DB2 for AIX requesters, packages and tables should be in the same collection. If you have to circumvent this, please see item number 4 on page 243 under 8.2.6.2, "Approaches."

- Duplicate object names are not allowed in a single collection on DB2 for OS/400 because a collection on DB2 for OS/400 is an object rather than just a qualifier, as on DB2 for MVS/ESA and SQL/DS. Thus collection DRDAX5 cannot hold package DRDASU2 for user DRDAX1 and package DRDASU2 for user DRDAX2. Anyone creating a new package for the same program could overwrite a package that was created by another requester for this DRDASU2 program.

8.2.6.2 Approaches

There are four different approaches you could use to resolve the differences between the DB2 for OS/400 as a server and other platforms:

1. Keep the collection containing the application tables together with all packages. Qualify each SQL statement and use different packages names for each location.

2. Map *all* incoming requests from an AR to a single user who also creates the packages in a single collection. This would also require different package names for each AS. The mapping could be done by putting in a default user in a communication entry of the communication subsystem (usually QCMN).
   This would cause a security exposure because all requesters would share one user and could corrupt the packages of other requesters. In addition, you would run with conversation level security(NONE).

3. A specific user (DRDAX5) creates packages and database tables in a unique collection on every requester location. Because duplicate names are not supported in a single collection on DB2 for OS/400, packages from other locations must have different names. The package name is determined by the user at bind time. Unqualified SQL statements would use DRDAX5 (the package owner) as the collection qualifier. Each AR's SQL packages would use collection DRDAX5 to locate SQL objects.

4. Keep SQL packages in location-specific collections and keep the application tables in another collection. DB2 for MVS/ESA, SQL/DS, and DB2 for OS/400 users specify a *default* collection ID during package creation. For DB2 for OS/2 and DB2 for AIX users, the DB2 for OS/400 administrator is required to change the ownership of those packages to the user with the name of the central collection (DRDAX5). This enables those users to execute their packages against the central database, as the package owner is used to qualify the table names.

8.2.6.3 Implementation

For our scenario we chose approach number 3 for the following reasons:

- Security can be assured.

- Access can be through unqualified table names.

- It required no change to our existing application code (at all requester locations).

The DB2 for OS/400 server and each requester will have the same administrator and multiple end users. The administrator is the person who has the right to create packages on each location. In our scenario we implemented the administrator and two end users. To implement central regional databases RCAS400 and SJAS400, we created the following application environment on our DB2 for OS/400 servers (RCAS400 on system SCHASM02 and SJAS400 on system SJAS400A):

User Profiles

- User profile DRDAX5 represents the database administrator. It owns the DRDAX5 collection, which holds the database tables, as well as each AR's SQL packages. It is also responsible for configuring connections and managing the application environment.

- Its user class is *PGMR.

- It has special authorities, *JOBCTL, and *SERVICE, to enable it to perform problem determination on the DRDA jobs and the communication links as well.

Figure 120 shows the most important parameters of the database administrator user profile.

```
User profile . . . . . . . . . . . . . . . . :   DRDAX5
Password.... . . . . . . . . . . . . . . . :   ABCXYZ
Status . . . . . . . . . . . . . . . . . . :   *ENABLED
User class . . . . . . . . . . . . . . . . :   *PGMR
Special authority  . . . . . . . . . . . . :   *JOBCTL
                                                *SERVICE
*SPLCTL
Current library  . . . . . . . . . . . . . :   DRDAX5
```

Figure 120. *Database Administrator User Profile*

Note: In fact this "administrator" must carry the name of collection DRDAX5, so it can be used by the requesters to default to the unqualified table names we used in our application.

- User profile DRDAX1 for each AR location end user. Those end users can only execute packages. They get access to the database tables in collection DRDAX5 through the DRDASU2 package that they are executing.
  Their user class is *USER. Figure 121 shows the most important parameters of the location user profile.

```
User profile . . . . . . . . . . . . . . . . :   DRDAX1
Password.... . . . . . . . . . . . . . . . :   REDBOOK
Status . . . . . . . . . . . . . . . . . . :   *ENABLED
User class . . . . . . . . . . . . . . . . :   *USER
Special authority  . . . . . . . . . . . . :   *NONE
Group profile  . .. . . . . . . . . . . . . :   *NONE
Owner  . . . . . . . . . . . . . . . . . . :   *USER
Group authority  . . . . . . . . . . . . . :   *NONE
```

Figure 121. *Location User Profile*

Collections

1. The main collection, DRDAX5, contains the application database tables and packages for our requesters. It was created by user DRDAX5 at all locations and therefore is owned by DRDAX5. The public authority is *USE. This authority is enough to have access to the database tables for our application, and it prevents users from adding or changing anything in the collection.

   Figure 122 shows the authorities on collection DRDAX5 before DB2 for OS/400 Version 3.

```
Object . . . . . . . :     DRDAX5          Object type . . :    *LIB
   Library  . . . . . :     QSYS            Owner  . . . . . :    DRDAX5

                 Object     ----Object-----  ----------Data-----------
   User          Authority  Opr  Mgt  Exist  Read  Add  Update  Delete
   DRDAX5        *ALL        X    X    X       X     X      X      X
   *PUBLIC       *USE        X                 X
```

Figure 122. Authorities on Collection DRDAX5

   The value for the public depends on the system value, QCRTAUT (Create default public authority), if not explicitly mentioned at creation time. In our case QCRTAUT had the value *CHANGE. Therefore we changed the *PUBLIC authority by using the GRTOBJAUT command.

2. A collection NULLID is required for DB2 for OS/2 and DB2 for AIX users for their initial connection. It was created with public authority *CHANGE.

Database Tables: The application tables were created manually using ISQL CREATE TABLE statements. One of the application samples performs multiple-site update. Therefore public authority was set to *USE (read-only), and explicit authority *CHANGE was granted to the various end users of our application.

Figure 123 on page 246 shows the authorities on the database tables in the DRDAX5 collection.

```
Object . . . . . . . :    PART_MAST        Object type . . :    *FILE
    Library  . . . . . :    DRDAX5           Owner  . . . . :     DRDAX5

                  Object    ----Object-----  ----------Data-----------
    User          Authority Opr  Mgt  Exist  Read  Add  Update  Delete
    DRDAX5        *ALL        X    X    X      X     X     X       X
    DRDAX1        *CHANGE     X                X     X     X       X
    DRDAX2        *CHANGE     X                X     X     X       X
    *PUBLIC       *USE        X                X
```

Figure 123. Authorities on the PART_MAST Database Table

8.2.7 Problem Determination

Figure 124 shows the major OS/400 components for DB2 for OS/400 as an AS. This figure is almost identical to Figure 116 on page 229. There are two different components.

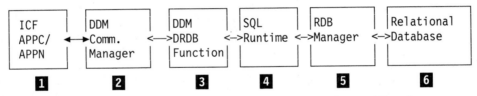

Figure 124. Components of DB2 for OS/400 Distributed Relational Database

1 ICF is the interface between the DDM Communications Manager and APPC/APPN.

2 DDM Communications Manager is used to send and receive DDM data streams to and from the AR. This manager is also responsible for starting and ending conversations and ensuring that conversations are shared when possible.

3 DDM Distributed Relational Database Function on the AS receives DDM commands, converts them into corresponding SQL operations, and sends them to SQL Runtime support.

4 SQL Runtime support on the AR executes the received SQL statements.

5 RDB Manager accesses the data and performs character translation using CCSIDs.

6 Relational Database contains our data.

When DB2 for OS/400 acts as an AS, application execution of the SQL statement in a package is the primary focal point for problem determination.

SQL packages define the access plan to the database of the remote user. The procedure described below will help the AR application programmer determine whether the application executes correctly and the access to the database is optimized.

You can evaluate the structure and performance of the SQL statements in a package using information messages put in the JOBLOG by the RDB manager. The database manager issues the message for a program when running in debug mode. The DB2 for OS/400 AS recognizes a special TPN that causes the AS to send a message to the system operator and then wait for a reply. This allows the server job to be put in debug mode.

The following steps stop the DB2 for OS/400 server job and start it in debug mode.

Note: The steps require that a user ID or user ID and password combination be sent on the connection, depending on the conversation security level.

1. Specify QCNTSRVC as the TPN at the AR

   - DB2 for OS/400 AR specifies QCNTSRVC on the TNSPGM of the Change RDB Directory Entry (CHGRBDIRE) command for the DB2 for OS/400 server location.

   - SQL/DS VM AR changes the UCOMDIR NAMES file and specifies QCNTSRVC in the TPN tag. Then issue SET COMDIR RELOAD USER.

   - DB2 AR uses SPUFI to update the SYSIBM.SYSLOCATIONS table to specify QCNTSRVC in the LINKATTR column for the row containing the RDB_NAME of the DB2 for OS/400 AS. DB2 for MVS/ESA may have to be brought down for this to take effect.

   - DB2 for OS/2 DDCS/2 AR puts "D8,CNTSRVC" in the *Parameters* field of the Database Connection Services Directory entry for the AS/400.

   - DB2 for AIX DDCS/6000 AR puts the following value in the REMOTE TRANSACTION PROGRAM name (RTPN) field of the LU6.2 CPI Communications Side Information Profile for the DB2/400 application server: D8C3D5E3E2D9E5C3. This is the EBCDIC representation of QCNTSRVC. The user must be logged on as root to change this value.

2. When DB2 for OS/400 AS receives a TPN of QCNTSRVC, it sends a CPF9188 message to the system console (message queue QSYSOPR) and waits for a *G* reply to the message (the *G* means go or continue).

3. Before entering *G*, find the name of the server job by selecting HELP on the CPF9188 message. Issue a STRSRVJOB command for the server job.

4. Enter STRDBG to start the debug.

5. Reply to the CPF9188 message with a *G*.

After the application has run, you can view the JOBLOG for the server job to see SQL the debug messages. The JOBLOG contains messages about how each SQL statement ran in the job. For each SQL statement there is an indication of the SQLCODE. You can also evaluate the structure and performance of the given SQL statements in the job by using the performance information messages that are also placed in the JOBLOG when running in debug mode. Chapter 14 of the *SAA SQL/400 Programmers Guide* provides a list of the messages that the database manager can send.

Chapter 9. VM and VSE Platforms

In this chapter we discuss the tasks involved to enable SQL/DS for VM to perform the DRDA AR functions. We also discuss the tasks involved to enable SQL/DS for VM and SQL/DS for VSE to perform the DRDA AS functions.

All the tasks completed for the VM and VSE platforms were carried out at the ITSO located in Boeblingen.

9.1 VM AR

In this section we present the definitions and our suggestions for setting up an SQL/DS DRDA environment under a VM operating system. VSE currently supports the AS role only, so in this section we deal with the AR definitions for VM only. A previous knowledge of DRDA is assumed. For more information about VM AR refer to the standard literature and the following two publications:

- *Setup and Usage of SQL/DS in a DRDA Environment*
- *DRDA Client/Server Application Scenarios for VM and VSE*

In our environment, VM is an AR to

- DB2 for MVS/ESA
- DB2 for OS/400
- SQL/DS for VSE
- DB2 for OS/2
- DB2 for AIX

9.1.1 Operating System Definitions

The operating system used was VM/ESA 1.2 with the required software for DRDA implementation, that is, SQL/DS 3.4, VTAM 3.4, and AVS/VM.

9.1.1.1 Database and AVS Machines

The SQL/DS database and AVS machines are exactly the same as those shown for the AS. Please see Figure 132 on page 265 and Figure 133 on page 266 for their directory entries.

Note: When SQL/DS is an AR *only*, neither a local database machine nor a local database is needed.

9.1.1.2 CMS User Machine

Figure 125 shows the entries for an AR virtual machine.

```
USER SQLUSER AMPS1020 8M 16M G
  ACCOUNT SQLUSER
  OPTION MAXCON 26
  IUCV ANY
  IPL   CMS
  CONSOLE 009 3215
  SPOOL   00C 2540 READER *
  SPOOL   00D 2540 PUNCH A
  SPOOL   00E 1403
  LINK MAINT    190  190 RR
  LINK MAINT    19D  19D RR
  LINK MAINT    19E  19E RR
  LINK MAINT    900  900 RR
  LINK MAINT    901  901 RR
  LINK S34VMDB6 195  195 RR
MDISK  191 9345 0232 010 IS9PP2 MW RSQL WSQL MSQL
```

Figure 125. USER DIRECT Entry for a VM AR

9.1.1.3 CMS COMDIR Entries

To communicate with an AS, the communications directory (COMDIR) must be defined. There are two types of COMDIR: the SCOMDIR (valid for the whole system), and the UCOMDIR (for the user only). We used the UCOMDIR shown in Figure 126 on page 251.

```
:NICK.CENTDB2
            :TPN."6DB
            :LUNAME.IPFA2GL4 SCLUDB41
            :MODENAME.IBMRDBM
            :SECURITY.PGM
            :USERID.DRDAX1
            :PASSWORD.REDBOOk
            :DBNAME.CENTDB2    <====== DB2 database
:NICK.SJ2SMPL
            :TPN.DB22TPN
            :LUNAME.IPFA2GL4 SC02130I
            :MODENAME.IBMRDBM
            :SECURITY.PGM
            :USERID.USERID
            :PASSWORD.PASSWORD
            :DBNAME.SJ2SMPL     <====== DB2 for OS/2 database
:NICK.SJ6SMPL
            :TPN.DB26TPN
            :LUNAME.IPFA2GL4 SC02131I
            :MODENAME.IBMRDBM
            :SECURITY.PGM
            :USERID.db2v2
            :PASSWORD.db2v2
            :DBNAME.SJ6SMPL     <====== DB2 for AIX database
:NICK.SJAS400
            :TPN."6DB
            :LUNAME.IPFA2GL4 SC02132I
            :MODENAME.IBMRDBM
            :SECURITY.PGM
            :USERID.DRDAX1
            :PASSWORD.REDBOOK
            :DBNAME.SJAS400     <====== DB2 for OS/400 database
:NICK.S34VSDB1
            :TPN.TPN1
            :LUNAME.IPFA2GL4 IPFA21CD
            :MODENAME.IBMRDBM
            :SECURITY.PGM
            :USERID.DBREQ2
            :PASSWORD.SSMC1
            :DBNAME.S34VSDB1  <====== VSE SQL/DS database
```

Figure 126. UCOMDIR NAMES File with AS Definitions

9.1.2 Network Definitions

Establishing connections between locations across a multiple-network environment requires agreement among locations on many coordinated tasks; a previous knowledge of SNA connectivity is assumed and is not covered here.

Our environment involved two VTAM domains, as shown in Figure 25 on page 77, to pass requests through the IBM backbone network.

The definitions for these domains are essentially the same specified to set up the AS environment. Please refer to "Network Definitions" on page 267 for more details.

Because the remote servers were located in a different network than the AR, we defined the remote network IDs and their related cross-domain resources as shown in Figure 127.

```
          VBUILD TYPE=CDRSC
          NETWORK NETID=USIBMSC
SCLUDB3A  CDRSC
SCLUDB41  CDRSC
SCHASM01  CDRSC
SCHASM02  CDRSC
```

Figure 127. CDRSDRDA VTAMLST

9.1.3 Database Definitions

An existing SQL/DS can be used by installing DRDA AR support and setting the SQLINIT parameter PROTOCOL to AUTO.

9.1.3.1 Installing DRDA Code

Installing the DRDA code is an optional customization step after the installation of the base code. The DRDA code can be installed (and removed) by using the SQL/DS ARISDBMA EXEC for AS support, AR support, or both. The increased processing required for DRDA operations requires additional storage, so the machine's virtual storage may have to be increased.

For the use of the ARISDBMA EXEC please refer to Figure 138 on page 270 and the related description.

9.1.3.2 SQLINIT

The SQLINIT EXEC initializes a user machine for SQL/DS access. With this EXEC, users specify the default database they want to access and any special options to be used for the access. If users want to access another database that is not the default established through SQLINIT, they can issue the SQL command CONNECT to access the other database.

The PROTOCOL parameter in the SQLINIT EXEC enables SQL/DS for DRDA and specifies which database access protocol is used when communicating with the AS. Valid values are

- SQLDS
- AUTO
- DRDA

SQLDS specifies that only private protocol is be used. If this option is specified, the AR connects only to an SQL/DS AS because the SQL/DS-only protocol is used. SQLDS is the default value.

AUTO specifies that the AR is to use private flow when communicating with an SQL/DS AS and DRDA when communicating with a non-SQL/DS AS.

DRDA specifies that the AR has to use the DRDA flow with both SQL/DS and non-SQL/DS ASs.

9.1.3.3 ISQL on a Non-SQL/DS AS

Before using ISQL on a remote AS, you must first execute the steps listed below to create the ISQL package in the remote AS. You may also have to perform these steps if the remote system is another SQL/DS and the ISQL function is not present, either because it was not installed or has been removed. *Use of ISQL is not currently supported on the AS/400.*

First, you need to preprocess the DBS utility package on the non-SQL/DS AS and create the SQLDBA.DBSOPTIONS table on that AS. You can do this on the SQL/DS AR once you have obtained the necessary program bind and table creation privileges for your authorization ID on the target AS.

Do the following from an SQL/DS AR:

1. Establish the non-SQL/DS AS as the default AS and run the SQLINIT EXEC against it.

2. Link to the database machine's service disk, by entering

    ```
    LINK machid 193 193 RR
    ```

3. Access the service disk, by entering

    ```
    ACC 193 V
    ```

4. Preprocess the DBS utility, by entering

```
SQLPREP ASM PP (PREP=SQLDBA.ARIDSQL,BLOCK,ISOL(CS),NOPR,NOPU,
    CTOKEN(NO),ERROR) IN (ARIDSQLP MACRO V)
```

5. Create the SQLDBA.DBSOPTIONS table, by entering the following DBS utility commands:

```
SET ERRORMODE CONTINUE;

CREATE TABLE SQLDBA.DBSOPTIONS
  (SQLOPTION VAR CHAR  (18) NOT NULL,
   VALUE     VAR CHAR  (18) NOT NULL);

CREATE UNIQUE INDEX SQLDBA.DBSINDEX
  ON SQLDBA.DBSOPTIONS (SQLOPTION,VALUE);

INSERT INTO SQLDBA.DBSOPTIONS
  VALUES ('RELEASE','3.4.0');

COMMIT WORK;
```

SQLDBA.DBSOPTIONS tables

When using DB2 for OS/2 as a remote AS, you do not have to manually create the SQLDBA.DBSOPTIONS tables. You can execute the following command from an OS/2 command line on the remote AS:

sqldbsu *database_name*

where *database_name* is the name of the target database on the DB2 for OS/2 AS.

Do the following from an SQL/DS AR to load ISQL:

1. Run the SQLINIT EXEC to establish the non-SQL/DS AS as the default AS.

2. Link to the database machine's service disk by entering

```
LINK machid 193 193 RR
```

3. Access the service disk by entering

```
ACC 193 V
```

4. Issue the following CMS command:

```
FILEDEF ARIISQLM DISK ARIISQLM MACRO V
```

5. Issue the following DBS utility command to reload ISQL:

```
RELOAD PACKAGE (SQLDBA.ARIISQL) REPLACE KEEP INFILE (ARIISQLM);
```

6. Create the SQLDBA.ROUTINE table and any other *userID*.ROUTINE tables that you want.

```
 ┌─── SQLDBA.ROUTINE table ──────────────────────────────────────────

  When using DB2 for OS/2 as a remote AS, you do not have to manually create
  SQLDBA.ROUTINE tables.  You can execute the following command from an OS/2
  command line on the remote AS:

    isql database_name

  where database_name is the name of the target database on the DB2 for OS/2 AS.

```

For more information about the DBS utility and ISQL on a non-SQL/DS AS, please see *SQL/DS System Administration for IBM VM Systems* and *DB2 For OS/2 Installation and Operation Guide*.

9.1.4 DBSU

See 9.1.3.3, "ISQL on a Non-SQL/DS AS" on page 253 for the customization steps required to run DBSU against a non-SQL/DS AS. These steps are not required when accessing an SQL/DS AS. Figure 128 on page 256 shows an ISQL session acessing a remote non-SQL/DS AS.

```
Ready; T=0.01/0.01 11:13:26
isql
ARI0659I Line-edit symbols reset:
        LINEND=# LINEDEL=OFF CHARDEL=OFF
        ESCAPE=OFF TABCHAR=OFF
ARI0662I EMSG function value reset to ON.
ARI0320I The default server name is DBSRV4D.
ARI0499I Warning: Status Shared Segment is not loaded.
        Return Code = 4
ARI7716I User DBADMIN connected to server DBSRV4D. 1
ARI7399I The ISQL default profile values are in effect.
ARI7079I ISQL initialization complete.
ARI7080A Please enter an ISQL command or an SQL statement.
select name  from sysibm.systables 2
ARI7960I The query cost estimate for this SELECT statement is 1.
select * from syscat.tables 3
ARI7960I The query cost estimate for this SELECT statement is 1.
exit
ARI7601I ISQL ended normally on your request.
ARI0657I EMSG function value restored to TEXT.
ARI0660I Line-edit symbols restored:
        LINEND=# LINEDEL=¢ CHARDEL=@
        ESCAPE=" TABCHAR=ON
Ready; T=0.48/0.67 11:14:33
```

Figure 128. An ISQL Session against Remote Non-SQL/DS ASs

In Figure 128:

1 In our case **DBSRV4D** is a DB2 for OS/2 database server.

2 SYSIBM.SYSTABLES are DB2 for OS/2 base tables, not SQL/DS tables.

3 SYSCAT.TABLES is the DB2 for OS/2 catalog table as described in *DB2 Administration Guide for common servers*.

9.1.5 Security Requirements

When a remote system sends a request to SQL/DS for VM, it must satisfy the security requirements of the AR, the AS, and the network. You can categorize these requirements as follows:

- Selecting end-user names
- Network security parameters

- Database manager security

- Security subsystems

9.1.5.1 Selecting End-User Names

The end-user ID is a one- to eight-character string that must be unique in a particular operating system. It is difficult to have unique userids throughout an SNA network. To eliminate potential userid conflicts, SQL/DS for VM supports end-user name translation. This function is optional; you can activate it when required.

Inbound translation and outbound translation are supported. Outbound name translation is performed for the AR through the CMS COMDIR. The related entry in the COMDIR must specify :security.PGM. The userid specified for :userid and the password specified for :password in the COMDIR entry are communicated to the AS.

Figure 129 illustrates how outbound translation works. The user with userid DB2 on the local system is mapped to userid DB2V2 when he or she connects to the SJ6SMPL AS.

```
:NICK.SJ6SMPL
              :TPN.DB26TPN
              :LUNAME.IPFA2GL4 SC02131I
              :MODENAME.IBMRDBM
              :SECURITY.PGM
              :USERID.DB2V2
              :PASSWORD.DB2V2
              :DBNAME.SJ6SMPL    <====== DB2 for AIX database
```

Figure 129. Outbound Name Translation Using COMDIR

9.1.5.2 Network Security

The AR provides the end userid, the password (optionally), and the required LU.

DRDA provides three major network security features:

- Session-Level Security
  Controlled by the VERIFY parameter on the VTAM APPL statement

- Conversation-Level Security
  Specified in the CMS COMDIR

- Data Encryption
  Possible with VTAM 3.4 and later versions on MVS only.

DB2 for MVS/ESA security controls are defined by using VTAM parameters and rules that are recorded in the communications database (CDB) tables.

9.1.5.3 Session-Level Security

Session-level security is implemented through VTAM. It is also referred to as *partner LU verification*. If you want the partner LU (the LU that represents the AR) to be checked by RACF during session BIND processing, specify VERIFY=REQUIRED in the APPL definition for SQL/DS for VM. If you do not want to use this level of security, specify VERIFY=NONE.

9.1.5.4 Conversation-Level Security

You have to record the conversation-level security requirements of each AS in the AR's COMDIR. The AS dictates the security requirements.

The possible SNA conversation security levels you can specify for the COMDIR's SECURITY tag are

- SECURITY=SAME

  The connection is routed to the server using an already verified userid. The password is not sent. This applies when :SECURITY.SAME is specified in the COMDIR. In this case outbound name translation is not performed. The CMS user's logon userid is sent to the AS.

- SECURITY=PGM

  The connecting AR sends both a userid and password to the AS. This applies when :SECURITY.PGM is specified in the COMDIR. In this case outbound name translation is performed.

  The password can be specified in the password tag in the COMDIR or in the control program system directory by using the APPCPASS directory statement. Use the APPCPASS directory statement if you want to maximize password security. If there is no password in the COMDIR entry, the system directory (VM) is searched for an APPCPASS statement.

VM provides a flexible method of maximizing userid and password security. In the COMDIR you have the following options:

- Userid and password are specified.
  In this case no APPCPASS statement is necessary.

- Userid and password are both blank.
  In this case the userid and password are to be defined by the APPCPASS statement.

- Userid is blank.
  In this case the userid is to be defined by the APPCPASS statement.

- Password is blank.
  In this case the password is to be defined by the APPCPASS statement.

Figure 130 illustrates the case where the userid is stored in the COMDIR and the password is stored in the system (VM) directory.

```
:NICK.SJ6SMPL
            :TPN.DB26TPN
            :LUNAME.IPFA2GL4 SCO2131I
            :MODENAME.IBMRDBM
            :SECURITY.PGM
            :USERID.DB2V2
            :password.
            :DBNAME.SJ6SMPL
```

Figure 130. *COMDIR without a Password*

When SECURITY=PGM, APPC/VM reads the userid and password from the COMDIR; if one or both of tags are blanks, it searches through the system (VM) directory for the missing information.

The APPCPASS statement in our sample would look this:

   APPCPASS IPFA2GL4 SC02331I DB2V2 DB2V2PW

APPC/VM gets password DB2V2PW when it is requesting a connection through AVS gateway IPFA2GL4, partner LU SC02131I, and user DB2V2.

For more on security, please read "Setting up the AR in a VM Environment" in the *DRDA Connectivity Guide*.

For more on the AGW ADD USER command, please refer to *VM Connectivity Planning, Administration, and Operation*.

9.1.5.5 Database Manager Security

One way of controling access to each AS is through outbound name translation at the AR. However, the best way is to do come-from checking and inbound translation at the server because the COMDIR and the AR can be easily modified by the end user.
Other methods of controlling access to the AS are

- Application preprocessing

The remote application is preprocessed to a particular AS by using the SQL/DS for VM SQLPREP EXEC or the Database Service Utility (DBSU) RELOAD PACKAGE command. SQL/DS for VM does not restrict these functions.

When the package is reloaded, the owner of the package is assigned the run privilege. The userid must be known at the remote side (AS). The database administrator can reload a package as well.

In addition the AS may require additional privileges before the application program can be executed.

- Executing remote applications

    To run a remote application, the end user must have authority to run the related application (plan) at the remote AS. The plan owner is automatically granted the authority to run the plan. The other users must be granted the authority through the DB2 GRANT EXECUTE statement.

    The end users who are granted the authority to execute an application are automatically granted the authority to execute each statement contained in the application program. Thus the end users do not need any other privileges, such as table privileges.

9.1.5.6 Security Subsystem Use

SQL/DS for VM uses a security subsystem like RACF to check the userid and the password. As an AR, SQL/DS for VM does not have any direct calls to the security subsystem.

The security subsystem is indirectly used to identify the end user (userid and password) when end users are attached using CICS or VM.

VTAM can also invoke the security subsystem if you use SNA session-level security.

9.1.6 Common Errors

Typical error conditions you may encounter are:

- Wrong password or ID

    Each time a connection request is sent with a wrong password or a wrong userid, a communication error is received reporting SQLCODE = −30080 and SQLSTATE = 58019.

- Invalid TPN entry in the COMDIR

    If you specify an invalid TPN in the COMDIR, you will receive an SQLCODE = −940 and SQLSTATE = 52005 when you issue a CONNECT against that AS.

The same error message is received if the default TPN (X′07F6C4C2′) is misspelled. The default TPN is normally used by DB2 for MVS/ESA and DB2 for OS/400 servers; VM and VSE servers can specify a different TPN. The default TPN must be entered as the hexadecimal representation and appears as :TPN."6DB in the COMDIR, as X′07′ is an unprintable character.

To enter the default TPN in hexadecimal mode, you have to XEDIT the COMDIR file (SCOMDIR or UCOMDIR, as the case may be) as follows:

1. Enter XEDIT for the COMDIR file

2. Make the TPN tag line the current line

3. From the command line, issue SET VERIFY ON HEX 1 72

4. Enter hex values 07F6C4C2 in the appropriate columns

5. From the command line, issue SET VERIFY 1 72 and...

6. FILE

- SQLPREP error

When preprocessing the DBS utility against a DB2 for OS/2 AS, you might receive the error shown in Figure 131 on page 262.

```
ARIO7171 Start SQLPREP EXEC: 09/20/95 10:37:18 DST.
ARIO7131 Preprocessor ARIPRPA
         called with the following parameters:
PREP=SQLDBA.ARIDSQL,BLOCK,ISOL(CS),NOPR,NOPU,CTOKEN(NO),ERROR

ARIO512E An error has occurred.
         SQLCODE -4930 is received from the AS.
         Product  = OS/2 EE DB  Level = V02R01M0
         SQLERRP  = SQLJPSEM
         SQLSTATE =
         SQLERRD(1) = -12  SQLERRD(2) = 0  SQLERRD(3) = 0
         SQLERRD(4) = 0  SQLERRD(5) = 0 SQLERRD(6) = 0
         SQLWARN0 = ' '  SQLWARN1 = ' '  SQLWARN2 = ' '
         SQLWARN3 = ' '  SQLWARN4 = ' '  SQLWARN5 = ' '
         SQLWARN6 = ' '  SQLWARN7 = ' '  SQLWARN8 = ' '
         SQLWARN9 = ' '  SQLWARNA = ' '
         SQLERRM  = SQLERROR CONTINUE (DRDA Bind Option BNDC
                    RTCTL(BNDERRALW))
ARIO5471 - You did not declare any host variables in ARIDSQL.
ARIO5861 - Preprocessing ended with 1 errors and
         - 0 warnings.
ARIO5981 - The AS restored the package for
         - ARIDSQL or did not produce the package.

ARIO710E Errors occurred during SQLPREP EXEC processing.
ARIO7961 End SQLPREP EXEC: 09/20/95 10:37:32 DST
```

Figure 131. SQLPREP against a DB2 for OS/2 AS with ERROR Parameter

Remove the ERROR option from the SQLPREP command to execute this step successfully.

9.2 VM and VSE ASs

In this section we present the definitions and our suggestions for setting up an SQL/DS DRDA AS under both the VM and VSE operating systems. A previous knowledge of DRDA concepts is assumed.

For more information about VM and VSE as ASs, please refer to the DRDA literature and the following two publications:

- *Setup and Usage of SQL/DS in a DRDA Environment*
- *DRDA Client/Server Application Scenarios for VM and VSE*

In our environment, VM and VSE are ASs for applications running in the following RDBMS environments:

- DB2 for MVS/ESA
- DB2 for OS/400
- DB2 for AIX
- DB2 for OS/2
- SQL/DS for VM
- SQL/DS for VSE

When either VM or VSE are to work as DRDA ASs, the main connectivity topics to be addressed are

- Operating system definitions
- Network definitions
- Database definitions
- Security
- Common errors

The main tasks for implementing SQL/DS as a DRDA AS are described below.

9.2.1 VM AS

In this section we discuss the setup tasks required to enable SQL/DS for VM to perform AS functions to support remote DRDA clients. The tasks are basically the same regardless of the platform of the DRDA clients: to understand the security requirements and to grant RDBMS authorities.

The operating system used was VM/ESA 1.2 with the required software for DRDA implementation, that is, SQL/DS 3.4, VTAM 3.4 and AVS/VM. The tasks you must perform are

- Update control program system directory.
- Add VTAM definitions.
- Add SQL/DS DRDA support code

Establishing connections between locations across a multiple-network environment requires many tasks in project coordination and agreements; a previous knowledge of SNA connectivity is assumed and is not covered here.

In our local environment two VTAM domains were involved. For a better perspective, please refer to Figure 25 on page 77.

In the following paragraphs, we go through the main operating system and SNA definitions needed to get access from ARs to the SQL/DS database acting as the AS.

9.2.2 Operating System Definitions

From an operating system point of view, only the control program system directory has to be considered. The following entries must be present:

- GCS machine
- VTAM machine
- SQL/DS database machine
- AVS machine
- Userid and password for each AR

No special considerations apply to the GCS and VTAM entries.

9.2.3 Database Machine S34VMDB0 Entry (DRDA AS)

Figure 132 on page 265 shows the entry used for the S34VMDB0 virtual machine, which provides the AS function of DRDA.

```
USER S34VMDB0 xxxxx 7M 16M G
   ACCOUNT S34VMDB0
   OPTION MAXCONN 150 ACCT ECMODE
   IUCV *IDENT S34VMDB0 GLOBAL
   IUCV ALLOW
   IPL CMS
   CONSOLE 009 3215 T MAINT
   SPOOL 00C 2540 READER *
   SPOOL 00D 2540 PUNCH A
   SPOOL 00E 1403
   LINK MAINT     190 190 RR
   LINK MAINT     19D 19D RR
   LINK MAINT     19E 19E RR
  MDISK 191 3380 0481 10 IS2MD1 WR RSQL WSQL
  MDISK 193 3380 0094 65 IS2MD1  R RSQL WSQL
  MDISK 195 3380 0223 25 IS2MD1 MR ALL  WSQL MSQL
* DIRECTORY / LOG / DATA
  MDISK 200 3380 0060 34 IS2MD1  R RSQL WSQL
  MDISK 201 3380 1756 08 IS2MD1 MR
  MDISK 202 3380 0704 77 IS2MD1 MR
```

Figure 132. USER DIRECT Entry for the S34VMDB0 AS

The OPTION MAXCONN 150 ACCT ECMODE entry specifies the total number of possible connections to this virtual machine.

The IUCV *IDENT S34VMDB0 GLOBAL statement authorizes the database machine, as a resource owner, to connect to the VM Identify System Service (*IDENT). The name S34VMDB0 specifies the resource that the virtual machine is authorized to identify. This name must match the name of the database specified in the DBNAME parameter during execution of the database generation SQLDBINS EXEC and named in the DBNAME parameter of the SQLSTART EXEC that starts a VM application server. The GLOBAL parameter identifies this database machine as a global resource, which can be accessed from a different processor in the network.

The MDISK definitions we used correspond to the minidisk defaults used in *SQL/DS Installation for IBM VM Systems*:

- MDISK 191 ==> user work disk
- MDISK 193 ==> SQL/DS service disk
- MDISK 195 ==> SQL/DS production disk
- MDISK 200 ==> BDISK database DIRECTORY disk
- MDISK 201 ==> LOGDSK1 database LOG disk
- MDISK 203 ==> DDSK1 database DBEXTENT1 disk.

9.2.3.1 Entry for APPC VTAM Support (AVS)

Figure 133 shows the entry used for the AVSVM virtual machine, which provides the APPC VTAM support.

```
USER AVSVM xxxxx    2M 16M G 64
     ACCOUNT  AVSVM
     IUCV *IDENT GATEANY GATEWAY REVOKE
     IUCV ALLOW
     IUCV ANY
     OPTION COMSRV MAXCONN 20 ECMODE REALTIMER
     IPL      GCS PARM AUTOLOG
     CONSOLE  01F 3215 A MAINT
     SPOOL    00C 2540 READER A
     SPOOL    00D 2540 PUNCH A
     SPOOL    00E 1403
     LINK     GCS    595 595 RR
     LINK     MAINT  190 190 RR
     LINK     MAINT  19D 19D RR
     LINK     MAINT  19E 19E RR
     MDISK 191 3380 1637 0001 IS2VMA  MR    RPW WPW
```

Figure 133. *USER DIRECT Entry for the AVSVM Machine*

AVS is part of the VM operating system and handles communications between VM and non-VM systems in the SNA network.

AVS translates protocols between APPC/VM and APPC/VTAM and enables an APPC program in an SNA network to allocate conversations with global resources (APPC/VM programs).

AVS is a VTAM application that runs with VTAM in a separate virtual machine in the same Group Control System (GCS) group.

The IUCV *IDENT GATEANY GATEWAY REVOKE statement lets the AVS virtual machine connect to the Identify System Service (*IDENT) to identify gateways that are used to access resources in the SNA network. GATEANY lets the AVS virtual machine identify any gateway name.

The IUCV ALLOW statement allows the AVS virtual machine to connect to the database S34VMDB0, which is run by the server machine S34VMDB0 (in our case the control program userid for the database machine and the database name specified at generation time are the same).

9.2.3.2 AGWPROF GCS (for AVS Virtual Machine)

The AGWPROF GCS file (Figure 134) is executed at AVSVM startup time to activate the gateways. We omitted the CNOS commands because all partner LUs are independent, so sessions can be established without further commands. IPFA2GL3 and IPFA2GL4 are two LU 6.2 applications defined in a VTAM major node.

```
Trace 0
'AGW ACTIVATE  GATEWAY IPFA2GL3 GLOBAL'
'AGW ACTIVATE  GATEWAY IPFA2GL4 GLOBAL'
```

Figure 134. *AGWPROF GCS to Activate AVS Gateway*

9.2.3.3 Security Checking

We defined an entry as shown in Figure 135 for each application that has to access the SQL/DS VM database with SECURITY=PGM, that is, the application must specify both userid and password.

```
USER SJUS1 DRDA1A  2M 16M G
    ACCOUNT  1    XXXXXX
    IUCV ANY
```

Figure 135. *USER DIRECT Entry for Incoming AR*

9.2.4 Network Definitions

Figure 136 on page 268 shows the ADJSSCP tables we needed to find destination resources within our own network (DEIBMIPF) as well as in the other participating network (USIBMSC). IPFV2 is the VM SSCP, and IPFV2A is the VSE SSCP. Both SSCPs are connected through a VCTCA. IPF is a third SSCP, connected with the other two through a 3745 communications controller. IPF is also connected with the network in SNI mode to enable DRDA traffic with networks other than DEIBMIPF.

```
        VBUILD TYPE=ADJSSCP
        NETWORK
IPF     ADJCDRM
*
DEIBMIPF NETWORK NETID=DEIBMIPF
*
IPF     ADJCDRM
IPFV2   ADJCDRM
IPFV2A  ADJCDRM
*
```

Figure 136. SSCPDRDA VTAMLST

The IPF2AVS defines two applications, IPFA2GL3 and IPFA2GL4, which are LU 6.2s responsible for communicating with other operating systems (see Figure 137 on page 269). We used IPFA2GL3 for the VM AR to VSE and IPFA2GL4 for the VM AR to DB2 for MVS/ESA, DB2 for OS/2, DB2 for OS/400, and DB2 for AIX.

```
*******************************************************************
IPF2AVS   VBUILD TYPE=APPL
IPFA2GL3 APPL   APPC=YES,                                        X
                AUTHEXIT=YES,                                    X
                AUTOSES=20,                                      X
                DSESLIM=200,                                     X
                DMINWNL=100,                                     X
                DMINWNR=100,                                     X
                EAS=9999,                                        X
                MAXPVT=100K,                                     X
                SECACPT=ALREADYV,                                X
                VERIFY=NONE,                                     X
                VPACING=2,                                       X
                MODETAB=RDSTAB,                                  X
                DLOGMOD=IBMROS2,                                 X
                SYNCLVL=CONFIRM,                                 X
                OPERCNOS=ALLOW,                                  X
                PARSESS=YES
IPFA2GL4 APPL   APPC=YES,                                        X
                AUTHEXIT=YES,                                    X
                AUTOSES=20,                                      X
                DSESLIM=200,                                     X
                DMINWNL=100,                                     X
                DMINWNR=100,                                     X
                EAS=3999,                                        X
                MAXPVT=200K,                                     X
                SECACPT=ALREADYV,                                X
                VERIFY=NONE,                                     X
                VPACING=2,                                       X
                MODETAB=DRDAMOD,                                 X
                DLOGMOD=IBMRDBM,                                 X
                SYNCLVL=CONFIRM,                                 X
                OPERCNOS=ALLOW,                                  X
                PARSESS=YES
```

Figure 137. IPF2AVS VTAMLST

In our project, IPFA2GL4 was the local LU that established sessions and conversations with the following remote partner LUs:

- SCLUDB41   in Poughkeepsie (DB2 for MVS/ESA)

- SJ02130I   in San Jose   (DB2 for OS/2)

- SJ02131I   in San Jose   (DB2 for AIX)

- SC02132I   in San Jose   (DB2 for OS/400)

- SCHASM02   in Rochester   (DB2 for OS/400).

9.2.5 Database Definitions

SQL/DS has no special requirements other than DRDA AS support and setting the startup parameter PROTOCOL to AUTO.

9.2.5.1 Installing DRDA Code

Installing the DRDA code is an optional customization step after the installation of the base code. DRDA can be installed (and removed) by using the ARISDBMA EXEC for SQL/DS ASs, SQL/DS ARs, or both. The increased processing for distributed conversations requires a significant amount of storage, so the virtual storage of the database virtual machine must be increased.

Figure 138 shows the syntax of the ARISDBMA EXEC.

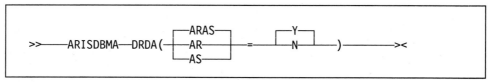

Figure 138. ARISDBMA EXEC Syntax

You can specify the following combinations of parameters:

ARAS=Y	Install the DRDA code for both the AS and the AR (this is the default)
ARAS=N	Remove the DRDA code from both the AS and AR
AS=Y	Install the DRDA code for the AS
AS=N	Remove the DRDA code from the AS
AR=Y	Install the DRDA code for the AR
AR=N	Remove the DRDA code from the AR

For AS support, only AS=Y need be selected; to add AR support, use ARAS=Y.

To access the DRDA code you *must* update (link-edit) the load library with the ARISSLKE EXEC. If any SQL/DS components were previously stored in saved segments, resave them because the sizes of the resource adapter and RDS increase when the DRDA code is installed.

9.2.5.2 SQLSTART

The PROTOCOL parameter in the SQLSTART startup EXEC enables SQL/DS for DRDA (see Table 22).

Table 22. SQL/DS DRDA Environment Parameters	
Parameter	**Default**
PROTOCOL=SQLDS | AUTO	SQLDS

We used PROTOCOL=AUTO to enable connection of both SQL/DS and non-SQL/DS ARs, the former using the private SQL/DS protocol, the latter using DRDA.

9.2.6 Security Requirements

When an AR routes a request to the SQL/DS for VM AS, the following security requirements for the server and the network apply:

- Selecting end-user names
- Network security parameters
- Database manager security
- Security subsystems

9.2.6.1 Selecting End-User Names

The end-user ID is a one- to eight-character string that must be unique in a particular operating system. It is difficult to have unique userids throughout an SNA network. Therefore the AS may get the same userids from different ARs. SQL/DS for VM optionally enables you to perform inbound translation under the following conditions:

- Inbound connection request comes through an AVS gateway.
- The AR must use conversation SECURITY=SAME (already verified).

   Note: : If SECURITY=PGM, the AR already has performed outbound name translation to ensure unique userids.

When SECURITY=SAME is specified, the AVS translation function is called, and a valid mapping must be found for each incoming connect request. The mapping information is specified at the AS by using the AGW ADD USERID command. This command enables you to specify a new userid for incoming userids. This new (translated) userid is not known in the local AVS machine. The new userid is used by SQL/DS for checking the user's privileges.

The AGW ADD USERID command adds a new entry in the AVS userid table. It provides you with flexibility to define mapping data as shown in the examples that follow. This AGW command enables all users to connect from IPFA2GL4 to this AS:

```
AGW ADD USERID IPFA2GL4 * =
```

This AGW command enables one specific user (DB2V2) from a specific requester (IPFA2GL4) to connect to this AS and defines IPDB2V2 as the new userid for the DB2V2 userid:

```
AGW ADD USERID IPFA2GL4 DB2V2 IPDB2V2
```

You can change actual AVS userid entries as follows:

- Delete an entry by using the AGW DELETE USERID command.

- Inactivate an entry by using the AGW STOP USERID command.

The following example shows how you could resolve a naming conflict using the inbound translation function of AVS. Suppose two users with userid DB2V2 exist. One exists in Toronto and one in Boeblingen, and both want to access the San Jose system. At the AS in San Jose, do the following to prevent the naming conflict:

- Use AGW ADD USERID TORONTO DB2V2 TDB2V2 to specify a new userid for the user in Toronto. It is not absolutely necessary to change the userid of the Boeblingen user because the userids are already unique when the Toronto entry is made.

- Use AGW ADD USERID TORONTO * = to allow all other users from Toronto to access the San Jose system with their userid.

- The DBA in San Jose must use the DB2 GRANT command to grant a set of privileges for the new (translated) userid (TDB2V2).

9.2.6.2 Network Security

DRDA (LU6.2) provides three basic network security features:

Session-Level Security
Controlled by the VERIFY parameter on the VTAM APPL statement

Conversation-Level Security
Specified in the control program system directory (COMDIR)

Data Encryption
Possible with VTAM 3.4 and later versions on MVS only.

9.2.6.3 Session-Level Security

Session level security is implemented through VTAM. It is also referred to as *partner LU verification.* If you want the partner LU (the LU that represents the AR) to be checked by RACF during session BIND processing, specify VERIFY=REQUIRED in the APPL definition for SQL/DS. If you do not want to use this level of security, specify VERIFY=NONE.

Use session-level security in nontrusted environments where, for example, you have OS/2 ARs. In this case this level of security together with the entries in the control program system directory is the way to ensure userid and password checking for SQL/DS for VM as an AS.

9.2.6.4 Conversation-Level Security

The ARs must send a userid and password to be checked during conversation allocation when you specify SECACPT=CONV in the APPL definition of the AS. In trusted environments we recommend that you use SECACPT=ALREADYV, which means that VTAM accepts either a userid and password, or a userid and an indication that this userid has been verified.

At least the userid must be sent to the VM AS. Security none is not accepted.

The userid and password are checked against the control program system directory. The userid alone (in the case of SECURITY=SAME) is checked against the AVS userid table.

It is therefore necessary to record the userids and passwords of the AR users in the control program system directory of the AS (SQL/DS for VM).

With the APPCPASS statement VM provides a method of storing userid and password for AR users in the CP system Directory.

The APPCPASS statement in our sample would look this:

```
APPCPASS IPFA2GL4 SC02331I DB2V2 DB2V2PW
```

This statement indicates that through AVS gateway IPFA2GL4 and partner LU SC02131I, the user with userid DB2V2 and password DB2V2PW is authorized.

For more on the AGW ADD USER command, please refer to *VM Connectivity Planning, Administration, and Operation.*

9.2.6.5 Database Manager Security

One way of controling access to each AS is through inbound name translation at the AS. Other methods of controlling access to the AS are:

- DB2 uses the userid provided by VM to check whether that user has CONNECT authority for the related database.

- Access privileges for objects of SQL/DS can be granted by the system administrator or by the owner of a particular object.

The basic objects the AS controls are

- Packages

  End users are authorized to create, replace, and run packages using the GRANT statement. The owner automatically is authorized to run or replace the package. With the GRANT EXECUTE statement, individual users or user groups get authorized to run a package (application) at the AS. To allow all users to run the package, the GRANT to PUBLIC statement is used.

  A package can contain

  - Static SQL statements
    End users who are granted the authority to execute a package are automatically granted the authority to execute each statement of the related application program. Thus end users do not need any table privileges if the package contains static SQL statements only.

  - Dynamic SQL statements
    The contents of a dynamic SQL statement are not known before execution. The application program builds the dynamic SQL statement and SQL dynamically preprocesses the statement using SQL PREPARE or EXECUTE IMMEDIATE.

    For execution, the end user needs table privileges for all tables and SQL objects used in the application program.

- SQL objects
  These objects are tables, views, and synonyms. End users can be granted the authority to create delete, change, or read individual SQL objects. For dynamic SQL statements, this authority is required.

The AS can individually authorize users to bind packages, run packages, and use SQL objects.

9.2.6.6 Security Subsystem Use
SQL/DS for VM uses a security subsystem like RACF to check the user ID and the password. As an AR, SQL/DS for VM does not have any direct calls to the security subsystem.

The security subsystem is indirectly used to identify the end user (userid and password) when end users are attached using CICS or VM.

VTAM can also invoke the security subsystem if you use SNA session level security, which can be activated by the VERIFY parameter on the VTAM APPL statement.

9.2.7 Common Errors

Listed below are typical errors and misunderstandings in setting up DRDA AS environments.

- Starting SQL/DS without specifying PROTOCOL=AUTO. The default is PROTOCOL = SQLDS, in which case every unlike requester trying to connect to SQL/DS receives a general communications error, and no special messages are seen at the VM system components (VTAM, AVS, SQL/DS).

- Several VTAM sense codes are received each time the number of sessions established between resources in different networks reaches the limit specified in the NCP parameter, GWNAU. This is due to the high use of LU 6.2 sessions; the VTAM sense codes received should be 087D and/or 0805. One solution would be to increase the number specified for the GWNAU parameter in the NCP.

- Incoming requests from DDCS for AIX with security level SAME are rejected if the userid is in lowercase. AVS/VM expects it to be folded to uppercase.

- Message AGWVAF367S is received on the AVSVM console if a requester tries to connect with SECURITY=SAME and an AGW ADD USER command for that remote LU and its userid has not been issued to the local AVS gateway.

9.3 VSE AS

In this section we discuss the setup tasks required to enable SQL/DS for VSE to perform AS functions to support remote DRDA clients. The tasks are basically the same regardless of the platform of the DRDA clients: to understand the security requirements and to grant RDBMS authorities.

The operating system we used was VSE/ESA V1.3.0, running as a guest under VM/ESA 1.2, with the required software for DRDA implementation, that is, SQL/DS 3.4, VTAM 3.4, and CICS V2.2. The tasks you must perform are

- Update VM control program system directory if VSE runs as a guest under VM.

- Assemble all required CICS tables.

- Add VTAM definitions.

- Add SQL/DS DRDA support code.

Setting up a DRDA environment in VSE is similar to setting up a DRDA environment in VM and requires a similar understanding of SNA connectivity and networking. CICS skills are also needed, as CICS handles the requests from the ARs using LU 6.2 support.

Figure 139 on page 276 shows the VSE/ESA components involved in the DRDA implementation.

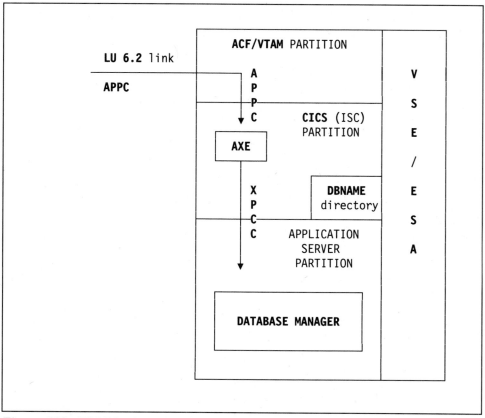

Figure 139. VSE/ESA Components in a DRDA Implementation

The following VSE/ESA components participate in the DRDA implementation:

- CICS/VSE Inter System Communications (ISC)

  To establish a DRDA environment, APPC (LU 6.2) connectivity between CICS/VSE and an LU on the AR system must be established. The CICS ISC component provides the SNA LU 6.2 (APPC) functions to the SQL/DS AS. CICS ISC must be activated (DFHSIT - ISC=YES) to use VSE DRDA.

  The CICS APPC service receives an APPC ALLOCATE verb with a TPN from an AR. CICS then verifies that an AXE transaction has been defined with this TPN (DFHPCT) and performs the security check.

If the security check is successful, CICS starts the AXE transaction, and it begins communicating with the database that corresponds to the TPN received through the APPC ALLOCATE verb.

The TPN transmitted by APPC ALLOCATE verb must have been defined in the DBNAME directory pointing to an operating SQL/DS AS within the VSE system (refer to Figure 142 on page 289).

- AXE Transaction

The APPC-XPCC-Exchange (AXE) transaction is a CICS transaction activated by the remote AR specifying a TPN.

The AXE program routes the DRDA data stream between the remote AR and the SQL/DS database manager using the CICS LU 6.2 support and the VSE XPCC functions. This transaction (program ARIAXED) is used as the "middleman" because CICS is the only VSE component that currently supports the APPC protocol. The AXE transaction is used to convert the DRDA APPC requests to XPCC requests (in both directions) between the CICS partition and a local VSE SQL server partition.

- ACF/VTAM

CICS (ISC) uses ACF/VTAM to establish or bind LU-to-LU sessions with the remote systems. The SQL/DS AS uses LU 6.2 basic conversations over these sessions to communicate with the remote DRDA ARs.

- DBNAME Directory

The DBNAME directory is used to map an incoming request for conversation allocation to a predefined AS identified by the incoming TPN.

As the DBNAME directory is used by all of the VSE partitions, it should be available in the shared virtual area (SVA) for performance reasons.

- XPCC

The XPCC (Cross Partition Communication Control) is the VSE macro interface that enables communication and data transfer between VSE partitions (that is, CICS/VSE to and from SQL/DS).

9.3.1 Operating System Definitions

When SQL/DS is initialized to support a DRDA AS, its partition size should be at least 6MB (8MB is better).

In our example, all SNA communications to the VSE/ESA guest (VSEANL13) go through the VCTCA. We added the VCTCA definitions for completeness.

- Define the CTCA to the VM VTAM machine.

```
USER VTAM XXXXXX 32M 32M G
* 5684095 ACF/VTAM for ESA
  ...
  SPECIAL 700 CTCA VSEANL13
  ...
```

- Define the CTCA to the VSE guest machine.

```
/* Profile EXEC for the 2nd level VSE/ESA machine: VSEANL13 */

'CP DEFINE CTCA AS 600 USER VTAM'
'CP COUPLE 600 TO VTAM 700'
'TERM CON 3270'
'CP IPL E00'
```

- ADD statement in the VSE IPL PROC.

```
  ...
ADD 600,CTCA,EML
  ...
```

9.3.2 Network Definitions: VTAM

The local network consists of three VTAM domains and four subareas.

- The VM VTAM major node definitions for VCTCA are

```
IPF2CTCA VTAMLST  Z1  F 80  Trunc=80 Size=11 Line=0 Col=1 Alt=0

|...+....1....+....2....+....3....+....4....+....5....+....6....+....7...
* * * Top of File * * *
         VBUILD TYPE=CA
VLG700    GROUP LNCTL=CTCA,              ** CHANNEL-TO-CHANNEL LINK **X
                DELAY=.020,                                       **X
                MAXBFRU=(2),                                      **X
                MIH=YES,                                          **X
                REPLYTO=25.5,                                     **X
                ISTATUS=ACTIVE                                    **
VCL700    LINE  ADDRESS=700,            ** DEFINE C-T-C LINK ADDR. **X
                ISTATUS=ACTIVE                                    **
VPU700    PU    PUTYPE=4,               ** DEFINE C-T-C LINK STA.  **X
                ISTATUS=ACTIVE                                    **
* * * End of File * * *
```

- The VSE VTAM major node definitions for VCTCA are

```
// JOB PHVTMCTC
// EXEC LIBR,PARM='MSHP'
ACCESS SUBLIB=PRD2.CONFIG
DELETE VTMCTCA.SAVE
RENAME VTMCTCA.B:VTMCTCA.SAVE
CATALOG     VTMCTCA.B         REPLACE=YES
VTMCTCA  VBUILD TYPE=CA
VLG600    GROUP LNCTL=CTCA,                                 C
                DELAY=.020,                                 C
                MAXBFRU=(2),                                C
                MIH=YES,                                    C
                REPLYTO=25.5,                               C
                ISTATUS=ACTIVE
VCL600    LINE  ADDRESS=600,                                C
                ISTATUS=ACTIVE
VPU600    PU    PUTYPE=4,                                   C
                ISTATUS=ACTIVE
/+
```

- The VTMADJ is

```
CATALOG     VTMADJ.B         REPLACE=YES
VTMADJ   VBUILD TYPE=ADJSSCP
         NETWORK
IPF       ADJCDRM
DEIBMIPF NETWORK=DEIBMIPF
IPF       ADJCDRM
IPFV2     ADJCDRM
IPFV2A    ADJCDRM
```

- The target CICS subsystem in VSE/ESA (VSEANL13) is

```
IPFA21CD APPL  ACBNAME=IPFA21CD,                            C
               AUTH=(ACQ,PASS,VPACE),                       C
               APPC=NO,                                     C
               SONSCIP=YES,                                 C
               EAS=30,                                      C
               PARSESS=YES,                                 C
               VPACING=0
```

IPFA21CD is defined to VSE VTAM. Note that APPC=NO and PARSESS=YES
should be specified.

9.3.3 Networking Definitions: CICS

The CICS partition to be used for this DRDA connection must have LU 6.2 links to remote systems with the ARs. The *CICS/VSE Intercommunication Guide* contains additional information about defining and establishing such links.

To prepare CICS to contribute to DRDA, the following tables must be customized to enable the LU 6.2 support:

DFHSIT ==> (ISC support)

DFHPPT ==> (ARICAXED program)

DFHPCT ==> (TPN)

DFHTST ==> (ARICAXED error logging)

DFHSNT ==> (userids and passwords for requesters)

DFHTCT ==> (connections and sessions)

The screens from page 280 to page 287 illustrate the CICS tables used in our environment.

- DFHSIT

```
        DFHSIT TYPE=CSECT,                                          *
              ...
              APPLID=IPFA21CD,   DRDA CICS APPLICATION NAME         *
              DUMP=NO,           DRDA IDUMP IN ABEND SITUATIONS     *
              GRPLIST=VSELIST,   DRDA GROUP LIST FOR DRDA CICS      *
              ISC=YES,           DRDA    INTERSYSTEM COMMUNICATION  *
              PCT=DR,            DRDA TPNs INCLUDED                 *
              PPT=DR,            DRDA ARICAXED INCLUDED             *
              SUFFIX=DR,         DRDA                               *
              TST=DR,            DRDA    TEMP STORAGE TABLE INCLUDED *
              ...
              DUMMY=DUMMY                TO END MACRO
        END   DFHSITBA
```

- APPLID
  The CICS APPLID is used to define the CICS application to VTAM. It is also needed when defining a remote access to specify

  - the partner LU (DDCS for OS/2)

  - the LU name (CM/2)

  which must be used to access the SQL/DS DRDA AS.

- ISC support (ISC=YES)
  LU 6.2 links are supported through CICS ISC.

- DFHSNT

  There is one entry for each remote user allowed to connect to the DRDA server.

```
*--------------------------------------------------------------------*
*              REMOTE USER for DRDA ACCESS                           *
*--------------------------------------------------------------------*
          DFHSNT TYPE=ENTRY,                                          C
                 USERID=SJUS1,                                        C
                 PASSWRD=DRDA1A,                                      C
                 RSLKEY=0
```

The DFHSNT entry is needed when an outside AR attempts a connect, as CICS checks in the DFHSNT for the validity of USERID and PASSWORD, or USERID only, depending on the DRDA security level issued by the AR (PGM or SAME). The security can be upgraded with VTAM, but we did not do that.

- DFHTST

  An entry must be provided to support the ARICAXED error logging.

```
*--------------------------------------------------------------------*
*         LOCAL ENTRIES SHOULD BE PLACED BELOW THIS BOX              *
*--------------------------------------------------------------------*
          SPACE 3
          DFHTST TYPE=RECOVERY,                                       C
                 DATAID=ARIAXELG
*--------------------------------------------------------------------*
*         LOCAL ENTRIES SHOULD BE PLACED ABOVE THIS BOX              *
*--------------------------------------------------------------------*
```

Our customization of the program properties table (DFHPPT), the program control table (DFHPCT), and the terminal control table (DFHTCT) follows. Although these tables can be macro defined, RDO definition is recommended as described below.

To easily manage the DRDA entries we recommend that you define them in a unique group.

Note: This group has been called "DRDA" in the ITSO system.

- DRDA definitions

  The CEDA DEFINE command is used to define the following resources:

  - AXE program

  - TPN transactions

  - LU 6.2 connections

  - LU 6.2 sessions

- DRDA LIST creation

To install the DRDA group at CICS initialization, add it to the current LIST (VSELIST).

We defined a group (DRDA) in order to put all DRDA definitions together:

```
CEDA ADD GR(DRDA) LIST(DRDALIST)

CEDA APPEND LIST(DRDALIST) TO (VSELIST)
```

— DRDA group installation
  If a DRDA test is needed before you have stopped CICS, the newly created DRDA group must be installed in the current CICS session.

```
CEDA INSTALL GR(DRDA)
```

The screen captures from the RDO process are shown below.

- An entry must be defined for the AXE program (ARICAXED).

  Define ARICAXED program:

```
CEDA  Define
  PROGram        : ARICAXED
  Group          : DRDA
  Language       : Assembler      CObol | Assembler | C | Pli | Rpg
  RELoad         : No             No | Yes
  RESident       : Yes            No | Yes
  RSl            : 00             0-24 | Public
  Status         : Enabled        Enabled | Disabled
REMOTE ATTRIBUTES
  REMOTESystem   :
  REMOTEName     :
  Transid        :
  Executionset   : Fullapi        Fullapi | Dplsubset
```

- LU 6.2 links (connections and sessions) must be defined for each remote LU.

  Define DRC1 connection to LU IPFA2GL3:

```
CEDA  DEFine
  Connection     : DRC1
  Group          : DRDA
CONNECTION IDENTIFIERS
  Netname      ==> IPFA2GL3
  INDsys       ==>
REMOTE ATTRIBUTES
```

```
REMOTESystem ==>
REMOTEName   ==>
CONNECTION PROPERTIES
ACcessmethod ==> Vtam          Vtam | IRc | INdirect
Protocol     ==> Appc          Appc | Lu61
SInglesess   ==> No            No | Yes
Datastream   ==> User          User | 3270 | SCs | STrfield | Lms
RECordformat ==> U             U | Vb
OPERATIONAL PROPERTIES
AUtoconnect  ==> yes            No | Yes | All
INService    ==> Yes            Yes | No
SECURITY
 SEcurityname ==>
 ATtachsec    ==> verify        Local | Identify | Verify
 Bindpassword ==>               PASSWORD NOT SPECIFIED
```

Note: Use ATtachsec ==> Identify to allow security=SAME.
Use ATtachsec ==> Verify to enforce security=PGM.

Define DRS1 session for connection DRC1:

```
CEDA  DEFine
 Sessions     : DRS1
 Group        : DRDA
SESSION IDENTIFIERS
 Connection   : DRC1
 SESSName     :
 NETnameq     :
 MOdename     : IBMRDBM
SESSION PROPERTIES
 Protocol     : Appc              Appc | Lu61
 MAximum      : 00020 , 00010     0-32767
 RECEIVEPfx   :
 RECEIVECount : No                No | 1-999
 SENDPfx      :
 SENDCount    : No                No | 1-999
 SENDSize     : 04096             1-30720
 RECEIVESize  : 04096             1-30720
OPERATOR DEFAULTS
 OPERId       :
 OPERPriority : 000               0-255
 OPERRsl      : 0
 OPERSecurity : 1
 USERId       :
SESSION USAGES
 Transaction  :
 SESSPriority : 000               0-255
OPERATIONAL PROPERTIES
 Autoconnect  : Yes               No | Yes | All
 INservice    :                   No | Yes
 Buildchain   : Yes               Yes | No
 USERArealen  : 000               0-255
 IOarealen    : 00000 , 00000     0-32767
 RELreq       : No                No | Yes
 Discreq      : No                No | Yes
 NEPclass     : 000               0-255
RECOVERY
 RECOvoption  : Sysdefault        Sysdefault | None
```

Similarly, we defined connections and sessions for all remote LU 6.2 partners in the ITSCNET and USIBMSC networks.

Display connections using the master terminal transaction (CEMT):

```
I CONN
STATUS:   RESULTS - OVERTYPE TO MODIFY
 Conn(BOA1) Net(BOA3000K)      Ins Rel
 Conn(DRC1) Net(IPFA2GL3)      Ins Rel
 Conn(MMDR) Net(IPFA2GL4)      Ins Rel
 Conn(POK1) Net(SCLUDB3A)      Ins Rel
 Conn(ROC1) Net(SCHASM01)      Ins Rel
 Conn(ROC2) Net(SCHASM02)      Ins Rel
 Conn(SJC1) Net(SJA2108I)      Ins Rel
```

- All transaction codes (TPNs) that are available for DRDA users to access VSE SQL/DS DRDA servers must be defined.

Define TPN transaction TPN1 for remote access to ARICAXED program:

```
CEDA  DEFine
  TRansaction    : TPN1
  Group          : DRDA
  PROGram        : ARICAXED
  TWasize        : 00000          0-32767
  PROFile        : DFHCICST
  PArtitionset   :
  STatus         : Enabled        Enabled | Disabled
  PRIMedsize     : 00000          0-65520
REMOTE ATTRIBUTES
  DYnamic        : No             No | Yes
  REMOTESystem   :
  REMOTEName     :
  TRProf         :
  Localq         :                No | Yes
SCHEDULING
  PRIOrity       : 001            0-255
  TClass         : No             No | 1-10
ALIASES
  Alias          :
  TAskreq        :
  Xtranid        :
RECOVERY
  DTimout        : No             No | 1-7000
  Indoubt        : Backout        Backout | Commit | Wait
  REStart        : No             No | Yes
  SPurge         : No             No | Yes
  TPurge         : No             No | Yes
  DUmp           : Yes            Yes | No
  TRACe          : Yes            Yes | No
SECURITY
  Extsec         : No             No | Yes
  TRANsec        : 01             1-64
  RSL            : 00             0-24 | Public
  RSLC           : No             No | Yes | External
```

Display the ITSO DRDA group that has been defined:

```
EXP   GR(DRDA)
ENTER COMMANDS
  NAME        TYPE          GROUP                              DATE    T
  DRC1        CONNECTION    DRDA                               94.033  1
  1T20        CONNECTION    DRDA                               94.033  1
  ROC1        CONNECTION    DRDA                               94.033  1
  ROC2        CONNECTION    DRDA                               94.033  1
  POK1        CONNECTION    DRDA                               94.033  1
  SJC1        CONNECTION    DRDA                               94.033  1
  BOA1        CONNECTION    DRDA                               94.033  1
  MMDR        CONNECTION    DRDA                               94.033  1
  ARICAXED    PROGRAM       DRDA                               94.033  1
  DRS1        SESSIONS      DRDA                               94.033  1
  1T20        SESSIONS      DRDA                               94.033  1
  TPN1        TRANSACTION   DRDA                               94.033  1
  TPN2        TRANSACTION   DRDA                               94.033  1
  TPN3        TRANSACTION   DRDA                               94.033  1
  1T20        TRANSACTION   DRDA                               94.033  1
```

9.3.4 Database Definitions

The following tasks must be undertaken when installing SQL/DS:

- Adding DRDA AS support

- DBNAME Directory customization

- New startup parameters

The SQL/DS V3.R4 initial installation does not provide activation of the DRDA code. To function as a DRDA AS, the DRDA code must be activated to set up the VSE/ESA SQL/DS AS. This activation must be achieved for the systems that require the DRDA facility. Procedure ARIS342D has been provided for this purpose and can be executed at any time (see Figure 140 on page 288). The DRDA support is activated the next time the SQL/DS database manager is started.

```
* $$ JOB JNM=ARIS342D,CLASS=0,DISP=D
* ***********************************************************
* ARIS342D: LINK EDIT RDS WITH DRDA SERVER SUPPORT
* ***********************************************************
// JOB ARIS342D
// LIBDEF *,SEARCH=(PRD2.SQL340),CATALOG=PRD2.SQL340
// OPTION CATAL
 INCLUDE ARISLKRA
// EXEC   PGM=LNKEDT,PARM='MSHP'
/*
/&
* $$ EOJ
```

Figure 140. Procedure ARIS342D

To disable the DRDA server support, job control member ARIS343D can be executed at any time (see Figure 141). The DRDA support is removed the next time the AS is started.

```
* $$ JOB JNM=ARIS343D,CLASS=0,DISP=D
* ***********************************************************
* ARIS342D: LINK EDIT RDS WITHOUT DRDA SERVER SUPPORT
* ***********************************************************
// JOB ARIS343D
// LIBDEF *,SEARCH=(PRD2.SQL340),CATALOG=PRD2.SQL340
// OPTION CATAL
 INCLUDE ARISLKRD
// EXEC   PGM=LNKEDT,PARM='MSHP'
/*
/&
* $$ EOJ
```

Figure 141. Procedure ARIS343D

In the DBNAME directory, all application IDs and database names are provided together with the TPNs that must be defined in a DFHPCT entry to be available.

Figure 142 on page 289 shows the DBNAME directory we used.

```
****************************************************************
*TPN       APPLID      *DBNAME               PID  PRIV          *
*          1      1    22            3   44   5                 *
*2..5____0......7__12..............9___45___0_____           *
 TPN1     SYSARI01    S34VSDB1                                  
 TPN2     SYSARI02    S34VSDB2                                  
 TPN3     SYSARI01    S34VSDB1                    Y             
 AXE0     SYSARI01    S34VSDB1                                  
          SYSARI02    S34VSDB2            01                    
          SYSARI01    S34VSDB1            0B                    
          SYSARI03    S34VSDB0            05                    
          S34VMDB0    S34VMDB0                                  
          S34VMDB1    S34VMDB1                                  
          S34VMDB2    S34VMDB2                                  
 "D6B     SYSARI00    SQLDS                                     
```

Figure 142. DBNAME Directory

The following rules apply:

- An entry in the DBNAME directory for each TPN
  An entry must be defined for each TPN used by remote users. Multiple users can have access to the same TPN.

- Each TPN must be defined in DFHPCT.
  An entry for each TPN must be defined in DFHPCT. As the TPN is a CICS transaction name, it must be part of the DFHPCT table to be activated.

- Multiple TPNs to one APPLID
  Multiple TPNs can refer to the same APPLID. This could be very useful to give specific advantages to one user of a database server. The CICS transaction definition allows security (RSL) and class (TClass) to be defined at the transaction level. These features associated with a TPN can also be used to provide different uses of the AXE program to different users.

- Exclusive use of a real agent
  Exclusive use of a real agent can be associated with a TPN (TPN3). This privilege, marked with a *Yes* in column 50 of the TPN entry, is valid only for the DRDA environment. It gives the user of this TPN the privilege of having a real agent available for its exclusive use during its entire LU 6.2 conversation. TPNs with no exclusive privilege have their real agent released at the end of each unit of work.

- DBNAME to APPLID relationship should be constant.
  For example, in the DBNAME directory (Figure 142), the database with the DBNAME of S34VSDB1 always maps to the APPLID SYSARI01, and DBNAME S34VSDB2 always maps to SYSARI02.

APPLIDs and dynamic partitions

Be sure that you understand the implications of starting your SQL/DS AS in a dynamic partition. If SQL/DS is not started at VSE IPL time, other jobs starting in the same class could make SQL/DS go to a different partition number than the expected number inside the same class (for example, Y2 instead of Y1, which would mean your AR should be looking for APPLID SYSARI11 instead of SYSARI0F). The correlation between each partition name (BG, F7, and so on) and partition ID (00, 01, and so on) is hardcoded and does not follow a general rule. Use the partition ID as a suffix for SYSARIxx when you specify an APPLID in the DBNAME directory as SYSARI00, SYSARI01, and so on. For a list of the valid partition ID to partition name pairs, see Figure 15 in the *SQL/DS System Administration for VSE* manual.

The SQL/DS startup job stream must be updated to allow incoming DRDA ARs to access the VSE SQL/DS AS.

- New initialization parameter

  - RMTUSERS=nnnn

  RMTUSERS indicates the number of remote users that concurrently are authorized to access the SQL/DS AS. The allowable range of users is 0 through 65535.

  Note that this parameter has no default value. RMTUSERS must be coded to allow DRDA access. If this parameter is not specified or if its value is zero, remote users are not accepted.

The following example provides ten remote DRDA users.

```
// JOB S34VSDB2    START SQL/DS V3 R4 WITH 2MB DATA BUFFERS
// SETPFIX LIMIT=256K
// LIBDEF PROC,SEARCH=(PRD2.SQL340)
// EXEC  PROC=ARIS34PL   *-- SQL/DS PRODUCTION LIBRARY ID PROC
// EXEC  PROC=ARI34DB2   *-- SQL/DS DATABASE ID PROC
// EXEC  ARISQLDS,SIZE=AUTO,PARM=' DBNAME=S34VSDB2,PARMID=PARVSESW,     X
             RMTUSERS=10'

/*
/&
* $$ EOJ
```

The new SQL operator command, SHOW CONNECT, displays the status of remote users and provides the Rmtuser_ID (for connected remote users).

The Rmtuser_ID can be used when it is needed to force a remote user with the operator command:

FORCE RMTUSER Rmtuser_ID

Note: The FORCE command does not deallocate the LU 6.2 conversation. CEMT terminates the task for the AXE transaction (TPN), which results in a deallocate abend to the AR and an XPCC abnormal disconnect to the AS.

The database server operator can gather information about the remote users that are connected.

The following is an example of the output on your screen after you enter SHOW CONNECT:

```
01 20 SHOW CONNECT
02 Z1 020 STATUS OF CONNECTED SQL/DS USERS          1994-03-07  08:3
03 Z1 020    CHECKPOINT AGENT IS NOT ACTIVE.
04 Z1 020    USER ID: BOEUS1     SQL ID: BOEUS1
05 Z1 020       USER IS INACTIVE.
06 Z1 020            STATE STARTED: 1994-02-25  08:29:39
07 Z1 020            CONVERSATION STARTED: 1994-02-25  08:29:25
08 Z1 020            LUWID: SNANETID.IPFA2GL3.A72320746FC2.0001
09 Z1 020            EXTNAM: SQLUSER.1
10 Z1 020            REQUESTER: SQLDS/VM  V3.4.0   AT BOEVMIS2
11 Z1 020            RMTUSER ID: 1
12 Z1 020            LU NAME: IPFA21CD
13 Z1 020            TASK NO.: 0000135
14 Z1 020    0  SQL/DS REMOTE USERS ARE ACTIVE.
15 Z1 020    1  SQL/DS REMOTE USERS ARE INACTIVE.
16 Z1 020    52  SQL/DS AGENTS ARE AVAILABLE.
17 Z1 020    19  SQL/DS REMOTE CONNECTIONS ARE AVAILABLE.
18 Z1 020 ARI0065I SQL/DS OPERATOR COMMAND PROCESSING IS COMPLETE.
19
```

9.3.5 Security

In this section we provide a brief overview of our tests related to the applicable DRDA security combinations. The SQL/DS VSE AS depends on CICS for intersystem communication security.

CICS offers bind security, link security, and user security.

Bind security is an option to do a session-level LU-to-LU verification. At the AS you can use the CEDA DEFINE CONNECTION function to define a BINDPASSWORD. The password must be defined at the AR as well. It is 16 hexadecimal characters long and filled up by hexadecimal zeros from right to left in case of shorter passwords.

During bind, security is used to prevent unauthorized sessions with CICS from remote systems.

Link Security is used to limit access to specific transactions or resources.

You can define link security by

- Using the CICS sign-on table (DFHSNT; see Figure 143)

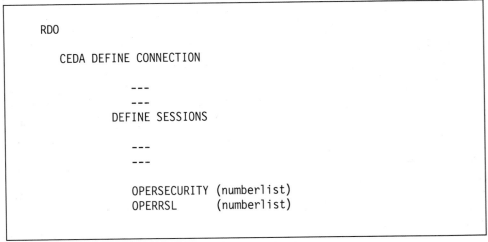

```
RDO

   CEDA DEFINE CONNECTION

          ---
          ---
          SECURITYNAME (name)
```

Figure 143. *Specifying Link Security with CICS Sign-On Table*

CICS matches this definition with the userids of the DFHSNT TYPE=ENTRY when the session is bound.

- Specifying security in the link definition

You can specify CICS security keys for each set of sessions by the means of the OPERSECURITY and OPERRSL operands as shown in Figure 144.

```
RDO

   CEDA DEFINE CONNECTION

          ---
          ---
          DEFINE SESSIONS

          ---
          ---

          OPERSECURITY (numberlist)
          OPERRSL      (numberlist)
```

Figure 144. *Define Link Security in the Link Definition*

For more about link security, refer to the *CICS/VSE Intercommunication Guide*.

The CICS implementation of the SNA LU 6.2 conversation level security provides end-user verification.

User security validates the userid with the CICS sign-on table (DFHSNT) before accepting a request to start a conversation. For example, DRDA ARs not defined in the CICS sign-on table (userid, password) are not allowed to attach an AXE transaction to start a conversation with the SQL/DS server.

User security for a remote system can be selected in the CEDA DEFINE CONNECTION command by using the ATTACHSEC parameter. The three levels of *attach security* are

- LOCAL
  Not supported by DRDA.

- IDENTIFY
  Equivalent to SECURITY=SAME (or already verified) in LU 6.2 terminology. Only the userid is required for the CICS sign-on process. With this level of security CICS trusts that the AR verified the users before allocation to the SQL/DS for VSE server.

- VERIFY
  Equivalent to SECURITY=PGM in LU 6.2 terminology. In this case CICS expects the remote system to send both the userid and password when allocating the conversation and rejects the connection if a password is not supplied.

The AS is responsible for managing the database resources and dictates which security the AR must provide. VM requesters, for example, must update the COMDIR accordingly to ensure that the required security data is communicated to the AR.

For further information about security, please read the chapter "Setting up the AS in a VSE Environment " in the *Connectivity Guide*. The AS dictates the security requirements.

9.3.5.1 Database Manager Security

Inbound or outbound userid translation is not supported by the VSE AS. CICS uses the userid as provided by AR. The AXE transaction passes the userid to SQL/DS for VSE. The userid must be defined in the SYSTEM.SYSUSERAUTH catalog table where you also can specify the related user authority.

The userid must have the connect authority for the database at the AS. This is checked by SQL/DS for VSE first. SQL/DS for VSE at the AS then checks the privileges that have been granted to the user by the database administrator. Access to database objects is controlled and managed by SQL/DS for VSE through a set of privileges.

The basic objects the AS controls are:

- Packages

End users are authorized to create, replace, and run packages using the GRANT statement. The owner is automatically authorized to run or replace the package. With the GRANT EXECUTE statement, individual users or user groups are authorized to run a package (application) at the AS. To allow all users to run the package, the GRANT to PUBLIC statement is used.

When an application is preprocessed a package is created that contains either

– Static SQL statements
  End users who are granted the authority to execute a package are automatically granted the authority to execute each statement of the related application program. Thus end users do not need any table privileges if the package contains static SQL statements only.

  or

– Dynamic SQL statements
  The contents of a dynamic SQL statement are not known before execution. The application program builds the dynamic SQL statement, and SQL/DS dynamically binds the statement.

  For execution, the end user needs table privileges for all tables and SQL objects used in the application program.

• SQL objects
  These objects are tables, views, synonyms, or aliases. End users can be granted the authority to create, delete, change, or read individual SQL objects. For dynamic SQL statements, this authority is required.

The AS can individually authorize users to bind packages, run packages, and use SQL objects.

For further information about security, please read the chapter "Setting up the AS in a VSE Environment" in the *Connectivity Guide*.

9.3.6 Common Errors

The following remarks are intended to help avoid typical errors and misunderstandings in setting up DRDA AS environments.

• If you start SQL/DS without specifying the RMTUSERS parameter, the default RMTUSERS=0 is assumed. In this case every AR trying to connect to SQL/DS will receive a general communication error.

• If you specify ATtachsec=Verify in the connection definition for a partner LU of an AR, that AR cannot connect with SECURITY=SAME.

Chapter 10. MVS Platform

DB2 for MVS/ESA is a robust database management system. Today many MVS customers use DB2 for MVS/ESA for application development and data management purposes. DB2 for MVS/ESA V3 already has full DRDA level 2 implementation with DUW and multiple-site update capability. Thus DB2 plays a very important role in client/server computing. Together with the improved availability, performance, and usability in V4, DB2 plays a strong role as the premier enterprise server.

As DB2 for MVS/ESA provides the foundation for data integrity and security in a distributed enterprise, we envisage that much of its participation will be as a database server. Because DB2 for MVS/ESA also supports the AR function, it can be a requester to any database server that provides DRDA AS function.

In this chapter we discuss the tasks to enable DB2 for MVS/ESA to perform the DRDA AS and AR functions. All tasks completed for the MVS platform were carried out on the DB2 system located in Poughkeepsie.

For the rest of this chapter, any references to *DB2* denote DB2 for MVS/ESA.

10.1 Defining DB2 to the Network

DB2 uses DDF to handle the communication between the local DB2 subsystem and remote database managers. DDF runs on a separate address space and interfaces with VTAM. To enable DB2 to participate in the connection with any DRDA partners, you must define the DB2 to VTAM and install the DDF facility. DDF is a prerequisite for DB2 for MVS/ESA to perform both the AR and AS functions.

10.1.1 Defining DB2 to VTAM

To make DB2 accessible through VTAM, DB2 must be defined as a VTAM application. This is achieved by a VTAM APPL statement, which contains the information required by VTAM, for example, the LU name and optionally the password. Figure 145 on page 296 shows the VTAM APPL statement for the DB2 system installed in Poughkeepsie. The VTAM APPL definition for DB2 is included in the major node definition.

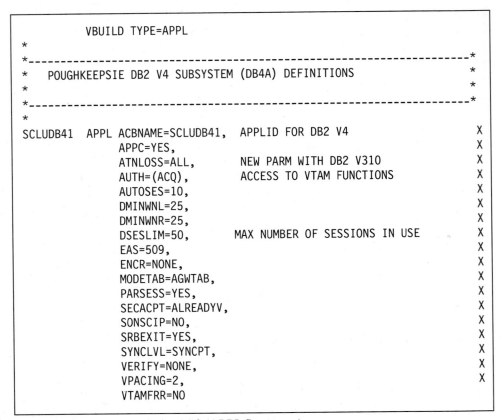

```
            VBUILD TYPE=APPL
    *
    *---------------------------------------------------------------*
    *   POUGHKEEPSIE DB2 V4 SUBSYSTEM (DB4A) DEFINITIONS            *
    *                                                               *
    *---------------------------------------------------------------*
    *
SCLUDB41  APPL ACBNAME=SCLUDB41,  APPLID FOR DB2 V4               X
               APPC=YES,                                          X
               ATNLOSS=ALL,       NEW PARM WITH DB2 V310          X
               AUTH=(ACQ),        ACCESS TO VTAM FUNCTIONS        X
               AUTOSES=10,                                        X
               DMINWNL=25,                                        X
               DMINWNR=25,                                        X
               DSESLIM=50,        MAX NUMBER OF SESSIONS IN USE   X
               EAS=509,                                           X
               ENCR=NONE,                                         X
               MODETAB=AGWTAB,                                    X
               PARSESS=YES,                                       X
               SECACPT=ALREADYV,                                  X
               SONSCIP=NO,                                        X
               SRBEXIT=YES,                                       X
               SYNCLVL=SYNCPT,                                    X
               VERIFY=NONE,                                       X
               VPACING=2,                                         X
               VTAMFRR=NO
```

Figure 145. Major Node for DB2 (APPL Statement)

The LU name of the DB2 system is the APPL statement label, which is set to SCLUDB41 as shown in Figure 145. Another way of specifying this value is to use the ACBNAME keyword option, which overrides the value in the statement label. Thus the absence of the line

```
ACBNAME=SCLUDB41
```

would indicate that the LU name equates to the label.

Note that the NETID value is not specified on the VTAM APPL statement, because VTAM implicitly assigns the NETID to the applications.

The DSELLIM parameter defines the default number of sessions limit for this DB2 subsystem as it communicates with any other system on a given mode. Use this parameter to protect the DB2 subsystem from being overloaded with requests from ARs. For example, you can assign a low number to DSELLIM to limit the number of simultaneous requests issued by a given AR and mode. You can use the CONVLIMIT column of the SYSLUMODES table to override this parameter value for a specific LU name (see 10.2.2.4, "SYSLUMODES" on page 304).

The SYNCLVL parameter is set to SYNCPT, which tells VTAM that this DB2 subsystem supports two-phase commit. Nevertheless DB2 still supports the non-two-phase commit process when communicating with those partners LUs that do not support two-phase commit.

The MODETAB parameter identifies the name of the VTAM logon mode table that you want DB2 to use. Only modes defined in this table are eligible for conversations created by this DB2. For more about modes see 10.1.1.1, "Mode."

The parameters in the VTAM APPL statement describe the communication characteristics of the DB2 for MVS/ESA system. These characteristics are applicable for connections to any remote partners. You can override the settings of some of these parameters at a specific partner LU name level (see 10.2.2, "Populating the CDB" on page 301).

For a discussion about the SECACPT and VERIFY parameters, see 10.3.2, "Security Considerations" on page 311. For detailed explanations of and recommendations for each option, refer to the *DB2 for MVS/ESA Installation Guide*.

10.1.1.1 Mode

A VTAM link between two LUs is a *session*. When a session is created, VTAM uses a mode name to identify the SNA session characteristics to use. Each mode name is associated with some communication characteristics such as

- Pacing
- RU sizes
- COS

Each mode name is defined in a log mode table, the name of which is referenced in the VTAM APPL statement (see Figure 145 on page 296). The mode name IBMRDB is the recommended name because it is used as a default for DRDA connections whenever you do not explicitly assign a mode to a session. To use it as a default, you must make sure that your system programmer adds it to your DB2 mode table. Figure 146 on page 298 shows the mode definition for the IBMRDB we used in Poughkeepsie.

```
IBMRDB     MODEENT LOGMODE=IBMRDB,      AGW (SLU) TO AGW (PLU)          X
               PSNDPAC=X'03',          PRIMARY SEND PACING COUNT      X
               SRCVPAC=X'03',          SECONDARY RECEIVE PACING COUNT X
               SSNDPAC=X'00',          SECONDARY SEND PACING COUNT    X
               TYPE=X'00',             NEGOTIATED BIND                X
               FMPROF=X'13',           FM PROFILE 19 LU 6.2           X
               TSPROF=X'07',           TS PROFILE 7 LU 6.2            X
               PRIPROT=X'B0',          PRIMARY NAU PROTOCOL           X
               SECPROT=X'B0',          SECONDARY NAU PROT             X
               RUSIZES=X'8989',        8 X 2**9 = 4096                X
               COMPROT=X'50B1',        COMMON NAU PROT                X
               PSERVIC=X'0602000000000000000002C00'    SYSMSG/Q MODEL
```

Figure 146. Mode Entry Used in Poughkeepsie VTAM

For explanations of and recommendations for each mode option, refer to the *DB2 for MVS/ESA Installation Guide.* In 10.3.1, "Populating the CDB" on page 310 we explain how to explicitly assign a mode to a session for DB2.

10.1.2 DDF Setup

To enable DB2 for MVS/ESA to participate in connections with any DRDA partners, DDF must be installed. DDF is an optional facility of DB2 that allows a DB2 application to access data at remote relational database systems that support DRDA. DDF also allows applications running in a remote DB2 for MVS/ESA or any AR environment that supports DRDA to access data in a DB2 subsystem.

DDF requires VTAM Version 3 Release 3 or later. In the subsequent discussion we assume that the appropriate version and release of VTAM is installed.

When DDF starts up, DB2 reads the DDF record from the bootstrap data set (BSDS) to obtain the following information, which is used by DDF to connect to VTAM:

- LU name for DB2

- RDB_NAME, which is referred to as *location name* in DB2

- The password used when connecting the DB2 to VTAM (optional depending on the VTAM requirement)

There are two ways to set up the definitions:

- If you choose to set up DDF during installation by running the installation CLIST, use the DSNTIPR ISPF panel to set up the definitions, as shown in Figure 147 on page 299.

```
DSNTIPR                        DISTRIBUTED DATA FACILITY
===>

Enter data below:

1 DDF STARTUP OPTION    ===> AUTO      NO, AUTO, or COMMAND
2 DB2 LOCATION NAME     ===> CENTDB2        The name other DB2s use to
                                            refer to this DB2
3 DB2 NETWORK LUNAME    ===> SCLUDB41  The name VTAM uses to refer to this DB2
4 DB2 NETWORK PASSWORD  ===>           Password for DB2's VTAM application
5 RLST ACCESS ERROR     ===>           NOLIMIT, NORUN, or 1-5000000
6 RESYNC INTERVAL       ===>           Minutes between resynchronization period
7 DDF THREADS           ===>           (ACTIVE or INACTIVE) Status of a
                                       database access thread that commits or
                                       rolls back and holds no database locks
                                       or cursors
8 DB2 GENERIC LUNAME    ===>           Generic VTAM LU name for this DB2
                                       subsystem or data sharing group
9 IDLE THREAD TIMEOUT   ===> 0         0 or seconds until dormant serve ACTIVE
                                       thread will be terminated (0-9999)


PRESS:  ENTER to continue   RETURN to exit   HELP for more information
```

Figure 147. Distributed Data Facility Panel: DSNTIPR

The definitions for the DB2 system in Poughkeepsie are shown in fields 2, 3, and 4. The location name is set to CENTDB2. The network LU name is set to SCLUDB41, which matches the value of the ACBNAME of the VTAM APPL statement. The password field is blank because a password is not specified in the VTAM APPL statement.

The input captured by the ISPF panel is used by an installation job to update the BSDS.

- If DB2 is already installed, you can use the change log inventory utility (DSNJU003) to directly update the information in the BSDS. Figure 148 on page 300 shows a job obtained from the DB2 SDSNSAMP library. In the sample job we updated the BSDS with location name CENTDB2 and LU name SCLUDB41.

```
//DSNJU003 JOB (999,POK),
//             'DB2 UTILITY',
//             CLASS=A,MSGCLASS=T,MSGLEVEL=(1,1),
//             NOTIFY=&SYSUID
//*--------------------------------------------------------------- */
//*        CHANGE LOG INVENTORY:
//*             UPDATE BSDS WITH PASSWORDS,
//*             UPDATE BSDS WITH DISTRIBUTED VALUES
//*--------------------------------------------------------------- */
//DSNTLOG EXEC PGM=DSNJU003,COND=(4,LT)
//STEPLIB   DD  DISP=SHR,DSN=DSN410.SDSNLOAD
//SYSUT1    DD  DISP=OLD,DSN=DSN410.BSDS01
//SYSUT2    DD  DISP=OLD,DSN=DSN410.BSDS02
//SYSPRINT DD  SYSOUT=*
//SYSUDUMP DD  SYSOUT=*
//SYSIN     DD  *
  DDF     LOCATION=CENTDB2,LUNAME=SCLUDB41
//*
```

Figure 148. *Change Log Inventory Utility*

Note that the location name must be unique in the network. It is referred to by other ARs that need to access this DB2. The location name of a DB2 must be defined as the

- *Target database* in the DCS directory on DDCS for OS/2 and DDCS for AIX
- *DBNAME* in the VM communication directory on SQL/DS for VM
- *Relational database* on the OS/400

There is no connection from DB2 for VSE because it does not support AR function.

10.2 MVS Application Requester

In this section we discuss the setup tasks required to enable DB2 for MVS/ESA to perform AR functions to access data in remote DRDA partners. The tasks are basically the same regardless of the platform of the DRDA partners: collect the network information of the partner and populate the communications database.

10.2.1 CDB

The *CDB* is a collection of tables that are used by the DDF to get information about communicating with other DRDA partners. The CDB is created during installation. It contains six tables, which can be maintained by using SQL statements. The tables are related through DB2 referential integrity, as shown in Figure 149 on page 301.

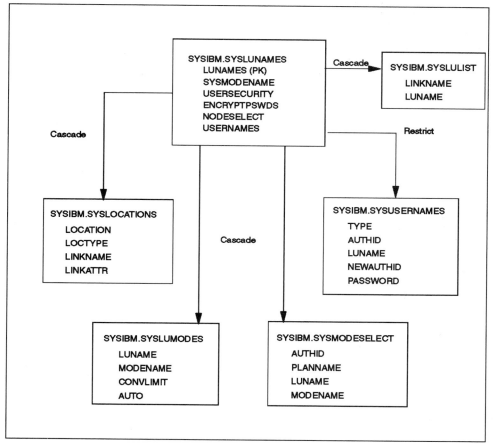

Figure 149. DB2 CDB Tables

The SYSLUNAMES table is the parent table for the other five tables based on its primary key column, LUNAME. This table contains the LU names of the target system to which this DB2 can connect; you must create a row for each remote server system.

10.2.2 Populating the CDB

To populate the CDB step, you must have information about the partner system, for example, the LU name, and the security requirements. For complete coverage of the CDB, refer to the *DB2 for MVS/ESA SQL Reference*.

10.2.2.1 SYSLUNAMES

The SYSLUNAMES table defines the security and mode requirements for conversations. This table must contain a row for each LU name associated with the remote system you want to access. Figure 150 on page 302 shows the partner LUs defined in our DB2 system in Poughkeepsie.

LUNAME	SYSMODENAME	USERSECURITY	ENCRYPTPSWDS	MODESELECT	USERNAMES	GENERIC
SC02130I		A			O	
SC02131I					O	
SC02132I		A			O	
IPFA2GL4					O	
IPFA21CD				Y	O	
SC06000I		A			O	

Figure 150. SYSIBM.SYSLUNAMES Table

We used outbound translation, as indicated by *O* in the USERNAMES column, because the userids for our initial connection testing were different across all database servers. Thus the userid and password were sent to the remote systems for validation. We used SECURITY=PROGRAM.

We chose to use a mode name other than the default for IPFA21CD, which is the LU name of the SQL/DS for VSE system in Boeblingen, hence the *Y* in the MODESELECT column. The actual mode name is defined in the SYSMODESELECT table. Refer to Figure 154 on page 304 to see how the specific mode name is assigned to SQL/DS for VSE.

The GENERIC column is new in DB2 V4. It is used for *data sharing* purposes. Each data sharing group can have a DB2 generic LU name associated with it. A *Y* in this column indicates that the VTAM generic LU name is specified in the LUNAME column of the table. This generic LU name will be used to access the remote server that belongs to the same data sharing group. As we did not connect to a data sharing group, the value defaulted to blank.

10.2.2.2 SYSLOCATIONS

The SYSLOCATIONS table maps the location name to the LU name. If the servers use nondefault TPN, the TPN is specified in the LINKATTR column. This table contains one row for each remote server. It must, together with the SYSLUNAMES table, be populated for each server. All other CDB table information is optional, depending on your communications and userid translation requirements. Figure 151 on page 303 shows the locations we used.

```
---------+---------+---------+---------+---------
LOCATION         LOCTYPE  LINKNAME  LINKATTR
---------+---------+---------+---------+---------
SJ2SMPL                   SC02130I  DB22TPN
SJ6SMPL                   SC02131I  DB26TPN
SJAS400                   SC02132I
S34VMDB0                  IPFA2GL4  S34VMDB0
S34VSDB1                  IPFA21CD  TPN1
RCAS400                   SC06000I
```

Figure 151. SYSIBM.SYSLOCATIONS Table

The values in the LOCATION column are the names used in the SQL CONNECT statements; they are the RDB_NAMEs.

10.2.2.3 SYSUSERNAMES

The SYSUSERNAMES table is used to manage userids by providing passwords and optionally userid translation for outbound requests. Userid translation is required to resolve naming conflicts between two database systems.

Outbound translation is activated for a connection to a server when its USERNAMES column in the SYSLUNAMES table is set to *O* or *B*. Figure 152 is an excerpt from our table.

```
---------+---------+---------+---------+-------
TYPE  AUTHID  LUNAME    NEWAUTHID  PASSWORD
---------+---------+---------+---------+-------
0             SC02130I  USERID    PSW1111
0             SC02131I  db2v2     PSW2222
0             SC02132I  QSECOFR   PSW3333
0             IPFA2GL4  SJUS1     PSW4444
0             IPFA21CD  DBSRV2    PSW5555
0             SC06000I  DRDARES3  PSW6666
```

Figure 152. SYSIBM.SYSUSERNAMES Table

In our test environment we chose to translate most of the IDs for each remote server to simplify administration.

Inbound translation is also supported for incoming requests; see 10.3.1.2, "SYSUSERNAMES" on page 311.

10.2.2.4 SYSLUMODES

The SYSLUMODES table is used by DDF at startup to negotiate session limits, a process called *change number of sessions* (CNOS). The value specified in the CONVLIMIT column defines the conversation limits for a specific combination of LUNAME and MODENAME; it overrides the DSESLIM parameter in VTAM APPL statement.

AUTO controls the preallocation of sessions during DDF startup. If you set AUTO to *Y*, DB2 allocates a number of sessions during DDF startup, the number is indicated by the value in CONVLIMIT. Figure 153 shows that the table is empty as we chose to use the DSESLIM value.

```
---------+---------+---------+--------
LUNAME    MODENAME CONVLIMIT AUTO
---------+---------+---------+--------
```

Figure 153. SYSIBM.SYSLUMODES Table

10.2.2.5 SYSMODESELECT

The SYSMODESELECT table associates a mode name with any conversation created for an outgoing SQL request to an LU. Figure 154 shows that instead of using the default mode, we chose to use mode name IBMRDBM when connecting to the SQL/DS for VSE system at Boeblingen. Note that any LU name defined in this table is associated with an entry defined in the SYSLOCATIONS table.

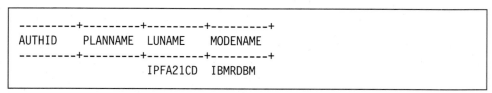

```
---------+---------+---------+---------+
AUTHID    PLANNAME LUNAME    MODENAME
---------+---------+---------+---------+
                   IPFA21CD  IBMRDBM
```

Figure 154. SYSIBM.SYSMODESELECT Table

10.2.2.6 SYSLULIST

The SYSLULIST table is a new table in DB2 for MVS/ESA V4. It supports the specification of multiple LU names for a given location. In our scenarios, we used a specific LU name for each remote location, so our table is empty, as shown in Figure 155 on page 305.

```
    ---------+---------+-
  LINKNAME  LUNAME
    ---------+---------+-
```

Figure 155. *SYSIBM.SYSLULIST Table*

If the remote servers were in a data sharing group, you could set the LINKNAME column to the value of the LINKNAME column of SYSLOCATIONS and the LUNAME column of the SYSLUNAMES. It can be set to any character string of up to 8 bytes. The LUNAMES column would contain the actual LU names of the DB2 systems in the data sharing group, one LU name for each row.

The SYSLULIST table is used when you want to suppress connection to a generic LU name. This is done by setting a blank value in the GENERIC column of the SYSLUNAMES table. DB2 for MVS/ESA chooses from the SYSLULIST table one LU name for the LINKNAME to establish a connection. This process is called *member-specific setup*. The member-specific setup requires that the group have workload management support, which is available in MVS/ESA V5.2

10.2.3 Testing the Connection

After the CDB tables are populated, you can test the connection by using the DB2-supplied program *SQL processing using file input* (SPUFI). SPUFI is a TSO ISPF program that provides an end-user interface for interactive SQL execution. SPUFI supports RUW only.

To use SPUFI to access a remote database, the SPUFI package must be bound to each of the remote database servers. Each of the packages must be included in the SPUFI plan.

We bound the SPUFI package, DSNESM68, to all of the remote database servers that are described in Chapter 4, "ITSO System Scenario" on page 65. Here is an excerpt from the job we used to perform remote bind to some database servers:

```
//STDRD3AB JOB (999,POK),
//         CLASS=A,MSGCLASS=T,MSGLEVEL=(1,1),NOTIFY=&SYSUID
//*
//*-----------------------------------------------------------
//*      BIND THE SPUFI PACKAGE TO REMOTE SERVERS
//*-----------------------------------------------------------
//STEP010   EXEC PGM=IKJEFT1A,DYNAMNBR=20
//STEPLIB   DD DSN=DSN410.SDSNLOAD,DISP=SHR
//SYSLIN    DD DUMMY
//SYSPRINT  DD SYSOUT=*
//DBRMLIB   DD DSN=DSN410.SDSNDBRM,DISP=SHR
//SYSTSPRT  DD SYSOUT=*
//SYSTSIN   DD *
```

```
DSN SYSTEM(DB41)
BIND PACKAGE(SJ2SMPL.DSNESPCS)  -
     OWNER(STDRD3A)             -
     QUALIFIER(USERID)          -
     MEMBER(DSNESM68)           -
     ISOLATION(CS)              -
     VALIDATE(BIND)             -
     RELEASE(COMMIT)            -
     CURRENTDATA(NO)            -
     ACTION(REPLACE)
BIND PACKAGE(SJ6SMPL.DSNESPCS)  -
     OWNER(STDRD3A)             -
     QUALIFIER(DB2V2)           -
     MEMBER(DSNESM68)           -
     ISOLATION(CS)              -
     VALIDATE(BIND)             -
     RELEASE(COMMIT)            -
     CURRENTDATA(NO)            -
     ACTION(REPLACE)
BIND PACKAGE(SJAS400.DSNESPCS)  -
     OWNER(STDRD3A)             -
     QUALIFIER(STDRD4A)         -
     MEMBER(DSNESM68)           -
     ISOLATION(CS)              -
     VALIDATE(BIND)             -
     RELEASE(COMMIT)            -
     CURRENTDATA(NO)            -
     ACTION(REPLACE)
BIND PACKAGE(S34VMDB0.SJUS1)    -
     OWNER(SJUS1)               -
     QUALIFIER(SJUS1)           -
     MEMBER(DSNESM68)           -
     ISOLATION(CS)              -
     VALIDATE(BIND)             -
     RELEASE(COMMIT)            -
     CURRENTDATA(NO)            -
     ACTION(REPLACE)

REBIND PLAN(DSNESPCS)               -
       PKLIST(DSNESPCS.*,           -
              SJ2SMPL.DSNESPCS.*,   -
              SJ6SMPL.DSNESPCS.*,   -
              SJAS400.DSNESPCS.*,   -
              S34VMDB0.SJUS1.*)     -
       ISOLATION(CS)
  END
/*
```

The BIND operation is not identical among all RDBMSs; hence, there are some points
you should be aware of when binding a package from DB2 for MVS/ESA to other
RDBMSs. Note that we used userid outbound translation from DB2 for MVS/ESA.
Table 23 on page 307 highlights the results of the DRDA bind operation on the
OWNER, QUALIFIER, and primary ID attributes in the AS platforms.

Table 23. *Remote Bind from DB2 for MVS/ESA: Results*

Target DBMS	Bind Operation Results
DB2 for OS/2 and AIX	• Packages do not have OWNER and QUALIFIER attributes. • OWNER and QUALIFIER parameters, if specified in the BIND command, must be set to the primary ID of the BIND process. • The primary ID becomes the BOUNDBY ID of the package.

DB2 for OS/400	• The value of OWNER, if specified in the BIND command, can be set to any valid user ID of the OS/400.
	• The OWNER, if specified in the BIND command, does not need authority to perform the SQL operations contained in the package; the authorization validation is performed against the primary ID of the BIND process.
	• QUALIFIER value does not undergo userid translation.
	  – For SQL statements that reference unqualified table (or view) names in the package, the tables are assumed to exist in a collection whose name matches the value of the QUALIFIER parameter.
	  – If you omit this parameter, the tables are assumed to exist in a collection whose name matches the primary ID of the BIND process.
	  – For packages that do not reference any table or view names, that is, all of the SQL statements are dynamically prepared, you can specify any character string for the QUALIFIER parameter; it does not have to be a valid userid in the OS/400 system.
	• The primary ID of the BIND process becomes the OWNER and CREATOR of the package.

SQL/DS for VM/ESA and VSE	• Packages do not have OWNER and QUALIFIER attributes. • OWNER and QUALIFIER parameters, if specified, must be set to the COLLECTION name of the package. • The COLLECTION name becomes the CREATOR of the package. • The COLLECTION name can be any character string of up to eight bytes long; it does not need to be a valid user ID in the VM/ESA or VSE systems.

Note: If you have updated CDB tables, you may or may not have to restart DDF, depending on which table has been changed. If SYSLUMODES is changed, you must stop and start DDF.

10.2.3.1 Using SPUFI

After you bind the SPUFI package to the remote AS, you can issue some dynamic SQL statements to test the connections. Figure 156 shows the SPUFI input panel. We specified the location name *SJ2SMPL* to connect to the DB2 for OS/2 system in San Jose.

```
DSNESP01                      SPUFI                          SSID: DB41
===>

  Enter the input data set name:        (Can be sequential or partitioned)
   1   DATA SET NAME ... ===> 'STDRD3A.DB2UTIL(TESTSQL)'
   2   VOLUME SERIAL ... ===>            (Enter if not cataloged)
   3   DATA SET PASSWORD ===>            (Enter if password protected)

  Enter the output data set name:       (Must be a sequential data set)
   4   DATA SET NAME ... ===> SPUFI.OUT

  Specify processing options:
   5   CHANGE DEFAULTS   ===> NO         (Y/N - Display SPUFI defaults panel?)
   6   EDIT INPUT ...... ===> *          (Y/N - Enter SQL statements?)
   7   EXECUTE ......... ===> YES        (Y/N - Execute SQL statements?)
   8   AUTOCOMMIT ...... ===> YES        (Y/N - Commit after successful run?)
   9   BROWSE OUTPUT ... ===> YES        (Y/N - Browse output data set?)

  For remote SQL processing:
  10   CONNECT LOCATION  ===> SJ2SMPL


  PRESS:  ENTER to process    END to exit          HELP for more information
```

Figure 156. SPUFI Input Panel

Figure 157 on page 309 shows the result of the SPUFI execution. See message DSNE625I for the results of the connection and message DSNE616I for the results of the SELECT statement execution.

```
******************************* Top of Data **************************
DSNE625I CONNECT TO LOCATION SJAS400 PERFORMED, SQLCODE IS 0
DSNE616I STATEMENT EXECUTION WAS SUCCESSFUL, SQLCODE IS 0
******************************* Top of Data *******************____+--
DSNE625I CONNECT TO LOCATION SJ2SMPL PERFORMED, SQLCODE IS 0
DSNE616I STATEMENT EXECUTION WAS SUCCESSFUL, SQLCODE IS 0
---------+---------+---------+---------+---------+---------+-----
SELECT * FROM USERID.ORG
---------+---------+---------+---------+---------+---------+-----
DEPTNUMB  DEPTNAME        MANAGER  DIVISION   LOCATION
---------+---------+---------+---------+---------+---------+-----
      10  Head Office         160  Corporate  New York
      15  New England          50  Eastern    Boston
      20  Mid Atlantic         10  Eastern    Washington
      38  South Atlantic       30  Eastern    Atlanta
      42  Great Lakes         100  Midwest    Chicago
      51  Plains              140  Midwest    Dallas
      66  Pacific             270  Western    San Francisco
      84  Mountain            290  Western    Denver
DSNE610I NUMBER OF ROWS DISPLAYED IS 8
DSNT404I SQLCODE =    100, SQLSTATE = 02000, NO DATA FROM OS/2
---------+---------+---------+---------+---------+---------+-----
DSNE617I COMMIT PERFORMED, SQLCODE IS 0
DSNE616I STATEMENT EXECUTION WAS SUCCESSFUL, SQLCODE IS 0
---------+---------+---------+---------+---------+---------+---------+--
```

Figure 157. SPUFI Output Panel

10.2.3.2 Security

The connections from DB2 for MVS/ESA to all remote ITSO ASs were established successfully using SECURITY=PROGRAM. If you want to switch to using SECURITY=SAME, the partner LU definition for the DB2 for MVS/ESA in the server system has to be adjusted.

For the OS/2 server system, make sure that in CM/2 the partner LU definition for the DB2 for MVS/ESA is created and the corresponding *Conversation security verification* field is checked.

For the AIX server system, make sure that in SNA Server/6000 the partner LU definition for the DB2 for MVS/ESA is created and the corresponding *Already Verified* field is set.

In our sample application scenarios, we switched to using SECURITY=SAME because we set up identical userids for application preparation and testing activities on all platforms. Hence outbound translation was no longer required. For the details on our sample application scenarios, refer to Chapter 12, "Application Structure" on page 351.

10.3 MVS Application Server

In this section we discuss the setup tasks required to enable DB2 for MVS/ESA to perform AS functions to support remote DRDA clients. The tasks are basically the same regardless of the platform of the DRDA clients: understand the security requirements because the CDB tables may have to be updated and grant DBMS authorities.

DDF is required to enable DB2 for MVS/ESA to perform AS functions. The DDF setup includes the definition of

- VTAM LU name for the DB2 system
- Location name
- Password (optionally)

The process of setting up the definitions is described in 10.1.2, "DDF Setup" on page 298. The location name and the LU name should be supplied to the ARs that require connectivity. In addition the ARs should be aware that DB2 for MVS/ESA uses the DRDA default TPN, which is a hexadecimal value of X′07F6C4C2′.

10.3.1 Populating the CDB

The changes required in the CDB depend on how much you want to deviate from the default settings. In our scenario all updates to the CDB were done when we set up the connections to the remote servers. See 10.2.2, "Populating the CDB" on page 301.

10.3.1.1 SYSLUNAMES

There are two ways to define AR LUs in the SYSLUNAMES table:

- DB2 can use a default row in which the LUNAME column is blank. DB2 uses this row for serving requests from all systems that are not explicitly listed in the SYSLUNAMES table.

  The default row is created by a installation job, but you can change the values for this row any time before starting DDF.

- Update the SYSLUNAMES table to define the requester LU name. This method is typically used when you want to override the default values. For example, if you have defined conversation-level security of already verified in the VTAM APPL statement for DB2 for MVS/ESA, you have to create an entry in the SYSLUNAMES table for those ARs for which you want program security level and set the USERSECURITY column to C.

In addition, if you want to use userid inbound translation, update the USERNAMES column with a value *I* or *B* (for inbound and outbound translation).

If the remote system is both an AR and AS, explicit definition is required, but only one row is required for each system. In our DB2 for MVS/ESA system, all remote partners were already defined when we set up the connections, so we did not have to change the SYSLUNAMES table; all remote systems used the defaults for ARs. Refer to Figure 150 on page 302 for the contents of the table.

10.3.1.2 SYSUSERNAMES
You can use this table to handle userid inbound translation.

We did not use userid inbound translation in our sample application scenarios. Figure 158 shows an example of the SYSUSERNAMES table when inbound translations are implemented.

```
---------+---------+---------+---------+-------
TYPE  AUTHID    LUNAME    NEWAUTHID  PASSWORD
---------+---------+---------+---------+-------
I               SC02130I  STDRD4A
I     DRDARES3  IPFA2GL4  STDRD3A
```

Figure 158. SYSUSERNAMES Table: Inbound Translation

The example shows that any userid originating from LUNAME SC02130I is translated to userid STDRD4A. Userid DRDARES3 originating from LUNAME IPFA2GL4 is translated to userid STDRD3A.

Note: You do not have to provide a password for an inbound-translated userid; there is no further authentication process after the inbound translation. Hence the PASSWORD column is blank. For more details on inbound translation, refer to 10.3.2.3, "The Processes" on page 314.

The remote request is, from this point onward, treated like a local sign-on. The IDs after the translations are used as input to the DB2 sign-on exit routine.

10.3.2 Security Considerations
When an AR routes a distributed database request to the AS, security is provided at the network level. DRDA supports three major network security features:

- Session-level security

  Session-level security is implemented through VTAM. It is also referred to as *partner LU verification*. If you want the partner LU to be checked by RACF during session BIND processing, specify VERIFY=REQUIRED in the APPL statement for the DB2 for MVS/ESA server. Otherwise specify VERIFY=NONE.

Figure 145 on page 296 shows that our system did not use session-level security.

- Conversation-level security

  SNA conversation level security provides a range of security options, two of which are supported by DRDA:

  - SECURITY=PGM

    With this option the AS demands that the userid and password be sent from the AR. This option overrides whatever you specify in the USERSECURITY column of the SYSLUNAMES table.

    After receiving the ID and password, DB2 for MVS/ESA passes them to a security subsystem such as RACF for validation.

  - SECURITY=SAME

    This option is also known as *already verified*. With this option the AS accepts either a userid and password, or a user ID with an indication that it already has been verified at the AR. If both userid and password are sent, DB2 for MVS/ESA processes them as if SECURITY=PGM was specified.

    This option is used when you specify *A* or a blank in the USERSECURITY column of the SYSLUNAMES table and SECACPT=ALREADYV in the VTAM APPL macro for DB2 for MVS/ESA.

  The SECURITY option can also be set as a system default by using the SECACPT parameter of the APPL statement for the DB2 for MVS/ESA server.

  If you want to use SECURITY=PGM, specify SECACPT=CONV. We recommend that you use SECACPT=ALREADYV, which is the SECURITY=SAME option. This gives you the best flexibility. If you require an individual AR to use SECURITY=PGM, set the USERSECURITY column to *C* in the corresponding row in the SYSLUNAMES table.

  Figure 145 on page 296 and Figure 150 on page 302 show that in our environment we used ALREADYV. Whenever a password is sent, RACF is invoked, and the userid and password are validated, even if you specified ALREADYV and *A* in the USERSECURITY column.

> **Maintain current level of security**
>
> DDCS for OS/2 V1.2 always sends a userid and password implementing SECURITY=PGM. DDCS for OS/2 V2.3 can implement SECURITY=SAME. If you want to enforce SECURITY=PGM while keeping the SECACPT=ALREADYV setting, you can update the SYSLUNAMES table with USERSECURITY=C for the blank LU row. Connections with any systems that require SECURITY=PGM should be defined explicitly in the table with USERSECURITY=C.

- Encryption

    Password encryption is a mechanism to protect the password that is sent across the network from being recognized in case it is captured by unauthorized processes.

    DB2 for MVS/ESA supports encrypted passwords. RACF handles the actual encryption process. The ENCRYPTPSWDS column in the SYSLUNAMES table is used to indicate whether passwords exchanged with this partner are encrypted. This option is supported only between two DB2 for MVS/ESA systems. The column is set to Y in both systems to enable encryption.

As the owner of the database resources, the AS can dictate the level of security it requires. In addition to the network security parameters, DB2 for MVS/ESA also uses external security systems, such as RACF, to authorize incoming userids.

10.3.2.1 Security Provided by RACF

During DB2 for MVS/ESA installation, several RACF profiles are defined to protect various DB2 resources. One of the profiles is ssid.DIST, where *ssid* represents the subsystem ID of DB2 for MVS/ESA. This profile protects DDF resources from unauthorized remote access.

Without correct authorization, remote users cannot initiate connection to the database server. To provide the necessary authorization to users you can permit the RACF profile to

- Specific userids

- RACF groups to which the users are connected

- Userids that come from a specific LU name

    For example, to permit access to DB2 DDF resources on subsystem DB41 when the request comes from user1 at LUNAME equal to SC02133I, issue the following RACF command:

```
PERMIT DB41.DIST CLASS(DSNR) ID(user1) ACCESS(READ) +
       WHEN(APPCPORT(SC02133I))
```

This is one way DB2 for MVS/ESA performs come-from checking. The other way is by using the CDB. Note that DB2 invokes RACF authorization checking before the inbound userid translation is performed. Ensure that users are authorized in RACF and the CDB if you use both methods.

10.3.2.2 Come-From Checking

Come-from checking allows the AS to perform authentication against the userid from a given AR. In addition it allows the AS to restrict which userids can come from a given AR. For example, the CENTDB2 server can restrict userid DRDARES3 to "come from" the LU SC02132I. If another AR attempts to send the userid DRDARES3, the server rejects the request, because the userid does not come from the correct network location.

The SYSLUNAMES and the SYSUSERNAMES tables provide come-from checking specifications.

10.3.2.3 The Processes

The userids in a network may not be unique. The management of userids becomes difficult when the network becomes large. The DB2 for MVS/ESA server provides inbound translation to maintain userid uniqueness.

You can enable inbound translation by setting the USERNAMES column of SYSLUNAMES to *I*. DB2 for MVS/ESA translates the userid coming from the ARs using the SYSUSERNAMES table. For an example, see 10.3.1.2, "SYSUSERNAMES" on page 311.

The inbound translation process searches for a row in the SYSUSERNAMES table, using the LU name and the userid. The search is done in the following sequence:

1. AUTHID.LUNAME—a specific end user from a specific AR

2. AUTHID.blank—a specific end user from any AR

3. blank.LUNAME—any end user from a specific AR

If no row matches the search criteria, access is denied. Validation of DB2 for MVS/ESA authorization is carried out by using the translated userid, which is found in the NEWAUTHID column.

Note: The original userid is checked against the DDF RACF profile, *ssid.DIST*, before the inbound translation takes place.

Figure 159 on page 315 shows the process of come-from checking on a DB2 for MVS/ESA system for a DDCS for OS/2 AR.

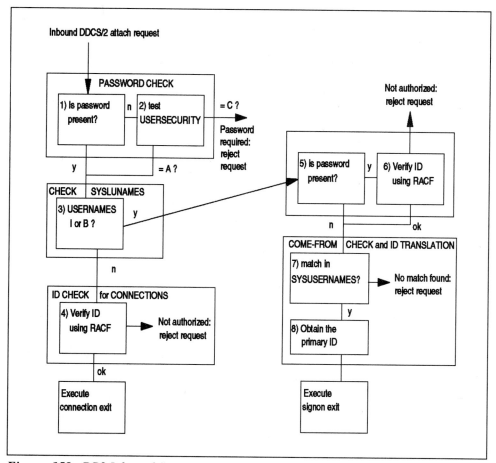

Figure 159. DB2 Inbound Security Processing

To highlight some important points about the come-from checking process:

- If a password is sent, RACF is always invoked before any userid translation that may be applicable for this ID.

- If the inbound translation is enabled, RACF is called only when a userid and a password are sent by the AR. If the AR sends only the userid, the inbound translation rules determine which users are allowed to connect.

- If inbound translation is not enabled, RACF is always invoked by DB2 for MVS/ESA to validate the userid, and the password if it is provided.

The inbound translation function provides the following capabilities:

- Maintains uniqueness for userids across different ARs

- Assigns a group of end users to a single ID to ease database security management

- Restricts userids allowed by a specific AR

- Restricts the allowed ARs for the AS

Maintaining userid uniqueness is a very important function, especially for large distributed database networks. A DB2 for MVS/ESA server can be accessed by many remote workstation clients, and these clients may be members of different and perhaps geographically dispersed LANs. It may not be practical or desirable to mandate that the logon userids are unique throughout the client network. You could use inbound translation to manage userid uniqueness *centrally* at the DB2 for MVS/ESA server location. For example, several users in the network may have the ID SMITH. The SYSUSERNAMES table could be used to provide a unique ID for every SMITH, perhaps by suffixing the name with a code that represents SMITH's home LAN, for example, SMITHSJ and SMITHPOK.

It may or may not be necessary to define each translated ID to RACF. This depends on your installation of the sign-on exit.

Whether the original ID or the translated ID is used to access DB2 for MVS/ESA managed data, you still require the DB2 privileges and authorities.

10.3.2.4 DBMS Security

As the owner of the database resources, DB2 for MVS/ESA controls the access to the resources. The resources are DB2 objects, for example, tables, views, synonyms, and aliases. The DRDA clients access these objects through packages.

A package is an executable module that contains SQL statements. The SQL statements can be static or dynamic. You can grant package privileges to a remote user with one or more of the following:

- BIND

  BIND allows users to bind and rebind an existing package. A new installation parameter, *BIND NEW PACKAGE*, comes with V4 of DB2 for MVS/ESA. If the parameter is set to BIND, users with the BIND package privilege can add a new version of a package. If you allow users to add new packages or a new version of a package, one of the following authorizations is required:

  - The BINDADD system privilege and the CREATE IN COLLECTION privilege

  - SYSADM or SYSCTRL authority

  - PACKADM authority for the collection or for all the collections

To create a package, users also need the relevant table or view authorizations required by the SQL statements in the package.

- COPY

  COPY allows users to copy a package from one collection to another.

- EXECUTE

  EXECUTE allows users to execute the package. If the packages contain dynamic SQL statements, users also need the relevant table or view authorizations required by the SQL statements in the package, unless you have the DYNAMICRULES option set to BIND in the BIND PLAN command. This setting causes DB2 for MVS/ESA to use the authorization ID of the plan or package owner for authorization checking of dynamic SQL statements.

You can provide package, table, and view authorities to users, using the SQL GRANT statements. For a detailed description of the GRANT statement, refer to *DB2 for MVS/ESA SQL Reference*.

Chapter 11. Application Development Considerations

This chapter contains some considerations on migrating DRDA level 1 applications to DRDA level 2 and porting DRDA applications across different DB2 platforms.

DRDA level 2 offers applications the ability to keep multiple connections active at the same time. You may need to redesign part of your application to take full advantage of this feature. However, in many cases you can migrate to the new functions in a rather smooth way and still achieve performance advantages.

Porting an application from one environment to another is a logical goal in a distributed environment. With careful research and planning, an existing DB2 for OS/2 application, for example, can be upgraded to access databases in a host system instead of, or in addition to, the DB2 for OS/2 database. Applications executing in a host environment may similarly be downsized to execute in a workstation environment, even retaining their host database access.

An understanding of application needs is important because they determine whether any trade-off is necessary for consistency within the environment as a whole. The more complex the environment, the more planning that must be done.

There are additional considerations concerned with coding constraints placed on applications as a result of their execution environment. For example, porting a PC-based Windows application to a 3270-based mainframe environment is difficult because of the terminal input/output inconsistency between the environments. These considerations are not within the scope of this book, but they are important. In this chapter we assume that your applications implement modular code for database access can be ported.

11.1 Migrating Applications to DRDA Level 2

In this section we give a brief overview and introduction of the DRDA level 2 implementation among the various DB2 platforms. DRDA level 2 allows a higher level of distribution compared to DRDA level 1. DRDA level 1 implemented *RUW*, whereas DRDA level 2 is the basis for *DUW*. Refer to 3.1.1, "Architectures Used to Access Distributed Data" on page 46 for details on the degrees of distribution.

11.1.1 DRDA Level 2: Introduction

DB2 for OS/400, DB2 for MVS/ESA, and DDCS for AIX V2.3 with the ENCINA product are the DB2 products that support multiple-site update in a heterogeneous environment. The next release of DDCS for AIX and DDCS for OS/2 will support multiple-site update in a heterogeneous environment. In the near future DB2 for OS/2 and DB2 for AIX will support multiple-site update in a heterogeneous environment. The versions of DB2 common server available at the time of writing provide support for DUW with DRDA single-site update. Also, multiple site update is supported in the DB2 common server platforms (non-DRDA). Refer to 12.7, "Multiple-Site Update for DB2 common server" on page 383.

Multiple-site update requires the following functions:

- *Two-phase commit* protocol to keep multiple databases in sync
- *SPM* to manage the two-phase commit protocol
- *New SQL statements* to manage multiple connections

11.1.2 Comparing DRDA Level 1 and DRDA Level 2

Accessing remote data under DRDA level 1 allows a single connection at a given time and given commit scope. To connect to a different AS, the application has to be in a connectable state, which can be achieved only by bringing the application to the beginning or end of a unit of work, that is, by issuing a ROLLBACK or COMMIT statement.

In DRDA level 2 you can connect to multiple servers, keeping multiple connections active at the same time. In this way, a single COMMIT scope can span multiple servers and include multiple SQL statements. Still, keep in mind that you cannot reference more than one server at a time in a single SQL statement.

SQL cursors are implicitly closed if you complete a transaction with a COMMIT or ROLLBACK statement, unless you specify a *WITH HOLD* clause on those platforms that support the clause in the SQL cursors declaration.

To see the differences between DRDA level 1 and DRDA level 2 from an application point of view refer to Figure 160 on page 321. Using three different units of work, the figure describes the different concepts of DUW and RUW.

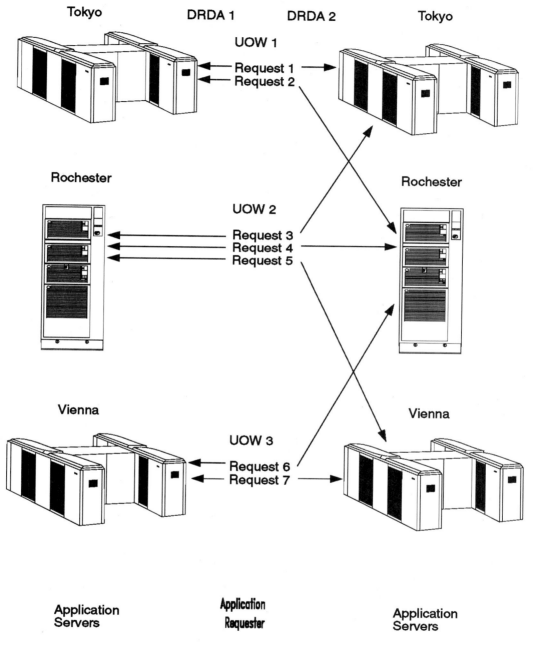

Figure 160. DUW and RUW

Note: The center of this figure shows three units of work. To the left the are the possible connections in a unit of work in DRDA level 1, and to the right are the additional possibilities in DRDA level 2. For example, for UOW1 using RUW, you can have several requests to the same location (Tokyo). For the same UOW1 using DUW, each request can be directed to a different location (Tokyo and Rochester).

11.1.3 Connection Management

Connection management is significantly enhanced for DRDA level 2. Because multiple active connections are allowed, application programmers must be able to change the current connection without previously disconnecting and without starting a new connection. In other words, they must be able to switch between two or more different connections for which active connections exist. For this reason, DRDA level 2 has introduced a significant change to the semantics of the SQL CONNECT statement. In DRDA level 2, for DB2 for OS/400 the SQL CONNECT statement can only be used to start a *new* connection. It must not be used to change the status of the current connection. If you try to issue a CONNECT statement toward a previously connected location, you get an SQL error, and the current connection is not changed.

To change the current connection and switch to another active connection, you must use the new SQL *SET CONNECTION* statement. The only case whereby a CONNECT statement changes the current connection is when a brand new connection is actually started, that is, when the CONNECT statement is successful. Depending on how you precompile or bind your application program, DB2 for MVS/ESA and DB2 common server behave the same way as DB2 for OS/400. Refer to 13.1.1, "Precompiling Your Program" on page 396 for DB2 common server and to 16.1.3.1, "Binding a Plan" on page 478 for DB2 for MVS/ESA.

In addition, DRDA level 2 connection management introduces a special SQL instruction to drop active connections. For DB2 for OS/400, you must use the SQL *RELEASE* statement to drop an active connection. Actually, the connection is dropped only at the subsequent transaction boundary. In DB2 for MVS/ESA and DB2 common server, connections are dropped depending on what you specify during precompile and bind.

Note that the DISCONNECT statement is

- Not valid for DB2 for OS/400 in a DRDA level 2 application
- Not supported by DB2 for MVS/ESA
- Supported by DB2 common server (RUW and DUW)

Unlike DRDA level 1, DRDA level 2 can take advantage of the services of an *SPM* to coordinate and carry out COMMIT and ROLLBACK statements among multiple ASs, thereby allowing an application program to maintain connections to perform work to multiple relational databases within the same unit of work.

At this time, for the DB2 family of products, only DB2 for OS/400, DB2 for MVS/ESA, and DDCS for AIX with the ENCINA product provide an SPM capable of working in a heterogeneous environment.

In summary, if you have to migrate a DRDA level 1 application to DRDA level 2, keep in mind the following considerations:

- To take full advantage of DRDA level 2, the structure of your transactions may need to be redesigned. In DRDA level 1, programmers are forced to conclude a transaction before starting a new connection. This limitation may have influenced the application design.

- Even if you do not change the logic of your programs, DRDA level 2 can still offer significant performance advantages. Issuing a SET CONNECTION statement is generally faster than starting a brand new connection.

- If the logic of your program is such that you know in advance which locations are accessed, you may want to prestart those connections and just use SET CONNECTION to the various locations. You also have to remove the DISCONNECT statements and RELEASE ALL the active connections before the application terminates.

- If the logic of your program is such that you cannot determine which connections are already active at a given time, for DB2 for OS/400, you should check the SQLSTATE after each CONNECT statement to determine whether the connection was already active and in that case issue a SET CONNECTION statement to the same location.

- Once you have fixed the various statements related to connection management, for DB2 for OS/400, you should make sure that the application does not expect that cursors are implicitly closed by DISCONNECT statements, because you will have removed those statements.

11.1.3.1 Connection States
DRDA level 2 introduces new connection states. A connection can be held or released and current or dormant (see Figure 161 on page 324).

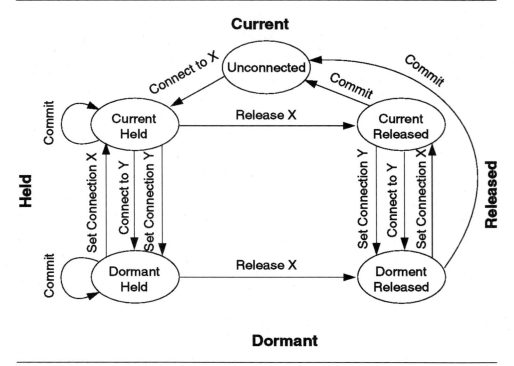

Figure 161. Connection States

Refer to Figure 161 for the discussion that follows. The figure is a general picture of the architecture. For DB2 for OS/400 the upper part, *Unconnected*, does not exist. Nevertheless it shows a state from where an initial connection can be made to remote servers and to which we return after all connections have ended and all work has been committed.

The CONNECT and RELEASE statements control whether a connection is in a held or released state.

- *Held state* means that a connection is not to be disconnected at the next commit operation. A connection in the released state cannot be put into held state.

- *Released state* means that a disconnect is to occur at the next successful commit operation (a rollback has no effect on connections). Therefore, a released state can be thought of as a pending disconnect.

A connection can remain in a released state across unit of work boundaries if a ROLLBACK statement is issued.

Regardless of whether a connection is in held or released state, a connection can also be in current or dormant state.

- *Current state* means that the connection is the connection used for SQL statements that are executed.

- *Dormant state* means that the connection is suspended. While the connection is in this state, SQL statements cannot use it. Nevertheless, SQL statements can always be executed against the current connection.

To change the state from dormant to current, use the SET CONNECTION statement (all platforms) or the CONNECT statement (DB2 for MVS/ESA and DB2 common server). The existing current connection becomes dormant. In fact there can be only one connection in a current state at a time. All others are in a dormant state.

For DB2 for OS/400, you cannot use the CONNECT statement to make a connection current. You must use the SET CONNECTION statement. The switch from a dormant to a current connection differs from the DB2 for MVS/ESA and DB2 common server implementation where a CONNECT to an already connected server can work as a SET CONNECTION. When a dormant connection becomes current in the same unit of work, all locks, cursors, and prepared statements are restored to reflect their last use when the connection was current. For DB2 for OS/400, connections are destroyed through the DISCONNECT statement in the DRDA level 1 connection. Once disconnected, an application must connect to the database again before it can direct SQL statements to it.

11.1.4 Two-Phase Commit Process

Synchronizing multiple databases requires more effort than when processing a single database. As we have multiple physical locations involved, the synchronization process is split into two phases. The problem to solve is what to do when one database has its changes committed and the other one does not and the communication link breaks down.

The benefit of two-phase commit is that multiple connections can be maintained, thus keeping data consistent across multiple ASs. In DRDA level 1, connections had to be disconnected and reestablished each time the application had to connect to a different AS.

When an application issues a COMMIT statement all connected databases must be coordinated to bring them to a consistent state. This condition, where all resources are in a consistent state, is called a *synchronization point*. The flows involved with the commitment of resources are dependent on the protection level of the LU 6.2 conversations:

- *Protected conversations* use *two-phase commit* (DRDA level 2) flows to commit the work.

- *Unprotected conversations* use *single-phase commit* (DRDA level 1) flows to commit the work.

The SPM component is used to control the two-phase commit flow. The SPM also controls rollback among the various protected resources. All changes are either committed or rolled back.

With distributed updates, SPMs on different systems cooperate to ensure that resources reach a consistent state. For more detailed information refer to the *DRDA Architecture Reference*. The example in Figure 162 shows the type of information that flows between the ARs and ASs to commit work on protected conversations.

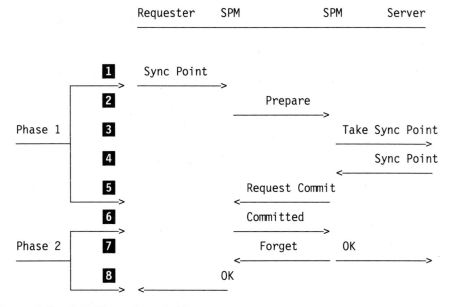

Figure 162. Two-Phase Commit Flow

Each AR and each AS has an SPM. All RDBMSs participating in this multiple-site update have to cooperate in order to ensure the synchronization.

Phase 1

1 The AR issues a COMMIT statement. This means that the application has reached a condition where all participating ASs and the AR are to be synchronized. The requester must wait until it receives the OK from its SPM.

2 The SPM of the AR sends a *Prepare to Commit* to the SPM of the servers.

3 All SPMs at the servers request to their corresponding ASs that the changes have been externalized. For DB2 for OS/400, the changes must be externalized on the journal receiver. For DB2 for MVS/ESA, the changes must be externalized to the log.

4 The servers return their OK to their SPMs.

5 The AS SPMs send a request commit to the AR SPM.

Phase 2

6 When the AR SPM receives the responses and logs them, the AS receives a *Committed* indication.

7 The server SPMs send *Forget* to the AR SPM and OK to their ASs. Everything has been synchronized now.

8 Finally the AR gets the OK from its SPM and can continue.

Note: The more ASs involved in a multiple-site update, the more messages have to flow. The messages require more resources, which causes additional communication line traffic.

11.1.5 DRDA Level 2 in a Heterogeneous Network

Not all DB2 platforms are provided with two-phase commit support, so you must be aware of some considerations when you mix different platforms in the same relational database network. In many cases, a CONNECT statement results in creating a connection that allows only read operations.

At CONNECT time, the AR establishes whether the AS can be updated or not. For instance, a DB2 for OS/400 AR connection to an AS that supports only single-phase commit is update capable if

- The program that initiated the connection was compiled with an isolation level other than *NONE,

and

- There are no other active connections, or all of them are read-only connections.

Note: COMMIT(*NONE) on DB2 for OS/400 means that no transaction isolation is done and no logs are written. It can only be used in a DB2 for OS/400-like environment. Refer also to Chapter 2 of the *Formal Register of Extensions and Differences in SQL*.

For DB2 for MVS/ESA AR a single-phase commit AS can be updated if this AS is the first connection in the unit of work. The rule of enabling updates to a single-phase AS will also be the rule for DB2 common server when it fully supports DRDA level 2.

For the time being, for DDCS for OS/2 or AIX (without the ENCINA product), the first server that is updated determines whether other servers can be updated; if the first server updated is a DB2 common server, any other DB2 common server can be updated, and DRDA connections are read-only. If the first server updated is a DRDA AS, it is the only server that can be updated; all other servers (DRDA or DB2 common server) become read-only. Also, DB2 for OS/2 and DB2 for AIX as DRDA ASs are considered single-phase commit (DRDA level 1).

As the services of an SPM are required when a protected conversation is used, a DRDA level 2 AR determines whether an SPM must be used as follows:

- When a single relational database is updated in each unit of work, an SPM is *not* required.

- When multiple relational databases are updated in one unit of work, an SPM *must* be used.

At connect time the AR determines whether or not an SPM must be used and the AS is updatable. The DRDA and commitment control protocols used depend on this decision.

Table 24 summarizes the general rule, valid across all DB2 platforms, for establishing the protocols to use. Flows can be mixed together.

Table 24. Mixing DRDA Levels			
Requester/Server	DRDA Level 1	DRDA Level 2 1PC	DRDA Level 2 2PC
DRDA level 1	DRDA level 1	DRDA level 1	DRDA level 1
DRDA level 2 1PC	DRDA level 1	DRDA level 2 1PC	DRDA level 2 1PC
DRDA level 2 2PC	DRDA level 1	DRDA level 2 1PC	DRDA level 2 2PC
Notes:			

- The left column contains the ARs. The upper row contains the ASs.
- 1PC = single-phase commit
- 2PC = two-phase commit

The table indicates

- AR is at DRDA level 1

  All ASs will use DRDA level 1 flow. This implies single-phase commit and unprotected conversations.

- AR is at DRDA level 2 supporting single-phase commit (1PC)

  When the AS is at DRDA level 1, DRDA level 1 protocol is used. All others use DRDA level 2 flow with single-phase commit.

- AR is at DRDA level 2 with two-phase commit (2PC)

When the AS is at DRDA level 1, DRDA level 1 flows are used. When the AS is at DRDA level 2 with single-phase commit capability, DRDA level 2 single-phase commit flow is used. When the AS is at DRDA level 2 with two-phase commit capability, DRDA level 2 two-phase commit flow is used.

11.2 Choice of Language

It is important to choose a development language that supports the application code across the range of platforms to which the application is intended to be ported. This language must also be supported by the database systems that the application intends to access. Table 25 shows a list of programming languages supported by each IBM SQL product.

C, COBOL, and Fortran cover the widest range of platforms and databases, so they are good choices when considering portability.

It is important to recognize that data can be accessed from a platform that does not necessarily support a particular language. For example, DRDA AR support is not implemented for the REXX language on AS/400, but a REXX application running on an OS/2 can certainly access data stored in DB2 for OS/400 through a DDCS/2 workstation.

Table 25 (Page 1 of 2). Programming Language Support					
Language	**DB2**	**SQL/DS**	**DB2 for OS/400**	**DB2 for OS/2**	**DB2 for AIX**
Assembler	X	X	—	—	—
Ada	V	—	—	—	—
APL	V	X	—	—	—
BASIC	V	X	—	—	—
C	X	X	X	X	X
COBOL	X	X	X	V	V
Fortran	X	X	X	V	X
PL/I	X	X	X	—	—
REXX	V	X	no DRDA AR support	X	X

Table 25 (Page 2 of 2). Programming Language Support					
Language	**DB2**	**SQL/DS**	**DB2 for OS/400**	**DB2 for OS/2**	**DB2 for AIX**
RPG	—	X	X	—	—

Notes:

- X denotes full support for the language by an IBM product.
- V denotes full support for the language by a third-party vendor product.
- —does not support the language.

Not all statements and options of a given language are supported on all platforms at all times. Variations can be expected because different products may be supplied by different vendors, or new releases of software containing a richer language set may not be available on all platforms at the same time. Protection from these differences might be obtained by selecting a compiler directive that limits the coding syntax to a particular standard.

We next present some considerations for C and COBOL. The considerations are presented as examples to illustrate that it is important not only to select a suitable language but also to understand any idiosyncrasies that can affect application portability and design.

11.2.1 C Considerations

The considerations mentioned in this section apply to using the C language to develop database applications that use embedded SQL.

11.2.1.1 Variant Characters

In C, a number of characters are used that belong to the variant character set. The variant character set consists of characters that change their code point based on the code page being used. In most cases trigraphs can be used instead of the variant characters to maintain uniformity of coding across platforms. Table 26 lists the trigraphs supported by each IBM SQL product.

Table 26 (Page 1 of 2). Trigraph Support						
Trigraph	**Char**	**DB2 for MVS**	**SQL/DS**	**DB2 for OS/400**	**DB2 for OS/2**	**DB2 for AIX**
??(	[	X	X	X	X	X
??)	]	X	X	X	X	X

Table 26 (Page 2 of 2). *Trigraph Support*

Trigraph	Char	DB2 for MVS	SQL/DS	DB2 for OS/400	DB2 for OS/2	DB2 for AIX
??<	{	X	X	X	X	X
??>	}	X	X	X	X	X
??′	^	T	T	T	T	T
??-	~	T	T	T	T	T
??!	|	T	T	T	T	T
??/	\	X	X	X	N	N
??=	#	T	T	X	T	T

Notes:

- X denotes full support.

- T tolerates trigraph but does no special processing.

- N does not support the trigraph.

11.2.1.2 NULL-Terminated Strings

The IBM-SQL standard for C requires that input host variables that are NULL-terminated are treated as varying length. The host variable value only includes those bytes before the NULL-terminator. The NULL-terminator is required. If it is not present, an error is returned. The IBM SQL standard for C requires that output host variables that are NULL-terminated are treated as fixed length. The host variable must be blank padded on assignment, and a null must be placed in the last byte position of the NULL-terminated host variable. In DB2 for OS/400, compliance is governed by the *CNULRQD parameter, used in the CRTSQLC precompiler. In DB2 for OS/2 and DB2 for AIX, compliance is governed by the /L and LANGLEVL parameters used in the precompilers.

11.2.1.3 Pointer Data Types

The degree of support for pointers in host variables varies among IBM SQL products:

- In DB2 for MVS/ESA, pointers can be used only in a descriptor name, and then only a one-level pointer is allowed.

- In SQL/DS, a one-level pointer can be used.

- DB2 for OS/400 supports pointers with more than one level, up to the limit of the C language.

- DB2 for OS/2 and DB2 for AIX support up to a ten-level pointer.

11.2.1.4 Miscellaneous

- Host structures are not supported by the DB2 for OS/2 and DB2 for AIX precompiler (in C).

- The C data type *int* is not supported for use in a host variable declaration.

- There is no exact equivalent in C for the PACKED data type. A host variable of type DOUBLE should be used to handle packed decimal columns. The C implementations for AS/400, ILE C/400, and DB2 for OS/400 support the PACKED data type.

- Single-precision floating point is not supported in C in the DB2 for OS/2 and DB2 for AIX application programs for host variable declarations.

11.2.2 COBOL Considerations

COMPUTATIONAL does not map to the same data type for each IBM SQL product. For COBOL/400, COMPUTATIONAL is equivalent to COMP-3 or PACKED-DECIMAL. In all other products COMPUTATIONAL is equivalent to COMP-4 or BINARY, which maps according to SMALLINT or INTEGER depending on its PICTURE clause.

SQL/DS requires the DECLARE CURSOR statement to be specified in the PROCEDURE DIVISION. In all other products the DECLARE CURSOR statement may also appear in the DATA DIVISION.

11.3 Choice of SQL

Some SQL statements differ among relational database products. SQL statements can be categorized as:

- SQL statements that conform to a particular standard

  These provide insurance for future requirements of the applications and allow the integration of new technology in a smoother fashion. In an expanding unlike database environment, this can be very important because it is fundamental to porting data from one type of database to another without affecting application programming code. The cost is in a possible loss of function. Most database systems have characteristics that are difficult to ignore and sometimes require the use of nonstandard SQL to exploit them.

- SQL statements that are common to multiple database systems

  If the environment is mature and reasonably stable, the use of nonstandard SQL might be considered low risk. It is quite legitimate to exploit the features of the environment in this case because application portability will be quite high.

- SQL statements that are unique to a subset of databases in the distributed environment

  The unique statements imply that portability is not possible in terms of SQL. Thus if the data moves to another database system, recoding of the SQL statements will be required. While this may be acceptable in a limited number of cases, the SQL statements should be treated as exceptions in a distributed database environment. For a database application that has this class of SQL statement within it, coding the statements into a separate application program enhances the portability of the application as a whole. Isolation of the exceptions in this way will make them easier to manage.

For reference purposes

- Table 27 lists the special registers supported by each IBM SQL product.
- Table 28 on page 334 lists the column functions supported by each IBM SQL product.
- Table 29 on page 334 lists the SQL statements supported by each IBM SQL product and commonly found in application programs.
- Table 30 on page 336 lists the scalar functions supported by each IBM SQL product.

Table 27 (Page 1 of 2). Special Registers Supported by IBM SQL Products					
	DB2 for MVS	**SQL/DS**	**DB2 for OS/400**	**DB2 for OS/2**	**DB2 for AIX**
CURRENT DATE	X	X	X	X	X
CURRENT DEGREE	X	—	—	—	—
CURRENT PACKAGESET	X	—	—	(1)	(1)
CURRENT SQLID	X	—	—	—	—
CURRENT SERVER (2)	X	X	X	X	X
CURRENT TIME	X	X	X	X	X
CURRENT TIMESTAMP	X	X	X	X	X

Table 27 (Page 2 of 2). *Special Registers Supported by IBM SQL Products*

	DB2 for MVS	SQL/DS	DB2 for OS/400	DB2 for OS/2	DB2 for AIX
CURRENT TIMEZONE	X	X	X	X	X
USER (3)	X	X	X	X	X

Notes:

- X denotes support for the SQL statement in some form.
- —does not support the SQL statement.

(1) DB2 for OS/2 and DB2 for AIX support the SET CURRENT PACKAGESET statement, but it is not implemented as a special register.

(2) The data type in DB2 for MVS/ESA is CHAR(16); in SQL/DS it is CHAR(18); and in DB2 for OS/400, DB2 for OS/2, and DB2 for AIX it is VARCHAR(18).

(3) The data type in DB2 for MVS/ESA and SQL/DS is CHAR(8); in DB2 for OS/400 it is VARCHAR(18); and in DB2 for OS/2 and DB2 for AIX it is VARCHAR(8).

Table 28. *Column Functions Supported by IBM SQL Products*

	DB2 for MVS	SQL/DS	DB2 for OS/400	DB2 for OS/2	DB2 for AIX
AVG	X	X	X	X	X
COUNT	X	X	X	X	X
MAX	X	X	X	X	X
MIN	X	X	X	X	X
SUM	X	X	X	X	X

Table 29 (Page 1 of 3). *SQL Statements Supported by IBM SQL Products*

	DB2 for MVS	SQL/DS	DB2 for OS/400	DB2 for OS/2	DB2 for AIX
BEGIN DECLARE	X	X	X	X	X
CLOSE	X	X	X	X	X
COMMIT	X	X	X	X	X
CONNECT	X	X	X	X	X

Table 29 (Page 2 of 3). *SQL Statements Supported by IBM SQL Products*

	DB2 for MVS	SQL/DS	DB2 for OS/400	DB2 for OS/2	DB2 for AIX
DECLARE CURSOR	X	X	X	X	X
DECLARE STATEMENT	X	—	X	—	—
DECLARE TABLE	X	—	—	—	—
DECLARE VARIABLE :c— :c—	X	—	—		
DELETE	X	X	X	X	X
DESCRIBE statement	X	X	X	X	X
DESCRIBE TABLE	X	—	X	—	—
END DECLARE	X	X	X	X	X
EXECUTE	X	X	X	X	X
EXECUTE IMMEDIATE	X	X	X	X	X
FETCH	X	X	X	X	X
INCLUDE	X	X	X	X	X
INSERT	X	X	X	X	X
LOCK DBSPACE	—	X	—	—	—
LOCK TABLE	X	X	X	X	X
OPEN	X	X	X	X	X
PREPARE	X	X	X	X	X
PUT	—	X	—	—	—
RELEASE	X	—	—	X	X
ROLLBACK	X	X	X	X	X
SELECT INTO	X	X	X	X	X
SET CONNECTION	X	—	—	X	X
SET register	X	—	—	—	—

Table 29 (Page 3 of 3). *SQL Statements Supported by IBM SQL Products*

	DB2 for MVS	SQL/DS	DB2 for OS/400	DB2 for OS/2	DB2 for AIX
SET host variable	X	—	—	—	—
UPDATE	X	X	X	X	X
WHENEVER	X	X	X	X	X

Notes:

- X denotes support for the SQL statement in some form.
- —does not support the SQL statement.

Table 30 (Page 1 of 2). *Scalar Functions Supported by IBM SQL Products*

	DB2 for MVS	SQL/DS	DB2 for OS/400	DB2 for OS/2	DB2 for AIX
ABSVAL	—	—	X	X	X
ACOST	—	—	X	—	—
ANTILOG	—	—	X	—	—
ASIN	—	—	X	X	X
ATAN	—	—	X	X	X
ATANH	—	—	X	—	—
CHAR(datetime)	X	X	X	X	X
CHAR(decimal)	X	X	—	X	X
COS	—	—	X	X	X
COSH	—	—	X	—	—
COT	—	—	X	X	X
DATE	X	X	X	X	X
DAY	X	X	X	X	X
DAYS	X	X	X	X	X
DECIMAL	X	X	X	X	X
DIGITS	X	X	X	X	X
EXP	—	—	X	X	X
FLOAT	X	X	X	X	X
HEX	X	X	X	X	X

Table 30 (Page 2 of 2). Scalar Functions Supported by IBM SQL Products

	DB2 for MVS	SQL/DS	DB2 for OS/400	DB2 for OS/2	DB2 for AIX
HOUR	X	X	X	X	X
INTEGER	X	X	X	X	X
LAND	—	—	X	—	—
LENGTH	X	X	X	X	X
LN	—	—	X	X	X
LNOT	—	—	X	—	—
LOG	—	—	X	X	X
LOR	—	—	X	—	—
MAX	—	—	X	X	X
MICROSECOND	X	X	X	X	X
MIN	—	—	X	X	X
MINUTE	X	X	X	X	X
MOD	—	—	X	—	—
MONTH	X	X	X	X	X
SECOND	X	X	X	X	X
SIN	—	—	X	X	X
SINH	—	—	X	—	—
SQRT	—	—	X	X	X
STRIP	—	X	X	—	—
SUBSTR	X	X	X	X	X
TAN	—	—	X	X	X
TANH	—	—	X	—	—
TIME	X	X	X	X	X
TIMESTAMP	X	X	X	X	X
TRANSLATE	—	X	X	X	X
VARGRAPHIC	X	X	—	X	X
XOR	—	—	X	—	—
YEAR	X	X	X	X	X
ZONED	—	—	X	—	—

11.3.1 SQL in a DDCS Environment

All IBM SQL products support the DML SELECT, INSERT, UPDATE, and DELETE statements and the cursor controlling statements of DECLARE CURSOR, OPEN, FETCH, and CLOSE. These SQL statements form the backbone of application programming in a relational database environment. Using the CONNECT, SET CONNECTION, COMMIT, and ROLLBACK SQL statements, applications can actively participate in a distributed relational database environment supported by DRDA. SQL statements do not necessarily execute where the application program is running. The DML statements actually execute on the database to which the application is connected at the time of statement execution. If the same statement were destined to execute on multiple database systems, the lowest common form of the statement that is supported by each of those database systems must be used. DDCS for OS/2 and DDCS for AIX fully support distributed static SQL and distributed dynamic SQL.

Application portability can be measured by how little change is required to move an application program from one environment to another. In the case of like environments, portability is not really an issue, and any of the methods listed below can be considered. In the case of unlike environments, when porting an application program, only the first method is available, because the output from one precompiler is not suitable for compilation and subsequent execution on a different platform because of architectural differences in the database APIs. There are three methods that may be considered:

1. Porting the base source code

2. Porting the precompiler generated modified source code

3. Porting the executable form of the application

11.3.1.1 Porting the Base Source Code

Porting the base source code requires the application to undergo the following on the destination platform:

- A precompile to generate a modified source file and a bind file

- A compile (and link) to generate an executable module

- A local bind (if local database access is required)

- A remote bind (if remote database access is required)

11.3.1.2 Porting the Modified Source Code

Porting the modified source code requires only a compile and link. The consistency tokens used for synchronization of the application program and the package are generated at precompile time, so token mismatch errors do not occur with remote database access. If the original bind file is available, it can be used to bind the package locally if required. If a local bind is required but the bind file is not available or not usable in the environment, porting the modified source file is not a viable option.

11.3.1.3 Porting the Executable Code

Porting the executable code is the simplest method. If the original bind file is available, it can be used to bind the package locally if required. If a local bind is required but the bind file is not available or not usable in the environment, porting the executable code is not an option.

Although this is the best way to port applications because of simplicity, it really works only when the operating systems are the same. Clearly, the best option is to port the executable form of the application. The next best option is to be in a position to port the executable code as soon as possible. This may mean creating a new version of the application, once for each type of platform, and then porting the executable modules between the individual machines belonging to a particular platform.

11.3.2 Connecting to Remote Databases

The CONNECT statement allows an application to route SQL calls to remote databases. CONNECT statement behavior and function vary depending on the local API and the DRDA level supported. When porting application programs that use CONNECT statements, care should be exercised to ensure that the application behaves in a desirable way on the destination system.

11.3.3 Terminating the Application

If an application uses DDCS to access a remote database through a CONNECT statement, either explicitly or implicitly, consideration should be given to coding a corresponding CONNECT RESET statement. The CONNECT RESET statement automatically invokes a COMMIT in the DDCS environment, when the application is using RUW, but not when it is using DUW.

If the application terminates normally without having specified a CONNECT RESET statement, DDCS automatically issues a CONNECT RESET on the application's behalf and COMMITs the RUW. If a program wants to have any remote database changes removed or undone, it should issue a ROLLBACK statement before terminating and before issuing any CONNECT RESET statement, when using RUW.

11.3.4 Handling Mixed Data

Mixed data is a term given to columns containing characters from both the single-byte character set (SBCS) and double-byte character set (DBCS).

EBCDIC on the host and ASCII on the workstation represent mixed data in different ways. When designing applications to use mixed data, size the column with consideration as to how much expansion may occur when switching between SBCS and DBCS. For each switch, add 2 bytes to the overall column length and set the host variable size to match the column size. Using variable length host variables in this situation improves the portability of the application.

11.3.5 Handling Long Data Fields

A column is considered long under the following conditions: DB2 for MVS/ESA long character strings are defined as VARCHAR(n), where n > 254, or VARGRAPHIC(n), where n > 127. LONG VARCHAR and LONG VARGRAPHIC can also be considered long if their actual length exceeds 254 bytes for character columns or 127 bytes for graphic columns.

DB2 for OS/400 long character strings are defined as VARCHAR(n), or CHAR(n), where n > 256, or VARGRAPHIC(n) or GRAPHIC(n), where n > 128. Other long character strings are defined as VARCHAR(n), where n > 254, or VARGRAPHIC(n), where n > 127. LONG VARCHAR and LONG VARGRAPHIC are considered long strings. All IBM SQL products place restrictions on the use of long columns, so careful planning is required when handling long strings in a distributed environment. Table 31 shows some of the restrictions for each IBM SQL product.

Table 31 (Page 1 of 2). Long String Restrictions on DML					
	DB2 for MVS	SQL/DS	DB2 for OS/400	DB2 for OS/2	DB2 for AIX
CHAR function	R	R	—	P	P
DATE/TIME functions	R	R	—	P	P
STRIP function	n/a	R	—	n/a	n/a
TRANSLATE function	n/a	R	—	P	P
VARGRAPHIC function	R	R	n/a	P	P
SUBSTR result	—	R	—	P	P
VALUE function/result	—	R	—	—	—
GROUP BY clause	R	R	—	R	R
ORDER BY clause	R	R	—	R	R

Table 31 (Page 2 of 2). *Long String Restrictions on DML*

	DB2 for MVS	SQL/DS	DB2 for OS/400	DB2 for OS/2	DB2 for AIX
SELECT DISTINCT	R	R	—	R	R
SUBSELECT	P	R	—	P	P
LIKE predicate	P	P	—	P	P
Column Functions	R	R	R	P	P
Concatenation	—	R	—	—	—

Notes:

- R indicates a restriction on the product.
- P indicates a partial restriction on the product.
- —no restrictions

11.3.6 SQLCA

Each IBM SQL product supports an SQLCA structure to communicate the results of SQL and database manager API calls to application programs. The names and the data types of each field in the SQLCA structure are the same in each product although some of the actual values may have a different meaning.

Variations are:

- DB2 for MVS/ESA, except when using C, provides an SQLEXT variable, which has now been functionally replaced by three extra SQLWARN indicators and a five-character SQLSTATE field.

- SQL/DS for VM does not generate a standard SQLCA for an INCLUDE SQLCA statement in a Fortran program.

- The PREP command (DB2 for OS/2) uses a parameter (/C) to indicate a standard SQLCA structure for Fortran programs. The default is to use the standard SQLCA format.

- The PREP command (DB2 for AIX) uses a parameter (SQLCA SAA) to indicate a standard SQLCA structure for Fortran programs. The default is to use the standard SQLCA format.

- For the SQLERRD fields, the third value consistently represents the number of rows affected by an INSERT, UPDATE, or DELETE SQL statement. All other fields are product specific but can convey the same meaning in more than one product.

- The SQLERRMC field usually contains a list of tokens separated by X′FF′. The tokens are used in message formatting routines to substitute for variables in error messages. Variations on this are:

    - DB2 for OS/400 returns message replace text instead of tokens except in response to a DRDA request, in which case the standard token list is returned.

    - DB2 for OS/2 and DB2 for AIX use a tokenized list but may use an X′FF′ to indicate a character token and an X′FE′ to indicate a numeric token.

- All IBM SQL products use the first SQLWARN field to indicate that at least one of the other SQLWARN indicators has been set. Other SQLWARN fields are product specific.

    There are error routines on some platforms that construct a very comprehensive message based on the contents of the SQLCA. Many customer installations also write their own error routine. It should be remembered that in a distributed environment, the error data returned in the SQLCA pertains to the system on which the statement was executed. Therefore, if a message formatting routine is available on the workstation and the SQL request went to the host, the message formatting routine may not construct a meaningful message because

- The SQLCODE does not necessarily convey the same meaning on the host as it does on the workstation.

- The SQLERRMC field contains tokens for the host format of the message, not the workstation format.

11.3.7 SQLCODE and SQLSTATE

Error handling in a distributed environment can be more complex than in a nondistributed environment.

There are three sources of error data to consider:

- Standard SQLCODE
- Mapped SQLCODE
- SQLSTATE variable

11.3.7.1 SQLCODE

All SQLCODE values conform to the following:

- If SQLCODE = 0, execution was successful.
- If SQLCODE > 0, execution was successful with a warning.
- If SQLCODE < 0, execution was not successful.

- If SQLCODE = +100, "no data" was found. In a cursor, this also signifies an end of record set condition.

Application programs that test for specific error conditions other than those listed above may need modifications to handle the same SQLCODEs originating from different database products.

11.3.7.2 Mapped SQLCODE

DDCS provides a mapping service that allows the SQLCODEs from the host databases to be converted to the workstation SQLCODEs. This mapping also converts the tokens in the SQLERRMC field of the SQLCA to a suitable workstation format. The principle behind the SQLCODE mapping facility is to allow applications developed on the workstation to execute without modification against host databases. DDCS translates the incoming DRDA server SQLCODE and SQLERRMC fields into their nearest equivalent on the workstation. If applications are explicitly testing for particular SQLCODE values, these values should be checked against the mapping files to ensure that the incoming DRDA SQLCODEs do in fact represent the same condition. Additionally, if the applications are ported from the workstation to the host environment, the SQLCODEs must to be rechecked to ensure that they mean the same thing in the host environment.

11.3.7.3 SQLSTATE

The SQLSTATE field of the SQLCA was introduced to allow all IBM SQL products to issue the same return code for the same type of error. The SQLSTATE values consist of a two-character class code, followed by a three-character subclass code value. Class code values represent classes of successful, successful with warnings, and unsuccessful SQL statement or API call conditions.

The SQLSTATE variable offers a consistent approach to error code handling in the distributed environment. Applications that check for particular SQLCODEs can be made more portable by altering the SQLCODE checking to SQLSTATE checking. However, although the SQLSTATE concept is good, it currently lacks the message texts and error token support that SQLCODEs provide.

11.3.8 Defining a Sort Order

Differences in collating sequences can cause undesirable results in queries and embedded SQL executed against multiple database systems. Character data is compared using a collating sequence. A collating sequence is an ordering for a set of characters that determines whether a particular character sorts higher, lower, or the same as another character. A single-byte character can be represented as a number between 0 and 255. This number is referred to as the code point of the character. A collating sequence orders these code points into a desirable sequence. The numerical value of a character's position within the collating sequence is referred to as the weight of the character. The same weight may apply to more than one character. A typical use of this is to give uppercase and lowercase alphabetic characters the same sorting sequence. When the code point and the weight values are identical throughout the collating sequence, the collating sequence is called an *identity sequence*.

Character comparisons are based on the weights of the characters. If nonunique weights are used, nonidentical characters may compare equally. For this reason, string comparison can be a two-phase process:

1. Compare the bytes of each string based on their weights.

2. If step 1 yielded equality, compare the bytes of each string based on their code point values.

If the collating sequence is the identity sequence, only the second step is performed. The collating sequence of a database affects

- The sequence of rows that qualify for SQL statements involving ordering criteria such as ORDER BY and GROUP BY clauses

- Qualifying rows selected by range predicates such as BETWEEN and GREATER THAN(>)

IBM SQL products use two main collating sequences:

- EBCDIC—used by DB2 for MVS/ESA, SQL/DS, and DB2 for OS/400

- ASCII—used by DB2 for AIX and DB2 for OS/2

Differences in these collating sequences affect only character data (that is CHAR, VARCHAR, and LONG VARCHAR type columns). The alphanumeric differences between these sequences are

- EBCDIC ...abc - xyz...ABC - XYZ...0-9...

- ASCII ...0 - 9...aAbBcC - xXyYzZ...

The traditional ASCII sequence is ...0 - 9...ABC - XYZ...abc - xyz... To minimize differences in query results, a user-defined collating sequence can be used in both DB2 for AIX and DB2 for OS/2 databases. The collating sequence for a database is defined at database creation time through an extension to the SQL CREATE DATABASE statement. Existing databases cannot have their collating sequence changed except by dropping the database and re-creating it.

Once a collating sequence is defined, all future character comparisons for that database are performed with that collating sequence. Potential problems may arise when

- An application merges sorted data originating from a source using a different collating sequence.

- An application makes assumptions about the ordering of data. For example, it assumes that numbers 0–9 are ranked lower than alphabetic characters A–Z or a–z.

11.3.9 Isolation

Different isolation levels are supported in IBM SQL products. Table 32 shows which products support which isolation levels.

Table 32. Isolation Levels Supported in IBM SQL Database Products					
	DB2 for MVS	SQL/DS	DB2 for OS/400	DB2 for OS/2	DB2 for AIX
Repeatable read	X	X	—	X	X
Read stability	—	—	X	X	X
Cursor stability	X	X	X	X	X
Uncommitted Read	X	—	X	X	X
No commit	—	—	X	—	—

Repeatable read ensures that

- Any row read during a unit of work is not changed by another process until the unit of work is complete.

- Any row changed by another process is not read until the other process completes its unit of work.

- The SQL statements issued are repeatable and produce the same results each time a given SQL SELECT statement is issued within the current unit of work.

Read stability ensures that

- Any row read during a unit of work is not changed by another process until the unit of work is complete.

- Any row changed by another process is not read until the other process completes its unit of work.

Read stability does not guarantee that the application will not see extra rows returned on repeated executions of a given SQL SELECT statement within the current unit of work. Extra rows may result from another process that is inserting data that meets current selection criteria.

Cursor stability ensures that

- Only the current row is not available for alteration by another process until the unit of work is complete.

- Any row changed by another process is not read until the other process completes its unit of work.

Uncommitted read allows

- Any row read during the current unit of work to be changed by another process.

- Any row that was changed by another process to be read.

No Commit. The rules are the same as for uncommitted read except

- COMMIT and ROLLBACK statements are not allowed.

- Changes are effectively committed at the end of each successful change operation and can be immediately accessed or changed by another process.

When an unsupported isolation level is requested by an AR, the AS escalates the isolation level to the next higher level.

11.3.10 Locking Considerations

All IBM SQL products support an explicit table lock through the LOCK TABLE SQL statement. If an explicit table lock is not requested, implicit locking on tables occurs during the execution of SQL statements. Although these are compatible within the IBM SQL product range, there can be differences in concurrency and deadlock potential because of differences in the duration and granularity of locks.

DB2 for MVS/ESA and DB2 common server use a timeout facility that controls how long a request for a lock waits until the request is rejected. Other databases wait indefinitely for the lock to be released.

DB2 for MVS/ESA can lock at the page level and so can lock rows that an application is not actually using. For DB2 for MVS/ESA Version 4, locking can be at the row level.

If an application relies on a database's implicit locking behavior, it may require reconsideration when participating in a distributed database environment because implicit locking might work differently on each platform.

11.3.11 Blocking

Blocking refers to the process whereby an AS responds to an AR with a block of rows for a cursor, as opposed to responding with only one row at a time. This can dramatically improve the network response time by reducing the amount of interactions between the AR and the AS.

When blocking is used,

1. The application program issues requests for cursor rows through the FETCH SQL statement.

2. The AR asks the AS for a block of rows if it has none in its buffers.

3. The AS initiates as many I/Os as required to fill the transfer block. This is defined by how many rows fit into the block and whether or not the end of the set has been reached.

4. The AS then sends this block of data back to the AR.

5. The AR then services consecutive fetch requests from its buffer until

   - The buffer is exhausted, in which case it requests another block from the AS.

   - The end of the set of records is reached.

When block fetch is used, performance will generally be substantially improved for most application programs retrieving large amounts of data through cursors. However, if the application fetches only the first few rows, performance may degrade as a result of using block fetch. This is because the first FETCH statement may take longer than normal as it may involve the selection of multiple rows. Block fetch comes in two varieties:

- *Limited Block Fetch:* With limited block fetch a single SNA APPC conversation is used for all requests and responses for participating cursors in an application program. This minimizes the overall requirement for APPC sessions. Processing between the AR and AS is synchronous. The AR issues a request to the AS for a block of cursor-related SQL data and waits for a response. After the AR receives the block of SQL data, it waits for the application program to finish fetching the rows in the data block before requesting another block from the AS.

- *Continuous Block Fetch:* Continuous block fetch allows one APPC session to be established for each eligible open cursor, as long as sufficient APPC sessions are available. For each eligible open cursor,

  - A request is sent from the AR to the AS.

  - The AS fills the data block with result rows and transmits the block back to the AR.

  Processing is asynchronous because the AS continues to fill and transmit the data blocks back to the AR until the prevailing SNA pacing limits are reached. If a session shortage arises, continuous block fetch falls back to limited block fetch.

DDCS uses a variation of limited block fetch. Refer to 2.1.7.5, "Prefetch" on page 20. DDCS supports the following blocking options:

- BLOCKING ALL—the target DBMS blocks ambiguous cursors.

- BLOCKING UNAMBIG—the target DBMS blocks only unambiguous cursors.

- BLOCKING NO—the target DBMS does not block cursors.

For a cursor to be eligible for block fetch, none of the following can be true:

- The cursor contains a FOR UPDATE OF clause.
- A static positioned DELETE or UPDATE statement references the cursor.
- The select list contains a long string (SQL/DS only).

A cursor is ambiguous when it cannot be determined at BIND time whether the cursor is read-only or used by UPDATE and DELETE. Host database systems consider that dynamic cursors are ambiguous. For simplicity, read-only cursors should be marked with a FOR FETCH ONLY clause, and update cursors should be marked with a FOR UPDATE OF clause. These clauses can then control the level of blocking an application does at a cursor level. If an update is attempted on a cursor that is using blocking, the update fails. DDCS uses the block size specified in the DB2 for OS/2 or DB2 for AIX configuration file for the RQRIOBLK field.

Cursors using block fetch operations are vulnerable to reading data that has already been changed. With block fetch, database access speeds ahead of the application to prefetch rows. Thus it is possible for the application to fetch rows that no longer exist or to miss recently inserted rows. This may be acceptable to the application. If it is not acceptable, block fetching should be disabled.

Again, the simplest method of controlling block fetch is to use the FOR FETCH ONLY and FOR UPDATE OF clauses. The latter can be used on a cursor even if updates will not be made through that cursor.

Chapter 12. Application Structure

This chapter provides several application examples using DRDA across the various DB2 family of products platforms. The purpose of this chapter is to provide application developers with a set of simple code samples highlighting the characteristics of the various DB2 family of products platforms as ASs and ARs. We intended to keep the code as simple and essential as possible. For this reason, the programs we provide are not meant to reproduce a real customer application environment (which would imply, for instance, a sophisticated user interface).

The samples discussed in this chapter are variations on the same logic. Once you understand the structure of the first program, you can easily follow the flow of the subsequent samples:

- A DRDA level 1 program accessing the various locations in read-only mode

- The same program as above, migrated to DRDA level 2

- A DRDA level 2 program performing database updates at a single site and accessing the other locations in read-only mode

- A DRDA level 2 program performing database updates at multiple sites in the same unit of work. This version of the program must be run on an AR supporting two-phase commit.

- The same as the previous program, modified so that it can be run on a requester that does not support two-phase commit.

12.1 SQL Tables Used by Application Programs

Throughout this chapter we intend to develop a simple order entry application. Our scenario is based on a hypothetical company that has a central database, where order fulfillment is performed, and various branch offices and warehouses. Our programs implement a simple ordering application for spare parts.

The sample programs we discuss rely on the following database tables:

- PART_MAST—Holds a description of each spare part with which the company deals (see Table 33 on page 352). A copy of this table resides at all locations and can contain parts that are not necessarily held in stock at that location.

- PART_STOCK—Holds a list of parts and their quantities that are currently held in stock at the location (see Table 34 on page 352). Each location has its own copy of this table.

- LOCATION—Holds the list of the location names (DBMS names) in our network of warehouses (see Table 35 on page 352). It also indicates whether a specific location runs an RDBMS that supports two-phase commit.

- ORDERTBL—Contains the orders for spare parts issued from the various branch offices (see Table 36). In our scenario, an order simply corresponds to a single row of this table. The order information includes the name of the warehouse where the order will be filled. This table is only needed at the central site.

Table 33. PART_MAST Table

PART_NUMB	SMALLINT
PART_DESC	CHAR(20)

Table 34. PART_STOCK Table

PART_NUMB	SMALLINT
PART_QTY	SMALLINT

Table 35. LOCATION Table

LOCATION	CHAR(8)
TWOPC	CHAR(1)

Note: The LOCATION column identifies whether a location supports DRDA level 2 (*Y*), DUW (*P*), or RUW only (*N*).

Table 36. ORDERTBL Table

ORD_NUMB	SMALLINT
PART_NUMB	SMALLINT
ORD_QTY	SMALLINT
ORD_TIME	TIMESTAMP
ORD_LOC	CHAR(8)

12.2 DRDA Level 1 Example

In this section we describe a simple DRDA level 1 application that will be the basis for the remaining examples. This program asks the user for a part number. It then accesses the local database to find the part description and displays it on the screen. The program then connects to the various locations to retrieve the quantity on hand for the requested part available at each warehouse. The quantity values are displayed on the screen.

This program has been tested on the following ARs:

- DB2 for OS/400
- DB2 for MVS
- DB2 for OS/2
- DB2 for AIX
- DB2 for VM

The program can access any AS supporting DRDA.

12.2.1 Program Pseudocode

The following pseudocode describes the functions of the program (referred to from now on as *PARTSTK*).

```
BEGIN PARTSTK

    Request the part number from user;
    CONNECT TO LOCAL;

    IF CONNECT OK
      BEGIN IF
        Get part description from PART_MAST;
        Print part description;
        Count the number of locations in LOCATION table;
        Get the locations from LOCATION table;
      END IF
    ELSE GOTO ERR_ROUTINE;

    FOR I=1 to number of locations
      BEGIN FOR
        CONNECT TO location
        IF connection to location is OK
          BEGIN IF
            Get the stock information from PART_STOCK table;
            IF OK print stock information on the screen;
            ELSE print ERROR in retrieving stock information;
          END IF
        ELSE  /* Connection to location failed */
          BEGIN ELSE
            Print ERROR in CONNECT;
            CONTINUE
          END ELSE
    END FOR I

    ERR_ROUTINE:
        Print error information;

END PARTSTK
```

12.3 Program Coding

Figure 163 on page 355 shows the PARTSTK source code when we used C and embedded SQL in the OS/2 environment.

```
1
#include <sqlcodes.h>
#include <sqlenv.h>
#include <sqlutil.h>
#include <sql.h>
#include <stdio.h>
#include <stdlib.h>
#include <string.h>

2 EXEC SQL INCLUDE SQLCA;


3 EXEC SQL WHENEVER SQLERROR    GOTO err_routine;
   EXEC SQL WHENEVER SQLWARNING CONTINUE;
   EXEC SQL WHENEVER NOT FOUND  CONTINUE;

4
EXEC SQL BEGIN DECLARE SECTION;
 short part_num;
 short part_qty;
 short part_reqd=0;
 char  part_desc[21]
 char  location[9];
 short locnum;
EXEC SQL END   DECLARE SECTION;

   5 char loc_list[23][9];
     int   i=0;
     int   j=0;
     int rc;
     char sqlstate_str[6];

main()
{

   sqlstate_str[5]='\0';

     printf(" Partstck program running..\n");
   6 printf(" Please enter part number:\n");
     gets(part_desc);part_reqd=atoi(part_desc);

     printf("  Connecting to LOCAL\n");
```

Figure 163 (Part 1 of 4). PARTSTK Program Sample Code (1)

```
7  EXEC SQL CONNECT TO LOCAL;

   printf("%s","\n  Connection to LOCAL established");
   printf("%s", "\n\n  Finding part description\n\n");

   EXEC SQL SELECT PART_NUMB, PART_DESC
       INTO :part_num, :part_desc
       FROM PART_MAST
      WHERE PART_NUMB = :part_reqd;
   if ((rc = strncmp(sqlca.sqlstate,"00000",5)) !=0) goto err_routine;

   printf("  Description selected for part: %d\n",part_num);
   printf("               description: %s\n",part_desc);
   printf(" \n");

8  EXEC SQL SELECT  COUNT(*) into :locnum FROM LOCATION;
9  EXEC SQL DECLARE loc_csr CURSOR FOR
   SELECT LOCATION
     FROM LOCATION;

   EXEC SQL OPEN loc_csr;
   for(i=0;i<=(locnum-1);++i) {
      EXEC SQL FETCH loc_csr INTO :location;

      for(j=7;location[j]==' ';j--) {
         location[j] = '\0';
      }
      strcpy(loc_list[i],location);
   }
   10  EXEC SQL CLOSE loc_csr;
      EXEC SQL COMMIT;
      EXEC SQL CONNECT RESET;
```

Figure 163 (Part 2 of 4). PARTSTK Program Sample Code (1)

```
11  for(i=0;i<=(locnum-1);++i)
      {
          strcpy(location,loc_list[i]);

      12  EXEC SQL WHENEVER SQLERROR CONTINUE;

      13  EXEC SQL CONNECT TO :location;

    14  if ((rc = strncmp(sqlca.sqlstate,"00000",5)) !=0)
       printf("\n\n  %s %s%s\n","Location ", location,  " not available   ");
       else
       {
         printf("%s%s\n", "\n  Connected to:  ", location);
         15  EXEC SQL
             SELECT PART_QTY
               INTO :part_qty
               FROM PART_STOCK
             WHERE PART_NUMB = :part_reqd;


         16  if ((rc = strncmp(sqlca.sqlstate,"00000",5)) !=0)
             {
               strncpy(sqlstate_str,sqlca.sqlstate,5);
               printf("\n   Error in receiving stock information from
               this location");
               printf("%s%s\n","  Sqlstate:".sqlstate_str);
               EXEC SQL CONNECT RESET;

             } /* END IF, sqlstate different from 0 */
      17  else printf("  Stock for %s is %d\n",location,part_qty);

      18  EXEC SQL COMMIT;
          EXEC SQL CONNECT RESET;

      } /* END ELSE, Connection OK */
   } /* END FOR, connecting to every location */
```

Figure 163 (Part 3 of 4). PARTSTK Program Sample Code (1)

```
    return(0);    /**** return code 0 = No errors, OK ****/


    /****                      ****/
    /**** Global error handling routine ****/
    /****                      ****/
    [19]
    err_routine:
      strncpy(sqlstate_str,sqlca.sqlstate,5);
      printf("An error has occured...\n");
      printf("         Sqlstate: %s\n",sqlstate_str);
      printf("         Sqlcaid: %s\n",sqlca.sqlcaid);
      printf("         Sqlcabc: %d\n",sqlca.sqlcabc);
      printf("         Sqlerrml: %d\n",sqlca.sqlerrml);
      printf("         Sqlerrmc: %s\n",sqlca.sqlerrmc);
      printf("         Sqlerrp: %s\n",sqlca.sqlerrp);
      printf("         Sqlerrd: %d\n",sqlca.sqlerrd);
      EXEC SQL CONNECT RESET;
      return(99);  /**** return code 99 = something failed ****/

    }  /* END MAIN */
```

Figure 163 (Part 4 of 4). PARTSTK Program Sample Code (1)

Notes for Figure 163 on page 355

1 The included files contain definitions of APIs, constraints, data structures, macros, and constants required by the application program.

2 The precompiler will generate a host-language-specific structure as a result of the EXEC SQL INCLUDE SQLCA statement. The SQLCA contains variables that are used by the RDBMS to provide an application program with the information about the execution of SQL statements and API calls.

3 The WHENEVER statements are directed to the precompiler for handling error conditions. They instruct the precompiler to automatically pass control to the error routine (err_routine) if the SQLSTATE reflects an error as a result of an SQL statement's execution.

4 Host variables are defined in a section within the bounds of the BEGIN DECLARE SECTION and the END DECLARE SECTION statements. Not all precompilers demand such a rigid placement of host variables. All IBM SQL precompilers support this method, so it is the most portable way of specifying host variables.

5 Variables that are used in a C program must be introduced before they are used. When introducing variables, the type of the variable is given first, followed by its name.

6 Part number is prompted from the user. It is stored to be used in the SQL statement to get the part description.

7 A connection to LOCAL is issued. The word LOCAL is arbitrary and needs a database alias LOCAL to exist in each local database directory. An SQL call is issued to retrieve the description of the part from the PART_MAST table.

8 An SQL call is issued to count the number of locations from the LOCATION table. This is a way to find out to how many locations the application program PARTSTK needs to connect. When a new location is added, PARTSTK does not have to be changed; only the LOCATION table must be updated.

9 A cursor is defined to retrieve all locations from the LOCATION table in a fetch loop and to store them in a character array.

10 When all locations are fetched and stored, the work is committed and the PARTSTK program disconnects from the location.

11 Next, the PARTSTK application program connects to all locations in a FOR-loop to get the part stock information. The loop is repeated until all locations are searched.

12 WHENEVER SQL ERROR CONTINUE is executed. This means that the global WHENEVER SQLERROR GOTO err_routine is overwritten and an implicit check of SQLSTATE is implemented after each execution of any SQL statement. This makes it possible to continue program execution easily after an SQL error. For example, if there is a communications error when executing a CONNECT statement, program execution does not stop and the connection to the next location can be tried.

13 A connect to a location is issued.

14 SQLSTATE is checked after the CONNECT statement. If it indicates an error, the user is informed that the location is not available, and the program continues and connects to the next location (= next execution of the FOR-loop).

15 If the connection is OK, an SQL call is issued to get the part stock information from the PART_STOCK table.

16 If SQLSTATE indicates that there was an error while retrieving the part stock information, the user is informed, the error code is printed on the screen, and the program continues by connecting to the next location (= next execution of the FOR-loop).

17 If the part stock information is retrieved properly, the application prints it out on the screen.

18 After the part stock information is retrieved from a location, the work is committed. After that the PARTSTK program disconnects from the location and continues to the next one (=next execution of the FOR-loop).

19 Err_routine is part of this application that is executed in some error situations. When the WHENEVER SQL ERROR statement indicates an error situation, err_routine is always executed. Also, if the retrieval of the part information from the local database LOCAL is unsuccessful, err_routine is executed.

12.4 Moving to DRDA Level 2

Even if your DRDA level 1 applications performs only read operations on the various databases in the network, as in the previous example, it may be worthwhile to migrate the applications to use the DRDA level 2 protocol for performance reasons.

In DRDA level 1, only one connection could be active, whereas DRDA level 2 allows the coexistence of multiple active connections. Switching from one location to another is much faster if you use DRDA level 2, especially if you have to access various locations multiple times in the same application. You can afford to keep the connections active and then use *SET CONNECTION* to set the current connection to locations to which you have already connected. This will save the time needed to perform a CONNECT RESET and issue the CONNECT again.

In our example, moving to DRDA level 2 did not really provide a performance improvement, because the program never went back to access a location that had been previously connected. However, look at the code in Figure 164 on page 361 to understand the steps required to migrate your DRDA level 1 applications to the DRDA level 2 protocol.

12.4.1 Program Pseudocode

The logic of the program is exactly the same as in the previous example. Refer to 12.2.1, "Program Pseudocode" on page 353 to understand the flow of the application.

12.4.2 Program Coding

Not many changes are needed to migrate the previous example to DRDA level 2. The changes are highlighted and explained right after the coding.

```
/* #include <sqlcodes.h>
#include <sqlenv.h>
#include <sqlutil.h>
#include <sql.h> */
#include <stdio.h>
#include <stdlib.h>
#include <string.h>

EXEC SQL INCLUDE SQLCA;


EXEC SQL WHENEVER SQLERROR    GOTO err_routine;
EXEC SQL WHENEVER SQLWARNING CONTINUE;
EXEC SQL WHENEVER NOT FOUND  CONTINUE;


EXEC SQL BEGIN DECLARE SECTION;
 char LOCAL[9] = "RCAS400";
 short part_num;
 short part_qty;
 short part_reqd=0;
 char  part_desc[21];
 char  location[9];
 char  user_id[11];
 char  pasw_id[11];
 short locnum;
EXEC SQL END   DECLARE SECTION;

  char loc_list[23][9];
     int  i=0;
     int  j=0;
     int rc;
     char sqlstate_str[6];
```

Figure 164 (Part 1 of 4). DRDASUTS: Moving to DRDA Level 2

```
main()
{

   sqlstate_str[5]='\0';

      printf(" Partstck program running..\n");
      printf(" Please enter your userid in uppercase...\n");
      gets(user_id);
      printf(" Please enter your password in uppercase...\n");
      gets(pasw_id);
      printf(" Please enter part number:\n");
      gets(part_desc);part_reqd=atoi(part_desc);

      printf("  Connecting to LOCAL\n");
   EXEC SQL WHENEVER SQLERROR   CONTINUE; ▇1
   EXEC SQL CONNECT TO :LOCAL
            USER   :user_id
            USING :pasw_id;
   if ((rc = strncmp(sqlca.sqlstate,"08002",5)) ==0)  ▇2
      EXEC SQL SET CONNECTION :LOCAL;
      EXEC SQL WHENEVER SQLERROR   GOTO err_routine;

   printf("%s","\n Connection to LOCAL established");
   printf("%s", "\n\n  Finding part description\n\n");

   EXEC SQL SELECT PART_NUMB, PART_DESC
        INTO :part_num, :part_desc
        FROM PART_MAST
      WHERE PART_NUMB = :part_reqd;
   if ((rc = strncmp(sqlca.sqlstate,"00000",5)) !=0) goto err_routine;
   printf(" Description selected for part: %d\n",part_num);
   printf("                description: %s\n",part_desc);
   printf(" \n");
```

Figure 164 (Part 2 of 4). DRDASUTS: Moving to DRDA Level 2

```
      EXEC SQL SELECT  COUNT(*) into :locnum FROM LOCATION;
      EXEC SQL DECLARE loc_csr CURSOR FOR
       SELECT LOCATION
         FROM LOCATION ;
      EXEC SQL OPEN loc_csr;
      for(i=0;i<=(locnum-1);++i) {
         EXEC SQL FETCH loc_csr INTO :location;
         for(j=7;location[j]==' ';j--) {
            location[j] = '\0';
         }
         strcpy(loc_list[i],location);
       }
          EXEC SQL CLOSE loc_csr;
/*                                                              */
/* The Connection is not closed here, because now we are using DRDA2 */
/*                                                              */
      for(i=0;i<=(locnum-1);++i)
        {
         strcpy(location,loc_list[i]);

         EXEC SQL WHENEVER SQLERROR CONTINUE;  [1]

         EXEC SQL CONNECT TO :location
               USER  :user_id
               USING :pasw_id;
         printf("SQLCODE = %d\n", sqlca.sqlcode);
         if ((rc = strncmp(sqlca.sqlstate,"08002",5)) ==0)
               EXEC SQL SET CONNECTION :location;  [3]
               /* If sqlstate=08002 the connection has already been
                  established. We need to set the current connection
               */
         EXEC SQL WHENEVER SQLERROR   GOTO err_routine;

      if ((rc = strncmp(sqlca.sqlstate,"00000",5)) !=0)
         printf("\n\n  %s %s%s\n","Location ", location,  " not available   ");
         else
         {
           printf("%s%s\n", "\n  Connected to:  ", location);
```

Figure 164 (Part 3 of 4). *DRDASUTS: Moving to DRDA Level 2*

```
                    EXEC SQL
                    SELECT PART_QTY
                      INTO :part_qty
                      FROM PART_STOCK
                      WHERE PART_NUMB = :part_reqd;

           if ((rc = strncmp(sqlca.sqlstate,"00000",5)) !=0)
               {
                   strncpy(sqlstate_str,sqlca.sqlstate,5);
                   printf("\n   Error in receiving stock information from\
                   this location");
                   printf("%s%s\n","   Sqlstate:", sqlstate_str);
       /*    EXEC SQL CONNECT RESET;*/ ▊4
       /*    Not needed in DRDA-2   */

               } /* END IF, sqlstate different from 0 */
         else printf("  Stock for %s is %d\n",location,part_qty);
       } /* END ELSE, Connection OK */
    } /* END FOR, connecting to every location */

    EXEC SQL COMMIT;
    return(0);   /**** return code 0 = No errors, OK ****/

    /****                          ****/
    /**** Global error handling routine ****/
    /****                          ****/
  err_routine:
    strncpy(sqlstate_str,sqlca.sqlstate,5);
    printf("An error has occurred...\n"); /*... Changed ....*/
    printf("          SQLCODE: %d\n", SQLCODE);
    printf("          Sqlstate: %s\n",sqlstate_str);
    printf("          Sqlcaid: %s\n",sqlca.sqlcaid);
    printf("          Sqlcabc: %d\n",sqlca.sqlcabc);
    printf("          Sqlerrml: %d\n",sqlca.sqlerrml);
    printf("          Sqlerrmc: %s\n",sqlca.sqlerrmc);
    printf("          Sqlerrp: %s\n",sqlca.sqlerrp);
    printf("          Sqlerrd: %d\n",sqlca.sqlerrd);
    EXEC SQL RELEASE ALL;
    EXEC SQL ROLLBACK;
    return(99);  /**** return code 99 = something failed ****/

  } /* END MAIN */
```

Figure 164 (Part 4 of 4). DRDASUTS: Moving to DRDA Level 2

Notes for Figure 164 on page 361

1 We have to disable the current exception handler because the following SQL CONNECT statement may generate an error if the connection already exists. In that case, we just want to set the current connection to that location. We will monitor this specific error in the program.

2 This statement checks the *sqlstate* to verify whether the connection already exists. The corresponding value of the *sqlstate* is 08002. If the test determines that the connection is already active, we have to make sure that the current connection points to that location. This can be achieved by issuing a *SET CONNECTION* SQL statement.

3 This statement will be executed if the program finds active connections. In that case, performance will be significantly faster than when starting a brand new connection is required. Active connections can be maintained across program invocations. If you run this program multiple times, you will notice that the first run will activate the connections and the subsequent executions will proceed faster than the first, because they will take advantage of the existing connections.

4 The *CONNECT RESET* statement is no longer needed because DRDA level 2 supports multiple active connections.

12.5 DRDA Level 2 Single-Site Update

In this section, we take a further step in implementing DRDA level 2 function within our example. We intend to modify our program so that an order can be created as a result of the processing. In our scenario, an order is represented by a record in the *ORDERTBL* table. The program will therefore create a new record in the ORDERTBL table residing at the central database (*CENTDB2*).

Here is a quick explanation of the logic of the new version of the program, which now implements *single-site update* logic in our DRDA level 2 network

- The user will be prompted for the part number and the quantity to be ordered.
- The program first connects to the central database to make sure the location is accessed in read/write mode.
- The program reads the LOCATION table.
- The program connects to all locations.
- The location with the highest quantity of the requested item is identified.
- An order is then created at the central database containing the part number, the quantity, the current time stamp, and the name of the location we selected.
- The program then commits the transaction.

There are some considerations we want to point out before we discuss the actual coding.

The *single-site update* scenario is particularly important because it can be implemented and run on any AR supporting DUW. All of the IBM DB2 family of products support single-site update, with the exception of SQL/DS for VM and SQL/DS for VSE. At the time of writing, DDCS for OS/2 and DDCS for AIX support single-site update only with DRDA databases in a DUW because they do not provide support for two-phase commit in a heterogeneous network of DRDA level 2 systems. Thus out of the multiple DRDA connections that can be established, only one of them supports read and write operations. The remaining active connections support only read operations. However, DB2 common server allows multiple-site updates if all involved RDBMSs use the private protocol; all involved RDBMSs are DB2 common servers.

If executing the program from a DRDA level 2 AR and connecting to a DRDA level 1 and DRDA level 2 AS, you should pay special attention to the sequence of the *CONNECT* statements because that sequence determines which location will be accessed in read/write mode. In particular, the first connection to be established will always be update capable. Therefore, it is crucial that the first connection occurs against the central database, which is where we will create the new order record.

If executing the program from a DB2 common server AR, the order of the *CONNECT* statement is not important, but the first update is important. If the first update is to a DRDA AS, then this is the only server that can be updated. If the first update is to a DB2 common server, then all DB2 common servers can be updated and all DRDA ASs are read-only.

12.5.1 Program Pseudocode
The following pseudocode describes the application flow.

```
BEGIN PARTSTK

    Request the part number from user;
    Request the quantity to be ordered;
    RELEASE ALL the existing connections;
    CONNECT TO CENTDB2;

    IF CONNECT OK
      BEGIN IF
        CONNECT TO LOCAL;
          IF CONNECT OK
            BEGIN IF
              Get part description from PART_MAST;
              Print part description;
              Count the number of locations in LOCATION table;
              Get the locations from LOCATION table;
            END IF
          ELSE GOTO ERR_ROUTINE;
    ELSE GOTO ERR_ROUTINE;

    FOR I=1 to number of locations
      BEGIN FOR
        CONNECT TO location
        IF connection to location is OK
          BEGIN IF
            Get the stock information from PART_STOCK table;
            IF OK print stock information on the screen;
            Determine the location with the maximum amount of
              the requested part and save it in MAXLOC
            ELSE print ERROR in retrieving stock information;
          END IF
        ELSE  /* Connection to location failed */
          BEGIN ELSE
            Print ERROR in CONNECT;
            CONTINUE
          END ELSE
    END FOR I
    SET CONNECTION CENTDB2;
    INSERT new order row INTO ORDERTBL;
    COMMIT;
```

```
ERR_ROUTINE:
        Print error information;

END PARTSTK
```

12.5.2 Program Coding

Figure 165 on page 369 shows the program coding from DRDASU2, an evolution of the previous program. The changes we introduced are highlighted and explained below.

1 Since we want to be able to control which connection will be read/write capable, we have to make sure that no existing connections have read/write privileges. For this reason, we drop all existing connections at the beginning of the program. The *RELEASE ALL* statement followed by a COMMIT serves this purpose. If no active connections exist when the program is called, the COMMIT statement would fail, generating an SQLERROR. For this reason, we temporarily disable the exception handler.

2 This statement activates the first connection in this application. The connection is directed to the central database and will have read/write privileges. Currently, if the program runs on a DB2 common server and actually performs updates in this DRDA AS, all remaining connections **3** and **4** will be read-only. Because DB2 common server will support DRDA level 2 in the future, it is therefore critical, for compatibility purposes, that the first connection is directed to the central database, where we will create the new order.

5 The connection to the central database is already active. We just have to switch back to it with a *SET CONNECTION* statement before inserting a new row into the ORDERTBL table. We will then commit the transaction.

```
/*This program uses the DRDA-2 Connection Manager and performs a      */
/*database update on a single site in a DRDA-2 network.  The program */
/*first connects to the central database server (CENTDB2) to ensure  */
/*that the connection is read/write  capable.  It will then connect  */
/*to the local database manager to read the table where the locations*/
/*are registered. The program will also determine which location has */
/*the highest amount of the requested part item and generate a new   */
/*order at the central site.  It will finally commit the transaction.*/
/*This program can run off any Application Requester supporting       */
/*DRDA-2. 2-Phase commitment control support is not required for this*/
/*program to run successfully.  */

/* #include <sqlcodes.h>
#include <sqlenv.h>
#include <sqlutil.h>
#include <sql.h> */
#include <stdio.h>
#include <stdlib.h>
#include <string.h>

EXEC SQL INCLUDE SQLCA;

EXEC SQL WHENEVER SQLERROR   GOTO err_routine;
EXEC SQL WHENEVER SQLWARNING CONTINUE;
EXEC SQL WHENEVER NOT FOUND  CONTINUE;


EXEC SQL BEGIN DECLARE SECTION;
 char LOCAL[9] = "RCAS400"; /*... Changed ....*/
 char POK[9] = "CENTDB2"; /*... Changed ....*/
 short new_ord_numb;
 short part_num;
 short part_qty;
 short part_reqd=0;
 short ord_qtyd=0;
 char  partnums[5];
 char  ord_qty[5];
 char  part_desc[21];
 char  location[9];
 char  maxloc[9];
 char  user_id[11];
 char  pasw_id[11];
 short locnum;
 short max_part_qty = 0;
 EXEC SQL END   DECLARE SECTION;
```

Figure 165 (Part 1 of 6). DRDASU2: DRDA Level 2 Single-Site Update

```
   char loc_list[23][9];
      int   i=0;
      int   j=0;
      int rc;
      char sqlstate_str[6];
main()
{

   sqlstate_str[5]='\0';

      EXEC SQL RELEASE ALL;
      EXEC SQL whenever SQLERROR continue;  ■1
      EXEC SQL COMMIT;
      EXEC SQL whenever SQLERROR GOTO err_routine;

      /* RELEASE ALL AND COMMIT, to make sure there are no */
      /* active   connections                             */

      printf(" Partstck program running..\n");
      printf(" Please enter your userid in uppercase...\n");
      gets(user_id);
      printf(" Please enter your password in uppercase...\n");
      gets(pasw_id);
      printf(" Please enter part number:\n");
      gets(partnums);part_reqd=atoi(partnums);
      printf(" Please enter order quantity:\n");
      gets(ord_qty);ord_qtyd=atoi(ord_qty);
      printf("  Connecting to Order Center POK..\n");

   EXEC SQL WHENEVER SQLERROR  CONTINUE;
   EXEC SQL CONNECT TO :POK  ■2
            USER   :user_id
            USING :pasw_id;
      printf("SQLCODE %d \n", sqlca.sqlcode);   /*MONITOR SQLCODE*/
      if ((rc = strncmp(sqlca.sqlstate,"08002",5)) ==0)
   EXEC SQL WHENEVER SQLERROR   GOTO err_routine;
```

Figure 165 (Part 2 of 6). DRDASU2: DRDA Level 2 Single-Site Update

```
    printf("%s","\n  Connection to Order Center established");

    printf("  Connecting to LOCAL..\n");
EXEC SQL WHENEVER SQLERROR  CONTINUE;
EXEC SQL CONNECT TO :LOCAL 3
        USER  :user_id
        USING :pasw_id;
  printf("SQLCODE %d \n", sqlca.sqlcode);  /*MONITOR SQLCODE*/
  if ((rc = strncmp(sqlca.sqlstate,"08002",5)) ==0)
    EXEC SQL SET CONNECTION :LOCAL;
EXEC SQL WHENEVER SQLERROR   GOTO err_routine;
printf("%s","\n  Connection to LOCAL established");
printf("%s", "\n\n  Finding part description\n\n");

EXEC SQL SELECT PART_NUMB, PART_DESC
    INTO :part_num, :part_desc
    FROM PART_MAST
    WHERE PART_NUMB = :part_reqd;
if ((rc = strncmp(sqlca.sqlstate,"00000",5)) !=0) goto err_routine;

printf("  Description selected for part: %d\n",part_num);
printf("              description: %s\n",part_desc);
printf(" \n");

EXEC SQL SELECT  COUNT(*) into :locnum FROM LOCATION;
EXEC SQL DECLARE loc_csr CURSOR FOR
 SELECT LOCATION
   FROM LOCATION;

EXEC SQL OPEN loc_csr;
for(i=0;i<=(locnum-1);++i) {
   EXEC SQL FETCH loc_csr INTO :location;

   for(j=7;location[j]==' ';j--) {
       location[j] = '\0';
   }
   strcpy(loc_list[i],location);
}
```

Figure 165 (Part 3 of 6). DRDASU2: DRDA Level 2 Single-Site Update

```
      EXEC SQL CLOSE loc_csr;
/*                                                                    */
/* The Connection is not close here, because now we are using DRDA2*/
/*                                                                    */
   for(i=0;i<=(locnum-1);++i)
     {
      strcpy(location,loc_list[i]);

      EXEC SQL WHENEVER SQLERROR CONTINUE;

      EXEC SQL CONNECT TO :location  4
            USER   :user_id
            USING :pasw_id;
      printf("SQLCODE %d \n", sqlca.sqlcode); /*MONITOR SQLCODE*/

   if ((rc = strncmp(sqlca.sqlstate,"08002",5)) ==0)
            EXEC SQL SET CONNECTION :location;
            /* If sqlstate= 08002 the connection has already been
               established. We need to set the current connection
            */
      EXEC SQL WHENEVER SQLERROR   GOTO err_routine;

   if ((rc = strncmp(sqlca.sqlstate,"00000",5)) !=0)
      printf("\n\n  %s %s%s\n","Location ", location,  " not available   ");
      else
      {
        printf("%s%s\n", "\n  Connected to:  ", location);
            EXEC SQL
            SELECT PART_QTY
              INTO :part_qty
              FROM PART_STOCK
            WHERE PART_NUMB = :part_reqd;
```

Figure 165 (Part 4 of 6). DRDASU2: DRDA Level 2 Single-Site Update

```
        if ((rc = strncmp(sqlca.sqlstate,"00000",5)) !=0)
          {
            strncpy(sqlstate_str,sqlca.sqlstate,5);
            printf("\n   Error in receiving stock information from\
            this location");
            printf("%s%s\n","   Sqlstate:", sqlstate_str);
/*      EXEC SQL CONNECT RESET;*/
/*      Not needed in DRDA-2   */

          } /* END IF, sqlstate different from 0 */
    else  {
            printf("  Stock for %s is %d\n",location,part_qty);
            if (part_qty > max_part_qty)
              {
                max_part_qty = part_qty;
                strncpy(maxloc, location, 9);
              }
          } /* End else */

  } /* END ELSE, Connection OK */
} /* END FOR, connecting to every location */
printf("Location with the most items: %9.9s\n", maxloc);
if(max_part_qty < ord_qtyd)
    {
    printf("Quantity not available at any location\n");
    }
else
    {
    printf("Creating an order...\n");
    EXEC SQL set connection :POK; 5
     printf("SQLCODE %d \n", sqlca.sqlcode); /*MONITOR SQLCODE*/
    EXEC SQL select max(ord_numb) + 1
            into :new_ord_numb from ORDERTBL;
            /* Generate a new order number....*/
    EXEC SQL insert into ORDERTBL
            values(:new_ord_numb, :part_reqd, :ord_qtyd,
                CURRENT TIMESTAMP, :maxloc);
            /* Insert the new order...*/
    }
```

Figure 165 (Part 5 of 6). DRDASU2: DRDA Level 2 Single-Site Update

```
   EXEC SQL COMMIT;
   return(0);   /**** return code 0 = No errors, OK ****/


   /****                        ****/
   /**** Global error handling routine ****/
   /****                        ****/
err_routine:
   strncpy(sqlstate_str,sqlca.sqlstate,5);
   printf("An error has occurred...\n"); /*... Changed ....*/
   printf("            SQLCODE: %d\n", SQLCODE);
   printf("            Sqlstate: %s\n",sqlstate_str);
   printf("            Sqlcaid: %s\n",sqlca.sqlcaid);
   printf("            Sqlcabc: %d\n",sqlca.sqlcabc);
   printf("            Sqlerrml: %d\n",sqlca.sqlerrml);
   printf("            Sqlerrmc: %s\n",sqlca.sqlerrmc);
   printf("            Sqlerrp: %s\n",sqlca.sqlerrp);
   printf("            Sqlerrd: %d\n",sqlca.sqlerrd);
   EXEC SQL RELEASE ALL;
   EXEC SQL whenever SQLERROR continue;
   EXEC SQL ROLLBACK;
   EXEC SQL whenever SQLERROR GOTO err_routine;
   return(99);  /**** return code 99 = something failed ****/

}  /* END MAIN */
```

Figure 165 (Part 6 of 6). DRDASU2: DRDA Level 2 Single-Site Update

12.6 DRDA Level 2 Multiple-Site Update

In this section we show how our example can be extended to perform multiple update operations on different locations within the same unit of work. This version of the program exploits the DRDA level 2 support provided by some of the DB2 platforms, specifically DB2 for OS/400 and DB2 for MVS/ESA. For this reason, this version of the program can be run only in a network of DB2 for OS/400 and DB2 for MVS/ESA platforms. Either platform can be chosen as an AR or an AS. In our *LOCATION* table, the locations that support two-phase commit with SPM and therefore DRDA level 2 are identified by the value *Y* in the *TWOPC* column. The program has been modified to select only those locations when the table is loaded into memory.

In the scenario where the AR and all ASs support DRDA level 2, the sequence of the CONNECT statements does not really matter, and all connections will be read/write capable.

The logic of the program has been modified so that at the end of the processing a new order will be created at the central site, and the stock quantity at the location for which the order has been issued will be updated. The program will commit both operations by using two-phase commit.

The program could also access DRDA level 1 ASs in read-only mode, as long as the first connection was for a DRDA level 2.

12.6.1 Program Pseudocode

The following pseudocode describes the logical structure of the multiple-site update example.

```
BEGIN PARTSTK

    Request the part number from user;
    Request the quantity to be ordered;
    RELEASE ALL the existing connections;
    CONNECT TO CENTDB2;

    IF CONNECT OK
      BEGIN IF
        CONNECT TO LOCAL;
          IF CONNECT OK
            BEGIN IF
              Get part description from PART_MAST;
              Print part description;
              Count the number of locations in LOCATION table;
              Get the locations from LOCATION table;
            END IF
          ELSE GOTO ERR_ROUTINE;
    ELSE GOTO ERR_ROUTINE;

    FOR I=1 to number of locations
      BEGIN FOR
        CONNECT TO location
        IF connection to location is OK
          BEGIN IF
            Get the stock information from PART_STOCK table;
            Determine the location with the maximum amount of
              the requested part and save it in MAXLOC
            IF OK print stock information on the screen;
            ELSE print ERROR in retrieving stock information;
          END IF
        ELSE  /* Connection to location failed */
          BEGIN ELSE
            Print ERROR in CONNECT;
            CONTINUE
          END ELSE
    END FOR I
    SET CONNECTION CENTDB2;
    INSERT new order row INTO ORDERTBL;
    SET CONNECTION TO MAXLOC;
    UPDATE PART_STOCK decreasing the stock quantity by the
      requested amount;
    COMMIT;
```

```
    ERR_ROUTINE:
        Print error information;

END PARTSTK
```

12.6.2 Program Coding

Figure 166 on page 378 shows the MSUTWOPC program, which is meant to run in a network of systems that support two-phase commit. For this reason, the program is not subject to the same constraints as the previous version. The single-site update limitation can be removed, and the sequence of *CONNECT* statements is not relevant to determining which connections have read/write privileges. The differences between this program and the previous examples are highlighted and explained below.

1 This group of statements is not strictly needed. We preserved them to minimize the changes, but in practice you would not have to drop active connections in this scenario.

2 We connect to the central database and this connection will be read/write capable. Because we run this program under the assumption that all platforms involved support two-phase commit, all subsequent connections (**3**) will have read/write privileges.

4 We want to involve only two-phase commit capabilities. For this reason, we introduced a selection criterion (WHERE TWOPC="Y"). The LOCATION table needs to reflect which locations run a RDBMS that supports DRDA level 2 and flag those locations with a *Y* in the TWOPC field.

5 This statement creates a new order row in the ORDERTBL table at the central site.

6 This statement updates the inventory information at the location that was selected to fill the order. That location, in general, will not coincide with the central location, where we just created a new order. The *COMMIT* operation following this statement will therefore require two-phase commit support to be carried out.

```
/*This program is meant to run on an Application Requester which    */
/*will be accessed in read/write mode. The program reads the table  */
/*containing all the Application Server locations from the local     */
/*relational database. The program will create an order for the      */
/*requested part at the central database (CENTDB2) and will update   */
/*the inventory information (part quantity) at the location where the*/
/*desired part was found. It will then commit the transaction using  */
/*2 - Phase Commitment Control.                                       */
/*It is required that all the Application Requesters as well as the   */
/*Application Servers provide the 2-Phase Commitment Control support  */
/*for this program to run successfully.  Only 2PC capable locations   */
/*will be selected (TWOPC = 'Y')                                      */

/* #include <sqlcodes.h>
#include <sqlenv.h>
#include <sqlutil.h>
#include <sql.h> */
#include <stdio.h>
#include <stdlib.h>
#include <string.h>

EXEC SQL INCLUDE SQLCA;

EXEC SQL WHENEVER SQLERROR   GOTO err_routine;
EXEC SQL WHENEVER SQLWARNING CONTINUE;
EXEC SQL WHENEVER NOT FOUND  CONTINUE;

EXEC SQL BEGIN DECLARE SECTION;
 char LOCAL[9] = "RCAS400";
 char POK[9] = "CENTDB2";
 short new_ord_numb;
 short part_num;
 short part_qty;
 short part_reqd=0;
 short ord_qtyd=0;
 char  partnums[5];
 char  ord_qty[5];
 char  part_desc[21];
 char  location[9];
 char  maxloc[9];
 char  user_id[11];
 char  pasw_id[11];
 short locnum;
 short max_part_qty = 0;
EXEC SQL END   DECLARE SECTION;
```

Figure 166 (Part 1 of 6). MSUTWOPC: DRDA Level 2 Multiple-Site Update

```
   char loc_list[23][9];
      int  i=0;
      int  j=0;
      int rc;
      char sqlstate_str[6];
main()
{

   sqlstate_str[5]='\0';

    EXEC SQL RELEASE ALL;
    EXEC SQL whenever SQLERROR continue;  ▐1▌
    EXEC SQL COMMIT;
    EXEC SQL whenever SQLERROR GOTO err_routine;

    /* RELEASE ALL AND COMMIT to make sure there are no */
    /* active connections                              */

    printf(" Partstok program running..\n");
    printf(" Please enter your userid in uppercase...\n");
    gets(user_id);
    printf(" Please enter your password in uppercase...\n");
    gets(pasw_id);
    printf(" Please enter part number:\n");
    gets(partnums);part_reqd=atoi(partnums);
    printf(" Please enter order quantity:\n");
    gets(ord_qty);ord_qtyd=atoi(ord_qty);
    printf("  Connecting to Order Center POK..\n");

  EXEC SQL WHENEVER SQLERROR  CONTINUE;
  EXEC SQL CONNECT TO :POK  ▐2▌
          USER   :user_id
          USING :pasw_id;
    printf("SQLCODE %d \n", sqlca.sqlcode);   /*MONITOR SQLCODE*/
    if ((rc = strncmp(sqlca.sqlstate,"08002",5)) ==0) {
    printf("%s","\n  Connection to Order Center established");
    }
    else
  EXEC SQL WHENEVER SQLERROR   GOTO err_routine;

    printf("  Connecting to LOCAL..\n");
```

Figure 166 (Part 2 of 6). MSUTWOPC: DRDA Level 2 Multiple-Site Update

```
EXEC SQL WHENEVER SQLERROR  CONTINUE;
EXEC SQL CONNECT TO :LOCAL  3
        USER  :user_id
        USING :pasw_id;
  printf("SQLCODE %d \n", sqlca.sqlcode);  /*MONITOR SQLCODE*/
  if ((rc = strncmp(sqlca.sqlstate,"08002",5)) ==0)
EXEC SQL SET CONNECTION :LOCAL;
EXEC SQL WHENEVER SQLERROR  GOTO err_routine;
printf("%s","\n  Connection to LOCAL established");
printf("%s", "\n\n  Finding part description\n\n");

EXEC SQL SELECT PART_NUMB, PART_DESC
    INTO :part_num, :part_desc
    FROM PART_MAST
    WHERE PART_NUMB = :part_reqd;

if ((rc = strncmp(sqlca.sqlstate,"00000",5)) !=0) goto err_routine;

printf("  Description selected for part: %d\n",part_num);
printf("                description: %s\n",part_desc);
printf(" \n");

EXEC SQL SELECT  COUNT(*) into :locnum FROM LOCATION;
EXEC SQL DECLARE loc_csr CURSOR FOR
 SELECT LOCATION
    FROM LOCATION WHERE TWOPC = 'Y' FOR FETCH ONLY;  4

EXEC SQL OPEN loc_csr;
for(i=0;i<=(locnum-1);++i) {
   EXEC SQL FETCH loc_csr INTO :location;

   for(j=7;location[j]==' ';j--) {
      location[j] = '\0';
   }
   strcpy(loc_list[i],location);
}
```

Figure 166 (Part 3 of 6). MSUTWOPC: DRDA Level 2 Multiple-Site Update

```
      EXEC SQL CLOSE loc_csr;
/*                                                                */
/* The Connection is not ended here, because we are using DRDA2*/
/*                                                                */
   for(i=0;i<=(locnum-1);++i)
    {
    strcpy(location,loc_list[i]);

    EXEC SQL WHENEVER SQLERROR CONTINUE;

    EXEC SQL CONNECT TO :location
         USER  :user_id
         USING :pasw_id;
    printf("SQLCODE %d \n", sqlca.sqlcode); /*MONITOR SQLCODE*/

  if ((rc = strncmp(sqlca.sqlstate,"08002",5)) ==0)
         EXEC SQL SET CONNECTION :location;
       /* If sqlstate= 08002 the connection has already been
          established. We just need to set the current connection.
       */
    EXEC SQL WHENEVER SQLERROR   GOTO err_routine;
  if ((rc = strncmp(sqlca.sqlstate,"00000",5)) !=0)
   printf("\n\n  %s %s%s\n","Location ", location,  " not available  ");
   else
   {
     printf("%s%s\n", "\n  Connected to:  ", location);
         EXEC SQL
         SELECT PART_QTY
           INTO :part_qty
           FROM PART_STOCK
         WHERE PART_NUMB = :part_reqd;
```

Figure 166 (Part 4 of 6). MSUTWOPC: DRDA Level 2 Multiple-Site Update

```
        if ((rc = strncmp(sqlca.sqlstate,"00000",5)) !=0)
            {
            strncpy(sqlstate_str,sqlca.sqlstate,5);
            printf("\n   Error in receiving stock information from\
            this location");
            printf("%s%s\n","   Sqlstate:", sqlstate_str);

            } /* END IF, sqlstate different from 0 */
    else    {
            printf("  Stock for %s is %d\n",location,part_qty);
            if (part_qty > max_part_qty)
              {
                max_part_qty = part_qty;
                strncpy(maxloc, location, 9);
                }
            } /* End else */

  } /* END ELSE, Connection OK */
} /* END FOR, connecting to every location */
printf("Location with the most items: %9.9s\n", maxloc);
if(max_part_qty < ord_qtyd)
    {
    printf("Quantity not available at any location\n");
    }
else
    {
    printf("Creating an order...\n");
    EXEC SQL set connection :POK;
     printf("SQLCODE %d \n", sqlca.sqlcode); /*MONITOR SQLCODE*/
    EXEC SQL select max(ord_numb) + 1
            into :new_ord_numb from ORDERTBL;
            /* Generate a new order number....*/
    EXEC SQL insert into ORDERTBL ⬛5
            values(:new_ord_numb, :part_reqd, :ord_qtyd,
                CURRENT TIMESTAMP, :maxloc);
            /* Insert the new order...*/

    EXEC SQL set connection :maxloc;
    EXEC SQL update PART_STOCK set PART_QTY = PART_QTY-:ord_qtyd
            WHERE PART_NUMB = :part_reqd; ⬛6
            /* Update the inventory at the location for which
                the order was issued                      */

    }
```

Figure 166 (Part 5 of 6). MSUTWOPC: DRDA Level 2 Multiple-Site Update

```
      EXEC SQL COMMIT; /* Two phase commit */
      return(0);    /**** return code 0 = No errors, OK ****/


      /****                              ****/
      /**** Global error handling routine ****/
      /****                              ****/
    err_routine:
      strncpy(sqlstate_str,sqlca.sqlstate,5);
      printf("An error has occurred...\n"); /*... Changed ....*/
      printf("          SQLCODE:  %d\n", SQLCODE);
      printf("          Sqlstate: %s\n",sqlstate_str);
      printf("          Sqlcaid: %s\n",sqlca.sqlcaid);
      printf("          Sqlcabc: %d\n",sqlca.sqlcabc);
      printf("          Sqlerrml: %d\n",sqlca.sqlerrml);
      printf("          Sqlerrmc: %s\n",sqlca.sqlerrmc);
      printf("          Sqlerrp: %s\n",sqlca.sqlerrp);
      printf("          Sqlerrd: %d\n",sqlca.sqlerrd);
      EXEC SQL RELEASE ALL;
      EXEC SQL whenever SQLERROR continue;
      EXEC SQL ROLLBACK;
      EXEC SQL whenever SQLERROR GOTO err_routine;
      return(99);  /**** return code 99 = something failed ****/

    }  /* END MAIN */
```

Figure 166 (Part 6 of 6). MSUTWOPC: DRDA Level 2 Multiple-Site Update

12.7 Multiple-Site Update for DB2 common server

The two-phase commit implemented by DRDA level 2 compliant databases is not yet available in DB2 common servers, because the services of an SPM are not yet provided. Nevertheless DB2 common servers provide their own protocol to support two-phase commit.

To coordinate multiple-site update between DB2 commons servers, the transaction monitor (TM) function has been implemented in the DB2 common server platforms.

The TM components are the following:

- *Coordinator*

    The coordinator of the two-phase commit process is the program itself. To give your program the required coordination abilities, you have to prepare it with the PREP command option, SYNCPOINT TWOPHASE.

- *Database Protection Services (DPS)*

  This is the function responsible for transaction management in each database.

- *TM database*

  This is a database used for logging and recovery by the TM in the two-phase commit process. The TM database is determined at the database client by the database manager configuration parameter, *TM_DATABASE*. There are some considerations associated with the TM database:

  - Can be a local or remote DB2 common server database.

  - Cannot be a DRDA database.

  - Is used as a logger and as a coordinator of the unit of work.

  - The TM_DATABASE value can be any valid database alias name, or 1ST_CONN, indicating that the first database connected performs the TM database function.

  - The TM databases must be able to connect to all databases accessed by the application. All databases accessed by the application must be able to connect to the TM database.

  See the *DB2 Administration Guide for common servers* for more information on the TM_DATABASE parameter.

- *Resynchronization manager*

  This is the function responsible for carrying out crash recovery if the two-phase commit process does not complete successfully.

Currently in a unit of work an application executing in DB2 common server is allowed one of the following:

- Update several DB2 common servers and read-only from several DRDA ASs.

- Update in one DRDA AS, read from several ASs, read from several DB2 common servers.

If the application is executing in an AIX platform using the services of ENCINA, full DRDA level 2 support is provided.

DB2 common server, acting as a DRDA AS, is currently a DRDA level 1.

12.7.1 Program Pseudocode

Figure 167 on page 385 shows the pseudocode describing the logical structure of our multiple-site update sample for DB2 common servers. In fact the logic of this program is exactly the same as the logic of the DRDA level 2 sample program.

```
BEGIN PARTSTK

    Request the user ID from user;
    Request the password from user;
    Request the product_id to be ordered;
    Request the quantity to be ordered;
    RELEASE ALL the existing connections;
    CONNECT TO SJ6SMPL;

    IF CONNECT OK
      BEGIN IF
        CONNECT TO LOCAL;
          IF CONNECT OK
            BEGIN IF
              Get part description from PART_MAST;
              Print part description;
              Count the number of locations in LOCATION table;
              Get the locations from LOCATION table;
            END IF
          ELSE GOTO ERR_ROUTINE;
    ELSE GOTO ERR_ROUTINE;

    FOR I=1 to number of locations
      BEGIN FOR
        CONNECT TO location
        IF connection to location is OK
          BEGIN IF
            Get the stock information from PART_STOCK table;
            Determine the location with the maximum amount of
              the requested part and save it in MAXLOC
            IF OK print stock information on the screen;
            ELSE print ERROR in retrieving stock information;
          END IF
        ELSE  /* Connection to location failed */
          BEGIN ELSE
            Print ERROR in CONNECT;
            CONTINUE
          END ELSE
    END FOR I
    SET CONNECTION SJ6SMPL;
    INSERT new order row INTO ORDERTBL;
    SET CONNECTION TO MAXLOC;
    UPDATE PART_STOCK decreasing the stock quantity by the
      requested amount;
    COMMIT;
```

Figure 167 (Part 1 of 2). Multiple-Site Update Pseudocode: DB2 common servers

```
      ERR_ROUTINE:
           Print error information;

  END PARTSTK
```

Figure 167 (Part 2 of 2). Multiple-Site Update Pseudocode: DB2 common servers

12.7.2 Program Coding

Program MSUPP2PC (Figure 169 on page 388) is meant to run in a network of systems that support the two-phase commit provided by DB2 common servers.

As stated before, the logic of this program is the same as the logic for the DRDA level 2 sample program. Nevertheless there are some minor differences in the program coding itself. These differences are highlighted and explained below.

1 We connect to the central database, and this connection is read/write capable. The central site for our program is the DB2 for AIX in San Jose, so we connect to SJ6SMPL. Because we run this program under the assumption that all platforms involved support DB2 common server two-phase commit, all subsequent connections (**2**) are read/write capable.

3 We can involve only locations with DB2 common server two-phase commit capabilities. For this reason, we introduced a selection criterion (WHERE TWOPC=P). The LOCATION table must reflect which locations run an RDBMS that supports DB2 common server two-phase commit private protocol and flag those locations with a *P* in the TWOPC field.

Figure 168 shows the LOCATION table.

```
LOCATION TWOPC
-------- -----
SJ2SMPL  P
RCAS400  Y
SJAS400  Y
CENTDB2  Y
SJ6SMPL  P
S34VMDBO N
S34VSDB1 N
```

Figure 168. MSUPP2PC: LOCATION Table Contents

4 This statement creates a new order row in the ORDERTBL table at the central site, which is SJ6SMPL in this case.

5 This statement updates the inventory information at the location that was selected to fill the order. That location, in general, does not coincide with the central location, where we just created a new order. The *COMMIT* statement following this statement therefore requires DB2 common server two-phase commit support to be carried out.

```
/*This program is meant to run on an Application Requester which   */
/*will be accessed in read/write mode. The program reads the table   */
/*containing all the Application Server locations from the local    */
/*relational database. The program will create an order for the    */
/*requested part at the central database (SJ6SMPL) and will update   */
/*the inventory information (part quantity) at the location where the*/
/*desired part was found. It will then commit the transaction using  */
/*2 - Phase Commitment Control provided by DB2 common server     */
/*It is required that all the Application Requesters as well as the  */
/*Application Servers provide the 2-Phase Commitment Control support */
/*provided for DB2 common server, for this program to run succesfully*/
/*Only 2PC capable locations will be selected (TWOPC = 'P') */

/* #include <sqlcodes.h>
#include <sqlenv.h>
#include <sqlutil.h>
#include <sql.h> */

#include <stdio.h>
#include <stdlib.h>
#include <string.h>

EXEC SQL INCLUDE SQLCA;

EXEC SQL WHENEVER SQLERROR   GOTO err_routine;
EXEC SQL WHENEVER SQLWARNING CONTINUE;
EXEC SQL WHENEVER NOT FOUND  CONTINUE;

EXEC SQL BEGIN DECLARE SECTION;
 char LOCAL[9] = "SJ2SMPL";
 char SJ6[9] = "SJ6SMPL";
 short new_ord_numb;
 short part_num;
 short part_qty;
 short part_reqd=0;
 short ord_qtyd=0;
 char  partnums[5];
 char  ord_qty[5];
 char  part_desc[21];
 char  location[9];
 char  maxloc[9];
 char  user_id[11];
 char  pasw_id[11];
 short locnum;
 short max_part_qty = 0;
 EXEC SQL END   DECLARE SECTION;
```

Figure 169 (Part 1 of 6). MSUPP2PC: Multiple-Site   Update   Example—DB2 common servers

```
  char loc_list[23][9];
    int  i=0;
    int  j=0;
    int rc;
    char sqlstate_str[6];
main()
{

  sqlstate_str[5]='\0';

    EXEC SQL RELEASE ALL;
    EXEC SQL whenever SQLERROR continue;
    EXEC SQL COMMIT;
    EXEC SQL whenever SQLERROR GOTO err_routine;

    /* RELEASE ALL AND COMMIT to make sure there are no */
    /* active connections                              */

    printf(" Partstok program running..\n");
    printf(" Please enter your userid in uppercase...\n");
    gets(user_id);
    printf(" Please enter your password in uppercase...\n");
    gets(pasw_id);
    printf(" Please enter part number:\n");
    gets(partnums);part_reqd=atoi(partnums);
    printf(" Please enter order quantity:\n");
    gets(ord_qty);ord_qtyd=atoi(ord_qty);
    printf("  Connecting to Order Center SJ6..\n");

  EXEC SQL WHENEVER SQLERROR  CONTINUE;
  EXEC SQL CONNECT TO :SJ6 ∎1
          USER  :user_id
          USING :pasw_id;
    printf("SQLCODE %d \n", sqlca.sqlcode);   /*MONITOR SQLCODE*/
    if ((rc = strncmp(sqlca.sqlstate,"08002",5)) ==0) {
    printf("%s","\n Connection to Order Center established");
    }
    else
  EXEC SQL WHENEVER SQLERROR   GOTO err_routine;
```

Figure 169 (Part 2 of 6). *MSUPP2PC: Multiple-Site Update Example—DB2 common servers*

```
     printf(" Connecting to LOCAL..\n");

EXEC SQL WHENEVER SQLERROR  CONTINUE;
EXEC SQL CONNECT TO :LOCAL  2
        USER  :user_id
        USING :pasw_id;
  printf("SQLCODE %d \n", sqlca.sqlcode);  /*MONITOR SQLCODE*/
  if ((rc = strncmp(sqlca.sqlstate,"08002",5)) ==0)
EXEC SQL SET CONNECTION :LOCAL;
EXEC SQL WHENEVER SQLERROR  GOTO err_routine;
printf("%s","\n Connection to LOCAL established");
printf("%s", "\n\n  Finding part description\n\n");

EXEC SQL SELECT PART_NUMB, PART_DESC
    INTO :part_num, :part_desc
    FROM PART_MAST
    WHERE PART_NUMB = :part_reqd;

if ((rc = strncmp(sqlca.sqlstate,"00000",5)) !=0) goto err_routine;

printf(" Description selected for part: %d\n",part_num);
printf("              description: %s\n",part_desc);
printf(" \n");

EXEC SQL SELECT  COUNT(*) into :locnum FROM LOCATION;
EXEC SQL DECLARE loc_csr CURSOR FOR
 SELECT LOCATION
   FROM LOCATION WHERE TWOPC = 'P' FOR FETCH ONLY;  3

EXEC SQL OPEN loc_csr;
for(i=0;i<=(locnum-1);++i) {
   EXEC SQL FETCH loc_csr INTO :location;

   for(j=7;location[j]==' ';j--) {
       location[j] = '\0';
   }
   strcpy(loc_list[i],location);
}
```

Figure 169 (Part 3 of 6). MSUPP2PC: Multiple-Site Update Example—DB2 common servers

```
     EXEC SQL CLOSE loc_csr;
/*                                                               */
/* The Connection is not ended here, because we are using DRDA2*/
/*                                                               */
   for(i=0;i<=(locnum-1);++i)
     {
     strcpy(location,loc_list[i]);

     EXEC SQL WHENEVER SQLERROR CONTINUE;

     EXEC SQL CONNECT TO :location
         USER  :user_id
         USING :pasw_id;
     printf("SQLCODE %d \n", sqlca.sqlcode); /*MONITOR SQLCODE*/

   if ((rc = strncmp(sqlca.sqlstate,"08002",5)) ==0)
           EXEC SQL SET CONNECTION :location;
         /* If sqlstate= 08002 the connection has already been
            established. We just need to set the current connection.
         */
     EXEC SQL WHENEVER SQLERROR   GOTO err_routine;
   if ((rc = strncmp(sqlca.sqlstate,"00000",5)) !=0)
     printf("\n\n  %s %s%s\n","Location ", location, " not available    ");
     else
     {
       printf("%s%s\n", "\n  Connected to:  ", location);
           EXEC SQL
           SELECT PART_QTY
             INTO :part_qty
             FROM PART_STOCK
             WHERE PART_NUMB = :part_reqd;
```

Figure 169 (Part 4 of 6). MSUPP2PC: Multiple-Site   Update   Example—DB2 common servers

```
        if ((rc = strncmp(sqlca.sqlstate,"00000",5)) !=0)
            {
             strncpy(sqlstate_str,sqlca.sqlstate,5);
             printf("\n   Error in receiving stock information from\
             this location");
             printf("%s%s\n","   Sqlstate:", sqlstate_str);

            } /* END IF, sqlstate different from 0 */
    else   {
             printf("  Stock for %s is %d\n",location,part_qty);
             if (part_qty > max_part_qty)
               {
                max_part_qty = part_qty;
                strncpy(maxloc, location, 9);
                }
            } /* End else */

   } /* END ELSE, Connection OK */
} /* END FOR, connecting to every location */

printf("Location with the most items: %9.9s\n", maxloc);
if(max_part_qty < ord_qtyd)
    {
    printf("Quantity not available at any location\n");
    }
else
    {
    printf("Creating an order...\n");
    EXEC SQL set connection :SJ6;
     printf("SQLCODE %d \n", sqlca.sqlcode); /*MONITOR SQLCODE*/
    EXEC SQL select max(ord_numb) + 1
            into :new_ord_numb from ORDERTBL;
            /* Generate a new order number....*/
    EXEC SQL insert into ORDERTBL  4
            values(:new_ord_numb, :part_reqd, :ord_qtyd,
                  CURRENT TIMESTAMP, :maxloc);
            /* Insert the new order...*/

    EXEC SQL set connection :maxloc;
    EXEC SQL update PART_STOCK set PART_QTY = PART_QTY-:ord_qtyd
            WHERE PART_NUMB = :part_reqd;  5
             /* Update the inventory at the location for which
                the order was issued                         */

    }
```

Figure 169 (Part 5 of 6). *MSUPP2PC: Multiple-Site   Update   Example—DB2 common servers*

```
    EXEC SQL COMMIT; /* Two phase commit */
    return(0);    /**** return code 0 = No errors, OK ****/


    /****                          ****/
    /**** Global error handling routine ****/
    /****                          ****/
err_routine:
    strncpy(sqlstate_str,sqlca.sqlstate,5);
    printf("An error has occurred...\n"); /*... Changed ....*/
    printf("          SQLCODE: %d\n", SQLCODE);
    printf("          Sqlstate: %s\n",sqlstate_str);
    printf("          Sqlcaid: %s\n",sqlca.sqlcaid);
    printf("          Sqlcabc: %d\n",sqlca.sqlcabc);
    printf("          Sqlerrml: %d\n",sqlca.sqlerrml);
    printf("          Sqlerrmc: %s\n",sqlca.sqlerrmc);
    printf("          Sqlerrp: %s\n",sqlca.sqlerrp);
    printf("          Sqlerrd: %d\n",sqlca.sqlerrd);
    EXEC SQL RELEASE ALL;
    EXEC SQL whenever SQLERROR continue;
    EXEC SQL ROLLBACK;
    EXEC SQL whenever SQLERROR GOTO err_routine;
    return(99); /**** return code 99 = something failed ****/

} /* END MAIN */
```

Figure 169 (Part 6 of 6). *MSUPP2PC: Multiple-Site   Update   Example—DB2 common servers*

Chapter 13. Program Preparation: DB2 common server

In this chapter we describe the steps required to prepare a DB2 common server program meant to access data in different DB2 database servers. The style of program preparation described refers to programs developed using static and dynamic embedded SQL statements. This chapter does not provide information about CLI programming, which does not require a program to be precompiled and bound.

In the first section of this chapter we describe the process and concepts of DB2 common server program preparation. The second section contains the steps we took to prepare our sample programs in the following SDK application environments:

- SDK for OS/2

- SDK for AIX

- SDK for Windows

- SDK/DOS

Refer to 2.1.5, "Software Developer's Kit" on page 16 for more information on SDK.

13.1 Process Description and Concepts

The most frequently used technique for coding programs accessing DB2 databases is embedded SQL statements in the body of the program. This technique requires, besides the usual compiling and linking steps, two additional tasks: precompilation and binding.

Precompilation is the first step in the process of preparing a DB2 common server program. Precompilation is required to change SQL statements into language recognized by your compiler, so that you can compile and link your program to create an executable module.

Besides the creation of an executable module, you have to bind a package to each server that your DB2 common server program accesses.

Binding is the process that creates a usable control structure containing the access paths to data required by the SQL statements in your program. Such a structure is called a *package*. It can be implicitly created during precompilation or explicitly created by a BIND command.

Figure 170 on page 396 illustrates the DB2 common server program preparation process.

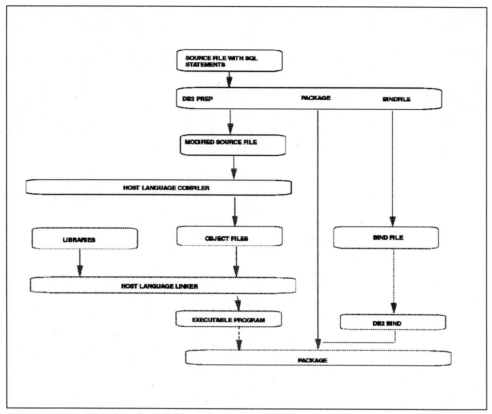

Figure 170. DB2 Common Server Program Preparation

In the following sections, we describe program preparation steps in more detail.

13.1.1 Precompiling Your Program

The precompiler converts source program SQL statements into comments and generates the DB2 run-time API calls for those statements, thus creating a modified source file to be processed by the compiler. The precompiler also generates a message file, a package, and/or a bind file, depending the PREP command options you use.

The syntax of the PREP command for DB2 common server is as follows:

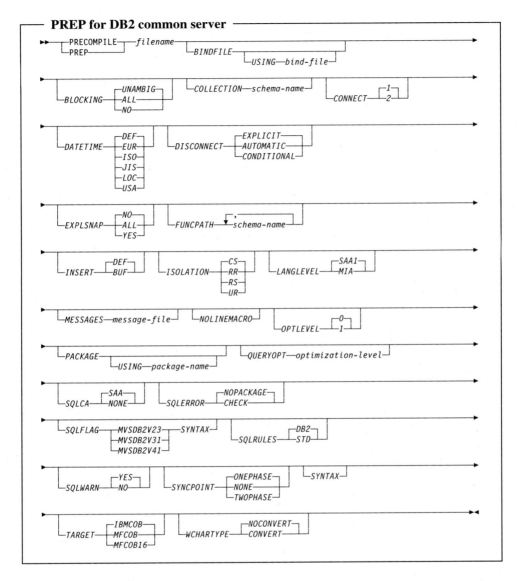

PREP for DB2 common server

```
>>─┬─PRECOMPILE─┬──filename─────────────────────────────────────────────────>
   └─PREP───────┘      └─BINDFILE─┬────────────────────────┬─┘
                                  └─USING──bind-file─┘

>──┬──────────────────────────┬──┬───────────────────────────────┬──┬──────────────────┬──>
   └─BLOCKING─┬─UNAMBIG─┬──┘  └─COLLECTION──schema-name─┘  └─CONNECT─┬─1─┬─┘
             ├─ALL─────┤                                            └─2─┘
             └─NO──────┘

>──┬───────────────────┬──┬────────────────────────────┬──>
   └─DATETIME─┬─DEF─┬─┘  └─DISCONNECT─┬─EXPLICIT───┬─┘
             ├─EUR─┤                 ├─AUTOMATIC──┤
             ├─ISO─┤                 └─CONDITIONAL┘
             ├─JIS─┤
             ├─LOC─┤
             └─USA─┘

>──┬──────────────────┬──┬──────────────────────────┬──>
   └─EXPLSNAP─┬─NO──┬─┘  └─FUNCPATH──┬┬──schema-name─┬─┘
             ├─ALL─┤              └──,──────────┘
             └─YES─┘

>──┬─────────────────┬──┬──────────────────────┬──┬──────────────────┬──>
   └─INSERT─┬─DEF─┬─┘  └─ISOLATION─┬─CS─┬─┘  └─LANGLEVEL─┬─SAA1─┬─┘
          └─BUF─┘               ├─RR─┤              └─MIA──┘
                                ├─RS─┤
                                └─UR─┘

>──┬──────────────────────────────┬──┬───────────────┬──┬─────────────────┬──>
   └─MESSAGES──message-file─┘  └─NOLINEMACRO─┘  └─OPTLEVEL─┬─0─┬─┘
                                                         └─1─┘

>──┬──────────────────────────────────────┬──┬─────────────────────────────────────┬──>
   └─PACKAGE─┬──────────────────────────┬─┘  └─QUERYOPT──optimization-level─┘
            └─USING──package-name─┘

>──┬────────────────────┬──┬──────────────────────────┬──>
   └─SQLCA─┬─SAA──┬─┘  └─SQLERROR─┬─NOPACKAGE─┬─┘
          └─NONE─┘              └─CHECK─────┘

>──┬───────────────────────────────────────────┬──>
   └─SQLFLAG─┬─MVSDB2V23─┬──SYNTAX─┬───────────────────────┬─┘
            ├─MVSDB2V31─┤        └─SQLRULES─┬─DB2─┬─┘
            └─MVSDB2V41─┘                  └─STD─┘

>──┬───────────────────┬──┬─────────────────────────┬──┬─────────┬──>
   └─SQLWARN─┬─YES─┬─┘  └─SYNCPOINT─┬─ONEPHASE─┬─┘  └─SYNTAX─┘
            └─NO──┘              ├─NONE─────┤
                                └─TWOPHASE─┘

>──┬──────────────────────┬──┬────────────────────────┬──><
   └─TARGET─┬─IBMCOB──┬─┘  └─WCHARTYPE─┬─NOCONVERT─┬─┘
          ├─MFCOB───┤                └─CONVERT───┘
          └─MFCOB16─┘
```

The syntax of the PREP command for DRDA database servers is shown in Figure 171 on page 398 and Figure 172 on page 399.

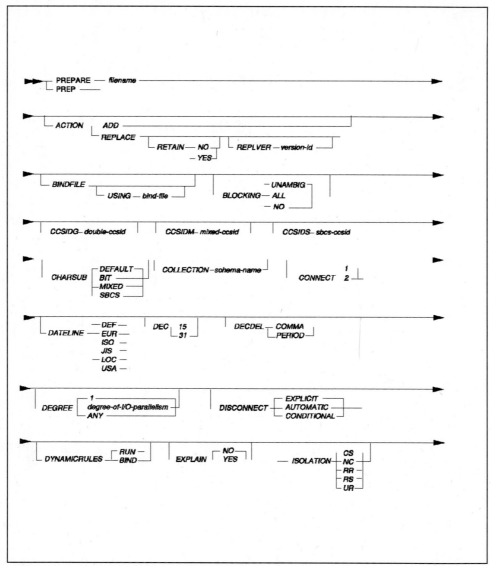

Figure 171. *PREP for DRDA Servers - Command Syntax - First Part*

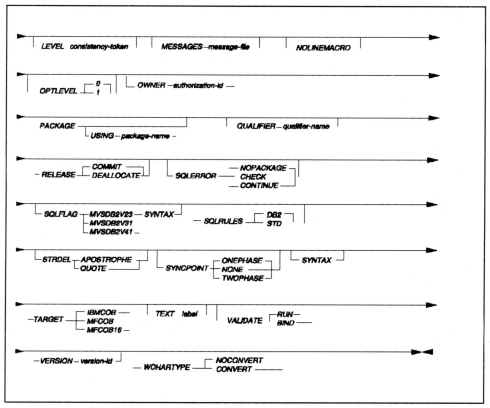

Figure 172. PREP for DRDA Servers - Command Syntax - Second Part

Note that not all options of the PREP command are available in the DRDA environment area supported by the DB2 common server engine, even though DB2 common server provides DRDA AS functionality.

The PREP command options that are relevant when precompiling a program coded to access distributed data are

- *filename*

    This is the file name that contains the source of the program you are precompiling. To specify to the precompiler the programming language used to code your program, use the file extension shown in Table 37 on page 400.

Table 37. *Valid File Name Extensions for the DB2 PREP Command: Source File*

	SDK for AIX	SDK for OS/2	SDK for Windows	SDK/DOS
COBOL	.sqb	.sqb	.sqb	Not supported
Fortran	.sqf	.sqf	Not supported	Not supported
.C	.sqc	.sqc	.sqc	.sqc
C++	.sqC	.sqx	.sqx	Not supported

The file extension of the modified source file depends on the programming language used. Table 38 lists the valid file extensions the precompiler gives to the modified source file.

Table 38. *Valid File Name Extensions for the DB2 PREP Command: Modified Source File*

	SDK for AIX	SDK for OS/2	SDK for Windows	SDK/DOS
COBOL	.cbl	.cbl	.cbl	Not supported
Fortran	.f	.for	Not supported	Not supported
.C	.c	.c	.c	.c
C++	.C	.cxx	.cxx	Not supported

- *ACTION*

  Indicates whether you are replacing an already existing package or creating a new package. This parameter is not supported when creating a package for DB2 common server. Valid values are:

  - *ADD*

    Adds a new object but does not replace an existing object.

  - *REPLACE*

    If a package with the same name exists, it is replaced. If not, a new package is created. Valid values are

    - *RETAIN*

      Indicates whether EXECUTE authorities are to be preserved when a package is replaced. Valid values are

      - *NO*

      - *YES*

   - *REPLVER version-id*

     Replaces a specific version of the package, identified by *version-id*. If the package with the specified *version-id* does not exist, the bind fails.

- *BINDFILE bind-file*

Indicates the precompiler to create a bind file. This option defers the creation of a package, unless the *PACKAGE* option is also specified, which causes the creation of both a package and a bind file.

The bind file name defaults to the program name, plus the .bnd file extension, unless you specify the option *USING bind-file*, where bind-file is the name you choose for your bind file. You must explicitly declare the .bnd extension in this case. If path is not specified, the bind file is created in the current directory.

- *COLLECTION schema-name*

The collection identifier for your package. If not specified, it defaults to the authorization ID creating the package. See 13.1.4, "Collection Considerations" on page 411 for more information about collections.

- *CONNECT*

Valid values are

   – *1*

     This value allows your application to connect to only one database server in the same unit of work. Support for RUW is provided.

   – *2*

     This value allows your application to connect to more than one database server in the same unit of work. Support for DUW is provided.

- *DISCONNECT*

Determines which connections to destroy during COMMIT statement execution. Valid values are

   – *AUTOMATIC*

     Destroys all remote connections.

   – *CONDITIONAL*

     Destroys all remote connections, unless an open cursor defined as WITH HOLD is associated with the connection.

   – *EXPLICIT*

Destroys only connections in the release pending state. The release pending state is set by issuing the RELEASE statement in your program, allowing you maximum flexibility for controlling remote connections.

- *ISOLATION*

Defines the degree of isolation of an application process executing concurrently with other application processes. Valid values are:

- *CS Cursor Stability*

- *NC No Commit*

  This isolation level is not supported by DB2 common server.

- *RR Repeatable Read*

- *RS Read Stability*

- *UC Uncommitted Read*

- *MESSAGES message-file*

Specifies the destination for warning, error, and completion status messages.

- *OWNER authorization ID*

Designates the owner of the package. If not specified, it defaults to the primary ID issuing the PREP command. This option is not valid when creating a package for DB2 common server.

- *PACKAGE using package-name*

Indicates to the precompiler to create a package. A package is also created if you omit *package, bindfile,* or *syntax.*

The package name defaults to the program name unless you specify the option *USING package-name* where package-name is the name you choose for your package. The package name is folded to uppercase.

- *QUALIFIER qualifier-name*

Is the implicit qualifier for unqualified names of tables, views, and indexes in the package. The default is the owner's authorization ID. This option is not valid when creating a package for DB2 common server.

- *SQLERROR*

Indicates whether to create a package and/or a bind file if SQL errors are detected. Valid values are

- *CHECK*

  Indicates that the target system performs all syntax and semantics checks on the SQL statements being bound. This option provides you with the ability to check your program SQL statements against the target system, but a package is not created.

  - *CONTINUE*

    Indicates the creation of a package and/or a bind file, even if SQL errors are detected. This option does not prevent the statements in error from failing during run time. This value is not valid when creating a package for DB2 common server.

  - *NOPACKAGE*

    Indicates not to create a package if SQL errors are detected.

- *SQLRULES*

  Indicates whether you can execute a type 2 CONNECT statement to an existing SQL connection. A type 2 CONNECT statement allows you to connect to more than one database server in the same unit of work. Valid values are

  - *DB2*

    No error occurs if the CONNECT statement identifies an existing SQL connection. The CONNECT or the SET CONNECTION statement makes an existing connection the current connection.

  - *STD*

    An error occurs if the CONNECT statement identifies an existing SQL connection. In this case, to make an existing connection the current connection, you must use the SET CONNECTION statement.

- *SYNCPOINT*

  Indicates how COMMITs or ROLLBACKs are to be coordinated among multiple database connections. Valid values are

  - *NONE*

    Specifies that a TM is not to be used to perform two-phase commit. There is no enforcement of single updater, multiple reader, so the application is responsible for recovery if any COMMIT or ROLLBACK fails.

  - *ONEPHASE*

    Specifies that a TM is not to be used to perform two-phase commit. Nevertheless, enforcement of single updater, multiple reader is provided.

  - *TWOPHASE*

    Specifies that the TM is required to coordinate two-phase commits among those databases that support this protocol.

- *SYNTAX*

Used to check the validity of the SQL statements in the source file. Suppresses the creation of a package or a bind file. If package option is specified, it is ignored.

- *VALIDATE*

  Indicates whether a check operation should be executed at run time if errors of the type OBJECT NOT FOUND and/or NOT AUTHORIZED were found during precompilation. This option is not valid when creating a package and/or bind file for DB2 common server. Valid values are

  - *BIND*

    If errors of the type OBJECT NOT FOUND and/or NOT AUTHORIZED are detected, the process of precompilation does not create a package, unless you use the SQLERROR CONTINUE option. The SQLERROR CONTINUE option does not prevent the statements in error from failing during run time.

  - *RUN*

    If errors of the type OBJECT NOT FOUND and/or NOT AUTHORIZED are detected during precompilation, this option indicates that DRDA database servers are to create a package and check the existence and/or authorization of objects during run time.

See the *DB2 Command Reference for common servers* for more information about the PREP command.

13.1.1.1 Precompilation Considerations

When you precompile a program, the modified source and messages are generated at the client workstation, but some bind validation has to be executed on the server. Therefore when precompiling a program, you must be connected to a database server either explicitly or implicitly.

As stated before, you can implicitly bind a package through the use of the PREP command or defer its creation until a DB2 BIND command is issued. Deferring the creation of a package can be very useful when you have to create the same package in several locations, when the database server required is down, or when you want to create a package without providing source code to end users.

To defer the creation of a package, you have to create a bind file. The bind file is the input for the BIND command. Refer to 13.1.3, "Creating a Package through the BIND Command" on page 405 for an explanation of the BIND command.

13.1.2 Creating an Executable Module for Your Program

To create an executable module for your program, you must perform two tasks: compile and link. *Compile* uses the modified source file generated during precompilation to create an object module. This module is used for further processing during the link step.

Link uses the object module created during compilation to create an executable file. This executable file contains the appropriate links to allow your application to interface with host language library APIs and the database manager APIs required for your operating environment.

13.1.3 Creating a Package through the BIND Command

In this section we describe the process required to explicitly create a package by using the BIND command.

The creation of a package using the BIND command is a two-phase process. The first phase is the creation of a bind file. The second phase is to bind the package, using the bind file created in the first phase.

13.1.3.1 Creating the Bind File

A bind file contains the data required to create a package. To create a bind file use the PREP command as follows:

- *Connect to a database server*

  To execute a PREP command, you should be connected to a database server, because some validation is performed on the database server side.

- *Indicate the precompiler to create a bind file*

  Specify the precompile option BINDFILE to indicate to the precompiler that a bind file is to be created. If you omit the PACKAGE option, package creation is deferred, and certain objects' existence and authorization SQLCODES are treated as warnings. Thus you can successfully create a bind file, even if

  - You do not have the authorizations required to execute the SQL statements being precompiled,

  - The referred objects are not defined in the database to which you are connected,

    or

  - You are not connected to the database where the package is to be eventually executed.

The precompile option values used to create a bind file are implicitly used when binding a package, unless you explicitly override one of the values. This applies for options such as COLLECTION, OWNER, and QUALIFIER, which are valid for both PREP and BIND commands, giving you the ability to create the same package with different options in different locations.

Refer to 13.1.1, "Precompiling Your Program" on page 396 for a description of the PREP command options most commonly used to create a program that is coded to access distributed data.

13.1.3.2 Creating the Package

To create a package, use the BIND command as follows:

- *Connect to a database server*

  When creating a package, the database server to which you connect is the location where the package is to be bound.

  To successfully bind a package in a DB2 common server database, all the referred objects, such as tables and views, should be defined in the database, and all the required authorizations should be held by the authorization ID executing the bind operation.

  You can successfully bind a package in a DRDA database server, however, even if not all of the referred objects are found, and/or not all of the required authorizations are held during bind time. This can be achieved by using the VALIDATE RUN bind option.

- *Issue the BIND command*

  Use the bind file created with the PREP command to bind a package in the location to which you are connected.

The syntax of the BIND command for DB2 common server is as follows:

BIND for DB2 common server

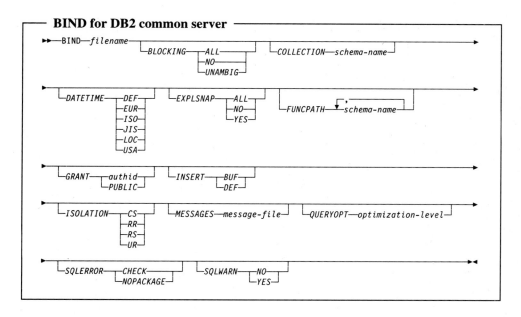

The syntax of the BIND command for DRDA database servers is as follows:

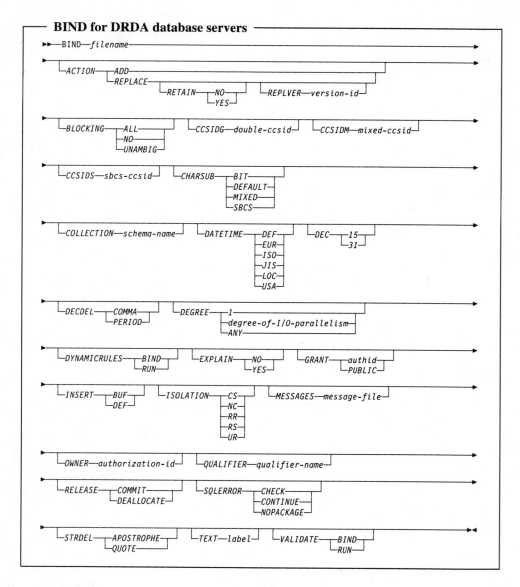

BIND for DRDA database servers

```
►►──BIND──filename────────────────────────────────────────────────────►

►───┬─────────────────────────────────────────────────────────────────►
    └─ACTION──┬─ADD─────────────────────────────────────────┬──
              └─REPLACE──┬──────────────────────────────────┘
                         └─RETAIN──┬─NO──┬──┬────────────────────────┐
                                   └─YES─┘  └─REPLVER──version-id─┘

►───┬──────────────────────────────────────────────────────────────────►
    └─BLOCKING──┬─ALL─────┬──  ─CCSIDG──double-ccsid─   ─CCSIDM──mixed-ccsid─
               ├─NO──────┤
               └─UNAMBIG─┘

►───┬───────────────────────────────────────────────────────────────────►
    └─CCSIDS──sbcs-ccsid─   ─CHARSUB──┬─BIT─────┬──
                                      ├─DEFAULT─┤
                                      ├─MIXED───┤
                                      └─SBCS────┘

►───┬────────────────────────────────────────────────────────────────────►
    └─COLLECTION──schema-name─   ─DATETIME──┬─DEF─┬──  ─DEC──┬─15─┬─
                                            ├─EUR─┤         └─31─┘
                                            ├─ISO─┤
                                            ├─JIS─┤
                                            ├─LOC─┤
                                            └─USA─┘

►───┬─────────────────────────────────────────────────────────────────────►
    └─DECDEL──┬─COMMA──┬──  ─DEGREE──┬─1────────────────────────┬─
              └─PERIOD─┘             ├─degree-of-I/O-parallelism─┤
                                     └─ANY──────────────────────┘

►───┬──────────────────────────────────────────────────────────────────────►
    └─DYNAMICRULES──┬─BIND─┬──  ─EXPLAIN──┬─NO──┬──  ─GRANT──┬─authid─┬─
                    └─RUN──┘              └─YES─┘            └─PUBLIC─┘

►───┬───────────────────────────────────────────────────────────────────────►
    └─INSERT──┬─BUF─┬──  ─ISOLATION──┬─CS─┬──  ─MESSAGES──message-file─
              └─DEF─┘                ├─NC─┤
                                     ├─RR─┤
                                     ├─RS─┤
                                     └─UR─┘

►───┬────────────────────────────────────────────────────────────────────────►
    └─OWNER──authorization-id─   ─QUALIFIER──qualifier-name─

►───┬─────────────────────────────────────────────────────────────────────────►
    └─RELEASE──┬─COMMIT─────┬──  ─SQLERROR──┬─CHECK─────┬─
               └─DEALLOCATE─┘               ├─CONTINUE──┤
                                            └─NOPACKAGE─┘

►───┬──────────────────────────────────────────────────────────────────►◄
    └─STRDEL──┬─APOSTROPHE─┬──  ─TEXT──label─   ─VALIDATE──┬─BIND─┬─
              └─QUOTE──────┘                               └─RUN──┘
```

The following BIND command options are relevant when you create a package used in a program coded to access distributed data:

- *filename*

  Is the name of a bind file generated during precompilation or a file that contains a list of names of several bind files.

Bind file extension should be *.bnd*.

If using a list of bind files, the file name specification must be preceded by a @ character.

- *ACTION*

Indicates whether you are replacing an already existing package or creating a new package. This option is not supported when creating a package for DB2 common server. Valid values are

  - *ADD*

    Adds a new object but does not replace an existing object.

  - *REPLACE*

    If a package with the same name exists, it is replaced. If not, a new package is created. Valid values are

    - *RETAIN*

      Indicates whether EXECUTE authorities are to be preserved when a package is replaced. Valid values are

      - *NO*

      - *YES*

    - *REPLVER version-id*

      Replaces a specific version of the package, identified by *version-id*. If the package with the specified *version-id* does not exist, the bind fails.

- *COLLECTION schema-name*

  The collection identifier for your package. If not specified, it defaults to the authorization ID creating the package. Refer to 13.1.4, "Collection Considerations" on page 411 for more information about collections.

- *GRANT*

  Grants EXECUTE and BIND privileges on the package to a specific authorization ID, a group ID, or PUBLIC. Valid values are

  - *authid*

    The name of an authorization ID or a group ID.

  - *PUBLIC*

- *ISOLATION*

  Defines the degree of isolation of an application process executing concurrently with other application processes. Valid values are

- *CS Cursor Stability*
- *NC No Commit*

  This isolation level is not supported by DB2 common server.

- *RR Repeatable Read*
- *RS Read Stability*
- *UC Uncommitted Read*

- *MESSAGES message-file*

  Specifies the destination for warning, error, and completion status messages.

- *OWNER authorization ID*

  Designates the owner of the package. If not specified, it defaults to the primary ID issuing the BIND command. This option is not valid when creating a package to DB2 common server.

- *QUALIFIER qualifier-name*

  Is the implicit qualifier for unqualified names of tables, views, and indexes in the package. The default is the owner's authorization ID. This option is not valid when creating a package for DB2 common server.

- *SQLERROR*

  Indicates whether to create a package if SQL errors are detected. Valid values are

  - *CHECK*

    Indicates that the target system performs all syntax and semantics checks on the SQL statements being bound. This option provides you with the ability to check your program SQL statements against the target system, but a package is not created when using it.

  - *CONTINUE*

    Indicates the creation of a package, even if SQL errors are detected. This option does not prevent the statements in error from failing during run time. This value is not valid when creating a package for DB2 common server.

  - *NOPACKAGE*

    Indicates not to create a package if SQL errors are detected.

See the *DB2 Command Reference for common servers* for more information about the BIND commands.

13.1.4 Collection Considerations

The specification of a collection is a new option in the DB2 PREP and BIND commands.

When you precompile a program, the collection name (default or explicitly specified) is carried through the linking process and is part of the executable file. This information is hardcoded in the executable, and you cannot change it.

When you bind a package, you can specify a different collection name from the name used in the precompile process, although this specification does not change the hardcoded collection name in the executable. To activate the use of a package from a collection different from the collection used during the precompile step, you have a new SQL command, SET CURRENT PACKAGESET. This command can only be embedded in the program.

The following scenario exemplifies the use of the COLLECTION option during the bind process together with the new SET CURRENT PACKAGET command. Assume you have a program, PROG1, that executes in a DB2 common server client and has access to the following servers:

- Two DB2 common servers
- One DB2 for MVS/ESA
- One DB2 for OS/400

The collection (package schema for DB2 common server) names for the package must be as shown in Table 39.

Table 39. *Collection Names for Servers*

Server	RDB_NAME	Collection Name
DB2 common server 1	DBCS1	COLCS1
DB2 common server 2	DBCS2	COLCS2
DB2 for MVS/ESA	DBMVS	COLMVS
DB2 for OS/400	DB400	COL400

When you precompile PROG1, you specify for COLLECTION one of the collection names, for example, COLCS1. Then, when you bind the package to the other servers, you specify the corresponding collection name.

COLCS1 is still hardcoded in the executable, so it is not enough for you to specify the corresponding collection name during the bind process to the other servers. You must also dynamically change the collection name using the SET CURRENT PACKAGESET in your program. Here is an example of the pseudocode for PROG1:

```
CONNECT TO DBCS1
SET CURRENT PACKAGESET COLCS1
SELECT ......
  ........
CONNECT TO DBCS2
SET CURRENT PACKAGESET COLCS2
SELECT ......
  .....
CONNECT TO DBMVS
SET CURRENT PACKAGESET COLMVS
SELECT ......
  .....
CONNECT TO DB400
SET CURRENT PACKAGESET COL400
SELECT ......
```

13.2 Preparing the Sample Programs

Although the options to precompile or bind the same DB2 program in AIX, OS/2, or Windows are the same, there are certain differences in the process used for each platform. In this section we look at these platform-related differences, describing the steps we took to prepare our sample programs.

We also describe the specific options required to use the two-phase commit private protocol of DB2 common server and the available options to prepare a DOS program.

Refer to 12.7, "Multiple-Site Update for DB2 common server" on page 383 for a description of DB2 common server two-phase commit private protocol.

Table 40 lists the programs created in SDK for AIX, SDK for OS/2, and SDK for Windows.

Table 40. *Sample Programs: Distribution Levels*	
Program Name	**Description**
DRDASUTS	Multiple-site read
DRDASU2	Multiple-site read, single-site update

Table 41 on page 413 lists the database servers we connect to in these programs.

Table 41. Database Servers for the Sample Programs

Database Server	Location Name
DB2 for MVS/ESA	CENTDB2
SQL/DS for VM	S34VMDB0
SQL/DS for VSE	S34VSDB1
DB2 for OS/400—San Jose	SJAS400
DB2 for OS/400—Rochester	RCAS400
DB2 for AIX—San Jose	SJ6SMPL
DB2 for OS/2—San Jose	SJ2SMPL

Refer to Chapter 12, "Application Structure" on page 351 for more information about programs.

13.2.1 SDK for OS/2

From now on, our description of the sample program preparation concentrates on program DRDASU2. The program was coded in C on an AS/400 platform and then ported to OS/2.

Even though there was no need to change the source code to get DRDASU2 running on this platform, here are some factors to consider when using NetBIOS to connect to a server and executing a DUW application.

The default for the maximum number of NetBIOS connections (MAX_NETBIOS_CONNECTIONS) is 1. If your application is using DUW, you have to increase MAX_NETBIOS_CONNECTIONS because each CONNECT statement counts as one NetBIOS session. If a CONNECT type 2 is to be used from your program, you must issue a call to *sqlsetc DB2 API* to increase the MAX_NETBIOS_CONNECTIONS. Refer to the *DB2 API Reference for common servers* for the required details on this DB2 API. If a CONNECT type 2 is to be used from the CLP, you must use the *DB2 SET CLIENT* command from the command line to increase the MAX_NETBIOS_CONNECTIONS. Because we were trying to reduce program portability efforts, we decided to catalog our OS/2 databases using TCP/IP nodes. Also, if a CONNECT type 2 is to be used from the CLP, you must use the *DB2 SET CLIENT* command from the command line. Refer to *DB2 Command Reference for common servers* for the required details on this command.

To prepare our sample programs, we created a command file (.cmd) to perform the following tasks:

- Connect to SJ2SMPL and create a bind file and a package.

- Compile and link the program to create an executable file.

- Connect to each location and create a package from the bind file.

Figure 173 shows the command file we used.

```
/*    */
db2 'connect to sj2smpl user drdax5 using password'
db2 'prep drdasu2.sqx bind file collection drdax5 package using os2su2
connect 2 sqlrules std'
icc  '-C+ -O- -Ti+ drdasu2.cxx'
link386 '/NOI /DEBUG /ST:32000 /PM:VIO drdasu2.obj,,,db2api;'
db2 'connect reset';
db2 'connect to sj2smpl user drdax5 using password'
db2 'grant execute on package os2su2 to public';
db2 'connect reset';
db2 'connect to sjas400 user drdax5 using password';
db2 'bind drdasu2.bnd grant public';
db2 'connect reset';
db2 'connect to sj6smpl user drdax5 using password';
db2 'bind drdasu2.bnd grant public';
db2 'connect reset';
db2 'connect to rcas400 user drdax5 using password';
db2 'bind drdasu2.bnd grant public';
db2 'connect reset';
db2 'connect to db41pok user drdax5 using password';
db2 'bind drdasu2.bnd  grant public';
db2 'connect reset';
db2 'connect to s34vmdb0 user sjus1 using password';
db2 'bind drdasu2.bnd  grant public sqlerror continue';
db2 'connect reset';
db2 'connect to s34vsdb1 user dbsrv2 using password';
db2 'bind drdasu2.bnd  grant public sqlerror continue';
db2 'connect reset';
```

Figure 173. Command File to Prepare Program DRDASU2: SDK for OS/2

We ran this command file from an OS/2 session to create the packages that DRDASU2 requires. In a command file, every DB2 command must be preceded by the DB2 keyword, indicating to OS/2 to forward those commands to the OS/2 database server.

13.2.1.1 Creating a Bind File and an Executable Module

We required a bind file to create a package in each database server accessed by DRDASU2. To create the DRDASU2 bind file, we executed the commands shown in Figure 174 on page 415.

```
db2 'connect to sj2smpl user drdax5 using password'
db2 'prep drdasu2.sqx bind file collection drdax5 package using os2su2
connect 2 sqlrules std'
```

Figure 174. DRDASU2 Bind File Creation Commands

A connection is established to SJ2SMPL, using the userid DRDAX5, which has DBADM authority in this database server and is the creator of the order entry application tables in every location accessed by the program. Refer to Chapter 12, "Application Structure" on page 351 for more information about the sample application tables.

Then a PREP command is issued to create the objects shown in Table 42.

Table 42. *PREP Command Objects for DRDASU2*

Object Type	Object Name
Modified Source File	drdasu2.cxx
Bind File	drdasu2.bnd
Package	OS2SU2

We decided to create all of our sample application packages in collection DRDAX5. Since we wanted the collection name to be the same in all locations, we gave our packages a name different from the program name, thus preventing packages from overriding in the database servers' catalogs.

Note that we explicitly used the COLLECTION option, for the clarity of the sample, but this is not needed because the userid executing the PREP command is the default collection name if no collection is specified.

We used the PACKAGE option using os2su2 to create a package called os2su2 in the OS/2 platform. Since the package name is kept in the drdasu2.bnd bind file, the packages created from this bind file are to be called OS2SU2 in every platform.

Because program DRDASU2 uses DUW, we specified CONNECT 2. We specified SQLRULES STD to conform to SQL92, using SET CONNECTION to make a dormant connection current.

Figure 175 on page 416 shows the commands we used to create the executable module for DRDASU2.

```
icc  '-C+ -O- -Ti+ drdasu2.cxx'
link386 '/NOI /DEBUG /ST:32000 /PM:VIO drdasu2.obj,,,db2api;'
```

Figure 175. *Creating DRDASU2 Executable Module in OS/2*

We used the IBM C Set++ compiler command *icc* to compile the modified source file called drdasu2.cxx, thus generating an object module called drdasu2.obj, which is to be used in the link process. The options used to compile are as follows:

- -C+

  Perform compile only, no link.

- -O-

  No optimization.

- -Ti+

  Generate debugger information.

We used the 32-bit linker command, *link386*, to link the object module drdasu2.obj. The object module has to be linked to the DB2 for OS/2 db2api module and the appropriate C++ libraries to create the executable module called drdasu2.exe. The options used to link are as follows:

- /NOI

  Preserve case sensitivity.

- **/DEBUG**

  Include debugging information.

- /ST:32000

  Specify a stack size of at least 32,000.

- /PM:VIO

  Enable the program to run in an OS/2 window.

13.2.1.2 Binding a Package in DB2 for MVS/ESA

Figure 176 on page 417 shows the commands we used to bind package OS2SU2 to *DB2 for MVS/ESA*.

```
db2 'connect reset';
db2 'connect to db41pok user drdax5 using password';
db2 'bind drdasu2.bnd  grant public';
```

Figure 176. Bind Package for Location CENTDB2

A CONNECT RESET statement is issued to disconnect from a previous connection, then a connection is established to DB41POK. Both CENTDB2 and DB41POK point to the same DB2 for MVS/ESA AS through the OS/2 DDCS gateway. Connecting to CENTDB2 would have accomplished the creation of package os2su2 in DB2 for MVS/ESA as well. We used different alias names to illustrate the facility of cataloging the same database with different alias names.

Figure 177 shows the database directory entries for both the CENTDB2 and DB41POK databases in our OS/2 client.

```
Database 13 entry:
  Database alias              = DB41POK
  Database name               = DB41POK
  Node name                   = SJ2TCPIP
  Database release level      = 6.00
  Comment                     =
  Directory entry type        = Remote
  Authentication              = DCS

Database 19 entry:
  Database alias              = CENTDB2
  Database name               = DB41POK
  Node name                   = SJ2TCPIP
  Database release level      = 6.00
  Comment                     =
  Directory entry type        = Remote
  Authentication              = DCS
```

Figure 177. OS/2 Client Database Directory Entries

To connect to DB2 for MVS/ESA, we used DRDAX5, which has SYSADM authority and is the creator of the order entry tables in this platform.

The BIND PACKAGE command used the drdasu2.bnd bind file to create package OS2SU2 in DB2 for MVS/ESA. Figure 178 on page 418 shows the entry for package OS2SU2 in the SYSIBM.SYSPACKAGE catalog table of DB2 for MVS/ESA.

```
COLLID              NAME      OWNER     CREATOR   QUALIFIER
------------------  --------  --------  --------  ---------
DRDAX5              OS2SU2    DRDAX5    DRDAX5    DRDAX5
```

Figure 178. SYSIBM.SYSPACKAGE of DB2 for MVS/ESA: OS2SU2 Package

Table 43 shows how some PREP and BIND PACKAGE parameters map to some of the columns of the DB2 for MVS/ESA SYSIBM.SYSPACKAGE table.

Table 43. PREP and BIND Options Mapping to DB2 for MVS/ESA

Parameter	Maps to:	Considerations
COLLECTION	COLLID	Can be provided during precompilation and overridden during bind
PACKAGE	NAME	Can be provided only during precompilation; cannot be overridden
OWNER	OWNER	The userid binding the package, unless a different value is specified during precompilation and/or bind
Primary ID	CREATOR	The userid binding the package
QUALIFIER	QUALIFIER	The userid binding the package, unless a different value is specified during precompilation and/or bind

You have to grant appropriate users with authority to execute every package you create. You can do this by connecting to the database server where the package is created and issuing the appropriate GRANT command, or by using the *grant* option in your BIND PACKAGE command.

We decided to use the *grant public* BIND command option to grant execute authority to public on package OS2SU2 on DB2 for MVS/ESA.

13.2.1.3 DB2 for OS/400

In Figure 179 on page 419 we show the commands we used to bind package OS2SU2 to DB2 for OS/400 in San Jose and in Rochester.

```
db2 'connect reset';
db2 'connect to sjas400 user drdax5 using password';
db2 'bind drdasu2.bnd grant public';
db2 'connect reset';
db2 'connect to rcas400 user drdax5 using password';
db2 'bind drdasu2.bnd grant public';
```

Figure 179. Bind Package OS2SU2 for Location SJAS400

A CONNECT RESET command is issued to disconnect from a previous connection; then a connection is established to SJAS400, and a BIND command is executed. After that, another CONNECT RESET command is issued, and a connection is established to RCAS400 in order to create a package in this location as well.

To connect to DB2 for OS/400, we used user DRDAX5 in both locations, San Jose and Rochester.

The user class for DRDAX5 is *PGMR, and it has the required authorizations to use and create objects in collection DRDAX5 in both the San Jose and Rochester systems.

See *Programmer Authority* in 8.2.5.3, "Programmer Authority" on page 241 for more information about authorizations in the OS/400 environment.

The BIND PACKAGE command used the drdasu2.bnd bind file to create package OS2SU2 in both the San Jose and Rochester databases.

Figure 180 shows the entry for package OS2SU2 in the QSYS2.SYSPACKAGES catalog table of DB2 for OS/400 in San Jose.

```
PACKAGE_NAME PACKAGE_SCHEMA PACKAGE_OWNER PACKAGE_CREATOR DEFAULT-SCHEMA
------------ -------------- ------------- --------------- --------------
OS2SU2       DRDAX5         DRDAX5        DRDAX5          DRDAX5
```

Figure 180. QSYS2.SYSPACKAGES of DB2 for OS/400: San Jose

Figure 181 on page 420 shows the entry for package OS2SU2 in the QSYS2.SYSPACKAGES catalog table of DB2 for OS/400 in Rochester.

```
 ┌────────────────────────────────────────────────────────────────────────────┐
 │ PACKAGE_NAME PACKAGE_SCHEMA PACKAGE_OWNER PACKAGE_CREATOR DEFAULT-SCHEMA      │
 │ ------------ -------------- ------------- --------------- --------------      │
 │ OS2SU2       DRDAX5         DRDAX5        DRDAX5          DRDAX5              │
 └────────────────────────────────────────────────────────────────────────────┘
```

Figure 181. QSYS2.SYSPACKAGES of DB2 for OS/400: Rochester

Table 44 shows how some PREP and BIND PACKAGE parameters map to some of the columns of the DB2 for OS/400 QSYS2.SYSPACKAGES table.

Table 44. PREP and Bind Options Mapping to DB2 for OS/400

Parameter	Maps to:	Considerations
QUALIFIER	DEFAULT_SCHEMA	Can be provided during precompilation and overridden during bind. If specified, it becomes the implicit qualifier for unqualified objects
OWNER	PACKAGE_OWNER	The userid binding the package
COLLECTION	PACKAGE_SCHEMA	Can be provided during precompilation and overridden during bind, but a collection with the specified name must exist in OS/400
Primary ID	PACKAGE_CREATOR	The userid binding the package. If qualifier is not specified, it becomes the qualifier for unqualified objects

You have to grant appropriate users with authority to execute every package you create. You can do this by connecting to the database server where the package is created and issuing the appropriate GRANT command, or by using the *grant* option in your BIND PACKAGE command.

We decided to use the *grant public* BIND command option to grant execute authority to public on package OS2SU2 on the DB2 for OS/400 in both San Jose and in Rochester.

13.2.1.4 SQL/DS for VM and VSE

Figure 182 on page 421 shows the commands we used to bind package OS2SU2 to SQL/DS for VM.

```
db2 'connect reset';
db2 'connect to s34vmdb0 user sjus1 using password';
db2 'bind drdasu2.bnd  grant public sqlerror continue';
```

Figure 182. Bind Package OS2SU2 for Location S34VMDB0

A CONNECT RESET command is issued to disconnect from a previous connection; then a connection is established to S34VMDB0, using user SJUS1, which has DBA authority.

The BIND PACKAGE command used the drdasu2.bnd bind file to create package OS2SU2 in SQL/DS for VM. Figure 183 shows the entry for package OS2SU2 in the SYSTEM.SYSACCESS catalog table of SQL/DS for VM.

```
TNAME              CREATOR
------------------ --------
OS2SU2             DRDAX5
```

Figure 183. SYSTEM.SYSACCESS of SQL/DS for VM: OS2SU2 Package

Figure 184 shows the commands we used to bind package OS2SU2 to SQL/DS for VSE.

```
db2 'connect reset';
db2 'connect to s34vsdb1 user dbsrv2 using password';
db2 'bind drdasu2.bnd  grant public sqlerror continue';
```

Figure 184. Bind Package OS2SU2 for Location S34VSDB1

A CONNECT RESET command is issued to disconnect from a previous connection, then a connection is established to S34VSDB1, using user DBSRV2, which has DBA authority.

The BIND PACKAGE command used the drdasu2.bnd bind file to create package OS2SU2 in SQL/DS for VSE. Figure 185 shows the entry for package OS2SU2 in the SYSTEM.SYSACCESS catalog table of SQL/DS for VSE.

```
TNAME              CREATOR
------------------ --------
OS2SU2             DRDAX5
```

Figure 185. SYSTEM.SYSACCESS of SQL/DS for VSE

The collection name specified during precompilation maps to the CREATOR column in the SQL/DS for VSE SYSTEM.SYSACCESS table. It becomes the implicit qualifier for unqualified objects in the corresponding package.

Because our collection name is DRDAX5, the unqualified objects in these two packages are qualified by DRDAX5 regardless of the primary ID used to bind the packages. Thus the order entry application tables for SQL/DS for VM and VSE should be created with CREATOR name DRDAX5.

You have to grant appropriate users the authority to execute every package you create. You can do this by connecting to the database server where the package is created and issuing thee appropriate GRANT command, or by using the *grant* option in your BIND PACKAGE command.

We decided to use the *grant public* BIND command option to grant execute authority to public on package OS2SU2 in both SQL/DS for VM and SQL/DS for VSE.

The *SQLERROR CONTINUE* option was used for these two platforms because the *FOR FETCH ONLY* option is not valid when preparing a program in SQL/DS, but it is accepted when binding or executing from an AR. In this way the packages were successfully created and executed in these platforms.

13.2.1.5 DB2 common server
Figure 186 shows the commands we used to bind package OS2SU2 to DB2 for AIX.

```
db2 'connect reset';
db2 'connect to sj6smpl user drdax5 using password';
db2 'bind drdasu2.bnd  grant public';
```

Figure 186. Bind Package OS2SU2 for Location SJ6SMPL

A CONNECT RESET command is issued to disconnect from a previous connection, then a connection to SJ6SMPL is established, using user DRDAX5, which has DBADM authority and is the creator of the order entry application tables in this platform.

The BIND PACKAGE command used the drdasu2.bnd bind file to create package OS2SU2 in DB2 for AIX. Figure 187 on page 423 shows the entry for package OS2SU2 in the SYSCAT.PACKAGES catalog table of DB2 for AIX.

```
PKGNAME   PKGSCHEMA BOUNDBY
--------  --------- --------
OS2SU2    DRDAX5    DRDAX5
```

Figure 187. SYSCAT.PACKAGES of DB2 for AIX: OS2SU2 Package

Figure 188 shows the commands we used to bind package OS2SU2 to DB2 for OS/2.

```
db2 'connect to sj2smpl user drdax5 using password'
db2 'prep drdasu2.sqx bind file collection drdax5 package using os2su2
connect 2 sqlrules std'
```

Figure 188. Bind Package OS2SU2 for Location SJ2SMPL

Because program DRDASU2 accesses DB2 for OS/2, we had to create a package in this
location as well. In fact such a package was created during precompilation time because
we used the *PACKAGE using* option.

The command file issues a connect to DB2 for OS/2 using user DRDAX5, which has
DBADM authority and is the creator of the order entry tables in this platform.

The PREP command created package OS2SU2 in DB2 for OS/2. Figure 189 shows the
entry for package OS2SU2 in the SYSCAT.PACKAGES catalog table of DB2 for OS/2.

```
PKGNAME   PKGSCHEMA BOUNDBY
--------  --------- --------
OS2SU2    DRDAX5    DRDAX5
```

Figure 189. SYSCAT.PACKAGES of DB2 for OS/2: OS2SU2 Package

For DB2 common server, the userid binding the package maps to the BOUNDBY
column of SYSCAT.PACKAGES. The BOUNDBY value is the qualifier of unqualified
objects in the corresponding package.

You do not have the option to change a qualifier, because DB2 common server does not
support the QUALIFIER option.

You have to grant appropriate users the authority to execute every package you create.
You can do this by connecting to the database server where the package is created and
issuing the appropriate GRANT command, or by using the *grant* option in your BIND
PACKAGE command.

We decided to use the *grant public* BIND command option to grant execute authority to public on package OS2SU2 on DB2 for AIX.

To grant execute authority on package OS2SU2 on DB2 for OS/2, we decided to execute the appropriate GRANT command as shown in Figure 190.

```
db2 'connect reset';
db2 'connect to sj2smpl user drdax5 using password'
db2 'grant execute on package os2su2 to public';
```

Figure 190. GRANT Command for Package OS2SU2 in DB2 for OS/2

13.2.2 SDK for Windows

As stated before, the program preparation steps for SDK for Windows, SDK for OS/2, and SDK for AIX are pretty much the same. The differences relate more to the operating system than to the DB2 commands used to prepare a program with embedded SQL.

In our Windows client we chose TCP/IP for the communication protocol with the server workstation and opted to have Microsoft Visual C++ as our programming environment. The considerations we made to select these two options are the following:

- TCP/IP for DOS

  We used the TCP/IP protocol in our Windows client to preserve program portability as much as possible. There are some NetBIOS considerations regarding DUW programs that affect the way you code this kind of program. Refer to 13.2.1, "SDK for OS/2" on page 413 for more details on this.

- Microsoft Visual C++

  We used C to develop our sample programs, so we needed a C compiler. We decided to use Microsoft Visual C++ because it provides the C compiler and a tool called WXServer, which we used to facilitate the program preparation process of our sample programs.

13.2.2.1 WXServer Usage

For a production environment, you may want to use a tool that helps you ease the DB2 program preparation process.

WXServer provides the environment to run Windows programs from a DOS session. Using WXServer, you can create batch files that contain the DB2 PREP and BIND commands, along with Microsoft C++ compile and link commands, thus creating an automated procedure to prepare your programs.

13.2.2.2 Creating Packages and an Executable Module: A Sample

We prepared a batch file called drdapru2.bat, which contains the DB2 precompile, DB2 bind, compile, and link processes.

To run the drdapru2.bat file in a Windows environment, we executed the following steps:

1. Started the wxsrvr.exe program

2. Ran the drdapru2.bat file.

   Note that when the DB2 precompile and bind processes have completed, you have to initiate the compile and link process by reactivating the DRDAPRU2 program.

Figure 191 on page 426 shows the drdapru2.bat file and highlights some commands for further explanation.

```
@echo off
echo 1 connect to sj2smpl user drdax5 using password > preptmp1
echo 2 prep drdasu2.sqx bindfile package using winsu2
collection drdax5 connect 2 sqlrules std NOLINEMACRO >> preptmp1
echo 3 grant execute on package winsu2 to public >> preptmp1
echo connect reset >> preptmp1
4
echo connect to rcas400 user drdax5 using password >> preptmp1
echo bind drdasu2.bnd grant public >> preptmp1
echo connect reset >> preptmp1
5
echo connect to sj6smpl user drdax5 using password >> preptmp1
echo bind drdasu2.bnd grant public >> preptmp1
echo connect reset >> preptmp1
5
echo connect to centdb2 user drdax5 using password >> preptmp1
echo bind drdasu2.bnd grant public >> preptmp1
echo connect reset >> preptmp1
5
echo connect to sjas400 user drdax5 using password >> preptmp1
echo bind drdasu2.bnd grant public >> preptmp1
echo connect reset >> preptmp1
5
echo connect to s34vmdb0 user sjus1 using drda1a >> preptmp1
echo bind drdasu2.bnd grant public sqlerror continue >> preptmp1
echo connect reset >> preptmp1
5
echo connect to s34vsdb1 user dbsrv2 using ssmc1 >> preptmp1
echo bind drdasu2.bnd grant public sqlerror continue >> preptmp1
echo connect reset >> preptmp1
echo 6 QUIT >> preptmp1
7 wx db2w -f 8 preptmp1
9 cl /c /Gy /ALw /W3 /Mq /DDB2WIN drdasu2.cxx
10 link /ST:32000 /SE:400 /NOD  drdasu2.obj,drdasu2.exe,
drdasu2.map,db2w+llibcewq+libw+oldnames;
@echo on
```

Figure 191. Batch File to Prepare Program DRDASU2

Note that the DB2 commands in this batch file are inserted in a file called PREPTMP1,
which is later sent to the SDK for Windows CLP for execution.

1 Issues a CONNECT statement to SJ2SMPL using userid DRDAX5

2 This PREP command creates the following objects:

- A package called *WINSU2* in SJ2SMPL location
- A bindfile called *drdasu2.bnd*
- A modified source code called *drdasu2.cxx*.

3 This command grants package WINSU2 execution to public.

4 A connection to RCAS400 is established to create package WINSU2 in this location.

5 Note that the CONNECT, BIND, and CONNECT RESET commands are issued for every location where package WINSU2 is required, and that the grant option is used to allow users the execution of the packages.

6 A QUIT command is issued to exit the SDK for Windows CLP.

7 This command invokes the SDK for Windows CLP and passes file PREPTMP1 **8** as a parameter.

9 This command compiles file drdasu2.cxx and generates file drdasu2.obj, which is then **10** linked to finally create an executable file called drdasu2.exe.

13.2.2.3 The Packages

The BIND PACKAGE commands issued in the drdapru2.bat batch file used the drdasu2.bnd bind file to create package WINSU2 in all locations, except SJ2SMPL, where the package was created by the PREP command itself.

Figure 192 shows the entry for package WINSU2 in the SYSIBM.SYSPACKAGE catalog table of DB2 for MVS/ESA.

```
COLLID              NAME      OWNER     CREATOR   QUALIFIER
------------------  --------  --------  --------  ---------
DRDAX5              WINSU2    DRDAX5    DRDAX5    DRDAX5
```

Figure 192. SYSIBM.SYSPACKAGE of DB2 for MVS/ESA: WINSU2 Package

Refer to 13.2.1.2, "Binding a Package in DB2 for MVS/ESA" on page 416 for more details on the options used to create packages for the MVS/ESA platform.

Figure 193 on page 428 shows the entry for package WINSU2 in the QSYS2.SYSPACKAGES catalog table of DB2 for OS/400 in San Jose.

```
 PACKAGE_NAME PACKAGE_SCHEMA PACKAGE_OWNER PACKAGE_CREATOR DEFAULT-SCHEMA
 ------------ -------------- ------------- --------------- --------------
 WINSU2       DRDAX5         DRDAX5        DRDAX5          DRDAX5
```

Figure 193. QSYS2.SYSPACKAGES of DB2 for OS/400: San Jose

Figure 194 shows the entry for package WINSU2 in the QSYS2.SYSPACKAGES catalog table of DB2 for OS/400 in Rochester.

```
 PACKAGE_NAME PACKAGE_SCHEMA PACKAGE_OWNER PACKAGE_CREATOR DEFAULT-SCHEMA
 ------------ -------------- ------------- --------------- --------------
 WINSU2       DRDAX5         DRDAX5        DRDAX5          DRDAX5
```

Figure 194. QSYS2.SYSPACKAGES of DB2 for OS/400: Rochester

Refer to 13.2.1.3, "DB2 for OS/400" on page 418 for more details on the options used to create packages for the AS/400 platform.

Figure 195 shows the entry for package WINSU2 in the SYSTEM.SYSACCESS catalog table of SQL/DS for VM.

```
 TNAME              CREATOR
 ------------------ --------
 WINSU2             DRDAX5
```

Figure 195. SYSTEM.SYSACCESS of SQL/DS for VM: WINSU2 Package

Figure 196 shows the entry for package WINSU2 in the SYSTEM.SYSACCESS catalog table of SQL/DS for VSE.

```
 TNAME              CREATOR
 ------------------ --------
 WINSU2             DRDAX5
```

Figure 196. SYSTEM.SYSACCESS of SQL/DS for VSE: WINSU2 Package

Refer to 13.2.1.4, "SQL/DS for VM and VSE" on page 420 for more details on the options used to create packages for the VM and VSE platforms.

Figure 197 on page 429 shows the entry for package WINSU2 in the SYSCAT.PACKAGES catalog table of DB2 for AIX.

```
PKGNAME   PKGSCHEMA BOUNDBY
--------  --------- --------
WINSU2    DRDAX5    DRDAX5
```

Figure 197. SYSCAT.PACKAGES of DB2 for AIX: WINSU2 Package

Figure 198 shows the entry for package WINSU2 in the SYSCAT.PACKAGES catalog table of DB2 for OS/2.

```
PKGNAME   PKGSCHEMA BOUNDBY
--------  --------- --------
WINSU2    DRDAX5    DRDAX5
```

Figure 198. SYSCAT.PACKAGES of DB2 for OS/2: WINSU2 Package

Refer to 13.2.1.5, "DB2 common server" on page 422 for more details on the options used to create packages for the AIX and OS/2 platforms.

13.2.3 SDK/DOS

A DOS requester does not support DUW, so we were unable to prepare our sample programs on this platform.

Nevertheless we illustrate the PREP and BIND commands options available for this platform and provide you with an example of a batch file you can use to prepare your programs in this environment.

The syntax for the PREP command in an SDK/DOS environment is the following:

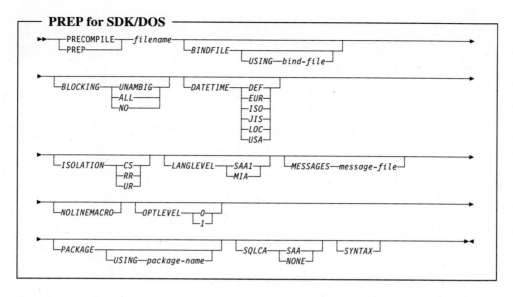

PREP for SDK/DOS

Note that such options as CONNECT, DISCONNECT, and SYNCPOINT and other PREP command options for DUW support are not available on this platform.

The syntax for the BIND command in an SDK/DOS environment is as follows:

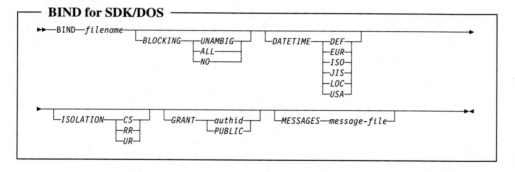

BIND for SDK/DOS

You must precompile and bind any DOS program that contains SQL statements, in addition to executing the appropriate compile and link steps.

Figure 199 on page 431 shows a batch (.bat) file to prepare a C program.

```
@echo off
echo connect to sample >> preptmp
echo prep program.sqc bind file NOLINEMACRO >> preptmp
echo bind program.bnd >> preptmp
echo quit >> preptmp
db2 < preptmp
erase preptmp
cl /c /Gy /AL /W3 /DDB2DOS program.c
link /ST:0x8192 /SE:400 /nod /noe program,,,llibce+db2sdk1+db2sdk2+
db2sdk3+db2util+db2prep=socket1+oldnames;
```

Figure 199. Sample Batch File to Prepare a DB2 Program Using SDK/DOS

This batch file inserts the CONNECT, PREP, and BIND DB2 commands in a file called preptmp, which is later passed to the DB2 CLP. After completion of the DB2 commands, control is given back to the batch file, and the compilation and link steps are executed.

The precompiler generates a modified source file called program.c, which is used for the compiler to generate an object module.

The linker generates the executable module, program.exe, by linking program.obj. The application object module must be linked together with the following database manager libraries:

- DB2SDK1.LIB
- DB2SDK2.LIB
- DB2SDK3.LIB
- DB2UTIL.LIB

Note that the link command should fit in a single line of the batch file.

Refer to the *Software Developer's Kit/DOS Programming Guide* for more information about DB2 program preparation on the DOS platform.

13.2.4 Using DB2 common server Two-phase Commit: An Example

DB2 for AIX and DB2 for OS/2 provide their own protocol to support two-phase commit processing.

In this section we describe the steps required to prepare program MSUPP2PC. Refer to 12.7, "Multiple-Site Update for DB2 common server" on page 383 for an explanation of the DB2 common server two-phase commit process and for more details on program MSUPP2PC.

13.2.4.1 Preparing the Program

Program MSUPP2PC was successfully prepared and tested on the following platforms: AIX, OS/2, and Windows.

Figure 200 shows the scenario to test MSUPP2PC in the AIX environment.

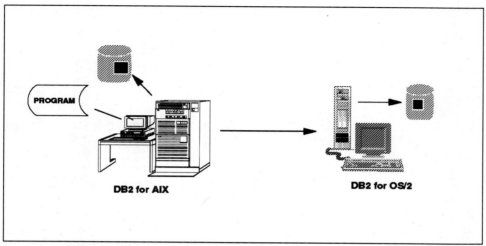

Figure 200. MSUPP2PC Execution Environment in AIX

In this case the requester program runs in the same AIX box where the DB2 for AIX resides. The AIX requester program accesses and updates data in both DB2 for AIX and DB2 for OS/2.

Figure 201 on page 433 shows the scenario to test MSUPP2PC in the Windows environment.

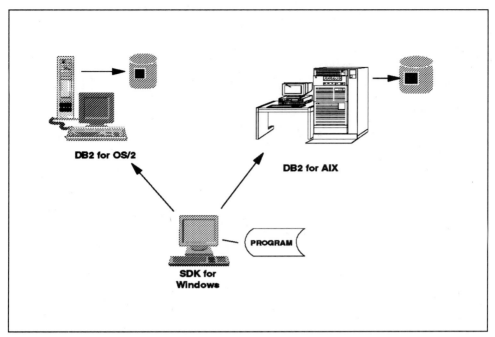

Figure 201. *MSUPP2PC Execution Environment in Windows*

In this case the client program executes on a separate DOS/Windows box running SDK for Windows. The Windows client accesses and updates data in both DB2 for AIX and DB2 for OS/2.

Figure 202 on page 434 shows the scenario to test MSUPP2PC in the OS/2 environment.

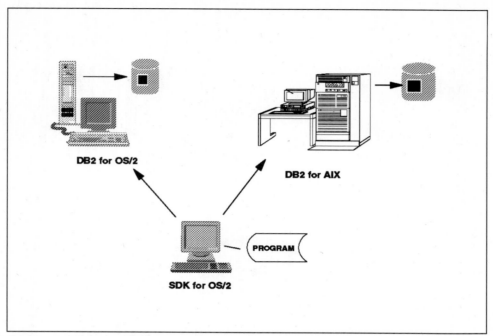

Figure 202. MSUPP2PC Execution Environment in OS/2

In this case the client program executes on a separate OS/2 running SDK for OS/2. The OS/2 client accesses and updates data in both DB2 for AIX and DB2 for OS/2. Let us concentrate on this scenario to describe the program preparation steps for MSUPP2PC.

We created a command file to perform all of the program preparation steps (see Figure 203 on page 435).

```
/*    */
1 db2 'connect to sj2smpl user drdax5 using password'
2 db2 'prep msupp2pc.sqx bind file collection drdax5 package using
os2pp2pc connect 2 sqlrules std syncpoint twophase';
3 db2 'grant execute on package os2pp2pc to public';
4 icc  '-C+ -O- -Ti+ msupp2pc.cxx'
5 link386 '/NOI /DEBUG /ST:32000 /PM:VIO msupp2pc.obj,,,
db2api;'
6 db2 'connect reset';
7 db2 'connect to sj6smpl user drdax5 using password';
8 db2 'bind msupp2pc.bnd grant public';
db2 'connect reset';
```

Figure 203. MSUPP2PC Program Preparation Command File

Notes for Figure 203

1 A connection is established to SJ2SMPL using userid DRDAX5, which has DBADM authority in this location and is the creator of the tables accessed in program MSUPP2PC.

2 A PREP command is issued to create a bind file, a package, and a modified source file called msupp2pc.cxx, which is used as input for the compile process.

3 Execution permit for the package is granted to public through the use of the GRANT command.

4 The compilation process creates an object module called msupp2pc.obj, which is used by the **5** linking process, which in turn creates the executable version of program msupp2pc.exe.

6 A CONNECT RESET command is issued to reset the previous connection to SJ2SMPL.

7 A connection is established to SJ6SMPL using userid DRDAX5, which has DBADM authority and is the creator of the tables accessed by program MSUPP2PC.

A package is created in SJ6SMPL through the **8** BIND command which uses the msupp2pc.bnd bind file. Execution permit is granted to public through the BIND command as well.

Because program MSUPP2PC was coded to use the two-phase commit process, implemented through DB2 common server, we had to indicate to the linker that the coordinator function should be included in the executable version of program

MSUPP2PC. Such an instruction was provided to the linker by using the *SYNCPOINT TWOPHASE* option of the PREP command.

In addition to the coordinator function linked to program MSUPP2PC, we had to specify a TM database.

13.2.4.2 Specifying the TM Database

To create the TM database, we updated the client database manager configuration, using the command illustrated in Figure 204.

```
UPDATE DATABASE MANAGER CONFIGURATION USING TM_DATABASE SJ2SMPL
```

Figure 204. UPDATE DATABASE MANAGER CONFIGURATION in an OS/2 Client

Figure 205 shows the database manager configuration parameter values for the OS/2 client.

```
            Database Manager Configuration
       Node type = Client
Database manager configuration release level        = 0x0600
Transaction processor monitor name       (TP_MON_NAME) =
Diagnostic error capture level              (DIAGLEVEL) = 3
Diagnostic data directory path                (DIAGPATH) =
SYSADM group name                         (SYSADM_GROUP) =
SYSCTRL group name                       (SYSCTRL_GROUP) =
SYSMAINT group name                     (SYSMAINT_GROUP) =
Directory cache support                      (DIR_CACHE) = NO
Max requester I/O block size (bytes)          (RQRIOBLK) = 32767
DOS requester I/O block size (bytes)      (DOS_RQRIOBLK) = 4096
DRDA services heap size (4KB)             (DRDA_HEAP_SZ) = 128
Transaction manager database name          (TM_DATABASE) = SJ2SMPL
Workstation name                                (NNAME) = MARCELA
Default accounting string              (DFT_ACCOUNT_STR) =
```

Figure 205. Database Manager Configuration for the OS/2 Client

Refer to 12.7, "Multiple-Site Update for DB2 common server" on page 383 for more details on the TM database and the DB2 common server two-phase commit.

13.2.5 SDK for AIX Program Preparation

Program preparation steps for SDK for AIX do not differ from those described for SDK for OS/2. What differs between the two platforms is the way in which commands have to be invoked, since invoking commands is an operating system dependent facility.

As for the other platforms in our scenario, besides creating a local database to be made available to the programs running on other platforms, we also performed all steps necessary to run the sample programs locally and have them access the remote databases (listed in Table 41 on page 413). We cataloged remote databases in the system database directory of DB2 for AIX using the same alias name as other AR platforms. We did this for simplicity. We could have chosen different names when cataloging a database server at the various locations without compromising the portability of the code. In fact, the programs pick up the database server names to which they have to connect from a local DB2 table, and these names are provided to the SQL CONNECT statements by means of a host variable.

As in OS/2, we created command files to perform the tasks requested by the program preparation process:

- Connect to SJ6SMPL and create a bind file (.bnd) and a package
- Compile and link the program to create an executable file
- Connect to each location and create a package from the bind file.

Figure 206 on page 438 shows an example of the command file we used.

```
db2 connect to sj6smpl user drdax5 using password
db2 prep drdasu2.sqc bindfile collection drdax5 \
    package using aixsu2 connect 2 sqlrules std

xlc -o drdasu2 drdasu2.c -I /u/db2v2/sqllib/include \
    -L /u/db2v2/sqllib/lib -ldb2

db2 connect reset
db2 connect to sj6smpl user drdax5 using password
db2 bind drdasu2.bnd blocking all grant public

db2 connect reset
db2 connect to sjas400 user drdax5 using password
db2 bind drdasu2.bnd blocking all grant public

db2 connect reset
db2 connect to sj2smpl user drdax5 using password
db2 bind drdasu2.bnd blocking all grant public

db2 connect reset
db2 connect to rcas400 user drdax5 using password
db2 bind drdasu2.bnd blocking all grant public

db2 connect reset
db2 connect to db41pok user drdax5 using password
db2 bind drdasu2.bnd blocking all grant public

db2 connect reset
db2 connect to s34vmdb0 user drdax5 using password
db2 bind drdasu2.bnd blocking all grant public

db2 connect reset
db2 connect to s34vsdb1 user drdax5 using password
db2 bind drdasu2.bnd blocking all grant public
```

Figure 206. *Command File to Prepare Program DRDASU2: SDK for AIX*

We run this command file from an AIX prompt to create the packages that DRDASU2 requires on the various platforms.

For the precompilation and bind steps, nothing differentiates the activities performed in AIX from those performed in OS/2.

For the compile and link steps, because there was no specific C++ code in the sample programs, in AIX we processed them as C programs. The services of the AIX C compiler and linker were invoked as shown in Figure 207 on page 439.

```
xlc -o drdasu2 drdasu2.c -I /u/db2v2/sqllib/include \
     -L /u/db2v2/sqllib/lib -ldb2
```

Figure 207. *Creating DRDASU2 Executable Module in AIX*

- -o

  Specifies the name of the executable module (drdasu2) to be obtained from the output file of the precompiler step (drdasu2.c)

- -I

  Specifies the path of DB2 include files

- -L

  Specifies the path of the DB2 run-time shared library

- -ldb2

  Specifies the link with the database manager library (libdb2.a)

Chapter 14. Program Preparation: DB2 for OS/400

This chapter provides information about preparing and running our applications on DB2 for OS/400. The programs reported in Chapter 12, "Application Structure" on page 351 were developed on the AS/400, and they are meant to run with very minor changes on the other platforms we dealt with.

14.1 Process Description and Concepts

This section provides a brief overview of the application development process required on the AS/400 system to create a DRDA application.

14.1.1 Editing Your Source Programs

On the AS/400, programs were developed using the C language with embedded SQL statements. We used the ILE C/400 compiler to create those programs.

The C source code was stored in a source file (QCSRC) residing in collection DRDAX5 on SCHASM02. The names of the file members match the names of the programs, as described in Chapter 12, "Application Structure" on page 351. DRDAX5 was also the userid of the programmer who created the programs.

Figure 208 shows the DRDAX5 user profile.

```
User profile . . . . . . . . . . . . . . . :   DRDAX5
Language identifier  . . . . . . . . . . . :   37 ▮1▮
Country identifier . . . . . . . . . . . . :   ENU
Coded character set identifier . . . . . . :   37 ▮1▮
```

Figure 208. DRDAX5 User Profile

14.1.2 CCSID Considerations

The userid was set up to support a CCSID and language ID supported by the other ASs. Figure 208 shows how to set the correct parameters for your user profiles on the AS/400 (▮1▮). Any object created on the AS/400 by DRDAX5 had implicitly defined a CCSID of 37. This circumvented any problems associated with creating distributed applications on multiple platforms and languages. The source file was also created with a CCSID of 37 to ensure that the ILE C/400 compiler used the correct coding for its special characters that are not in the invariant character set, for example, the "{" and "}".

14.1.3 Authority

Userid DRDAX5 was granted the authority to create and drop packages on each server. Refer to 8.1.3, "Security Requirements" on page 228 for information about security issues when DB2 for OS/400 is an AR.

14.1.4 Creating a Distributed Application

Three steps are required to create a distributed application on the AS/400:

1. Create the database tables in collection DRDAX5. They are entered by using ISQL. For their layout, please refer to 12.1, "SQL Tables Used by Application Programs" on page 351.

2. Precompile and compile the programs.

    On the AS/400 system, creating an application containing SQL statements implies an initial precompile step and a subsequent compile step. These two steps can be done separately, but more frequently you will issue a single command that performs both.

    However, during the precompile step, the SQL statements are replaced by CALL statements to the SQL interface module (QSQROUTE). Subsequently, the access plan is created. The access plan is stored into the program object at a later time. During the compile step, the source statements are actually converted by the compiler into executable form. We used the *CRTSQLCI* command to invoke the precompiler and the compiler.

    Note:

    Refer to *ILE Concepts*, and *ILE C/400 Programmers Guide* for more information about the program creation process.

3. Bind the application to the server using the Create SQL Package command (CRTSQLPKG).

    SQL uses the information collected during the precompile step to create an *access plan*. Also, when you use the CRTSQLPKG command in a distributed application, DRDA passes this information to the application server to create an *SQL package*. During package creation on the AS, an access plan is created for the package.

14.2 Precompile

The precompiler scans each statement of the application program source and does the following:

-   Looks for SQL statements and the definition of host variable names

- Verifies that each SQL statement is valid and free of syntax errors
- Validates the SQL statements using the description in the database
- Prepares each SQL statement for compilation in the host language
- Produces information about each precompiled SQL statement

The SQL precompile produces a listing and a temporary source file member. It can also produce the SQL package depending on the OPTION and RDB parameter of the CRTSQLxxx precompiler command. The precompiler listing shows each SQL source statement and points out whether any of those statements contain errors. If you also specify the *XREF option for the precompiler, you get a cross-reference listing that shows where SQL objects and host variables are used.

In the precompiler listing, errors are assigned a severity level. Error severity levels determine whether a compilation completes successfully. Severity 30 or higher indicates error conditions that must be corrected before the program will compile.

14.3 Creating the Sample Applications

In this section we describe the steps you have to take to create the sample applications discussed in Chapter 12, "Application Structure" on page 351 on an AS/400 AR.

14.3.1 Compile/Binding

We created our application samples by using the *CRTSQLCI* command. Typically, the precompiler would automatically call the host language compiler after the successful completion of a precompile which implies binding or package creation.

The following command shows how you can create program DRDASU2 in the DRDAX5 collection on SCHASM02. The same command can be used to create the other application samples.

```
CRTSQLCI  OBJ(DRDAX5/DRDASU2)
          SRCFILE(DRDAX5/QCSRC)
          COMMIT(*CS)            1
          OBJTYPE(*PGM)
          RDB(xxxxxxx)           2
          OPTION(*SQL)           3
          DFTRDBCOL(DRDAX5)      4
          GENLVL(30)             5
          DATFMT(*ISO)           6
          TIMFMT(*ISO)           6
          RDBCNNMTH(*DUW)        7
```

Notes for the CRTSQLCI command

1 SQL statements run under isolation level cursor stability. This applies only to SQL tables, views, and packages referred to in SQL statements. If the relational database specified on the RDB parameter is not on a DB2 for OS/400, *NONE cannot be specified.

2 This option indicates that the program is a distributed SQL program. The value that you specify is not really essential unless you want to take advantage of the *implicit connect* mechanism. We recommend that you specify the local relational database name, so that the application first connects to the local database when it is started.

3 The SQL naming convention to be used (collection name.table name). *SQL also specifies that SQL security conventions will be used. This requires that the owner of the program have the authority to the objects referred to by the static SQL statements in the program. The user of the program adopts the owner's authority when running in *SQL naming mode. When you create a program on a remote database other than DB2 for OS/400, you must specify *SQL. *SYS would indicate that the naming convention (library-name/file-name) to be used and therefore the server has to be a DB2 for OS/400. It also specifies that the user's authority to objects is used when executing SQL statements.

4 Specifies that DRDAX5 is the name of the collection identifier for our unqualified names of tables, views, indexes, and SQL packages. This parameter applies only to static SQL statements. This makes it easy to implement applications that do not point to particular collections on remote servers. The compiler also searches this collection for table, view, and index file definitions that are referenced in the SQL statements in the program.

5 The program fails if severity level 30 statements are encountered. Generally, any SQL statement that generates a severity level 30 or greater statement is not valid for any DRDA AS.

6 If the relational database specified on the RDB parameter refers to a platform that is not a DB2 for OS/400, the time and date format must be *ISO. Specifying values other than *ISO for this parameter would cause the package creation to fail on unlike ASs. You would obtain a DDM error code X'2121' at package creation time.

7 This parameter indicates whether your program uses the DRDA level 1 or DRDA level 2 connection manager. To enable the DRDA level 2 connection manager that allows using *SET CONNECTION* and *RELEASE* statements, you must make sure that DUW is specified here. This is the default value. By contrast, if you have to create a DRDA level 1 application on an AS/400 system running OS/400 V3R1 or higher, you must set this parameter value to RUW.

Figure 209 on page 445 shows the successfully compiled C source.

```
        #pragma linkage (QSQROUTE,OS) ▮1
        #pragma linkage (QSQLOPEN,OS) ▮1
        #pragma linkage (QSQLCLSE,OS) ▮1
        #pragma linkage (QSQLCMIT,OS) ▮1
        typedef struct
          { unsigned  char      sqlcaid[8];
                      long      sqlcabc;
                      long      sqlcode;
                      short     sqlerrml;
            unsigned  char      sqlerrmc[70];
            unsigned  char      sqlerrp[8];
                      long      sqlerrd[6];
            unsigned  char      sqlwarn[11];
            unsigned  char      sqlstate[5];
                   } SQLCA;
        void extern QSQROUTE(SQLCA *, ... );
        void extern QSQLOPEN(SQLCA *, ... );
        void extern QSQLCLSE(SQLCA *, ... );
        void extern QSQLCMIT(SQLCA *, ... );
    #include <string.h>
    /* #include <sqlcodes.h>
    #include <sqlenv.h>
    #include <sqlutil.h>
    #include <sql.h> */        ▮2
    #include <stdio.h>
    #include <stdlib.h>
    #include <string.h>

    /***$$$
    EXEC SQL INCLUDE SQLCA
    $$$***/
    #ifndef SQLCODE
    struct sqlca ▮3
      { unsigned  char      sqlcaid[8];
                  long      sqlcabc;
                  long      sqlcode;
                  short     sqlerrml;
        unsigned  char      sqlerrmc[70];
        unsigned  char      sqlerrp[8];
                  long      sqlerrd[6];
        unsigned  char      sqlwarn[11];
        unsigned  char      sqlstate[5];
               } ;
```

Figure 209 (Part 1 of 3). *Compile Listing for Program DRDASU2*

```
#define SQLCODE   sqlca.sqlcode
#define SQLWARN0 sqlca.sqlwarn[0]
#define SQLWARN1 sqlca.sqlwarn[1]
#define SQLWARN2 sqlca.sqlwarn[2]
#define SQLWARN3 sqlca.sqlwarn[3]
#define SQLWARN4 sqlca.sqlwarn[4]
#define SQLWARN5 sqlca.sqlwarn[5]
#define SQLWARN6 sqlca.sqlwarn[6]
#define SQLWARN7 sqlca.sqlwarn[7]
#define SQLWARN8 sqlca.sqlwarn[8]
#define SQLWARN9 sqlca.sqlwarn[9]
#define SQLWARNA sqlca.sqlwarn[10]
#define SQLSTATE sqlca.sqlstate
#endif
struct sqlca sqlca;

 .........
 .........
main()
{

 ........
 ........
/***$$$
   EXEC SQL CONNECT TO :LOCAL
           USER  :user_id
           USING :pasw_id
$$$***/
{
  sqlca.sqlerrd[5] =    15;
  QSQROUTE ((SQLCA * )&sqlca, LOCAL, user_id, pasw_id);
}
     printf("SQLCODE %d \n", sqlca.sqlcode);  /*MONITOR SQLCODE*/
     if ((rc = strncmp(sqlca.sqlstate,"08002",5)) ==0)
/***$$$
      EXEC SQL SET CONNECTION :LOCAL
$$$***/
{
  sqlca.sqlerrd[5] =    16;
  QSQROUTE ((SQLCA * )&sqlca, LOCAL); ■4
}
 .........
 .........
```

Figure 209 (Part 2 of 3). Compile Listing for Program DRDASU2

```
/***$$$
   EXEC SQL SELECT PART_NUMB, PART_DESC
        INTO :part_num, :part_desc
        FROM PART_MAST
       WHERE PART_NUMB = :part_reqd
$$$***/
{
static _Packed struct {
          short SQL_HEADER_LENGTH;
          short SQL_STMT_NUM;
          long SQL_INVOKE;
          char SQL_DATA_RETURNED;
          char SQL_RESERVED[55];
        short SQL_VAR_1;
        short SQL_VAR_2;
        char SQL_VAR_3[21];
} SQL_STRUCT = {64,    18,0,'0'};
  SQL_STRUCT.SQL_VAR_1 = part_reqd;
  sqlca.sqlerrd[5] = -7;
  QSQROUTE ((SQLCA * )&sqlca,&SQL_STRUCT); 4
  if (SQL_STRUCT.SQL_DATA_RETURNED == '1')
    {
      part_num = SQL_STRUCT.SQL_VAR_2;
      memcpy(part_desc,SQL_STRUCT.SQL_VAR_3,21);
    }
  if (SQLCODE < 0) goto  err_routine;
}
```

Figure 209 (Part 3 of 3). Compile Listing for Program DRDASU2

Notes for Figure 209 on page 445

1 Prior to OS/400 Version 3 Release 1, the ILE C/400 compiler replaced the SQL statements with call statements to the SQL interface module QSQROUTE. A pragma linkage statement indicates that this module is called within the program. Using Version 3 DB2 for OS/400 SQL precompilers, you will notice that additional programs such as QSQOPEN are called directly to shorten the call path and improve SQL performance.

2 These include files have been commented out for the AS/400 version of this program. The include files are needed in the DB2 for OS/2 and in the DB2 for AIX versions.

3 The SQLCA structure that is used to return SQLCODE was included by the ILE C/400 compiler.

4 This is an example of how the SQL precompiler resolves SQL statements into program calls to the appropriate SQL run-time programs.

14.3.2 Creating Packages

After the source was successfully compiled, an SQL package had to be created on each AS. The following command was used to create the package on a DB2 for OS/2 AS, identified by the relational database name *SJ2SMPL*.

```
CRTSQLPKG  PGM(DRDAX5/DRDASU2)
           RDB(SJ2SMPL)          1
           USER(*CURRENT)        2
           DFTRDBCOL(*NONE)      3
           TEXT(*BLANK)          4
           GENLVL(15)            5
```

Notes for the CRTSQLPKG command

1 Specifies the name of the remote database on which the package is created. In our example, this is San Jose's DB2 for OS/2 database. We also had to create the package on the following relational database servers:

- San Jose SJAS400 DB2 for OS/400
- San Jose SJ6SMPL DB2 for AIX
- Boeblingen DBSRV4D DB2 for OS/2
- Boeblingen BO6SMPL DB2 for AIX
- Boeblingen S34VSDB1 SQL/DS for VSE
- Boeblingen S34VMDB0 DB2 for VM
- Poughkeepsie CENTDB2 DB2 for MVS

2 Specifies the userid to be sent to the AS when starting the conversation. SECURITY(SAME) only requires that the userid be sent to create the package. In our scenario, we actually sent both the userid and the password. This parameter was not relevant to us.

3 The collection ID that is used to point to SQL objects when unqualified static SQL statements are executed. *PGM defaults to the collection name specified on the precompile. We specified *NONE and in that case the owner of the package became the default qualifier.

4 We recommend that you set the TEXT parameter to *BLANK. DB2 for AIX and DB2 for OS/2 do not support a description for the package, and the package creation might fail if you specify a value other than blank for this parameter.

5 When you create SQL programs and packages that are not on a DB2 for OS/400 and try to use SQL statements that are unique to that relational database, set GENLVL to 30. If a message is issued at this level, the statement is probably not valid for any relational database.

Figure 210 on page 449 shows the listing of the CRTSQLPKG command to create a package in DB2 for OS/2.

```
Program name.............DRDAX5/DRDASU2
Relational database.......SJ2SMPL
User ....................*CURRENT
Replace..................*YES
Default Collection........*NONE      ▮1
Generation level..........15
Object type..............*PGM
Module list..............*ALL
Source file..............DRDAX5/QCSRC
Member...................DRDASU2
                                        DIAGNOSTIC MESSAGES
MSG ID  SEV RECORD TEXT
SQL5057             SQL Package DRDASU2 in DRDAX5 created at SJ2SMPL from
                    program DRDASU2.
            * * * * * E N D  O F  L I S T I N G * * * * *
```

Figure 210. CRTSQLPKG Listing for DB2 for OS/2

Note for Figure 210 ▮1 Specifies the collection that unqualified SQL statements in the package should use to locate the SQL objects. In this example, *NONE indicates that the owner of the package is used as a default qualifier.

14.4 Running the Sample Applications

In this section we show how an end user can run program DRDASU2 on the AS/400 system. The same process applies to any other applications described in this book.

Userid DRDAX1 must sign on at a terminal connected to SCHASM02 and type CALL DRDAX5/DRDASU2. In this instance of the program execution (Figure 211 on page 450), part number 6666 was entered. The part was found on the local database, RCAS400, and the description displayed. Then each remote database was queried to determine the stock quantity at that location and select the location with the highest number of items. An order is generated for that location at the central site. The display refers to a run of the program with a subset of the database servers available.

```
   Partstck program running..
   Please enter your userid in uppercase...
> DRDAX5
   Please enter your password in uppercase...
> REDBOOK  ■1
   Please enter part number:
> 6666
   Please enter order quantity:
> 10
    Connecting to Order Center POK..
  SQLCODE 0  ■2
    Connecting to LOCAL..
  SQLCODE 0

    Connection to LOCAL established
    Finding part description

    Description selected for part: 6666
                 description: CARBURATOR


  SQLCODE 0

    Connected to:  SJ2SMPL
    Stock for SJ2SMPL is 325
  SQLCODE 0

    Connected to:  DBSRV4D
    Stock for DBSRV4D is 325
  SQLCODE −842  ■3

    Connected to:  CENTDB2
    Stock for CENTDB2 is 285
  SQLCODE −842

    Connected to:  RCAS400
    Stock for RCAS400 is 295
  Location with the most items:   SJ2SMPL
  Creating an order...
  SQLCODE 0
```

Figure 211. Display on SCHASM02 after Executing DRDASU2 Program

Notes for Figure 211

1 The password can be read because we did not try to hide it in designing our user interface. On the AS/400, using display files can easily solve this problem.

2 We display the SQLCODE values after every *CONNECT* statement. An SQLCODE equal to zero indicates that the connection has been started. In this case, the newly started connection also becomes the current connection.

3 On DB2 for OS/400, an SQLCODE equal to -842 indicates that there is an active connection to the location to which the program is trying to connect. In this case, the state of the current connection does not change, and a *SET CONNECTION* statement has to be issued.

14.4.1 Getting Information on Existing Applications

DB2/400 Version 3 provides a new PRTSQLINF command (Figure 212) which is used to obtain information about the embedded SQL statements in a program, SQL package, or service program. This information includes the SQL statements, the access plans used during the running of the statement, and a list of the command parameters used to precompile the source member for the object.

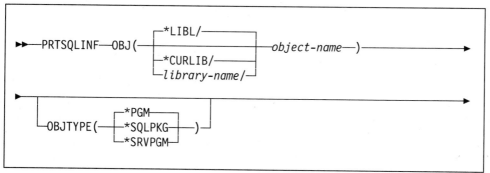

Figure 212. PRTSQLINF Command Syntax

Command parameters:

- OBJ

  - object-name. The name of the program or SQL package.

  - *LIBL. The library list is used to find the OBJ.

  - library-name. The name of the library containing the OBJ.

  - *CURLIB. The library specified as the user's current library contains the OBJ.

- OBJTYPE

  - *PGM. The OBJ parameter specifies the name of a program.

- *SQLPKG. The OBJ parameter specifies the name of an SQL package.

- *SRVPGM. The OBJ parameter specifies the name of a service program.

14.4.2 Customizing Applications for the AS/400

In this section we explain how we used some AS/400 features to improve the user interface of our application samples. We focus on one of our programs (PARTSTK), but the enhancements can easily be extended to the remaining application samples.

Some changes were made to the PARTSTK application on the DB2 for OS/400 to provide a familiar screen interface:

1. The PARTSTK program was logically split into two separate programs, PARTS1 and PARTS11. The PARTS1 program connected to the local database and returned the description and quantity to a screen. If the user chose to search the other locations for the quantity, the PARTS11 program was called.

2. A new program, PARTSC, was created to provide the screen interface and call programs PARTS1 and PARTS 11.

3. The PARTS11 program had to be created as a distributed database program because it was responsible for getting part quantity information from the remote databases.

4. A new field was added to the LOCATION table in collection DEALROCH on SCHASM02 (see Figure 213). The field was used to provide the user with a more descriptive name than the network remote database name for each server when the PARTS11 program was executed.

```
Please Enter Part Number:        10
Description:              OIL FILTER              Local Quantity: 1




F3 - Exit        F10 - Search Remote Locations              F12 - Return
```

Figure 213. Display on SCHASM02 after Executing PARTSC Program

If the user presses F10, PARTSC calls PARTS11 and the screen shown in Figure 214 on page 453 is displayed.

```
   Connected to:  POK.,NY-REGIONAL PARTS
Stock Quantity is 56

   Connected to:  GER. SQL/DS-PARTS CENTER
Stock Quantity is 1000

   Connected to:  ROCH.,MN REGIONAL PARTS
Stock Quantity is 10

   Connected to:  SQL/DS-VM GERMANY PARTS
Stock Quantity is 4321

Press ENTER to end terminal session.
```

Figure 214. Display on SCHASM02 after Executing PARTS11 Program

Notes for Figure 214

- Time and programmer skills were limiting factors in enhancing the program further. Additional enhancements planned were

  - The ability of the user to pick a remote location to query.

  - A subfile so the user could scroll each location to see the quantity for a part number in all locations.

  - A subfile so the user could scroll through all of the parts at a remote location.

- DB2 for OS/400 and ILE C/400 get along quite nicely.

- The source debugger proved quite helpful in navigating through our first attempt to write or modify a C program.

14.5 DB2 for OS/400 Package Management

Adding a new AS to the network can require a change to the application if server names are hardcoded. Certainly a package has to be created on that new server. As the number of ASs that contain SQL packages created by the AS/400 increases, package management issues relating to consistency, creation, and deletion become extremely important.

14.5.1.1 Considerations

Recompiling an AR application requires recreating the SQL packages on the RDBs accessed by the DRDA application. The *consistency token* is checked at execution time, and the requester program and remote SQL package must match or execution is halted with SQLSTATE 51003. The remote SQL packages must be re-created from the current version of the requester program.

Note: The consistency token has the same meaning as the record format level check on a traditional AS/400 database.

During this project we had to re-create our application several times and we were confronted with the following questions:

- When an application that requires an SQL package to be re-created is changed, what can be done to ensure that all the packages are successfully created before the changed requester application goes into production?

- How does the programmer determine on which RDBs a program needs an SQL package re-created? Should we use the RDB directory entries or is it more likely that some applications will deal only with certain RDBs? In this case, a mechanism is needed to cross-reference distributed database programs and the RDBs they require.

- Should a mechanism be put in place to periodically query remote databases and automatically re-create all packages?

- When a requester application is taken out of production, what happens to the packages on the AS?

- What process should exist to include and exclude new or obsolete RDBs?

14.5.1.2 Possible Solutions

- Maintain a table that cross-references requester program names with the RDBs that it uses. A compilation procedure would need to be created that would query this table and create packages on the appropriate RDBs.

- The approach we decided to implement was to re-create or create the packages during execution of the requester application. When the package was not found or a consistency token did not match, an exit could be coded to re-create the package on that RDB.

14.5.1.3 Finding Packages

Package information on different AS platforms is stored in different places. Below are the table names where package information can be found on the AS in our scenario.

On DB2 for OS/400 You can retrieve information about existing SQL packages

- From the SYSPACKAGE view in each collection.

- From the SYSPACKAGE view of the systemwide SQL catalog, located in the QSYS2 library.

- Directly from the QSYS/QADBPKG cross-reference file, which contains information about all existing packages on the system. This file can also be accessed by SQL.

On DB2 for MVS/ESA and DB2 common server platforms   Information   about packages is stored centrally in the SYSIBM.SYSPACKAGE table.

On SQL/DS for VM and SQL/DS for VSE   The package information is stored in a central table called SYSTEM.SYSACCESS. You should use the WHERE clause (CREATOR=xxxx) to avoid the long list of AVAILABLE rows. To see all packages, use WHERE TNAME NOT LIKE '%AVAIL%'.

14.5.1.4 Implementation
An AS/400 program with embedded SQL statements can create SQL packages for itself at the AR location at execution time.

The following COBOL example shows how package creation can be automated. The CRTSQLPKG CL command cannot be used directly in a COBOL program. However, there are several ways to issue a CL command from within a program:

- Call the QCMDEXEC API, which allows execution of a CL command. The command interface QCMDEXEC module can be called in COBOL, but it requires extensive string handling.

- Call a CL program containing the command to be executed. We show this alternative in our example, because it allows simple parameter passing and error handling.

- Call a local stored procedure through an SQL CALL statement.

When a package is not found or there is a consistency token error, DB2 for OS/400 returns SQLSTATE 51002 and 51003, respectively.

In the code fragment in Figure 215 on page 456 we show only the parts relevant for package creation. The program name for the example shown in Figure 215 on page 456 is *AORDER*.

```
1   01  CRTPKG-PARMS
2       05 CRTPKG-PACKAGE-NAME  PIC  X(10) VALUE 'AORDER'.
        05 CRTPKG-RDB-INFO.
3          06 RDB              PIC  X(8) VALUE 'RCAS400'
3        06 USER           PIC  X(8) VALUE 'DRDAX5'
3          06 PASSWORD         PIC  X(8) VALUE 'pwd'
4          05 CRTPKG-RETURN-CODE  PIC  X(7).
        ***********************
        EXEC SQL   CONNECT TO :RDB
5            USER :USER USING :PASSWORD
        END-EXEC.

A   SELECT-PART-STOCK.
        EXEC SQL
6          SELECT PART_NUM, PART_EOQ
                    INTO :WS-P-NUM, :WS-P-EOQ
          FROM   PART_STOCK
          WHERE  PART_NUM = :WS-P-NUM
        END-EXEC.
7          IF SQLSTATE = '51002'
7          OR SQLSTATE = '51003'
          PERFORM CREATE-PACKAGE THRU CREATE-PACKAGE-EXIT
A            GO TO SELECT-PART-STOCK
        ELSE GO TO ERROR
        END-IF.

     CREATE-PACKAGE.
8          EXEC SQL  COMMIT  END-EXEC.
9          CALL 'CRTPKG'  USING CRTPKG-PARMS.
     CREATE-PACKAGE-EXIT.      EXIT.
```

Figure 215. *Package Creation Example in COBOL*

Notes for Figure 215

1 These are the parameters passed to the CRTSQLPKG command.

2 Variable CRTPKG-PACKAGE-NAME must be the name of this program. Otherwise the CRTSQLPKG command would fail because the program name is used by the command.

3 Variable CRTPKG-RDB-INFO contains the RDB_NAME, userid, and password. We coded the userid and password as we ran with conversation security level PROGRAM. For simplicity's sake, we hardcoded the values within the program itself.

4 Variable CRTPKG-RETURN-CODE is passed so that the CL program could return the SQLSTATE in case the package creation failed.

5 We use conversation security level PROGRAM. Therefore we use CONNECT with user ID and password to connect to RCAS400.

6 The SELECT will fail when the package does not exist on RCAS400.

7 The first time we access the table on RCAS400, we receive SQLSTATE 51002 as the package does not exist there. A consistency token mismatch would return SQLSTATE 51003 from DB2 for MVS/ESA and an SQLSTATE 51003 from SQL/DS.

8 A COMMIT is required to enter a connectable state.

9 The program creates the package by calling a CL program

A This program retries the SELECT.

Figure 216 shows the CL program, CRTPKG, which creates a package on an AS.

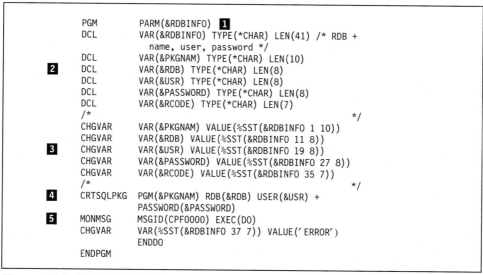

```
        PGM       PARM(&RDBINFO) ▪1
        DCL       VAR(&RDBINFO) TYPE(*CHAR) LEN(41) /* RDB +
                    name, user, password */
        DCL       VAR(&PKGNAM) TYPE(*CHAR) LEN(10)
 ▪2     DCL       VAR(&RDB) TYPE(*CHAR) LEN(8)
        DCL       VAR(&USR) TYPE(*CHAR) LEN(8)
        DCL       VAR(&PASSWORD) TYPE(*CHAR) LEN(8)
        DCL       VAR(&RCODE) TYPE(*CHAR) LEN(7)
        /*                                                    */
        CHGVAR    VAR(&PKGNAM) VALUE(%SST(&RDBINFO 1 10))
        CHGVAR    VAR(&RDB) VALUE(%SST(&RDBINFO 11 8))
 ▪3     CHGVAR    VAR(&USR) VALUE(%SST(&RDBINFO 19 8))
        CHGVAR    VAR(&PASSWORD) VALUE(%SST(&RDBINFO 27 8))
        CHGVAR    VAR(&RCODE) VALUE(%SST(&RDBINFO 35 7))
        /*                                                    */
 ▪4     CRTSQLPKG PGM(&PKGNAM) RDB(&RDB) USER(&USR) +
                    PASSWORD(&PASSWORD)
 ▪5     MONMSG    MSGID(CPF0000) EXEC(DO)
        CHGVAR    VAR(%SST(&RDBINFO 37 7)) VALUE('ERROR')
                  ENDDO
        ENDPGM
```

Figure 216. The CRTPKG Control Language Program

Notes for Figure 216

1 The input parameters from the caller.

2 Declare variables.

3 We extract the variables from the input parameter RDBINFO.

4 The package is created.

5 In case of an error we insert a value in the RCODE part of the RDBINFO parameter (see Table 45 on page 458).

Table 45. Input Parameters for CRTPKG

Position	Length	Label	Content
1	10	PKGNAM	Package name. Also the name of the calling program
11	8	RDB	The name of the AS where the package is to be created
19	8	USR	The collection ID or user name
27	8	PASSWORD	
37	7	RCODE	A return code

The CRTSQLPKG can fail for several reasons:

- Connection failure: We could try to reestablish the connection by retrieving the LU name from the RDB directory, then executing the VRYCFGSTS command against that LU. The question is, how to retrieve the LU name? The RDB directory is stored in QSYS/QADBXRDBD. We could now code a loop in our CL program, reading record after record until the RDB_NAME is found. Another (easier) approach is probably to pass a specific return code to the calling program which had to connect to the local database and executed an SQL SELECT statement against the RDB directory (file QADBXRDBD in library QSYS), and finally called CRTPKG again.

- The user does not have the proper authority to create packages or the package may be created with the wrong userid. This could be a reason to hardcode the userid and password in a table.

Chapter 15. Program Preparation: SQL/DS

This chapter contains guidelines for implementing and migrating applications coded on other platforms and intending to access SQL/DS (that is, SQL/DS as a DRDA AS) as well as "home-grown" applications in SQL/DS in need of interaction with the RDBMSs of other platforms (SQL/DS as a DRDA AR). Reviewing these guidelines before planning for your application could save you a lot of trouble when porting to other DRDA platforms.

You also might find the guidelines useful even if you are only working with SQL/DS on both the AR and AS ends. You will hardly sacrifice any functions at all, and, should you have to migrate a platform at a given location at some future date, the maintenance impact on your application will be minimal.

Generally speaking, you are well advised to stick to SAA SQL as much as possible, even if it means coding an extra line or two. You will pay for every platform-specific "goody" you may have included in your code at migration time!

As SQL/DS is not DRDA level 2 compliant at the time of writing, you cannot use the DRDA level 2 SQL command. Thus you do not have to deal with the additional complexity of maintaining the connection logic and data integrity among different sites.

15.1 Catalog Requirements

This section is written for SQL/DS-based system programmers and application programmers who want to access remote DRDA ASs and already have a working knowledge of DRDA.

Take a look at your application's catalog access requirements, if any. All RDBMSs are not created equal, and you will have to modify your SQL code if you relied on information from the SQL/DS catalog tables.

Table 46 shows the SQL/DS catalog tables and their equivalents on non-SQL/DS ASs.

Table 46 (Page 1 of 3). SQL/DS Catalog Tables and Their Equivalents on Non-SQL/DS ASs				
	SQL/DS Catalog	**DB2 for MVS/ESA**	**DB2 for OS/400**	**DB2 common server (Note 1)**
Authorization	SYSUSERAUTH SYSUSERLIST	SYSUSERAUTH	N/A, use EDTOBJAUT command	DBAUTH

	SQL/DS Catalog	DB2 for MVS/ESA	DB2 for OS/400	DB2 common server (Note 1)
Character conversion	SYSSTRINGS	SYSSTRINGS	(See Note 2)	(See Note 6)
Character set	SYSCHARSETS		(See Note 2)	(See Note 6)
Coded character set identifiers	SYSCCSIDS SYSSTRINGS		(See Note 2)	(See Note 6)
column SYSCOLUMNS SYSKEYCOLS	SYSCOLUMNS SYSCOLUMNS SYSKEYS		SYSCOLUMNS SYSCOLUMNS SYSKEYS	COLUMNS COLUMNS KEYCOLUSE
Column update privilege	SYSCOLAUTH	SYSCOLAUTH	N/A	N/A
Column with field procedure	SYSFIELDS	SYSFIELDS	(See Note 3)	
Constraint	SYSKEYS SYSKEYS SYSRELS SYSTABLESPACE	(See Note 4)	SYSKEYS SYSCST SYSCSTCOL SYSCSTDEP SYSKEYCST	CHECKS COLCHECKS KEYCOLUSE CONSTDEP TABCONST REFERENCES
dbspace	SYSDBSPACES SYSUSAGE SYSDROP	SYSTABLESPACE (See Note 5)	N/A	TABLESPACES
dbspace waiting to be dropped	SYSDROP	N/A	N/A	N/A
Default	SYSOPTIONS	N/A	N/A, use WRKSYSVAL command	N/A
Dropped dbspace	SYSDROP	N/A	N/A	N/A
Dropped table	SYSDROP	N/A	N/A	N/A
Field procedures	SYSFPARMS SYSFIELDS	SYSFIELDS	(See Note 3)	
Foreign key	SYSKEYS	SYSFOREIGNKEYS	SYSKEYS SYSKEYCST	TABCONST
Index	SYSINDEXES SYSUSAGE	SYSINDEXES SYSINDEXPART	SYSINDEXES SYSKEYS	INDEXES INDEXAUTH
Index column statistics	SYSCOLSTATS SYSCOLUMNS SYSINDEXES	SYSCOLUMNS SYSINDEXES	N/A	(see note 1) **SYSSTAT**.INDEXES **SYSSTAT**.COLUMNS
Key	SYSKEYS	SYSINDEXES	SYSINDEXES SYSKEYCST	INDEXES
Key column	SYSKEYCOLS		SYSKEYS	INDEXES
Language for character set	SYSLANGUAGE		N/A, use QLANGID system value	
Option	SYSOPTIONS		N/A	
Package	SYSACCESS SYSUSAGE	SYSPACKAGE SYSPACKDEP SYSPACKSTMT SYSPACKLIST (See Note 3)	SYSPACKAGE	PACKAGES PACKAGEAUTH PACKAGEDEP STATEMENTS
Package run privilege	SYSPROGAUTH	SYSPACKAUTH	N/A, use EDTOBJAUT command PACKAGEAUTH	
Password	SYSUSERAUTH		N/A	N/A

	SQL/DS Catalog	DB2 for MVS/ESA	DB2 for OS/400	DB2 common server (Note 1)
Primary key	SYSKEYS	SYSKEYS	SYSKEYCST	INDEXES
Privilege	SYSCOLAUTH SYSPROGAUTH SYSTABAUTH	SYSCOLAUTH SYSPACKAUTH SYSTABAUTH	N/A, use EDTOBJAUT command	DBAUTH TABAUTH PACKAGEAUTH INDEXAUTH
Statistics	SYSCATALOG SYSCOLSTATS SYSCOLUMNS SYSDBSPACES SYSINDEXES	SYSTABLES SYSTABLEPART SYSCOLUMNS SYSTABLESPACE SYSINDEXES SYSINDEXPART	N/A	(see Note 1) COLDIST
Synonym	SYSSYNONYMS	SYSSYNONYMS	N/A	TABLES
Table	SYSCATALOG SYSCOLUMNS SYSUSAGE	SYSTABLES SYSTABLEPART SYSPACKDEP	SYSTABLES SYSCOLUMNS	TABLES TABCONST
Table privilege	SYSTABAUTH	SYSTABAUTH	N/A, use EDTOBJAUT command	TABAUTH
Table waiting to be dropped	SYSDROP	N/A	N/A	N/A
Unique constraint	SYSKEYS	SYSKEYS	SYSCST	REFERENCES
View	SYSVIEWS SYSCATALOG SYSCOLUMNS SYSACCESS SYSUSAGE	SYSVIEWS SYSVIEWDEP SYSPACKDEP	SYSVIEWS SYSVIEWDEP SYSCOLUMNS	VIEWS VIEWDEP TABLES
View privilege	SYSTABAUTH	SYSTABAUTH	(See Note 2)	TABAUTH

Notes:

1. The DB2 common server database manager maintains two sets of system catalog views. The system catalog views are updated during normal operation in response to SQL statements. The system catalog views cannot be modified by using normal SQL data manipulation commands, with the exception of some specific updatable catalog views.

   The catalog views are supported in addition to the catalog base tables from Version 1, enabling existing applications to continue to run.

   The views are within the **SYSCAT** schema. SELECT privilege on all views is granted to PUBLIC by default. Application programs should be written to those views.

   A second set of views within the **SYSSTAT** schema contains statistical information used by the optimizer. hose views contain some updatable columns.

   Please see *DB2 Administration Guide for common servers* for more information about catalog views.

2. DB2 for OS/400 supports character conversion, character sets, and CCSIDs. Information can be found in the SYSCOLUMNS catalog view on a file level, in system values QCCSID, QLANGID, and QCHRID on a system level, and in the job attributes on a job level.

3. Field procedures are not currently supported on DB2 for OS/400.

4. Package structure is different in DB2 for MVS/ESA and can be made up of one DBRM.

5. Table spaces in DB2 for MVS/ESA are similar to SQL/DS table spaces, but there are also important differences. DB2 for MVS/ESA indexes do not share table spaces with tables, as SQL/DS does.

6. See *DDCS User* for conversions between ASCII code pages and EBCDIC host CCSIDs.

The DB2 for OS/400 catalog tables listed in this table apply for OS/400 Version 3. Not all tables are available in earlier releases.

The contents and structure of the catalog tables are not the same across DRDA ASs.

15.1.1.1 Catalog Access in Your Code
• SYSTEM.SYSCATALOG

– You can find SYSTEM.SYSCATALOG's most important information in the DB2 for OS/400's *collection-name*.SYSTABLES, with column NAME instead of TNAME listing the table names. You still have the REMARKS and LABEL columns as in SQL/DS.

Note: Before DB2 for OS/400 Version 3, the scope of catalog tables was restricted to a specific collection. With Version 3 this limitation is lifted. In collection (library) QSYS2, you can now find a set of views that enables you to retrieve systemwide information.

– You can find this information in SYSIBM.SYSTABLES in the DB2 for MVS/ESA catalog.

– SYSCAT.TABLES in DB2 common server provides information on *schema*.TABLES, which is the qualified name of the table. TABNAME and DEFINER correspond to TNAME and CREATOR of the SYSTEM.SYSTABLES SQL/DS catalog table.

• SYSTEM.SYSCOLUMNS

– SYSTEM.SYSCOLUMNS corresponds to *collection-name*.SYSCOLUMNS in DB2 for OS/400, except for the clustering information and other SQL/DS-only information the optimizer needs there for its own use under VM and VSE. DB2 for OS/400 relies on OS/400 system functions for optimization, and the information used by the optimizer is not in the DB2 for OS/400 catalog views.

– You can find information used by the optimizer in the SYSIBM.SYSTABLES DB2 for MVS/ESA catalog table.

– SYSCAT.COLUMNS in DB2 common server contains the same information.

You might find it worthwhile to port most, if not all, of your catalog work out of your application into a separate module. In this way your base source code can remain virtually unchanged no matter which platform you run against and have separate modules customized for each individual platform that are coded when needed.

15.1.1.2 Catalog Locks
• DB2 for OS/400

When porting to an AS/400 environment, you can be more liberal with catalog access than under SQL/DS as far as catalog locking is concerned. The catalog you perceive in DB2 for OS/400 is not really used by the system; it is there for information purposes only and is not subject to the same locking restrictions you would come across in SQL/DS.

• DB2 for MVS

DB2 performs catalog locking for system functions along similar lines to SQL/DS. DB2 databases are usually on a vaster scale than SQL/DS databases and typically involve many more concurrent users. Therefore, more care must be exercised when querying the DB2 catalog from interactive utilities. This is especially true for SQL/DS's ISQL, which does not release all locks on the object being viewed until an end-of-data condition is found or the user issues an END command.

- DB2 common server

All considerations about catalog locking in SQL/DS apply to DB2 common server as the DB2 common server locking mechanism has been updated to offer at least the same level of locking function as the locking mechanism in SQL/DS.

15.1.1.3 Catalog Contents
- DB2 for OS/400

The DB2 for OS/400 Version 3 catalog includes the following catalog views: SYSCOLUMNS, SYSINDEXES, SYSPACKAGE, SYSTABLES, SYSVIEWDEP, SYSVIEWS, SYSCST, SYSCSTCOL, SYSCSTDEP, SYSKEYCST, and SYSREFCST. Not all listed views are available in earlier releases. To obtain information about all tables, packages, views, indexes, and constraints on the AS/400, system qualify your query with QSYS2. To restrict your retrieval to a certain collection, qualify your query with this collection name.

- DB2 common server

The DB2 common server catalog contains views spread between two schema. Views under the SYSCAT schema contain information readable by every user (SELECT has been granted to PUBLIC). Views under the SYSSTAT schema contain statistical information used by the optimizer for accessing data. Those views are readable by users, and some of them are updatable by administrators to help prototype system response (see *DB2 Administration Guide for common servers*).

15.1.1.4 Object Qualification in DB2 for OS/400
The collection name is the object qualifier in DB2 for OS/400. For more on the DB2 for OS/400 catalog, please see *DB2/400 SQL Programming Version 3*. DB2 for OS/400 also maintains a set of catalog tables stored in the system's QSYS library.

15.1.1.5 Catalog Usage
- DB2 for OS/400

For those of you who are familiar with the SQL/DS catalog, the DB2 for OS/400 catalog views environment seems more spartan. Many of the columns containing data for the optimizer's use are missing, and you might wonder where many of the tables have gone. In fact they are inside the OS/400 itself. AS/400 gets its optimization parameters from internal tables, not from the DB2 for OS/400 catalog. The same holds for many other values SQL/DS users associate with the database.

Database functions are architected all the way into OS/400, reaching right into the microcode for some functions. All OS/400 processing and storage are managed in terms of database objects. You can think of the entire OS/400 address as one big database, parts of which can be accessed by the user and yield meaningful information, parts of which, although visible, are not necessarily relevant to the user, and parts of which are totally irrelevant to the user's application.

It is, for example, perfectly possible to get access to OS/400 system critical objects with SQL statements if you have enough authority. However, *never* play with any of those objects, especially those whose names start with *Q*, unless you know exactly what you are doing.

- DB2 common server

DB2 common server maintains two sets of views based on top of the primary table from Version 1 to facilitate compatibility with other running programs.

Views in the SYSCAT schema provide the same kind of information as those views provided by the SQL/DS catalog tables. The SYSCAT views have to be accessed from your application.

Views from the SYSSTAT schema (updatable views) contain statistical information used by the optimizer. Some columns in these views can be changed to investigate the performance of hypothetical databases. Before changing any statistics for the first time, we suggest that you issue the RUNSTATS command so that all statistics will reflect the current state. For more information, including rules for updating catalog statistics, see *DB2 Administration Guide for common servers.*

15.1.2 Other Platform-Specific Definitions

We suggest that you group your platform-dependent initialization and system programming code, such as ACQUIRE DBSPACE statements, in an external module. In this way your mainstream code, which is what you really care about in the first place, can stay nice and clean and portable as far as SAA is concerned.

15.1.2.1 CREATE TABLE

The CREATE TABLE statement has implementation differences among the current DRDA platforms:

- DB2 for OS/400 does not support the IN clause. The table name's qualifier is used for the collection name. There are also collection default values depending on whether the statement is static or dynamic.

  For more on object qualifiers in DB2 for OS/400, please refer to *DB2/400 SQL Programming Version 3* and *DB2/400 SQL Reference Version 3.*

- In DB2 for MVS environments, the IN clause refers to a table space (similar to SQL/DS's DBSPACE), which can be explicitly assigned to either a dedicated VSAM data set or a storage group (the recommended option). A storage group is the DB2 version of an SQL/DS storage pool. DB2 creates a table space in a system default database if none is specified in the IN clause.

- In DB2 common server environments, the IN clause refers to a table space that corresponds to SQL/DS's DBSPACE. It identifies the table space in which the table will be created. The table space must exist. If another table space is not specified, all table parts are stored in this table space. If the IN clause is not specified, the table is created in a table space created by the authorization ID. If the table space is not found, the table is placed in the default table space, USERSPACE1. If USERSPACE1 has been dropped, the table creation fails.

  tablespace-options specifies the table spaces in which indexes and/or long column values will be stored. See CREATE TABLESPACE in the *DB2 SQL Reference for common server* for more details.

  INDEX IN tablespace-name identifies the table space in which any indexes on the table will be created. This option is allowed only when the primary table space specified in the IN clause is a database managed space (DMS) table space. The specified table space must exist and be a REGULAR DMS table space.

  Note: You can specify which table space will contain a table's index only when you create the table.

15.1.2.2 Locking
Normally you would not consider locking when coding an application. Should your application rely on SQL/DS's row-level locking to access neighboring rows at the same time from different agents, however, keep in mind that DB2 for MVS/ESA locks to the page level and in Version 4 also to the row level.

15.1.2.3 Clustering
To earmark an index for clustering, use the CLUSTER clause in the DB2 for MVS/ESA CREATE INDEX statement.

DB2 for MVS/ESA also lets you select a new clustering index with less trouble than SQL/DS (without the SQL/DS Master product, at least). Specify a new clustering index in an ALTER INDEX statement to have it scheduled for the next time a DB2 for MVS/ESA REORG is run.

15.1.2.4 Partitioned Table Spaces
To maximize availability during whole-table locks during scans or maintenance activities, DB2 offers *partitioned table spaces*, where you can split your table space into independent parts according to the value range of the clustering index and have, at worst, each *segment* locked separately, rather than the whole table space. This option is valid for normal application SQL access and for backup or reorganization purposes.

Consider implementing partitioned table spaces for large tables.

DB2 common server offers you also the possibility to separate the indexes and any LONG column (LONG VARCHAR, LONG VARGRAPHIC, LOB data types, or distinct types with any of these as source types) from the actual table space containing data. See 15.1.2.1, "CREATE TABLE" on page 464

15.1.2.5 COMMIT Processing

If you are issuing COMMITs from your application, make sure you are consistent in your application's isolation level when running on a remote server. Cursor Stability and Repeatable Read are the most commonly found options.

When you prep from SQL/DS against a DB2 for OS/400 server requesting ISOL(RR), the tables are locked until the query is closed. If the cursor is read-only, the table is locked *shared, no update* (*SHRNUP). In update mode the table is locked *exclusive, read allowed* (*EXCLRD). A warning SQLCODE +595 along with SQLSTATE 01526 to signal the different isolation level are issued (see Figure 217).

```
    ARI0513I A warning has occurred.
             SQLCODE 595 is received from the application server.
             Product  = OS/400      Level = V02R03M0
             SQLERRP  =
             SQLSTATE = 01526
             SQLERRD(1) = 0  SQLERRD(2) = 0  SQLERRD(3) = 0
             SQLERRD(4) = 0  SQLERRD(5) = 0 SQLERRD(6) = 0
             SQLWARN0 = ' '  SQLWARN1 = ' '  SQLWARN2 = ' '
             SQLWARN3 = ' '  SQLWARN4 = ' '  SQLWARN5 = ' '
             SQLWARN6 = ' '  SQLWARN7 = ' '  SQLWARN8 = ' '
             SQLWARN9 = ' '  SQLWARNA = ' '
             SQLERRM  =
```

Figure 217. Isolation Level Escalation Warning on a DB2 for OS/400 AS

15.1.2.6 EXPLAIN Function

The EXPLAIN function provides useful information about how individual SQL DML statements are resolved. It is supported in both DB2 and SQL/DS. It loads data into special tables for either individual statements issued against a VM SQL/DS from ISQL (with the EXPLAIN ISQL command) or for whole programs when they are prepped from SQL/DS with the EXPLAIN(YES) preprocessor option.

EXPLAIN is not part of the DRDA architecture, although other platforms supply similar information through their own implementations:

- DB2 for MVS/ESA supports the EXPLAIN function for interactive commands and whole programs.

  Although the function is referred to by the same name on both DB2 and SQL/DS, you should be aware of the fact that the information supplied by the DB2 EXPLAIN is in a different format than the information supplied by SQL/DS EXPLAIN. DB2 for MVS/ESA loads EXPLAIN information into a single table, as opposed to the four tables in SQL/DS, and does not deliver cost information.

  For more on EXPLAIN function differences, please refer to Section 6.5.42, "EXPLAIN," in the *Formal Register of Extensions and Differences in SQL*.

- DB2 for OS/400 provides similar information as to SQL statement optimization in the form of messages when the application is run under debug mode with the STRDBG CL command, but you obviously have to create the program on OS/400. With DB2 for OS/400 Version 3, the new PRTSQLINF command can be used to specify the object name and type of object (program, SQL package, or service program). A listing of the SQL statements, access plan information, and the *Create SQL Program* (CRTSQLxxx, where xxx refers to the host language) command used to invoke the program will be created.

- DB2 common server provides a new graphical tool to optimize your SQL statements to run against a DB2 common server database. You can use this new interface to explain each of your statements on a DB2 common server to optimize them for that specific environment. For more information about the new visual explain tool, please refer to Appendix J of the *DB2 Administration Guide for common servers*.

15.2 Preparing the Sample Applications

Please refer to 11.2, "Choice of Language" on page 329 for information about high-level programming language support on other platforms and the programming language to select for your application.

15.2.1 Syntax

Note: This project has investigated C code with embedded SQL/DS AR statements in VM, but *not* in VSE, as the AR function is not supported on VSE at the time of writing.

- C Language #include Files

  If you received C code from OS/2, comment out the #include <sql*.*> files; they are not meant for preprocessing under SQL/DS's preprocessor and will give you error messages because they are neither present nor welcome in VM.

- Square brackets

In C source files the CHAR data type followed by a number enclosed in square brackets identifies an *array*, which is C's way of calling the SQL/DS CHARACTER(n) data type. The square brackets may not map properly across systems, being a frequent cause for syntax errors, even if they display correctly.

Also, the square brackets may map differently on different screens. In our project, square brackets displayed properly on a 3472-M InfoWindow terminal with APL keyboard but had incorrect hex values and required editing in HEX mode.

Use the XEDIT CMS editor in HEX mode to verify the byte value of the suspect characters:

```
SET HEX ON
SET VER 1 30 HEX 1 30
```

Columns 1 through 30 will display in both EBCDIC and hexadecimal.

You can now test whether your file's square brackets map to hex 'AD' for opening brackets and hex 'BD' for closing brackets and then edit your source file accordingly. You will see in the EBCDIC part the changes made in the HEX part.

- CONNECT

The CONNECT statement with userid and password, namely, CONNECT userid IDENTIFIED BY password, is valid only in SQL/DS and is not supported by DRDA.

The DRDA-supported CONNECT statement, CONNECT to dbname USER userid USING password, is not supported by SQL/DS.

DRDA level 2 CONNECT statements such as SET CONNECTION and CONNECT RESET are not supported by SQL/DS.

- SQL object names

When specifying object names, keep in mind that DB2 for OS/400 currently accepts a maximum length of 10 bytes.

15.2.2 Process Description and Concepts

15.2.2.1 SQLINIT
You must run the SQLINIT EXEC pointing to the right database. Do not forget PROTOCOL(AUTO)) before you preprocess your application:

SQLINIT DBNAME(target_database) PROTOCOL(AUTO)

Note: If DBNAME points to a *remote* database, an ARI warning will be issued to the effect that the database was not generated on your processor (see Figure 218 on page 469).

```
sqlinit db(centdb2)
ARIO717I Start SQLINIT EXEC: 10/04/95 15:54:09 CET.
ARI6042I Warning: Application server CENTDB2 has not been
         generated on this processor. Ignore this
         message if the server has been defined as a
         global resource on another processor.
ARIO320I The default server name is CENTDB2.
ARIO796I End SQLINIT EXEC: 10/04/95 15:54:10 CET
Ready; T=0.21/0.25 15:54:10
```

Figure 218. Response to the SQLINIT EXEC against a Remote DB2 for MVS/ESA AS

15.2.3 Preprocessing

You must load a copy of the package matching your code into each database participating in your application. You can

1. List the databases in the DBList parameter for the SQLPREP EXEC, or include the database names in a CMS file named in the DBFile parameter.

2. Preprocess your program against each of the platforms involved in your application, issuing a separate SQLINIT before reissuing each SQLPREP command.

   Notes:

   • Userid

     When prepping from SQL/DS to a peer, you have the option to add a userid and password that will override your VM (or VSE) logon ID. Neither DB2 for MVS/ESA nor DB2 for OS/400 allows this; you have to set your userid before preprocess, in either the COMDIR (with SECURITY=PGM) or the CP directory (SECURITY=SAME).

   • QUALIFIER preprocessor option

     When prepping from SQL/DS to a non-SQL/DS AS, you can add the QUALIFIER preprocessor option. This lets you specify a default qualifier for the objects referred to in your package; this qualifier need not be a userid.

   • CTOKEN

     You can prep against different platforms with different qualifiers and do a single compile. You must also specify CTOKEN(NO), in the preprocessor options to generate a blank consistency token. Otherwise your application will fail at execution time with a token mismatch error.

     We found this technique useful as an alternative to a rebind on a remote AS to match the default qualifier with that required by each server.

When specifying CTOKEN(NO) make sure your packages and code match. Running an application with nonmatching packages can produce unpredictable results.

3. RELOAD PACKAGE and UNLOAD PACKAGE

You can use the RELOAD PACKAGE function of the SQL/DS DBSU utility to reload packages generated on SQL/DS to remote DRDA database servers, either SQL/DS or non-SQL/DS. The syntax for RELOAD PACKAGE is

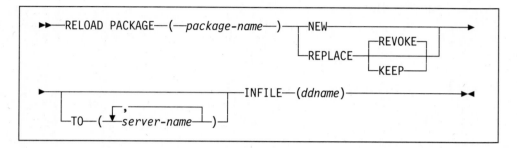

INFILE points to a file containing the package put there by the UNLOAD PACKAGE of the DBSU utility. The syntax for UNLOAD PACKAGE is

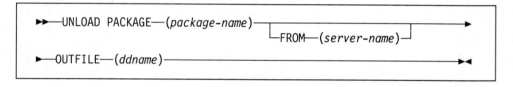

For more information about UNLOAD PACKAGE and RELOAD PACKAGE DBSU commands, see the *SQL/DS Database Services Utility for IBM VM Systems*.

Before you can use the DBS utility commands on a remote non-SQL/DS AS, you must first preprocess the DBS utility package on the non-SQL/DS AS and then create the SQLDBA.DBSOPTIONS table on that AS. ISQL is usually the first package you RELOAD on a remote non-SQL/DS AS.

Please refer to 9.1.3.3, "ISQL on a Non-SQL/DS AS" on page 253 for the customization steps to preprocess the DBS utility package and RELOAD ISQL package on a non-SQL/D AS.

15.2.3.1 Compiling

We compiled our C program by issuing

```
EXEC CC  fn ft fm
```

15.2.4 DRDASU2 Sample Application

Figure 219 shows the statements used to preprocess the DRDASU2 sample application on DB2 for OS/2 and the console listing it produced.

```
Ready; T=0.01/0.01 12:07:57
sqlprep c PP (PREP=DRDAX5.VMOSU2,ISOL(CS),CTOKEN(NO)) IN (DRDASU2
SQC A)
 PU (VMOSU2 SQP a) DBL(DBSRV4D) 1
ARI0717I Start SQLPREP EXEC: 10/10/95 12:08:02 CET.

ARI0717I Start SQLINIT EXEC: 10/10/95 12:08:02 CET.
ARI6042I Warning: Application server DBSRV4D has not been
         generated on this processor. Ignore this
         message if the server has been defined as a
         global resource on another processor.
ARI0320I The default server name is DBSRV4D.
ARI0796I End SQLINIT EXEC: 10/10/95 12:08:02 CET

ARI0700I SQLINIT on DBSRV4D successful. 2

ARI0320I The default server name is DBSRV4D.
ARI0663I FILEDEFS in effect are:
SYSIN    DISK      DRDASU2 SQC      A1
SYSPRINT DISK      DRDASU2 LISTPREP A1
SYSPUNCH DISK      VMOSU2  SQP      A1
ARISQLLD DISK      ARISQLLD LOADLIB Q1
ARI0713I Preprocessor ARIPRPB
         called with the following parameters:
 ....... PREP=DRDAX5.VMOSU2,ISOL(CS),CTOKEN(NO)
ARI0499I Warning: Status Shared Segment is not loaded.
         Return Code = 4

ARI0703I Preprocessing on DBSRV4D successful.

ARI0708I All SQLPREP EXEC processing completed successfully.
ARI0796I End SQLPREP EXEC: 10/10/95 12:08:09 CET
Ready; T=1.09/1.29 12:08:09
```

Figure 219. SQLPREP EXEC against a DB2 for OS/2 AS

Notes for Figure 219

1 The *DBL* option specifies the names of the databases you want to access. This option triggers an automatic SQLINIT statement for each database listed under this option.

2 Successful execution of the automatic SQLINIT triggered by the DBL option of the SQLPREP command. Remember that you will log on to the remote system using the userid and password defined in the COMDIR.

To verify the status of our package on the remote database server, we issued the command shown in Figure 220

```
Ready; T=0.01/0.01 15:54:04
isql
ARI0659I Line-edit symbols reset:
        LINEND=# LINEDEL=OFF CHARDEL=OFF
        ESCAPE=OFF TABCHAR=OFF
ARI0662I EMSG function value reset to ON.
ARI0320I The default server name is DBSRV4D.
ARI0499I Warning: Status Shared Segment is not loaded.
        Return Code = 4
ARI7716I User DRDAX5 connected to server DBSRV4D.
1
ARI7399I The ISQL default profile values are in effect.
ARI7079I ISQL initialization complete.
ARI7080A Please enter an ISQL command or an SQL statement.
select pkgschema, pkgname, boundby, valid,isolation,last_bind_time
from
syscat.packages where pkgschema = 'DRDAX5' order by 6  2

ARI7960I The query cost estimate for this SELECT statement is 1.

        The result is shown in the following screen


exit
ARI7601I ISQL ended normally on your request.
ARI0657I EMSG function value restored to TEXT.
ARI0660I Line-edit symbols restored:
        LINEND=# LINEDEL=¢ CHARDEL=@
        ESCAPE=" TABCHAR=ON
Ready; T=0.36/0.52 15:54:37
```

Figure 220. Inquiry on Remote DB2 for OS/2 Package Table

Notes for Figure 220

1 DRDAX5 is the userid used in the UCOMDIR directory. It is inserted in the BOUNDBY column in the package table of the DB2 for OS/2 server as shown in Figure 221.

2 SYSCAT.PACKAGES table corresponds to the SYSTEM.SYSACCESS SQL/DS catalog table. Please refer to the *DB2 Administration Guide for common servers* for a description of DB2 common server catalog tables.

```
 PKGSCHEMA   PKGNAME    BOUNDBY    VALID   ISOLATION  LAST_BIND_TIME
 ---------   --------   --------   -----   ---------
 ----------------------
 DRDAX5      MSUONEPC   DRDAX5     Y       CS
 1995-09-27-16.03.06.38
 DRDAX5      AIX2SUTS   DBADMIN    Y       CS
 1995-09-28-18.52.18.03
 DRDAX5      AIX2SU2    DBADMIN    Y       CS
 1995-09-28-18.52.44.69
 DRDAX5      VMOSUT     DBADMIN    Y       CS
 1995-10-05-17.38.38.79
 DRDAX5      DRDASU2    DRDAX5     Y       UR
 1995-10-05-23.56.01.69
 DRDAX5      BOSONEPC   DRDAX5     Y       CS
 1995-10-09-10.58.47.16
 DRDAX5      BIXSU2     DRDAX5     Y       CS
 1995-10-09-11.25.31.60
 DRDAX5      BIXONEPC   DRDAX5     Y       CS
 1995-10-10-11.49.26.25
 DRDAX5      VMOSU2     DRDAX5     Y       CS
 1995-10-10-16.26.01.12
  * End of Result *** 9 Rows Displayed ***Cost Estimate is
 1*************
```

Figure 221. Packages in Remote DB2 for OS/2 Package Table

Chapter 16. Program Preparation: DB2 for MVS/ESA

In this chapter we describe the steps required to prepare a DB2 for MVS/ESA application designed to access data in different database servers.

The chapter is divided into two main sections. In the first section we describe the general process of DB2 for MVS/ESA program preparation. In the second section we describe the process we followed to prepare our sample programs.

16.1 Process Description and Concepts

Because DB2 programs contain SQL statements, DB2 program preparation involves the typical compile and link-edit steps as well as the DB2 precompile and bind steps.

Figure 222 shows the DB2 for MVS/ESA program preparation process.

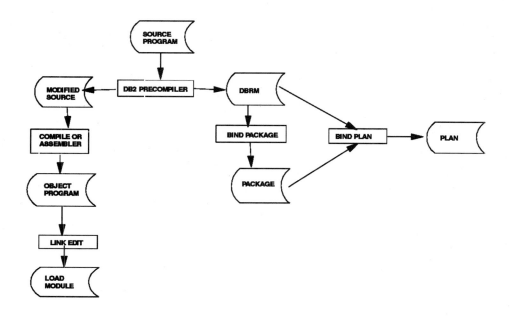

Figure 222. DB2 for MVS/ESA Program Preparation

16.1.1 Precompiling Your Program

Precompilation is required to change SQL statements into a language recognized by your compiler and assembler. Precompilation should take place before you create your load module and usually before you create a plan.

Precompilation uses the programming language statements and the embedded SQL statements in the program source code to perform the following functions:

- Translate embedded SQL statements into comments and calls to the DB2 language interface to create a modified source code file. The modified source code file is the input for the compilation process. Refer to 16.1.2, "Creating a Load Module for Your Program" on page 477 for further details.

- Extract SQL statements and host variables to create a DBRM. The DBRM contains the extracted SQL statements and host variables, along with information that identifies the program and ties the DBRM to the translated source statements. The DBRM is the input for the bind process. Refer to 16.1.3, "Creating a Plan for Your Program" on page 477 for further information.

Because the precompiler does not refer to DB2 catalog tables, DB2 does not validate the tables and columns used in your program. If you code SQL DECLARE TABLE statements in your program, the precompiler validates tables and columns against the table declarations provided.

You can control the way the precompiler interprets its input and presents its output by specifying precompiler options when invoking it. The host language, decimal separators, and SQL rules are examples of precompiler options.

The following two precompiler options are relevant when precompiling a program coded to access distributed data:

- *CONNECT*
    - Specify *CONNECT(2)* explicitly or by default.

      This option allows your application to connect to more than one database server in the same unit of work.
    - Specify *CONNECT(1)* explicitly.

      This option allows your application to connect to only one database server in one unit of work.
- *SQL*
    - Specify *SQL(ALL)* explicitly.

      SQL(ALL) allows the precompiler to accept any statement that obeys DRDA rules. Use this option if your application connects to a database server other than DB2 for MVS/ESA or to DB2 for MVS/ESA in addition to other database servers.

- Specify *SQL(DB2)* explicitly or by default.

  When SQL(DB2) is specified, the precompiler rejects any statement that does not obey DB2 for MVS/ESA rules. Use this option if your application connects only to DB2 for MVS/ESA.

See the *DB2 for MVS/ESA Application Programming and SQL Guide* for more information about precompiler options.

16.1.2 Creating a Load Module for Your Program

Compile and link edit are two separate steps in the process of creating your application load module.

The *compile* process uses the modified source code file created during precompilation to check the syntax of the host language and creates an object program. This object program is the input for the link-edit step.

The *link-edit* process uses the object program created during compilation to create an executable load file. The executable load file contains the appropriate links to allow your application to interface with the DB2 subsystem. The DB2 interface module to which you link depends on the application execution environment you choose for your application: TSO, Batch, CICS, or IMS.

See the *DB2 for MVS/ESA Application Programming and SQL Guide* for more information about link editing.

16.1.3 Creating a Plan for Your Program

SQL statements must have an access path to data. *Binding* is the process that creates access paths. It converts the output of the precompiler into a usable control structure, called a *package* or a *plan*.

In this section we define what plans and packages are, explain the differences between them, describe the commands to bind them, and explain how to create a plan for a program that accesses distributed data.

A *plan* is a control structure required to allocate DB2 resources and support SQL requests made at run time. To execute a DB2 for MVS/ESA application, you must have a plan.

A *package* is a control structure containing the required information to execute the SQL statements included in the associated program. In a DRDA environment, you must bind a package to a plan in order to execute the package.

Table 47 on page 478 presents the major differences between packages and plans.

Table 47. Packages and Plans

Package	Plan
Optional when accessing DB2 for MVS/ESA local data	Compulsory for a DB2 for MVS/ESA application
Compulsory when accessing distributed data through DRDA	Compulsory for a DB2 for MVS/ESA application
Cannot be run directly, must be bound in a plan	Can be run directly by naming it in a RUN subcommand
Contains only one DBRM	Contains at least one package or at least one directly bound DBRM
Options of BIND PACKAGE apply only to the package	Options of BIND PLAN apply to all DBRMs directly bound in the plan
Should be bound at the location where it runs	Can only be bound locally
Should be bound into a collection	Does not need a collection to be bound

16.1.3.1 Binding a Plan

A DB2 for MVS/ESA program always requires a plan, regardless of the location of the data that it accesses. A plan for a program accessing distributed data through DRDA must include a package for each remote location that your program accesses.

Use the *BIND PLAN* command to include your DBRMs and/or packages in a plan. The syntax for this command is shown in Figure 223 on page 479.

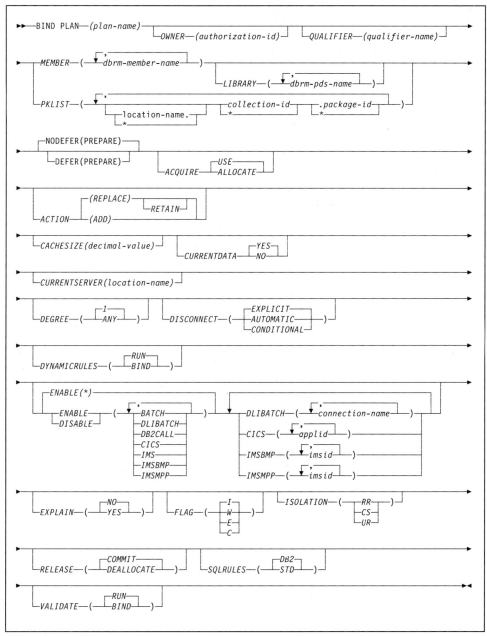

Figure 223. BIND PLAN Syntax

The following BIND PLAN options are relevant when including packages in a plan, as well as the options related to distributed data access:

- *OWNER*

  Determines the authorization ID of the owner of the plan. The default value is the primary ID of the user binding the plan.

- *QUALIFIER*

  Is the implicit qualifier for unqualified names of tables, views, and indexes in the packages. The default is the owner's authorization ID.

- *MEMBER*

  The name or names of the DBRMs you are including in the plan.

- *PKLIST(location-name.collection-id.package-id)*

  The name or names of the packages you are including in the plan. The valid values for the package name are

  - *location-name*

    Is the location name of the database server where the package is created. You can use either a particular location name or an asterisk (*), or you can omit this part of the package name. The default for location name is the local database server. If you use an asterisk, the location name is provided by the CURRENT SERVER special register at execution time. The CURRENT SERVER special register also indicates that this plan can use this package in any location. If you use a particular location name, then that database server should be defined in the SYSLOCATIONS catalog table.

  - *collection-id*

    Is the name of the collection containing the package. You can use a particular collection name or an asterisk; there is no default. If you specify an asterisk, the package name is provided by the CURRENT PACKAGESET special register at execution time. The CURRENT PACKAGESET special register also indicates that this plan can use this package from any collection.

  - *package-id*

    Names a particular package or specifies, by the asterisk, all packages in the collection.

- *CURRENTSERVER*

  Determines the location to connect to before running the plan. A connect type 1 is issued, preventing your application from using DUW support.

- *DISCONNECT*

Determines which connections to destroy during COMMIT statement execution. Valid values are

- *(EXPLICIT)*

  Destroys only connections in the release pending state. The release pending state is set by issuing the RELEASE statement in your program. The RELEASE statement allows you maximum flexibility for controlling remote connections.

- *(AUTOMATIC)*

  Destroys all remote connections.

- *(CONDITIONAL)*

  Destroys all remote connections, unless an open cursor defined as WITH HOLD is associated with the connection.

- *ISOLATION*

  Defines the degree of isolation of an application process executing concurrently with other application processes. Valid values are

  - *(RR) Repeatable Read*

    Locks only rows read during the transaction and keeps records locked until the transaction commits. Prevents the applications process from reading rows changed by other application until those changes are committed.

  - *(CS) Cursor Stability*

    Maintains locks on the current and previously changed rows only.

  - *(UR) Uncommitted Read*

    Neither acquires nor examines database locks. This isolation level applies only for read-only operations.

- *SQLRULES*

  Indicates whether you can execute a type 2 CONNECT statement to an existing SQL connection, according to DB2 rules. A type 2 CONNECT statement allows you to connect to more than one database server in the same unit of work. Valid values are

  - *(DB2)*

    No error occurs if the CONNECT statement identifies an existing SQL connection. CONNECT makes the existing connection the current connection.

  - *(STD)*

    An error occurs if the CONNECT statement identifies an existing SQL connection. To make an existing connection the current connection, you must use the SET CONNECTION statement.

See the *DB2 for MVS/ESA Command Reference* for more information about the BIND PLAN command.

16.1.3.2 Binding a Package

A package *may* be used to ease the process of DB2 program change management. A package *should* be used when preparing an application that will access distributed data through DRDA.

Use the *BIND PACKAGE* command to bind your DBRM into a package. The syntax for this command is shown in Figure 224 on page 483.

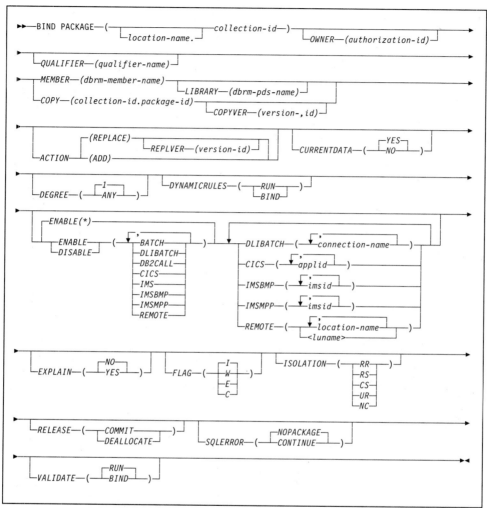

Figure 224. *BIND PACKAGE Syntax*

The following BIND PACKAGE options are relevant when binding a package to a remote location:

- *location-name*

  The name of the location where you want to bind the package. The location name must be defined in the CDB, specifically, in the SYSIBM.SYSLOCATIONS table.

- *collection-id*

  The collection of the package. This value is compulsory.

- *OWNER*

  Determines the authorization ID of the owner of the package. This value is subject to translation when sent to the remote location.

- *QUALIFIER*

  Is the implicit qualifier for unqualified names of tables, views, and indexes in the packages. This value is *not* subject to translation when sent to the remote location.

- *MEMBER*

  Is the name of the DBRM you are including in the package. You can include only one DBRM. The DBRM name becomes the package name. This option is mutually exclusive with the COPY option.

- *COPY*

  Is the name of a local package to be copied in the package you are binding. Access paths are re-created in the copy. This option is mutually exclusive with the MEMBER option.

- *ACTION*

  Indicates whether you are replacing an already existing package or creating a new package. Valid values are:

  - *(REPLACE)*

    If a package with the same name exists, it is replaced. If not, a new package is created.

  - *(REPLACE) REPLVER(version-id)*

    Replaces a specific version of the package, identified by *version-id*. If the package with the specified *version-id* does not exist, the bind fails.

  - *(ADD)*

    Adds a new object but does not replace an existing object.

- *ISOLATION*

  Defines the degree of isolation of an application process executing concurrently with other application processes. Valid values are:

  - *(RR) Repeatable Read*

    Locks only rows read during the transaction and keeps records locked until the transaction commits. Prevents the application process from reading rows changed by other applications until those changes are committed.

  - *(RS) Read Stability*

Locks only rows read during the transaction and keeps records locked until the transaction commits. This option is not supported by DB2 for MVS/ESA. It is used on packages bound to other database servers. If the remote server does not support this isolation level, it uses RR.

- *(CS) Cursor Stability*

  Maintains locks on the current and previously changed rows only.

- *(UR) Uncommitted Read*

  Neither acquires nor examines database locks. This isolation level applies only for read-only operations.

- *(NC) No Commit*

  Does not acquire locks and disables transaction management. This option is not supported by DB2 for MVS/ESA. It is used on packages bound to other database servers. If the remote server does not support this isolation level, it uses UR.

- *SQLERROR*

  Indicates whether or not to create a package if SQL errors occur. Valid values are:

  - *(NOPACKAGE)*

    Indicates not to create a package if SQL errors occur.

  - *(CONTINUE)*

    Indicates to create a package even if SQL errors occur. This option does not prevent the statements in error from failing during run time.

- *VALIDATE*

  Indicates whether a check operation should be executed at run time, if errors of the type OBJECT NOT FOUND and/or NOT AUTHORIZED are detected during the bind or rebind operations. Valid values are:

  - *(RUN)*

    If errors of the type OBJECT NOT FOUND and/or NOT AUTHORIZED are detected during bind or rebind processing, this option indicates that DB2 should create a package and check the existence of the objects and/or authorization during run time.

  - *(BIND)*

    If errors of the type OBJECT NOT FOUND and/or NOT AUTHORIZED are detected, the process of bind or rebind does not create a package, unless you use the SQLERROR(CONTINUE) option. The SQLERROR(CONTINUE) option does not prevent the statements in error from failing during run time, however.

See the *DB2 for MVS/ESA Command Reference* for more information about the BIND PACKAGE command.

16.1.3.3 Preparing Programs to Access Distributed Data

The process of preparing a program that accesses distributed data is much like the process of preparing of a program that accesses only local data.

In this section we address the steps and options you can use to prepare your program to access distributed data. We assume that the program you are preparing uses application-directed access, that is, your program explicitly connects to each new server by executing the CONNECT statement.

- *Precompiling your program*

  If your application requires DUW support, use the CONNECT(2) option. Use CONNECT(1) if your application requires RUW support.

  If your application accesses database servers different from DB2 for MVS/ESA, use SQL(ALL). Use SQL(DB2) if your application accesses only DB2 for MVS/ESA database servers.

- *Creating a load module for your program*

  Create your load module as usual.

- *Creating a plan for your program*

  Your program should have a plan that includes all packages for the remote locations to which it connects. It should include the DBRMs and/or packages if it connects to the local DB2 for MVS/ESA as well.

  Use the BIND PLAN option, DISCONNECT(EXPLICIT), if your program explicitly issues RELEASE statements.

  Use SQLRULES(STD) if you want the CONNECT statement to return an error code if the connection you are trying to establish is already in place.

  Refer to 16.1.3.1, "Binding a Plan" on page 478 for more information about bind options.

- *Creating the remote packages for your plan*

  To create a remote package, take the following issues into consideration:

  Make sure that the locations for which you are creating the packages exist in the SYSIBM.SYSLOCATIONS table of the CDB.

  Check the userid you sent to the remote location; it may affect the values you use in your BIND PACKAGE command. Refer to 16.2.2, "Binding Packages for Each Site" on page 489 for more information.

Remember that bind package options affect only the package you are creating. Thus you can create a plan that includes packages bound with different options to address the fact that dissimilar database servers may not support the same SQL statement clauses or the same prepare and/or bind options.

When you bind a package for a remote location, the remote location checks for the appropriate authorities to create a package, reads and updates the catalogs, and builds a package. Therefore you have to be aware of the authorities you require to create a package for a remote location, and that the DB2 for MVS/ESA catalogs are not updated when you create a remote package.

If you have to create the same package in different locations, but you get SQL errors when binding the package for some of the locations, you can use the SQLERROR(CONTINUE) option for this specific location. Note that this option does not prevent the statements in error from failing during run time.

For some database servers, the implicit qualifier of the unqualified objects in your package is the primary ID executing the bind operations; for other database servers the collection ID is the implicit qualifier.

Refer to Table 48 for specific database server information about qualifying unqualified objects.

Table 48. Qualifying Unqualified Objects in a Package

Database Server	Implicit Qualifier
DB2 for MVS/ESA	Primary ID binding the package, unless qualifier is specified
DB2 for OS/400	Primary ID binding the package, unless qualifier is specified
SQL/DS for VM and VSE	Creator name, which can be the primary ID binding the package or the collection name.
DB2 for common server	Primary ID binding the package.

You can use the QUALIFIER bind package option to determine the qualifier for unqualified objects in your package. Note, however, that the behavior of this option differs according to the database server to which you are binding the package.

Refer to 16.2.2, "Binding Packages for Each Site" on page 489 for more information about the QUALIFIER option. Refer to 16.1.3.2, "Binding a Package" on page 482 for a description of the BIND PACKAGE command options.

16.2 Preparing the Sample Programs

To prepare our sample programs, we decided to create batch jobs, the most common way of preparing programs in a production environment. We created three different jobs to perform the following tasks.

- Precompile, compile, and link edit
- Bind packages
- Bind plan

For each program, we had to submit the precompile, compile, and link-edit job first to generate the DBRMs required for the bind jobs. We verified that the bind package and bind plan jobs can be submitted in any order. Table 49 lists the programs we prepared.

Table 49. *Sample Programs*

Program Name	Description
DRDASUTS	Multiple-site read
DRDASU2	Multiple-site read, single-site update
MSUTWOPC	Multiple-site update for DRDA 2 servers

Table 41 on page 413 lists the database servers we connected to in the programs.

Refer to Chapter 12, "Application Structure" on page 351 for more information about the programs.

From now on, our description of the program preparation relates to program DRDASUTS.

16.2.1 Creating Database Request Module and Load Module

We coded the DRDASUTS program in C on the AS/400 platform and then ported it to MVS. Given that we were trying to reduce program portability efforts to the maximum extent, we decided not to code SQL DECLARE TABLE statements in the program. As a result, our precompilation step ended with return code = 0 and warning message DSNH050I.

We had to make the following modifications to the programs:

- Change the right bracket to x'BD'.
- Change the left bracket to x'AD'.

- Change SQL statements to uppercase.

- Omit the USER and USING keywords, because the CONNECT statement cannot use them from the sample programs.

To create the DBRM and load module for DRDASUTS, we invoked DSNHC, the DB2 procedure to prepare programs written in C. Figure 225 shows a portion of the JCL.

```
000900 //PREPTS    EXEC DSNHC,MEM=DRDASUTS,
001000 //           COND=(4,LT),
001100 //           PARM.PC='HOST(C),SOURCE,XREF,SQL(ALL),STDSQL(NO),TW',
001200 //           PARM.C='SOURCE LIST MARGINS(1,72)',
001300 //           PARM.LKED='AMODE=31,RMODE=ANY,MAP'
001400 //PC.DBRMLIB  DD DSN=DSN410.DBRMLIB.DATA(MVSSUTS),
001500 //              DISP=SHR
```

Figure 225. Invoking DNHC for C Program Preparation

We created a DBRM called MVSSUTS to be used as the input for the bind steps.

The HOST(C) option indicates that DRDASUTS is written in C.

Because DRDASUTS requires DUW support, the CONNECT(2) option should be used. However, we did not use this option in our job, because 2 is the default value for the CONNECT option.

Because program DRDASUTS connects to DB2 for MVS/ESA and other database servers such as DB2 for OS/400 and DB2 common server, we used the SQL(ALL) option to instruct the precompiler to apply DRDA rules for the SQL statements in this program.

16.2.2 Binding Packages for Each Site

Program DRDASUTS connects to remote locations as well as to the local site, DB2 for MVS/ESA in this case. We decided to create a package for each remote location and to have a directly bound DBRM for the local site.

To bind our remote packages, we used the MVSSUTS DBRM. We logged on to TSO with userid DRDAX5, which was defined in all systems and became the primary ID for the bind process because we did not use DB2 for MVS/ESA outbound translation.

16.2.2.1 Binding Packages to DB2 common server

Figure 226 on page 490 shows the command we used to bind package MVSSUTS to DB2 for OS/2.

```
BIND PACKAGE(SJ2SMPL.DRDAX5) MEMBER(MVSSUTS) VALIDATE(BIND) -
ACTION(REPLACE) QUALIFIER(DRDAX5) OWNER(DRDAX5) ISOLATION(CS)
```

Figure 226. Bind Package MVSSUTS for Location SJ2SMPL

By using this command, we created a package called MVSSUTS in location SJ2SMPL, using a collection named DRDAX5. Figure 227 shows the entry for package MVSSUTS in the SYSCAT.PACKAGES catalog table of DB2 for OS/2.

```
PKGNAME   PKGSCHEMA BOUNDBY
--------  --------- --------
MVSSUTS   DRDAX5    DRDAX5
```

Figure 227. SYSCAT.PACKAGES Table of DB2 for OS/2

Figure 228 shows the command we used to bind package MVSSUTS to DB2 for AIX.

```
BIND PACKAGE(SJ6SMPL.DRDAX5) MEMBER(MVSSUTS) VALIDATE(BIND) -
ACTION(REPLACE) QUALIFIER(DRDAX5) OWNER(DRDAX5) ISOLATION(CS)
```

Figure 228. Bind Package MVSSUTS for Location SJ6SMPL

By using this command, we created a package called MVSSUTS in location SJ6SMPL, using a collection named DRDAX5. Figure 229 shows the entry for package MVSSUTS in the SYSCAT.PACKAGES catalog table of DB2 for AIX.

```
PKGNAME   PKGSCHEMA BOUNDBY
--------  --------- --------
MVSSUTS   DRDAX5    DRDAX5
```

Figure 229. SYSCAT.PACKAGES Table of DB2 for AIX

The VALIDATE(RUN), ACTION(ADD), and SQLERROR(CONTINUE) bind options are not valid when binding a package to DB2 common server. We had to explicitly use VALIDATE(BIND). ACTION(REPLACE) can be specified explicitly or by default.

VALIDATE(RUN) is not a valid option when binding a package for DB2 for common server. Thus for DB2 common server we had to create all of the tables required for the programs, even though they were not required to run the programs on DB2 for OS/2 and DB2 for AIX.

The primary ID we used to bind was DRDAX5, which maps to the BOUNDBY column in the SYSCAT.PACKAGES catalog table of DB2 for common server. The value of BOUNDBY represents the implicit qualifier for unqualified objects in the corresponding package. DRDAX5 is the implicit qualifier for unqualified objects in package MVSSUTS.

The values provided for QUALIFIER and OWNER depend on the userid issuing the bind. QUALIFIER and OWNER must match that userid, regardless of the method DB2 for MVS/ESA uses to send the userid to the remote location. Additionally, QUALIFIER and OWNER value specification depends on whether or not outbound translation is used.

Table 50 lists the valid values for QUALIFIER and OWNER.

Table 50. Valid Values for QUALIFIER and OWNER: DB2 common server

Bind Package Option	Outbound Translation Used	Outbound Translation Not Used
QUALIFIER	Required. Must match the userid in the SYSUSERNAMES CDB table for the corresponding LU	Optional. If provided, must be set to the primary ID doing the bind
OWNER	Optional. Must match the userid in the SYSUSERNAMES CDB table for the corresponding LU	Optional. If provided, must be set to the primary ID doing the bind

Refer to 10.2.2.3, "SYSUSERNAMES" on page 303 for an explanation of outbound translation.

16.2.2.2 Binding Packages to DB2 for OS/400

Figure 230 shows the command we used to bind package MVSSUTS to DB2 for OS/400 in San Jose.

```
BIND PACKAGE(SJAS400.DRDAX5) MEMBER(MVSSUTS) VALIDATE(RUN) -
ACTION(REPLACE) QUALIFIER(DRDAX5) ISOLATION(CS) SQLERROR(CONTINUE)
```

Figure 230. Bind Package MVSSUTS for Location SJAS400

By using this command, we created a package called MVSSUTS in location SJAS400, using a collection named DRDAX5. Figure 231 on page 492 shows the entry for package MVSSUTS in the QSYS2.SYSPACKAGES catalog table of DB2 for OS/400.

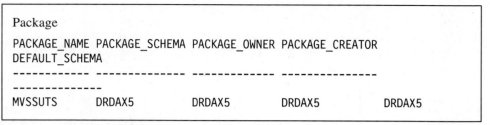

Figure 231. QSYS2.SYSPACKAGES Table of DB2 for OS/400 San Jose: MVSSUTS

Figure 232 shows the command we used to bind package MVSSUTS to DB2 for OS/400 in Rochester.

```
BIND PACKAGE(RCAS400.DRDAX5) MEMBER(MVSSUTS) VALIDATE(RUN) -
ACTION(REPLACE) QUALIFIER(DRDAX5) ISOLATION(CS) SQLERROR(CONTINUE)
```

Figure 232. Bind Package for Location RCAS400

By using this command, we created a package called MVSSUTS in location RCAS400, using a collection named DRDAX5. Figure 233 shows the entry for package MVSSUTS in the QSYS2.SYSPACKAGES catalog table of DB2 for OS/400.

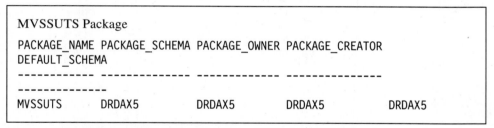

Figure 233. QSYS2.SYSPACKAGES Table of DB2 for OS/400 Rochester:

Table 51 on page 493 shows how some BIND PACKAGE parameters map to some of the columns of the OS/400 QSYS2.SYSPACKAGES catalog table.

Table 51. *Bind Package Parameters*

Bind Package Parameter	Maps to:	Considerations
QUALIFIER	DEFAULT_SCHEMA	If specified, it becomes the implicit qualifier for unqualified objects in the package.
OWNER	PACKAGE_OWNER	You should specify a valid AS/400 userid, but it always defaults to the primary ID.
COLLECTION	PACKAGE_SCHEMA	A collection with this name must exist in OS/400.
Primary ID	PACKAGE_CREATOR	If qualifier is not specified, creator becomes the implicit qualifier for unqualified objects in the package.

QUALIFIER and OWNER values do not depend on whether or not outbound translation is used.

16.2.2.3 Binding Packages to SQL/DS for VM and VSE

Figure 234 shows the command we used to bind package MVSSUTS to SQL/DS for VM.

```
BIND PACKAGE(S34VMDB0.DRDAX5) MEMBER(MVSSUTS) VALIDATE(RUN) -
ACTION(REPLACE) ISOLATION(CS) SQLERROR(CONTINUE) QUALIFIER(DRDAX5)
```

Figure 234. *Bind Package MVSSUTS for Location S34VMDB0*

By using this command, we created a package called MVSSUTS in location S34VMDB0, using a collection named DRDAX5. Figure 235 shows the entry for package MVSSUTS in the SYSTEM.SYSACCESS catalog table of SQL/DS for VM.

```
TNAME            CREATOR
------------------ --------
MVSSUTS          DRDAX5
```

Figure 235. *SYSTEM.SYSACCESS Table of SQL/DS for VM: MVSSUTS Package*

Figure 236 on page 494 shows the command we used to bind package MVSSUTS to SQL/DS for VSE.

```
BIND PACKAGE(S34VSDB1.DRDAX5) MEMBER(MVSSUTS) VALIDATE(RUN) -
ACTION(REPLACE) ISOLATION(CS) SQLERROR(CONTINUE) QUALIFIER(DRDAX5)
```

Figure 236. Bind Package MVSSUTS for Location S34VSDB1

By using this command, we created a package called MVSSUTS in location S34VSDB1, using a collection named DRDAX5. Figure 237 shows the entry for package MVSSUTS in the SYSTEM.SYSACCESS catalog table of SQL/DS for VSE.

```
TNAME               CREATOR
------------------  --------
MVSSUTS             DRDAX5
```

Figure 237. SYSTEM.SYSACCESS Table of SQL/DS for VSE

The collection name specified in the BIND PACKAGE command maps to the CREATOR column in the SQL/DS SYSTEM.SYSACCESS table. The value of CREATOR is the implicit qualifier for unqualified objects in the corresponding package. DRDAX5 is the implict qualifier for unqualified objects in package MVSSUTS.

OWNER and QUALIFIER options can be specified when binding to SQL/DS for VM and VSE, but they must match the collection name. Additionally QUALIFIER and OWNER values depend on whether or not outbound translation is used.

Table 52 shows the valid values for QUALIFIER and OWNER.

Table 52. Valid Values for QUALIFIER and OWNER: SQL/DS for VM and VSE		
Bind Package Option	**Outbound Translation Used**	**Outbound Translation Not Used**
QUALIFIER	Required. Must match both the userid in the SYSUSERNAMES CDB table for the corresponding LU and the collection name	Optional. If provided, must be set to the collection name
OWNER	Optional. Must match both the userid in the SYSUSERNAMES CDB table for the corresponding LU and the collection name	Optional. If provided, must be set to the collection name

Refer to 10.2.2.3, "SYSUSERNAMES" on page 303 for an explanation of outbound translation.

16.2.3 Binding a Plan in DB2 for MVS/ESA

The plan we created for program DRDASUTS includes all of the remote packages we built previously, plus one directly bound DBRM called MVSSUTS. Figure 238 shows the BIND PLAN command we executed.

```
BIND PLAN(MVSSUTS) MEMBER(MVSSUTS)                   -
                   PKLIST(SJ2SMPL.DRDAX5.MVSSUTS,    -
                          SJ6SMPL.DRDAX5.MVSSUTS,    -
                          SJAS400.DRDAX5.MVSSUTS,    -
                          RCAS400.DRDAX5.MVSSUTS,    -
                          S34VMDB0.DRDAX5.MVSSUTS,   -
                          S34VSDB1.DRDAX5.MVSSUTS)   -
                   ISOLATION(CS) QUALIFIER(DRDAX5) ACTION(REPLACE)
```

Figure 238. BIND PLAN Command for DB2 for MVS/ESA

The DISCONNECT(EXPLICIT) option is implicitly used in our BIND PLAN statement. Refer to 16.1.3.1, "Binding a Plan" on page 478 for more information.

To grant use of the plan to the appropriate users, we used the GRANT EXECUTE ON PLAN statement.

Chapter 17. Code Page Translation

Different systems represent data in different ways. When data is moved from one system to another, data conversion is sometimes required. DRDA products support data conversion.

The following terminology is used when data conversion is required in a DRDA environment:

- *Character set* is a defined set of characters, for example, the letters *A to Z, a to z*, and the digits *0 to 9*.

- *Code point* is a unique bit pattern that represents a character, for example, the configuration of bits X′C2′ can represent the letter *B*.

- *Code page* is a set of hexadecimal assignments (code points) for the characters in a character set. For single-byte characters a code page can be understood as a two-column table with up to 256 entries. Each table entry contains a character representation and its corresponding code point.

  As an example, the letter *A* is represented by code point X′C1′ in code page 437 and code point X′41′ in code page 850.

  The representation of character data depends on the encoding scheme. Here are some examples of encoding schemes:

  - Single-byte ASCII

  - Single-byte EBCDIC

  - Double-byte ASCII

  - Double-byte EBCDIC

- *Coded character set* is a set of rules that establish a character set and the one-to-one relationships between the characters of the set and their code points.

- *Coded character set ID (CCSID)* is the number assigned to a specific coded character set. It is a 2-byte binary number.

  You can think of a CCSID as a superset of code pages. As a matter of fact, wherever feasible, the CCSID is assigned the same value as the code page. However, the relationship between the two values cannot be maintained in all situations.

Conversion of numeric data depends on how a specific data type is represented at the sending and receiving system. This kind of conversion is built into the database products and is not subject to user changes.

Character conversion is done in accordance with CDRA. Bit data is not converted. Conversion is always done at the receiving system. You can do character conversion during remote processing when you send the data to the AS and again when the result is sent back to the AR. For example, if DDCS for OS/2 is used to access data in SQL/DS for VM,

- DDCS sends SQL statements and eventually data to SQL/DS.
- SQL/DS converts them to an EBCDIC CCSID and processes them.
- SQL/DS sends the results back to DDCS.
- DDCS converts the results to an ASCII or ISO code page.

Character conversion can affect performance and should be kept to a minimum. To avoid or minimize CCSID conversion, choose the same CCSID for the AS and AR, although this is not always possible. Investigate whether you can use the INTERNATIONAL (CCSID=500) character set when you are supporting different languages. This character set includes many different languages and as such helps minimize character conversion.

17.1 CHARNAME and CCSID in SQL/DS

The CHARNAME specification determines

- CCSID (500 is default)
- Classification table
- Translation table

To set the default CHARNAME as FRENCH for the AS, use SQLSTART (see Figure 239), SQLINIT, or SQLGLOB.

```
SQLSTART DB(SQLDBA) ID(MYBOOT) PARM(PARMID=WARM1,CHARNAME=FRENCH)
```

Figure 239. Starting the Application Server to Use the FRENCH Character Set

SQLINIT or SQLGLOB are also used to set the date and time formats and the PROTOCOL used. The protocol defines how the AR should communicate with the AS and can be set to

- SQL/DS to communicate with other SQL/DS systems. The AS defines the CCSID used by the AR. Therefore both the AS and AR must use the same CCSID.
- DRDA to communicate using only the DRDA protocol.

- AUTO to use the SQL/DS protocol when communicating with SQL/DS and DRDA when communicating with non-SQL/DS servers.

A character has a subtype attribute associated with it. Examples of character subtypes are

- SBCS
- DBCS
- Mixed
- Bit

Each database has a default character subtype that is related to the CCSID of the RDBMS. For SQL/DS, it is defined in the system catalog tables. The default subtype determines the default CCSID used.

17.1.1 CCSID at the AS

To display the actual values for the CCSID and CHARNAME, use SQLINIT with the QueRY parameter.

The actual CCSID is used to convert SQL statements and the constants that are part of the SQL statements.

The subtype specification belongs to the CCSID. It indicates to SQL/DS how to interpret character data, for example, as single-character data or mixed data. The defaults for CCSIDMIXED or CCSIDSBCS may vary according to the subtype value.

The default CCSID is used to

- Represent character data such as date, time, current user

- Present the results of scalar functions such as CHARS, DIGITS, and HEX

- For character columns when you create the table

17.1.2 CCSID at the AR

To minimize conversion, select a CHARNAME and CCSID that correspond to the application server. To display the actual values for the CCSID and CHARNAME, use SQLINIT with the QueRY parameter. The CHARNAME displayed is valid only when the PROTOCOL parameter is *not SQL/DS*. If PROTOCOL is SQL/DS, the CHARNAME of the connected server is displayed.

The database manager folds keywords to uppercase based on the default CHARNAME for SQL/DS defined on the SQLSTART initialization parameter. The database manager uses a specific set of characters when folding to uppercase. For example, all hexadecimal values in the ENGLISH character set that represent uppercase English letters are reserved. The database manager reserves hexadecimal values so it can correctly interpret SQL statements. Characters between delimited identifiers are not folded.

All characters have a classification code that can be used, for example, to determine which characters are reserved for the database manager and cannot be modified.

You should create your own CCSIDs only when absolutely necessary.

The absence of a character in the character set does not prevent you from using that character. You can define additional user-specific characters, but they can be used only for the character data and quoted IDs. They cannot be used for SQL/DS keywords or unquoted IDs.

If the CCSID is not supplied for SQL/DS in the SYSCHARSETS table, check the *Character Data Representation Architecture Level 1 Registry* for other predefined CCSIDs. If you find the CCSID there, use it.

17.2 SQL/DS System Catalog Tables for Code Page Support

In this section we describe the relational tables used by SQL/DS to manage code pages.

Figure 240 shows the SYSTEM.SYSOPTIONS catalog table. The CCSID and CHARNAME from this table are used if you do not override them during startup through the CHARNAME specification.

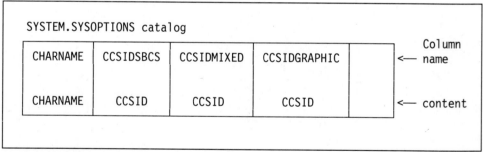

Figure 240. SYSTEM.SYSOPTIONS Catalog Table

Figure 241 on page 501 shows the SYSTEM.SYSCHARSET catalog table. This table contains all character sets available for this SQL/DS system and is used to check entered CHARNAMES. Before using a new character set, you must add it to this table. You can use the DB utility to load the character set. After you update SYSSTRINGS and SYSCCSIDS, you can use the character set in the SQLSTART EXEC.

The ENGLISH and the INTERNATIONAL character sets are defined in the database internally. New definitions for these character sets override the internal definitions.

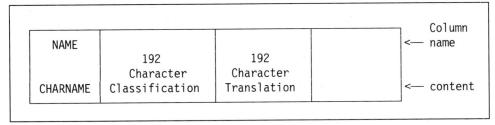

Figure 241. SYSTEM.SYSCHARSETS Catalog Table

Figure 242 shows the SYSTEM.SYSCCSIDS catalog table. This table contains new CCSIDs for a new character set. You have to update it when you define a new character set. Update it after adding a new character set to the SYSCHARSETS table.

The subtype of the CCSID can be single-byte, double-byte, or mixed. DBCSID and SBCSID specify the DBCS and the SBCS components for a mixed CCSID.

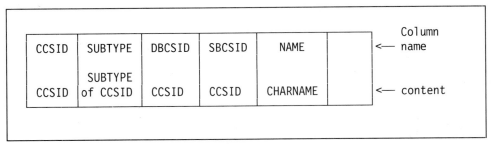

Figure 242. SYSTEM.SYSCCSIDS Catalog Table

Figure 243 on page 502 shows the SYSTEM.SYSSTRINGS catalog table. This table contains the conversion information and is also known as the *conversion selection table*. In this table you specify the CCSID conversions that are supported. You have to update the table when you define a new character set. Update it after adding a new character set to the SYSCHARSETS table.

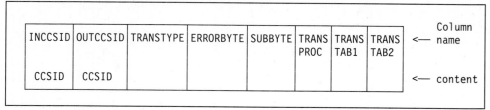

INCCSID	OUTCCSID	TRANSTYPE	ERRORBYTE	SUBBYTE	TRANS PROC	TRANS TAB1	TRANS TAB2	← name
CCSID	CCSID							← content

Figure 243. SYSTEM.SYSSTRINGS Catalog Table

Here is an explanation of the columns in the SYSSTRINGS table:

INCCSID CCSID of input character.

OUTCCSID CCSID of output character.

TRANSTYPE Identifies the conversion. SS for SBCS to SBCS. Other options are documented in the *SQL/DS System Administration for IBM VM Systems* manual.

ERRORBYTE Identifies characters that have no representation in the target code page. When such a translation occurs, an error occurs.

SUBBYTE Identifies characters that have no representation in the target code page. When such a translation occurs, a warning is issued.

TRANSPROC Identifies the conversion procedures used between the CCSIDs. Used for DBCS support.

TRANSTAB1 Represents the first 64 bytes of the conversion table.

TRANSTAB2 Represents the last 192 bytes of the conversion table.

A table similar to the SQL/DS SYSSTRINGS table is available in DB2 for MVS/ESA. Figure 244 shows the SYSTEM.SYSCOLUMNS catalog table. A CCSID can be defined for each column. If the value for a specific column is NULL, CCSID 500 is used.

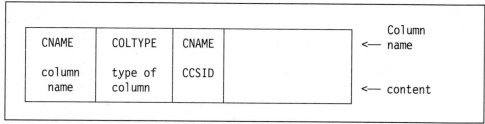

CNAME	COLTYPE	CNAME		← name
column name	type of column	CCSID		← content

Figure 244. SYSTEM.SYSCOLUMNS Catalog Table

Figure 245 on page 503 shows the ARISCCS macro file. The database manager uses this file to locate the current CHARNAME of the application server. The CMS ARISSCR, ARISCCS, and ARISSTR files are updated after all definitions are made in the system catalog tables. Use the ARISDBMA EXEC to update the CMS files.

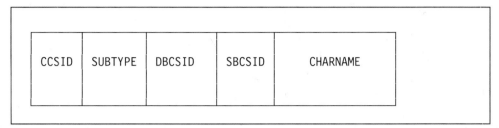

CCSID	SUBTYPE	DBCSID	SBCSID	CHARNAME

Figure 245. CMS ARISCCS Macro File.

For DB2 for MVS/ESA see the *DB2 for MVS/ESA Administration Guide*. For SQL/DS refer to *SQL/DS System Administration for VM Systems* or *SQL/DS System Administration for VSE*.

17.3 Defining Your Own Character Set

Follow these steps to define your own character set in SQL/DS:

1. Specify all characters in your set with their hexadecimal values in a matrix developed as shown in Figure 246 on page 504. First add the characters of the English character set; then add those that are specific to your character set.

		00				01				10				11				← Bits 0,1
		00	01	10	11	00	01	10	11	00	01	10	11	00	01	10	11	← 2,3
Bits 4567	HEX 1	0	1	2	3	4	5	6	7	8	9	A	B	C	D	E	F	← HEX 0
0000	0					SP	&	-										
0001	1							/		a	j			A	J		1	
0010	2									b	k	s		B	K	S	2	
0011	3									c	l	t		C	L	T	3	
0100	4									d	m	u		D	M	U	4	
0101	5									e	n	v		E	N	V	5	
0110	6									f	o	w		F	O	W	6	
0111	7									g	p	x		G	P	X	7	
1000	8									h	q	y		H	Q	Y	8	
1001	9									i	f	z		I	F	Z	9	
1010	A								:									
1011	B					.	$	,	#									
1100	C					<	.	%	@									
1101	D					(	)	_	′									
1110	E					+	;	>	=									
1111	F					I	;	>	=									

Figure 246. English Character Set (CCSID=37)

Figure 247 on page 505 shows how you might record the changes you want for the new code page.

```
X'4A', X'4F', X'5A', X'5B', X'5F', X'6A',
X'79', X'7B', X'7C', X'C0', X'D0'.
```

Figure 247. *Code Point Differences*

2. Classify each new or modified character.

   SQL/DS has 12 different character classifications to define how the character can be used in SQL statements. The character classifications are stored in an internal classification table. Review the classifications of the characters that differ from the English character set table. Only hexadecimal values that are currently classified as 0 can be classified as 3 and vice versa. Other changes are not allowed.

   - Classification 0 indicates unusable for keywords or unquoted identifiers.

   - Classification 3 indicates characters other than numerics, uppercase English alphabets, and underscores that are usable for unquoted identifiers.

   Figure 248 on page 506 and Figure 249 on page 507 show samples of hexadecimal value classifications. In addition to the classification code, enter the hexadecimal value of the character that is used for uppercase translation. If, for example, *a* is translated to *A* during uppercase translation, X'81' is translated to X'C1' (see English translation below).

Hex. Value	English Classif.	English Transl.	New Classif.	New Transl.
40	1	40		
41	0	41		
42	0	42		
43	0	43		
44	0	44		
45	0	45		
46	0	46		
47	0	47		
48	0	48		
49	0	49		
4A	0	4A	3	
4B	5	4B		
4C	6	4C		
4D	6	4D		
4E	6	4E		
4F	6	4F		
50	6	50		
51	0	51		
52	0	52		
53	0	53		
54	0	54		
55	0	55		
56	0	56		
57	0	57		
58	0	58		
59	0	59		
5A	0	5A		
5B	3	5B		
5C	6	5C		
5D	6	5D		
5E	6	5E		
5F	6	5F		
60	6	60		
61	6	61		
62	0	62		
63	0	63		
64	0	64		
65	0	65		
66	0	66		
67	0	67		
68	0	68		
69	0	69		
6A	0	6A	3	X'5B'
6B	6	6B		
6C	6	6C		
6D	B	6D		
6E	6	6E		
6F	6	6F		

Figure 248. Internal Classification Table for Hexadecimal Values (1)

Hex. Value	English Classif.	English Transl.	New Classif.	New Transl.
70	0	70		
71	0	61		
72	0	72		
73	0	73		
74	0	74		
75	0	75		
76	0	76		
77	0	77		
78	0	78		
79	0	79	3	X'7C'
7A	6	7A		
7B	3	7B		
7C	3	7C		
7D	2	7D		
7E	6	7E		
7F	7	7F		
80	0	80		
81	3	C1		
82	3	C2		
83	3	C3		
84	3	C4		
85	3	C5		
86	3	C6		
87	3	C7		
88	3	C8		
89	3	C9		
8A	0	8A		
8B	0	8B		
8C	0	8C		
8D	0	8D		
8E	0	8E		
8F	0	8F		
..	.	..	.	.....
..	.	..	.	.....
..	.	..	.	.....

Figure 249. Internal Classification Table for Hexadecimal Values (2)

Notes for Figure 248 on page 506 and Figure 249

- The hexadecimal values from X'00' to X'3F' are used by the database manager and have a classification of 0. You can set the remaining (192) hexadecimal values only. Therefore the characters in your set that have a hexadecimal value between X'00' and X'3F' can be used only as quoted identifiers.

- The hexadecimal values that represent uppercase English letters are reserved by the database manager and cannot be modified.

- All hexadecimal values classified as 0 or 3 in the English character set can be modified. All other hexadecimal values are reserved.

- Usually you would try to classify your letters in the alphabet as 3 because 0 would allow you to use these letters in quoted identifiers only. In our example in Figure 248 on page 506 X′4A was reclassified, because this hexadecimal value represents a letter in our alphabet.

- X′4F′ and X′5A are not reclassified because they are not members of our alphabet.

- X′5B′ is not reclassified because it is already classified as 3.

- X′5F′ is not reclassified because it cannot be reclassified.

- X′6A′ is reclassified to 3 because it is part of our alphabet. It is a lowercase letter. When it is translated to an uppercase letter, it should be translated to X′5B′. This translation value is also entered in the table. The same applies to X′79′.

3. Determine the hexadecimal values.

You have to determine the hexadecimal values to which lowercase letters are to be translated. This is not automatically known by the database manager. Some characters such as the dollar sign ($) may not have to be translated. If your alphabet has two new characters, which are represented by the hexadecimal values of X′6A′ and X′79′ (both lowercase letters), they should get translated to X′5B′ and X′7C′ when they are translated to uppercase characters. You should enter the translation values in the internal classification table for hexadecimal values.

After determining the hexadecimal values, verify that

- In all cases where you have classification 0, the hexadecimal values are translated to the identical hexadecimal value (like English).

- In all cases where you have classification 3, the hexadecimal values can be translated to any hexadecimal value.

4. Update the SYSTEM.SYSCHARSETS catalog table.

When you create a new character set, you must add it to the SYSTEM.SYSCHARSETS catalog table to make it known to the database manager. Use the INSERT function of the database manager. When you do this, you also define the name for the character set.

The easiest way to load a new character set is to modify a copy of the existing English character set. The ARISCHAR MACRO file contains these control statements. This macro is stored on the system disk. Figure 250 on page 509 shows a sample character set.

```
ARABIC              103300333305666663300333336366666663333333333066B663333333333063326733333333333333333333333333333333333333303333333333333333333333333003333
                    ="ØABCDEFGHI«»‰–··°JKLMNOPQR–ŒæŸÆ•·STUVWXYZi¿œ·‡„[£¥ﬁﬂ§¶¼½¾·‘’“”†{ABCDEFGHIôöòóõ}JKLMNOPQR·ûüùúÿ\STUVWXYZ·ÔäÒÓÕ0123456789
DANISH-NORWEGIAN    10333330333566666333333333003666666633333333366B660333333333306332673333333333300033003333333333000000033333333300033000000000000066
                    ="ØABCDEFGHI«»‰·‡·°JKLMNOPQR–ŒæŸÆ•·ÜSTUVWXYZi¿œ·‡„[£¥ﬁﬂ§¶¼½¾·‘’“”†#ABCDEFGHIÔäÒÓÕ$JKLMNOPQR·ÛüÙÚÿ\STUVWXYZ·ÔäÒÓÕ0123456789
ENGLISH             10000000000566666000000000063666666000000000066B66000000000000633267033333333300000000333333333000000003333333330000006000000000000
                    ="ØABCDEFGHI«»‰–··°JKLMNOPQR–ŒæŸÆ•·STUVWXYZi¿œ·‡„[£¥ﬁﬂ§¶¼½¾·‘’“”†{ABCDEFGHIôöòóõ}JKLMNOPQR·ûüùúÿ\STUVWXYZ·ÔäÒÓÕ0123456789
FINNISH-SWEDISH     10303330330566666033333330036666666333333333366B66303333333333633267333333333333000330033333333330030300333333333300033000000000000066
                    ="ØABCDEFGHI«»‰·‡·°JKLMNOPQR–ŒÆŸÆ•·ÜSTUVWXYZi¿œ·‡„[£¥ﬁﬂ§¶¼½¾·‘’“”†#ABCDEFGHIÔöÒÓÕ$JKLMNOPQR·ÛüÙÚÿ\STUVWXYZ·ÔäÒÓÕ0123456789
FRENCH              10000000000566666000000000003666666000000000366B66000000000000633267033333333300000000333333333000000003333333330000000000000000066
                    ="ØABCDEFGHI«»‰–··°JKLMNOPQR–ŒæŸÆ•·STUVWXYZi¿œ·‡„[£¥ﬁﬂ§¶¼½¾·‘’“”†EABCDEFGHIôöòóõEJKLMNOPQR·ûüùúÿCSTUVWXYZ·ÔäÒÓÕ0123456789
GERMAN              10000000003566666000000000033666666000000000366B66000000000000633267033333333300000000333333333000000003333333330000000000000000066
                    ="ØABCDEFGHI«»‰–··°JKLMNOPQR–ŒæŸÆ•·STUVWXYZi¿œ·‡„[£¥ﬁﬂ§¶¼½¾·‘’“”†¢ABCDEFGHIôöòóõ!JKLMNOPQR·ûüùúÿ\STUVWXYZ·ÔäÒÓÕ0123456789
GREEK               13333333330566666333333333303666666333333333666B66033303333306332670333333333333333303333333333333333003333333333333333303333333333
                    ="ØABCDEFGHIβäàáã°JKLMNOPQRåçñéêë·STUVWXYZèíöïìß[ÉöËÇÍÎÏÑÌ·ÂÄüÁÃ{ABCDEFGHIÅöòóõ}JKLMNOPQR·ûüùúÿ\STUVWXYZ·Ôä
HEBREW              13333333330566666333333333363666666333333333066B66030000000000633267033333333300000000333333333000000003333333330000006000000000000
                    ="ØABCDEFGHI«»‰–··°JKLMNOPQR–ŒæŸÆ•·STUVWXYZi¿œ·‡„[£¥ﬁﬂ§¶¼½¾·‘’“”†{ABCDEFGHIôöòóõ}JKLMNOPQR·ûüùúÿ\STUVWXYZ·ÔäÒÓÕ0123456789
INTERNATIONAL       10333333330566666333333333003666666333333333066B66333333333306332673333333333300033003333333333003030003333333330003300000000000066
                    ="ØABCDEFGHI«»‰–··°JKLMNOPQR–ŒÆŸÆ•·STUVWXYZi¿œ·‡„[£¥ﬁﬂ§¶¼½¾·‘’“”†{ABCDEFGHIÔäÒÓÕ}JKLMNOPQR·ÛÜÙÚÿ\STUVWXYZ·ÔäÒÓÕ0123456789
ITALIAN             10000000000566666000000000033666666000000000366B66000000000003633267033333333300000000333333333000000003333333330000000000000000066
                    ="ØABCDEFGHI«»‰–··°JKLMNOPQR–ŒæŸÆ•·ISTUVWXYZi¿œ·‡„[£¥ﬁﬂ§¶¼½¾·‘’“”†AABCDEFGHIôöòóõEJKLMNOPQR·ûüùúÿCSTUVWXYZ·ÔäÒÓÕ0123456789
JAPANESE-ENGLISH    10000333330566666333333333363666666333333333066B66333333333306332670333333333333333303333333333333333003333333333303360033333333
                    ="ØABCDEFGHI«»‰–··°JKLMNOPQR–ŒæŸÆ•·STUVWXYZi¿œ·‡„[£¥ﬁﬂ§¶¼½¾·‘’“”†{ABCDEFGHIôöòóõ}JKLMNOPQR·ûüùúÿ\STUVWXYZ·ÔäÒÓÕ0123456789
KATAKANA            10000333330566666333333030606666666333333333066B66033333333306332670333333333333333333333333303330033333333333333360033333333
                    ="Øabcdefghi«Q‰–··°jklmnopqr–RæŸÆ•·stuvwxyziSœ·‡„[£¥TUVWXYZ·‘’“”†{ABCDEFGHIôöòóõ}JKLMNOPQR·ûüùúÿ\STUVWXYZ·ÔäÒÓÕ0123456789
S-CHINESE           10333333330566666333333333063666666333333333066B66333333333306332673333333333300033003333333333003030003333333330003306000000000000
                    ="ØABCDEFGHI«»‰·‡·°JKLMNOPQR–ŒÆŸÆ•·STUVWXYZi¿œ·‡„[£¥ﬁﬂ§¶¼½¾·‘’“”†{ABCDEFGHIÔäÒÓÕ}JKLMNOPQR·ÛÜÙÚÿ\STUVWXYZ·ÔäÒÓÕ0123456789
SPANISH             10000000000566666000000000003666666000000000366B66000000000000633267033333333300000000333333333000000003333333330000000000000000066
                    ="ØABCDEFGHI«»‰–··°JKLMNOPQR–ŒæŸÆ•·STUVWXYZi¿œ·‡„[£¥ﬁﬂ§¶¼½¾·‘’“”†{ABCDEFGHIôöòóõ}JKLMNOPQR·ûüùúÿ\STUVWXYZ·ÔäÒÓÕ0123456789
TEST1               10000000000566666000000000063666666000000000066B66000000000000633267033333333300000000333333333000000003333333330000006000000000000
                    ="ØCBCDEFGHI«»‰–··°JKLMNOPQR–ŒæŸÆ•·STUVWXYZi¿œ·‡„[£¥ﬁﬂ§¶¼½¾·‘’“”†{CBCDEFGHIôöòóõ}JKLMNOPQR·ûüùúÿ\STUVWXYZ·ÔäÒÓÕ0123456789
```

Figure 250. *Sample of New Character Set TEST1*

Note: The first value in the INSERT statement is the name of the character set, followed by the 192 character classifications, followed by the 192 characters of the character translation table. The character translation table contains the translated characters, not the hexadecimal position of the characters.

5. Update the SYSTEM.SYSCCSIDS catalog table.

   Each new character set requires an entry in this table to identify the CCSID values related to the new character set. The INSERT statement would be similar to that shown in Figure 251.

```
INSERT INTO SYSTEM.SYSCCSIDS (CCSID,SUBTYPE,DBCSID,SBCSID,CHARNAME)
       VALUES (55789,
               'S',
               0,
               0,
               'TEST1')
```

Figure 251. *INSERT Statement to Add a New CCSID*

Figure 252 on page 510 shows the content of the ARISCCS MACRO It contains all available CCSIDs and their related CHARNAMEs. This file is updated at the very end, after all SYSTEM tables have been updated.

```
CCSID               CHARNAME
    SUBTYPE
-------------------------------------------
    37 S        0       0 ENGLISH
   273 S        0       0 GERMAN
   277 S        0       0 DANISH-NORWEGIAN
   278 S        0       0 FINNISH-SWEDISH
   280 S        0       0 ITALIAN
   284 S        0       0 SPANISH
   285 S        0       0 UK-ENGLISH
   290 S        0       0 290
   297 S        0       0 FRENCH
   420 S        0       0 ARABIC
   424 S        0       0 HEBREW
   500 S        0       0 INTERNATIONAL
   833 S        0       0 833
   836 S        0       0 836
   838 S        0       0 THAI
   870 S        0       0 870
   871 S        0       0 ICELANDIC
   875 S        0       0 GREEK
   930 M      290     300 930
   933 M      833     834 KOREAN
   935 M      836     837 S-CHINESE
   937 M    28709     835 T-CHINESE
   939 M     1027     300 939
  1027 S        0       0 1027
  5026 M      290    4396 KATAKANA
  5035 M     1027    4396 JAPANESE-ENGLISH
 28709 S        0       0 28709
 56789 S        0       0 TEST1
 65535 B        0       0
```

Figure 252. CCSID Definitions in the ARISCCS MACRO

Consider the following:

- The new CCSIDs must have a value within the 57,344 to 61,349 range, which is reserved for user-defined CCSIDs. Duplicate CCSIDs are not allowed.

- If your character set uses conversion tables provided by the CDRA registry, use the CCSIDs in those tables.

- CHARNAME must be the same as in the NAME column of the SYSTEM.SYSCHARSETS catalog table.

- Samples are found in the ARITPOP MACRO of the database manager.

6. Update the SYSTEM.SYSSTRINGS catalog table.

   You now must create the conversion table to allow conversions to and from the new CCSID. The tables that are used for conversion between two specific pairs of CCSID are stored in the SYSTEM.SYSSTRINGS table. The conversion tables for CDRA-supplied CCSIDs are provided by the CDRA registry.

   For your new CCSID, you must add a row for each conversion you want to support, both to and from the new CCSID.

   Each hexadecimal representation of each character in the source (IN) CCSID is mapped to each hexadecimal representation of each character in the target (OUT) CCSID (see Figure 253).

```
In CCSID 37  an '!' is represented by X'5A'
In CCSID 280 an '!' is represented by X'4F'

INCCSID = 37; OUTCCSID = 280;  90 is the position '5A' in the character
                               set table.
                               at offset 90 you define X'4F'(starting
                               with offset '0').
```

Figure 253. INCCSID and OUTCCSID Example

In cases where you have a column-specific CCSID, you have to provide for translation from the column CCSID to the database CCSID and from the database CCSID to the application-specific CCSID. You have to consider all applications (including the workstations) that will access the database. The code page translation from the workstation to the DRDA CCSID is done at the DRDA AS system. The translation from the DRDA AS CCSID to the code page of the workstation (application) is done at the workstation (not at the DRDA system).

Note: In SQL/DS you can create new code pages or modify code pages. In DB2 for workstations you cannot. Almost all current code pages are shipped with the workstation product. With a new code page, you can add data from the workstations. The translation from the workstation CCSID and the SQL/DS CCSID is done in SQL/DS. When you want to display (read) the data with the new CCSID, you get an error because the translation is done (according to DRDA) at the workstation and you cannot add or modify any workstation translation. The supported translations between code pages (at the workstation) and the CCSIDs on the DRDA database are described in the *DDCS User's Guide for DB2 common servers*

Examples of how to insert rows in the SYSTEM.SYSSTRINGS catalog can be found in the ARITPOP MACRO (part of SQL/DS) as shown in Figure 254 on page 513. You may have to use a hexadecimal editor to do the required editing work. Before you run the job, verify whether you want to execute the DELETE statements provided in the ARITPOP MACRO. Issue a COMMIT statement after you have made the updates.

```
CONNECT SQLDBA IDENTIFIED BY SQLDBAPW;
SET ERRORMODE CONTINUE;

INSERT INTO SYSTEM.SYSSTRINGS VALUES(37,280,'SS', NULL,NULL,' ',
'                              ü ä
                     ,
' βä{       .<(+ &! ë} Oe.ï |$*); -/  Ü  ñ Ñ ,%_>?  oe.      :  ''=''
fghi«»‰    jklmnopqr- Æ  stuvwxyzi ·‡Ù—#  @       ⌐ " † ABCDEFGHI
   JKLMNOPQR    ÿ  STUVWXYZ·ÔÄ ÓÕ0123456789 ÛÜÛ ');

INSERT INTO SYSTEM.SYSSTRINGS VALUES(37,500,'SS', NULL,NULL,' ',
'                          |  ü┼ä
                     ,
' β         .<(+ &⌐êë îÖï ß|$*); -  Ü   ñ   %_>? É oe.      :#@''=''
fghi«»     jklmnopqr- ŸÆ stuvwxyz   ‡Ù¬              {ABCDEFGHI
  }JKLMNOPQR    úÿ\ STUVWXYZ·ÔÄòÔ 0123456789 Û Ù ');

INSERT INTO SYSTEM.SYSSTRINGS VALUES(280,37,'SS', NULL,NULL,' ',
'                          |  ü┼ä
                     ,
' β {á  \  <(+  êë}îÖïß⌐$*); -/  Ü        ,%_>? ö            '=''
fghi  »    klmnopqr–Œ    stuvwxyzi  ‡Ù            ¬| "   ABCDEFGHI
   JKLMNOPQR    úÿ  STUVWXYZ·ÔÄòÔ 0123456789 ÛÜÛ ');

INSERT INTO SYSTEM.SYSCCSIDS VALUES(37,   'S',0,0,'ENGLISH');
INSERT INTO SYSTEM.SYSCCSIDS VALUES(280,  'S',0,0,'ITALIAN');
INSERT INTO SYSTEM.SYSCCSIDS VALUES(500,  'S',0,0,'INTERNATIONAL');
INSERT INTO SYSTEM.SYSCCSIDS VALUES(56789,'S',0,0,'TEST1');

UPDATE ALL STATISTICS FOR TABLE SYSTEM.SYSCCSIDS;
UPDATE ALL STATISTICS FOR TABLE SYSTEM.SYSSTRINGS;
COMMIT WORK;
```

Figure 254. INSERT Statements for SYSSTRINGS As Found in ARITPOP MACRO

7. Update the CCSID in the related CMS files.

Finally you must use the CCSID option of the ARISDBMA EXEC to load the CMS file that enables the use of the new character set (see Figure 255 on page 514).

```
ARISDBMA DB(xxxxxxxx) COMPONENT (CCSID)


Legend: xxxxxxx is the related database name
```

Figure 255. ARISDBMA EXEC to Load the CMS File

The information in SYSTEM.SYSCHARSETS, SYSTEM.SYSCCSIDS, and SYSTEM.SYSSTRINGS is copied into three CMS files, ARISSCR, ARISCCS, and ARISSTR, with the file type FLATFILE. Rename the CMS files with file type MACRO to any new file type.

After this, you rename the CMS files ARISSCR, ARISCCS, and ARISSTR with filetype FLATFILE and give them the new filetype MACRO. This procedure replaces the old ARISSCR, ARISCCS, ARISSTR files with the new created ones.

You have completed the definition of your new character set.

17.4 Code Page Considerations for DB2 common server

A code page maps each character from a character set to a numeric representation. The code page is identified by a number. The code page (and the country code) can be set in the database configuration file.

In DB2 common server it is not possible to define additional code pages or country codes. Almost all code pages used on workstations are already supported by DB2.

All SBCS conversion tables are carried internally and are not subject to change.

Character conversion occurs when you have different code pages and may occur when:

- A client has a code page that is different from the code page of the database.

  In UNIX-based environments the active code page is retrieved from the local environment variables. In OS/2 the active code page is retrieved from the CONFIG.SYS file. Use CHCP to check or change your current active code page. In DOS the active code page is retrieved from the CONFIG.SYS COUNTRY command. Use CHCP to check or change your current active code page. In Windows the active code page is either set by the DB2CODEPAGE environment variable or retrieved from the country ID in the WIN.INI file.

  Most of this conversion is done at the server. When the server is acting as a DDCS gateway to a DRDA AS, the conversion is done at the DRDA AS.

- An application has a code page that is different from the code page of the database.

  During precompile and bind you can define the code page that the application program uses. If you do not specify the code page during precompile and bind, the actual code page of your system is used. This may lead to unwanted conversions. We recommend that you specify the code page during precompile and bind.

- Data is imported with a code page that is different from the database code page.

  Most of this conversion is done at the client before the server is accessed, which might force a further conversion.

  Usually it is assumed that the exporting and importing applications use the same code page. An exception is the use of the PC/IXF format where the code page is part of the exported data and as such allows a code page conversion (when the FORCEIN option is not specified).

- Data is retrieved from a DRDA server. In this case the data is converted at the DDCS server.

Note that file names and BIT data like BLOB data are not converted.

Date and time formats are related to the country code of the application. During precompile and bind, you can override (define) this default.

Remote procedures must use the same code page as the accessed database. To ensure this, define the code page option during precompile and bind. Use CHCP to check your current active code page.

Avoid different code pages between bind and execution time. This can result in unpredictable results.

17.4.1 Programming Considerations

We strongly recommend that you precompile, bind, compile, and execute applications using the same code page. Conversions may be done during bind and execution, and different code pages would lead to errors. Any data obtained by an application is assumed to be in the code page of the application. This applies for file and user input.

The coding of SQL statements is not language dependent, so the statements can be coded in lowercase, uppercase, or mixed case.

This also applies to database objects. They must, however, belong to the extended character set supported by your code page.

Constants in static SQL statements are converted at bind time from the application code page to the database code page and are used at execution time. Use host variables that define these constants to avoid such conversions.

File names are not converted.

17.4.2 Coding Stored Procedures

You must ensure that data in the stored procedure have the same code page as in the database.

If the code page of the invoking program and the code page of the stored procedure are different, the data passed between the stored procedure and the invoking program must be character data.

Numeric data or data structures cannot be communicated when the client application has a different code page from the code page of the server. All data in the SQLDA is converted like character data if the client and server code pages differ. The only way to pass data is to define it as binary string data (use data type BLOB or define the character data as FOR BIT DATA).

The stored procedure must use the same code page as the database.

If the result of stored procedure processing is a character string, it is converted from the database code page to the application code page. Again, bit strings are not converted.

17.4.3 Terms Used

- *Code set* relates to the DB2 code page. It is a set of hexadecimal assignments (code points) for the characters in a character set. It can be defined in the database configuration file.

- *Code page* is like code set, but it is IBM defined and mapped from the operating system code set. It can be defined in the database configuration file.

- *Country code* is used by the database manager to provide country-specific support (date, time, or decimal point). It can be defined in the database configuration file.

- *Territory code* is used to define country parameter values. It can be defined in the database configuration file.

Appendix A. SNA Definitions and Connectivity Parameters

In this appendix we present some SNA definitions and explain their relationship to the DRDA connectivity parameters.

A.1 SNA Definitions

In this section we review some SNA concepts and definitions.

Physical unit (PU)

A physical unit (PU) is part of a device that performs control functions for the device. It takes action during device activation and deactivation, error recovery, and testing.

Logical unit (LU)

A logical unit (LU) is a user of the SNA network. It is the source of requests entering the network. An application running in the host, DB2 for MVS/ESA, for example, is considered an LU.

System services control point (SCCP)

The SSCP performs tasks such as starting and stopping resources, assisting in the establishment of a connection between LUs, and reacting to network problems.

Network Control Program (ACF/NCP)

The ACF/NCP is a product installed on the S/390* host to generate the Network Control Program load module, which is loaded from the host into a communication controller (3745, 3720, 3725, or 3705). The NCP controls the lines and the devices attached to it. It transfers data to and from the device and handles any errors that occur.

Network addressable unit (NAU)

NAUs are elements in the network that ACF/VTAM can address, such as an LU, PU, and SSCP.

Node

In SNA terms, a node is a physical device, such as a host processor, communication controller, terminal, or printer. In VTAM terms, a node is any point in a network defined by a symbolic name. There are major nodes and minor nodes.

Subarea addressing

A subarea is a portion of the network that has a boundary node and includes any peripheral nodes attached to the subarea node. SSCPs and NCPs are subarea nodes.

Domain

Domain is that part of a network that has been activated by one particular SSCP. There is only one SSCP in a domain.

Cross-domain resource manager (CDRM)

CDRM is a definition in VTAM of the SSCP in the other domains. A CDRM definition is necessary for cross-domain communication.

Cross-domain resource (CDRS)

CDRS is the definition in VTAM of a resource that resides outside the VTAM domain.

Session

A session is a logical connection between two NAUs.

Logon mode (LOGMODE)

The LOGMODE is used to determine the characteristics of a session. It includes class of service (COS), pacing, RU size, and protocol information.

Logon mode table (MODETAB)

The MODETAB is a table that contains the LOGMODE entries. There can be multiple MODETABs in an SSCP.

Request unit size (RU)

An RU is the part of a transmission flowing across the network that contains data for the use of the destination network node. The node can be an LU, PU, or SSCP. This parameter specifies the maximum length of data one LU can send to its session partner. It is specified in the LOGMODE definition.

For more information about SNA concepts and definitions, consult the relevant VTAM and NCP publications.

A.2 DRDA Connectivity Parameters

In this section we describe the most important SNA and DRDA parameters used to implement a DRDA network.

A.2.1 SNA Parameters

These parameters are used to establish the physical and logical connections in the SNA network.

Token-ring address

This address is used to identify a system in the token-ring network. In a client/server environment, the client or requester has to know how to get to the server, and the server has to know how to send the answer back to the client. This requires that all systems are defined by unique network addresses in the LAN.

Network node server address

This is the address of the token-ring card where the network connects to the host, for instance, the address for your IBM 3745 control unit.

IDBLK

This parameter is used by VTAM/NCP to identify the machine in a switched network. The value differs according to the type of equipment. For example, an OS/2 system is defined with the value 05D; an AIX system, as 071; and an AS/400 system, as 056.

IDNUM

This parameter is used by VTAM/NCP to identify the machine or a PU in a network.

MAXDATA/MAXBFRU

This parameter specifies the maximum message size that one system can send to another system. It affects the performance and system requirements of all participants in a conversation: the sender, the receiver, and other network components in between.

Network name

This parameter identifies the name of the network. The same physical network can provide connectivity for several logical networks. All nodes of a logical network have the same network name.

Control point

An SNA CP is an LU that is used to control all sessions between the different partners. On MVS and VM, we use the SSCP. The first qualifier of the control point name is the network name.

Logical unit name (LU)

An LU is a user of the SNA network. There are multiple types of LUs, and they can share the same SNA network. Each type represents a protocol that is used between different devices or programs. The most important LU type used in a DRDA network is the LU type 6.2 (LU 6.2).

The LU name consists of two qualifiers, each made up of a maximum of eight characters. The first qualifier is the network name and the second qualifier is the LU name itself.

Partner LU name

The partner LU is the remote logical unit in your network with which you want to communicate.

Local LU name

The local LU is the logical unit in your workstation that gives your transaction programs access to the network.

Mode name

The mode name is used to define commonly grouped transmission characteristics. It is important that the same mode name be defined and used in the DRDA server and DRDA requester. To establish a session the mode names must match at both ends. The commonly used name in a DRDA environment is IBMRDB. The mode entry is composed of multiple parameters used during the session negotiation. Parameter values are negotiated by the partners.

CPIC side information

In SNA, the profile that specifies the conversation characteristics to use when allocating a conversation with a remote transaction program. The profile is used by local transaction programs that communicate through CPI Communications. It specifies the partner LU name (the name of the connection profile that contains the remote LU name), the mode name, and the remote transaction program name.

Transaction program name (TPN)

A TPN is a program that uses APPC to communicate with a partner application program in the same node or at the partner node. It provides the necessary code to process the DRDA request on the target application server.

There are two basic TPNs:

- User transaction programs using APPC

- Service transaction programs providing service to other application programs

A.2.1.1 Connecting to VTAM

In the traditional networking environment, most resources are predefined in VTAM on the host system. All resources in the network are controlled by the host system. Over the years VTAM has added more and more dynamic definition capabilities, and today VTAM provides APPN capabilities.

Physical Unit (PU): There still must be definitions in the network that identify each workstation. This identification is called a physical unit (PU) and has to be defined in VTAM. Like any traditional definitions, it is a set of parameters identifying the resource and its characteristics. See the sample definition in Figure 256 on page 521.

```
SAMPLE PU DEFINITION FOR A SWITCHED MAJOR NODE (TRN)

CM2    PU    ADDR=10,
             IDBLK=05D,
             IDNUM=02130,
             CPNAME=SILVIO,
             DISCNT=NO,
             DYNLU=YES,
             IRETRY=YES,
             ISTATUS=ACTIVE,
             MAXDATA=1033,
             MAXOUT=7,
             MAXPATH=4,
             PACING=0,
             PUTYPE=2,
             MODETAB=IBMRDB,
             DLOGMOD=M2SDLCQ,
             USSTAB=US327X,
             VPACING=0
```

Figure 256. Example of a Real PU Definition in VTAM

The CP and PU are two different resources. When you start communications, your workstation sends an XID identifying it to the host. The XID is composed of the IDBLK and IDNUM parameters and the workstation's CPNAME. For CM/2 the CPNAME sent is the value you specify in the local node name field. If both nodes (host and CM/2) are APPN nodes and support CP-to-CP sessions, a CP-to-CP session is established through an LU 6.2 session.

In addition to the CP-to-CP session, CM/2 can also request an SSCP-to-PU session. The PU name is assigned by the host by matching a switched major node definition to either the IDBLK/IDNUM value or the CPNAME value in the XID sent by the workstation. Whether the host uses the IDBLK/IDNUM or CPNAME to match the definition is a VTAM option. The PU becomes an adjacent link station for the workstation's CP.

There is nothing to prevent you from having the same CPNAME and PU name. However, the VTAM documentation strongly discourages this because VTAM logic will cause some searches to fail if this is true.

Logical Unit (LU):   The next resource we need for our connection is the LU. The LU is a piece of code that acts as an interface between the application and the network. The LU ensures that requests from the application are transformed to something that can be understood by the partner at the other end. The LU type for DRDA connections is LU 6.2 used for program-to-program communication. For DRDA communication, we use independent LUs. An independent LU can issue a BIND to communicate with a destination LU by itself and does not have the services of the SSCP. The LU does not have to be defined in the VTAM definitions if you are using the *dynamic definition of independent LU* capability of VTAM; a dynamic independent LU definition will be added automatically to VTAM. With the recent versions of VTAM you can predefine this LU as a cross-domain resource (CDRSC) by using a PU macro.

A.2.2 RDB_Name Parameter

The RDB_NAME is a unique identifier for a database in your local database management system. The RDB_NAME is used to route SQL statements to the right destination. If the RDB_NAME points to a remote database system, you must associate this RDB_NAME with communication information to route the requests to the appropriate destination in the network.

- For a DB2 for MVS/ESA system, the RDB_Name is the location name. The DB2 location name is stored in the DB2 boot strap data set (BSDS).

- For SQL/DS, the RDB_Name is the database name defined during installation.

- For DB2/400, the RDB_Name is the relational database name that has the keyword *LOCAL for the remote location attribute.

- For DB2 common server, the RDB_Name is the database alias name in the database directory.

A.2.3 Cross-Reference

Table 53 on page 523, Table 54 on page 524, and Table 55 on page 524 show the host terminology for the SNA and DRDA connectivity parameters. We suggest that you use this terminology when you contact the person responsible for a given platform.

Table 53. *SNA Connectivity Parameters Cross-Reference*

Parameter	MVS	VM / VSE	OS/400	AIX	OS/2
TR Address	LOCADD (NCP)	LOCADD (NCP)	ADPTADR (local adapter address on line description)	Network Adapter Address	Network Adapter Address
IDBLK	IDBLK	IDBLK	part of EXCHID on line description	XID node ID	Node ID (hex)
IDNUM	IDNUM	IDNUM	part of EXCHID on line description	XID node ID	Node ID (hex)
MAXDATA	MAXDATA on NCP PCCU Macro	MAXDATA on NCP PCCU Macro	MAXFRAME on line description		Transmit Buffer Size
Partner TR Address	DIALNO	DIALNO	ADPTADR (LAN remote adapter address on controller description)	Remote Link Address	LAN Destination Address
Network Name	NETID	NETID	LCLNETID (use DSPNETA command)	Network Name	Network ID
Control Point Name	SSCPNAME	SSCPNAME	LCLCPNAME (use DSPNETA command)	Control Point Name	Local Node Name
Logical Unit Name	• VTAM APPL • DB2 BSDS	VTAM APPL	• LCLLOCNAME-default in Network Attributes • QAPPNLCL (if alias, use WRKCFGL command)	Local LU Name	Local LU Name
Partner LU Name	Communication database	COMDIR file	RMTLOCNAME (device description or configuration list)	Remote LU Name	Partner LU
Modename	• MODEENT • Communication database	• MODEENT • COMDIR file	Mode Description (MODE parameter on the ADDRDBDIRE command)	MODENAME	Transmit Service Mode
RUSIZE	RUSIZES	RUSIZES	MAXLENRU parameter on the CRTMODD command	Maximum RU Size	Maximum RU Size
PACING	• VTAM APPL VPACING • Nonzero SSNDPAC on VTAM MODEENT	• VTAM APPL VPACING • Nonzero SSNDPAC on VTAM MODEENT	INPACING parameter on the CRTMODD command	Receive Send Pacing	Receive Send Pacing
SNA Session-Level Security	VTAM APPL Verify	VTAM APPL Verify	• LOCPWD parameter on the CRTDEVAPPC command • Location password in configuration list QAPPNRMT	Session security supported in partner LU	LU-to-LU Security
AR can send SNA Security=SAME	• VTAM APPL=ALREADYV • USERSECURITY in SYSLUNAMES	VTAM	• SECURELOC(*YES) on the CRTDEVAPPC command or • *YES in column Secure Loc in configuration list	Conv. security level in partner LU	Conv. security level in partner LU

Table 54. DRDA AR Connectivity Parameters Cross-Reference

Parameter	MVS	VM	DB2/400	AIX	OS/2
Partner's RDB_NAME	Location Name in SYSLOCATIONS	COMDIR	RDB parameter on the ADDRDBDIRE command	Target database in DCS Directory	Target database in DCS Directory
TPN Local	'07',6DB	RESID / DBDIR	'07',6DB (defaults to special value *DRDA)	User TPN	User TPN
TPN Remote	LINKATTR column in SYSLOCATIONS	COMDIR	TNSPGM on ADDRDBDIRE, defaults to *DRDA	Side Info Profile	CPI-C Side Info Profile
USERID for requests sent to AS	RACF, or PASSWORD column in SYSUSERNAMES	COMDIR	User Profile or CONNECT statement	From CONNECT statement, or login, or instance-id	UPM logon or CONNECT statement

Note: VSE is not an application requester.

Table 55. DRDA AS Connectivity Parameters Cross-Reference

Parameter	MVS	VM / VSE	DB2/400	AIX	OS/2
Local RDB_NAME	Location Name in BSDS	RESID / DBDIR	RDB parameter on the ADDRDBDIRE command *LOCAL for remote location on the ADDRDBDIRE command	Alias in System Database Directory	Alias in System Database Directory

Appendix B. Problem Determination for DB2 common server

In this chapter we explain how you can tackle problems with DB2 or DDCS common server by using the facilities provided by the underlying operating environment, the products themselves, and additional products.

B.1 Addressing a Problem

In general, there are three ways in which you can address a problem:

- Develop a checklist that is common-sense driven
- Rely on what the system may have automatically logged
- Try to reproduce the problem (tracing)

The approach you choose will depend on what the problem is (at least what you know about it at the very beginning), how the system is configured, and your personal experiences and attitudes. A number of tools are available to assist you. For example, if you want to trace a connectivity problem, you can use the facilities provided by the network product and/or the DBMS (db2trc/db2drdat/ddcstrc).

Needless to say, always check SQLCODE (or SQLSTATE) after SQL processing, writing down its value (together with other helpful information).

B.2 Problem Type

In DB2 and DDCS common server, errors are mapped to messages in one of the following five categories:

- CLInnnnn: CLI messages
- DBAnnnnn: Database director and DBA utility messages
- DBInnnnn: Installation and configuration messages
- DB2nnnnn: CLP messages
- SQLnnnnn: SQL processing messages

To have an immediate understanding of an error, use the help information, which is available from the operating system command line prompt. For example, to obtain the text corresponding to message SQL30081, type

```
db2 ? SQL30081
```

If you have a graphical screen, you can navigate through the online documentation (just type *db2help* at a command line prompt).

B.3 Checklist

Checklists are helpful as a first attempt at problem determination. Through your experience with the DB2 common server products, you will acquire expertise that will enable you to complete and/or tune the checklists to your particular environment. This could prove sufficient in many situations, at least to fix problems whose causes are trivial or ordinary.

If, for example, you get a communication error from a DOS client trying to access a DB2 for AIX database, you first have to check if everything is OK with the network. If the connection is TCP/IP, from a DOS command prompt window you would probably issue a command similar to one of the following:

```
ping cayman
ping 9.113.36.198
```

assuming cayman and 9.113.36.198 are, respectively, the TCP/IP host name and address of the machine in which the DB2 server is running.

If everything is OK, you receive messages like these (to stop the sequence, press CTRL-C):

```
PING cayman.sanjose.ibm.com: 56 data bytes
64 bytes from 9.113.36.198: icmp_seq=0. time=0. ms
64 bytes from 9.113.36.198: icmp_seq=1. time=0. ms
64 bytes from 9.113.36.198: icmp_seq=2. time=0. ms

----cayman.sanjose.ibm.com PING Statistics----
3 packets transmitted, 3 packets received, 0% packet loss
round-trip (ms)  min/avg/max = 0/0/0
```

That check ensures you that you can reach the server machine over the network. Then, at the server machine, you can ensure that the DB2 instance owner is actually running the two AIX processes needed to serve TCP/IP client requests. The processes are named db2tcpm and db2tcpim. You can use the AIX ps command to check that processes are running:

```
ps -ef | grep db2tcp
```

You should see a couple of lines like the following:

```
db2v2 15242 13436   0 13:31:49      - 0:00 db2tcpcm
db2v2 15500 13436   0 13:31:49      - 0:00 db2tcpim
```

In our example, db2v2 is the instance owner; 15242 and 15500 are the AIX process IDs (PIDs) of the two processes, which have a common originator process whose PID is 13436.

You can then proceed to check the crux of the configurations (such as the TCP/IP ports in /etc/services).

The *DB2 Problem Determination Guide for common servers* contains samples of checklists that you can use to build checklists tailored to your needs.

B.4 Information Automatically Kept by the System

Version 2 of DB2 common server has introduced new facilities that enable the system to automatically store error logs, alerts, and dump files.

B.4.1 First Failure Data Capture (FFDC)

The FFDC facilities provide DB2 error logging and operating system error logging.

B.4.1.1 DB2 Error Logging

The placement and amount of the information automatically tracked by DB2 are ruled by two parameters:

DIAGPATH   Represents the fully qualified path in which the information is stored. In OS/2, if not specified, the system defaults DIAGPATH to one of the following names (depending on whether the DB2INSTPROF environment variable is set):

- x:\DB2INSTPROF\DB2INSTANCE

- x:\SQLLIB\DB2INSTANCE (when DB2INSTPROF is not set)

DB2INSTANCE is the environment variable holding the instance owner name; DB2INSTPROF holds the instance owner profile directory, and x: is the drive referenced in the DB2PATH environment variable (which holds the paths to DB2 executables).

In AIX, if not specified, the system defaults DIAGPATH to

- $INSTHOME/sqllib/db2dump

where $INSTHOME is the AIX home directory of the instance owner.

DIAGLEVEL   Represents the level of severity of the phenomena that are trapped:

- DIAGLEVEL (0): no data captured

- DIAGLEVEL (1): severe errors captured

- DIAGLEVEL (2): severe and nonsevere errors captured

- DIAGLEVEL (3): severe, nonsevere, and warning messages captured (default)

- DIAGLEVEL (4): severe, nonsevere, warning, and information messages captured

You can alter the values of DIAGPATH and DIAGLEVEL by means of the database director or from the command line as in this example (for the AIX platform):

```
db2 "update database manager configuration using DIAGPATH /tmp/db2diag"
```

Information trapped by FFDC DB2 error logging is stored in different files in the DIAGPATH directory:

DB2DIAG.LOG   A file holding a number of error messages depending on the threshold level set by DIAGLEVEL

DB2ALERT.LOG   A file holding alerts, that is, severe errors identified by a DIAxxxxx code and the location in which they have been reported. Alerts have matching entries in DB2DIAG.LOG and are reported to FFDC operating system error logging.

#####.DMP   Dump files with diagnostic information. Each file contains information related to an occurrence of a severe error. Information is in binary format, not suited to DBA analysis.

#####.TRP   (Available in DB2 for OS/2 only). Files with diagnostic information. Each file contains information related to an occurrence of a severe error. Information is in binary format, not suited to DBA analysis.

The system does not provide any facility to prune or remove any of these files; that has to be accomplished manually.

B.4.1.2 Operating System Error Logging

In addition to its own FFDC facilities, DB2 can use those provided by the underlying operating system:

- OS/2: First Failure Support Technology (FFST/2)

- AIX: system logger facility (SYSLOG)

Refer to the appropriate documentation to enable DB2 to access the native operating system capabilities.

In addition, AIX offers the capability to automatically create a *core* file in case of abend. This file, created in the current AIX directory, contains an image of the memory control blocks of the process abnormally terminated. The file can be accessed by the dbx command.

B.4.2 Integration with Other Products

If you are operating in a network, chances are that some products for network management (such as the IBM NetView family of products) are in place. You can take advantage of these products because DB2 provides the necessary interfaces to them. Thus you can set up an automated and sophisticated infrastructure to control your distributed (and possibly heterogeneous) environment.

The goal of this infrastructure is to be able to notify a system administrator (whether database or network administrator) that certain DB2 errors or conditions have been detected as well as track DB2 activities on a timely basis.

B.4.2.1 Simple Network Management Protocol (SNMP) Traps

SNMP compliance is particularly important because SNMP is an emerging standard proposed by the Internet Engineering Task Force (IETF) to address management of RDBMSs in a multiplatform, multivendor environment.

DB2 common server provides the capability to link to an SNMP agent by means of the DB2 SNMP subagent component that comes with the product. What flows from the DB2 SNMP subagent to the SNMP agent is called a *trap*.

A rich amount of information can be sent to the SNMP agent, going beyond errors and problem determination. A primary example is the ability to send performance information taken as snapshots of the database manager.

Note that the DB2 SNMP subagent is part of DB2, so possible errors it may encounter can be logged in DB2DIAG.LOG.

B.4.2.2 SNA Alerts

SNA alerts offer functions similar to SNMP traps. However, they are available only on the OS/2 version of DB2 common server.

B.5 Tracing

If the techniques previously described are not sufficient to fix a problem, consider activating tracing facilities and re-creating the problem.

DB2 and DDCS provide the following trace tools:

- db2trc and db2drdat (DB2)
- ddcstrc (DDCS)

When using these tools we suggest that you

- Reproduce the error in a situation similar to the situation when the problem originated
- Keep the general system load, including other DB2/DDCS applications, at a low level to isolate the problem and not overload the system (tracing is quite resource consuming)

Note that the above suggestions conflict, so you have to find the proper balance between them. If, for example, you are investigating the reason for a locking problem in a multiuser environment, you will most probably not be able to trap (reproduce) the problem if you just keep a single-user working.

B.5.1 DB2 Independent Trace Facility (db2trc)

DB2 common server provides db2trc as a powerful and flexible tool to track DB2 internal activities while reproducing an error. To invoke the tracing facility enter:

```
db2trc
```

at an operating system command line prompt. The facility is parameter driven; basically it allows you to specify the activities that have to be traced, where the information gathered should be stored, and the size of the output of the tracing process.

To use the tracing facilities, invoke db2trc with one of the available options, the most important of which are

db2trc on   Starts tracing. A number of flags can be given here.

db2trc dump   Dumps the output from memory to a binary file.

db2trc fmt   Formats a binary file to a text file.

db2trc flw   Formats a binary file to a text file showing the internal flow.

db2trc off   Stops tracing.

Refer to the *DB2 Problem Determination Guide for common servers* for a complete picture of the db2trc options. For quick help type

```
db2trc -u
```

at an operating system command line prompt.

Let us look at an example of a trace in the case of a connection from a DRDA AR to the DRDA AS facility of DB2 for AIX server (the syntax of the command would be slightly different with DB2 for OS/2).

```
        DRDA AR                    DB2 Server

                          1 db2trc on -l 5000000 -p 24863 -m *.*.75.*
2 "reproduce error"
                          3 db2trc dump dump_bin_file
                          4 db2trc off
                          5 db2trc fmt  dump_bin_file txt_file
                          6 db2trc flw  dump_bin_file flw_file
```

For this example:

1 Trace is activated. Here three options are used:

- -l: specifies the size in bytes of the trace buffer
- -p: specifies the PID of the particular process to be traced
- -m: inputs a 4-byte mask (bytes separated by commas):
    - 1′ byte: product to trace
    - 2′ byte: event types to be traced (system_error, api_errcode, ...)
    - 3′ byte: components to be traced
    - 4′ byte: set of functions to trace

    The values for the mask bytes are listed in the *DB2 Problem Determination Guide for common servers*. In our example, an asterisk (*), meaning every possible value, is given to all bytes but the third; 75 in the third byte relates to the DRDA AS function, which was the only one of interest for us. To track other functions together with 75, provide a list of values separated by commas.

2 At the DRDA AR, the action causing the problem is performed (attempt to reproduce the problem).

3 The trace image is dumped from memory to a binary disk file. This is done after the problem has actually been detected.

4 Trace is deactivated.

5 The binary file is formatted to a text file.

6 The binary file is formatted to a text file, showing the chain of the internal calls.

Here is an excerpt of the final output, showing how the drda_as function detected an SQL -811 error for the application traced:

```
DB2 fnc_data      drda_as                sqljg_sqlcagrp_len (1.35.75.108)
pid 24863; tid 1; cpid 0; sec 0; nsec 0; tpoint 179
SQLCA

SQLCAID:  SQLCA
SQLCABC:  136
SQLCODE:  -811
SQLERRML: 0
SQLERRMC:
SQLERRP:  SQLRITFT
SQLERRD 0->5 : FFFF877E, 00000000, 00000000, 00000000, 00000000, 00000000
SQLWARN(0->A):  ,  ,  ,  ,  ,  ,  ,  ,  ,  ,
SQLSTATE: 21000
```

As it appears, the process is quite straightforward. Note the following:

- In our example, because we expected the problem to be in a particular area, we could select which events to trace. In this way the trace process extracts only the relevant information.

- Tracing is written to memory. If that is not practical, switch to the option that writes directly to a file, as in this example:

    db2trc on -f /tmp/trace -m *.*.75.*

Writing directly to a file slows down the tracing process but sometimes may be the only affordable approach, especially if there are memory constraints.

- If, during the trace, you cannot reproduce the problem, you have to go back and reconsider what could differentiate the actual environment from the environment where the problem occurred. Nevertheless, what you find in the trace could prove helpful for understanding what is going on in the system when the action is performed.

B.5.2 DRDA Trace Facility (db2drdat and ddcstrc)

DB2 and DDCS provide, respectively, db2drdat and ddcstrc to trace problems encountered along DRDA connections. db2drdat has been introduced in version 2 of DB2 common server products as a means to trace DRDA flows exchanged between these products and other DRDA-compliant products. It offers the same functions of ddcstrc, the tracing facility in previous releases of DDCS. From now on, for the sake of simplicity, we use db2drdat only, but what is stated for db2drdat is also valid for ddcstrc.

Invoke db2drdat by entering

    db2drdat

at an operating system command line prompt. db2drdat works much in the same way as db2trc, but it focuses only on DRDA communications and so does not account for many features of a full RDBMS as DB2. Consequently, there is not a rich set of functions from which to select (as is possible with the mask option provide by the db2trc trace facility).

Basically, db2drdat can trace

- Messages exchanged between the DRDA AS function of DB2 common server and remote DRDA ARs
- Messages exchanged between DDCS (DRDA AR function of DB2 common server) and remote DRDA ASs

Note also that, although DDCS implements the DRDA AR function only, if you have a DB2 common server engine installed on the DDCS machine, ddcstrc can account for any DRDA request coming from remote DRDA ARs and directed to the DRDA AS function of DB2 common server.

You have two options when invoking db2drdat:

db2drdat on   Starts tracing. A number of flags can be given here.

db2drdat off   Stops tracing.

Here is an example of a trace in the case of a connection from DDCS for AIX to a DRDA AS (the syntax of the command would be slightly different with DDCS for OS/2):

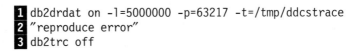

```
                   DDCS workstation

1  db2drdat on -l=5000000 -p=63217 -t=/tmp/ddcstrace
2  "reproduce error"
3  db2trc off
```

For this example:

1 Trace is activated. Here three options are used:

- -l: specifies the size in bytes of the trace buffer
- -p: specifies the PID of the particular process to be traced
- -t: specifies the trace output file

2 The action causing the problem is performed (attempt to reproduce the problem).

3 Trace is deactivated. This is done after the problem actually occurred.

Here is an extract of the final output, showing how the tracing function detects an SQL -204 (a nonexistent table name is specified in an SQL SELECT statement):

```
DB2 fnc_data      drda_as              sqljg_sqlcagrp_len (1.35.75.108)
pid 63217; tid 1; cpid 0; sec 0; nsec 0; tpoint 179
SQLCA

SQLCAID:  SQLCA
SQLCABC:  136
SQLCODE:  -204
SQLERRML: 16
SQLERRMC: DRDAX5.LOCATIONS
SQLERRP:  SQLNQ1FB
SQLERRD 0->5 : FFFF877E, 00000000, 00000000, 00000000, 00000000, 0000000A
SQLWARN(0->A):  ,  ,  ,  ,  ,  ,  ,  ,  ,  ,
SQLSTATE: 42704
```

For a complete picture of db2drdat capabilities, refer to the *DDCS User's Guide for common servers.*

For summary help, type

    db2drdat

at an operating system command line prompt.

B.5.3 SNA Trace

To trace problems in a connectivity scenario, it is often useful to use the mechanisms provided by the network software products. For DRDA connections involving DB2 common server products, use CM/2 (for DB2 and DDCS for OS/2) and SNA Server (for DB2 and DDCS for AIX). Our example refers to the AIX workstation located in San Jose connecting to the DB2 for MVS in Poughkeepsie.

B.5.3.1 Testing SNA Connection

To test the connectivity from the AIX workstation to the MVS platform from a pure SNA point of view, you must determine whether it is possible to establish an SNA session between the two LU 6.2s.

To do this, the *root* user has to perform the following tasks (which we report in the form of AIX commands, but SMIT offers equivalent functions):

- Start sna:

      sna -s

- Start the link station:

      sna -s l -p trlink **1**

- Start the session:

      sna -s s -ln SC02131I -pn USIBMSC.SCLUDB41 -m IBMRDB **2**

where

- **1** trlink is the link station used by DDCS for AIX.

- **2** SC02131I is the name of the LU 6.2 used by DDCS for AIX, and USIBMSC.SCLUDB41 is the fully qualified name (netid.luname) of the LU 6.2 used by DB2 for MVS/ESA.

If the connection has been successfully established, a message like the following is displayed:

```
Session started: Session ID = D1A3528A352C8D5F, Conversation group ID = 31
```

Note that in normal operations it is not necessary to explicitly start an SNA session in the way we have indicated. Once the link station is started, the system will automatically start a session when SQL CONNECT statements are issued to the DRDA AS.

B.5.3.2 Tracing SNA Connection

Whether or not an LU-to-LU connection has been successfully established, you may be interested in tracing the SNA flow exchanged over the network. SNA Server/6000 offers several tracing facilities to address the different aspects of the communications, such as SNA API and CPIC.

To configure SNA log files, use the following SMIT screens:

1. Communications Applications and Services

2. SNA Server/6000

3. Problem Determination Aids

4. Configure SNA Log and Trace Files

Figure 257 on page 536 shows the SMIT panel that displays. As you can see there are two service log files, which we describe below.

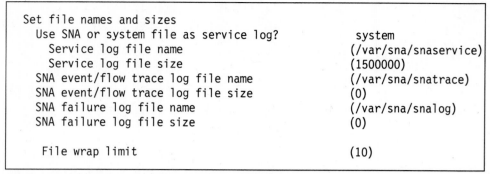

```
Set file names and sizes
   Use SNA or system file as service log?        system
     Service log file name                      (/var/sna/snaservice)
     Service log file size                       (1500000)
   SNA event/flow trace log file name            (/var/sna/snatrace)
   SNA event/flow trace log file size            (0)
   SNA failure log file name                     (/var/sna/snalog)
   SNA failure log file size                     (0)

   File wrap limit                                (10)
```

Figure 257. SNA Log and Trace File Configuration

SNA SNA Server/6000 data goes to a separate file. This option uses a generic trace channel obtained from the BOS. By default, this file includes all SNA Server/6000 data. You can also redirect SNA Server/6000 internal trace data and failure data to separate files. Choose this option if you have to use the BOS trace command for other application needs while SNA is running.

system SNA Server/6000 data goes to the AIX system event trace file. That file receives all trace channel zero data. If the system event trace daemon is not running, one is started. Choose this option to enable any SNA API tracing (command, generic, or CPIC) or to mix SNA trace data with trace data from other applications.

Assuming system file is the choice for the service log, here we show how the *root* user can invoke SNA tracing facilities from an AIX command prompt (the same is possible through the SMIT interface):

• Start SNA trace:

    `sna -trace only -l trlink -a on` **1**

• At this time, the error has to be reproduced (not necessarily by *root*). In our case, it is an SQL CONNECT statement issued while the DDF address space in DB2 for MVS/ESA is stopped.

• Stop SNA trace:

    `sna -trace off`

• Format sna trace:

    `trcrpt /var/sna/snaservice.x > /tmp/sna_trace` **2**

where

• **1** trlink is the link station used by DDCS.

- **2** /var/sna/snaservice.x is the name of the SNA trace file initialized at trace activation. trcrpt formats the trace file (in our example, redirects its output to a disk file).

Here is an excerpt from the formatted trace file:

```
Mon Oct 23 17:19:55 1995
System: AIX cayman Node: 4
Machine: 000060234200
Internet Address: 097124C6 9.113.36.198

Version: 2 Release: 2 Mod: 0 Fix: 0

/usr/bin/trace -a -j 27A,27B,271,325 -o /var/sna/snaservice.3 -L 1500000 -T 131072 -m Version: 2 Release: 2 Mod: 0 Fix: 0


ID     ELAPSED_SEC    DELTA_MSEC   APPL   SYSCALL KERNEL  INTERRUPT

                                    ...
                                    ...
                                    ...

271   18.496938496*                       AIXSNA  Ioctl SNA Resource Name: db41  1
271   18.496958464   0.019968             AIXSNA  Ioctl Exit - Reserved for CPI-C: 78   OK      <---
                                                  PID = 25248      CID = A2A6800
271   18.497010048   0.051584             AIXSNA  Ioctl Entry - CPI-C Allocate    <+++
                                                  PID = 25248      CID = A2A6800
271   18.497010048*                       AIXSNA  Ioctl SNA Resource Name: db41
271   18.497010048*                       AIXSNA  Allocate - input parameters:
                                                  type          = DEF_CONV
                                                  return_control = WHEN_SESSION_ALLOCATED
                                                  cgid          = 0
                                                  sess_type     = LU_LU
                                                  sync_level    = DEFAULT
                                                  rid           = 0000
271   18.497010048*                       AIXSNA  remote TP name =
271   18.497010048*                       AIXSNA  mode name      =
271   18.508829184   11.819136            AIXSNA  Mpx Entry       <+++
                                                  PGRP        = 33894
                                                  PID         = 33894
                                                  Device Num = 230000
271   18.508829184*                       AIXSNA  Mpx Channel Name: CNOSSourceTP
271   18.508849920   0.020736             AIXSNA  Mpx Request = Allocate new channel ID (CID)
271   18.508984832   0.134912             AIXSNA  Mpx Exit  OK      <---
                                                  PID = 33894      CID = A2A6400
271   18.509226752   0.241920             AIXSNA  Open Entry      <+++
                                                  PID = 33894      CID = A2A6400
271   18.509226752*                       AIXSNA  Open  SNA Resource Name: CNOSSourceTP
271   18.513006976   3.780224             AIXSNA  Open Exit  OK       <---
                                                  PID = 33894      CID = A2A6400
271   18.513112576   0.105600             AIXSNA  Ioctl Entry - Reserved for SSAPI: 111      <+++
                                                  PID = 33894      CID = A2A6400
271   18.513112576*                       AIXSNA  Ioctl SNA Resource Name: CNOSSourceTP
271   18.513152512   0.039936             AIXSNA  Ioctl Exit - Reserved for SSAPI: 111   OK       <---
                                                  PID = 33894      CID = A2A6400
271   18.513200384   0.047872             AIXSNA  Ioctl Entry - Set_Partner_LU_Name    <+++
                                                  PID = 33894      CID = A2A6400
271   18.513200384*                       AIXSNA  Ioctl SNA Resource Name: CNOSSourceTP
271   18.513200384*                       AIXSNA  Set_Partner_LU_Name - input parameters: USIBMSC.SCLUDB41  2
271   18.513254656   0.054272             AIXSNA  Ioctl Exit - Set_Partner_LU_Name   OK      <---
                                                  PID = 33894      CID = A2A6400
271   18.513300352   0.045696             AIXSNA  Ioctl Entry - Reserved for CNOS: 79    <+++
```

```
                                                        PID = 33894      CID = A2A6400
271    18.513300352*                            AIXSNA Ioctl SNA Resource Name: CNOSSourceTP
271    18.513323392      0.023040               AIXSNA Ioctl Exit - Reserved for CNOS: 79    OK         <---
                                                        PID = 33894      CID = A2A6400
271    18.513374208      0.050816               AIXSNA Ioctl Entry - Allocate       <+++
                                                        PID = 33894      CID = A2A6400
271    18.513374208*                            AIXSNA Ioctl SNA Resource Name: CNOSSourceTP
271    18.513374208*                            AIXSNA Allocate - input parameters:
                                                        type            = BASIC_CONV
                                                        return_control  = WHEN_SESSION_ALLOCATED
                                                        cgid            = 0
                                                        sess_type       = LU_LU
                                                        sync_level      = SYNC_NONE
                                                        rid             = 0000
271    18.513374208*                            AIXSNA  remote TP name  = 1
271    18.513374208*                            AIXSNA  mode name       = SNASVCMG   ▣3
27B    19.118749440      605.375232   Mon Oct 23 17:20:15 1995
                               --->Informational:
                                        Component: SNALNS  - LU Services
                                        file: xxxsmp72.c line: 143
                                        Origin:  Type: DF
                                        UNBIND_RQ received from partner LU. Type = f
                                        Sense code: 08570003   ▣4
                                        Local LU: USIBMSC.SCO2131I, Partner LU: USIBMSC.SCLUDB41. Mode: SNASVCMG
                                        CGID: 00000000
                                        Link Station: trlink
                                        ODAI = 1, OAF = X'02', DAF = X'01'
                                        Session ID: 01a3528a352cd032
27B    19.125782144      7.032704     Mon Oct 23 17:20:15 1995
                               ***>Failure: Resource error
                                        Failure ID: 0105-1137 Session deactivated and conversation terminated
                                        Component: SNAMDD  - Managing Device Driver
                                        file: lu6gsbid.c line: 448
                                        Message code: 112
271    19.127853184      2.071040               AIXSNA Ioctl Exit - Allocate    Failure, errno = 112      <---    ▣5
                                                        PID = 33894      CID = A2A6400
27B    19.128001408      0.148224     Mon Oct 23 17:20:15 1995
                               ***>Failure: System error
                                        Failure ID: 0105-1186 Severe failure in process CNOS request
                                        Component: SNACNOS - Change Number of Sessions
                                        file: cnosdmon.c line: 1698
                                        Errno: 112
                                        APPC: Allocate failed
271    19.128418176      0.416768               AIXSNA Close Entry       <+++
                                                        PID = 33894      CID = A2A6400
271    19.128418176*                            AIXSNA Close SNA Resource Name: CNOSSourceTP
271    19.128447744      0.029568               AIXSNA Close Exit  OK      <---
                                                        PID = 33894      CID = A2A6400
271    19.128489344      0.041600               AIXSNA Mpx Entry       <+++
                                                        PGRP          = 33894
                                                        PID           = 33894
                                                        Device Num = 230000
271    19.128489344*                            AIXSNA Mpx Channel Name:
271    19.128496768      0.007424               AIXSNA Mpx Request = Deallocate channel ID (CID)
271    19.128630016      0.133248               AIXSNA Mpx Exit  OK      <---
                                                        PID = 33894      CID = A2A6400
27B    19.131171200      2.541184     Mon Oct 23 17:20:15 1995
                               ***>Failure: TP error
                                        Component: SNACR   - Command Router
                                        file: xxxcrcnos.c line: 459
                                        Error/Message code: -113 (FFFFFF8F)
                                        Errno: 112
                                        mode - IBMRDB
```

```
                                        CNOS error encountered.
27B   19.133290240      2.119040    Mon Oct 23 17:20:15 1995
                                    ***>Failure: Software error
                                        Component: SNADD   - Presentation Services
                                        file: lu6gs62.c line: 2056
                                        Error/Message code: 0 (00000000)
                                        Errno: 112

27B   19.133380096      0.089856    Mon Oct 23 17:20:15 1995
                                    ***>Failure: Software error
                                        Component: SNADD   - Presentation Services
                                        file: lu6gs62.c line: 598
                                        Error/Message code: 0 (00000000)
                                        Errno: 112
                                        connection - db41
271   19.133565184      0.185088        AIXSNA Ioctl Exit - CPI-C Allocate   Failure, errno = 112      <---
                                            PID = 25248    CID = A2A6800
27B   19.154822400     21.257216    Mon Oct 23 17:20:15 1995
                                    --->Informational:
                                        Component: SNACR   - Command Router
                                        file: xxxcrec4.c line: 127
                                        Origin:  Type: 07
                                        Session Ending
                                        0105-2735 Session:DYNAMIC :trlink
                                        USIBMSC.SCO2131I/USIBMSC.SCLUDB41/SNASVCMG  has become inactive.
271   19.157225472      2.403072        AIXSNA Close Entry    <+++
                                            PID = 25248    CID = A2A6800
271   19.157225472*                     AIXSNA Close SNA Resource Name: db41
271   19.157256448      0.030976        AIXSNA Close Exit  OK      <---
                                            PID = 25248    CID = A2A6800
271   19.157301888      0.045440        AIXSNA Mpx Entry      <+++
                                            PGRP     = 25248
                                            PID      = 25248
                                            Device Num = 230000
271   19.157301888*                     AIXSNA Mpx Channel Name:
271   19.157308928      0.007040        AIXSNA Mpx Request = Deallocate channel ID (CID)
271   19.157447808      0.138880        AIXSNA Mpx Exit  OK      <---
                                            PID = 25248    CID = A2A6800
002   34.508521856  15351.074048        TRACE OFF channel 0
                                        Mon Oct 23 17:20:31 1995
```

For this example:

1 db41 is the symbolic destination name used when cataloging DB2 for MVS/ESA at the DDCS workstation (it matches an LU 6.2 Side Information Profile established in the SNA Server/6000 for DB2 for MVS/ESA.

2 USIBMSC.SCLUDB41 is the fully qualified LU 6.2 name of DB2 for MVS/ESA.

3 The AIXSNA mode name is SNASVCMG. It will change to IBMRDB if the connection is established.

4 08570003 is the VTAM sense code.

5 112 is the SNA API error code (it is reported in /usr/include/luxsna.h).

For comparison, here is the SNA trace when the connection is successfully established (DDF address space up):

```
Tue Oct 24 11:16:30 1995
System: AIX cayman Node: 4
Machine: 000060234200
Internet Address: 097124C6 9.113.36.198

Version: 2 Release: 2 Mod: 0 Fix: 0

/usr/bin/trace -a -j 27A,27B,271,325 -o /var/sna/snaservice.8 -L 1500000 -T 131072 -m Version: 2 Release: 2 Mod: 0 Fix: 0


ID    ELAPSED_SEC    DELTA_MSEC   APPL   SYSCALL KERNEL  INTERRUPT
                                   ...
                                   ...
                                   ...

271  19.337329920*                       AIXSNA Ioctl SNA Resource Name: db41
271  19.337350016    0.020096            AIXSNA Ioctl Exit - Reserved for CPI-C: 78   OK      <---
                                                PID = 27930    CID = A1DE800
271  19.337395840    0.045824            AIXSNA Ioctl Entry - CPI-C Allocate     <+++
                                                PID = 27930    CID = A1DE800
271  19.337395840*                       AIXSNA Ioctl SNA Resource Name: db41
271  19.337395840*                       AIXSNA Allocate - input parameters:
                                                type          = DEF_CONV
                                                return_control = WHEN_SESSION_ALLOCATED
                                                cgid          = 0
                                                sess_type     = LU_LU
                                                sync_level    = DEFAULT
                                                rid           = 0000
271  19.337395840*                       AIXSNA remote TP name =
271  19.337395840*                       AIXSNA mode name =
271  19.677909248    340.513408          AIXSNA Ioctl Exit - CPI-C Allocate   OK        <---  1
                                                PID = 27930    CID = A1DE800
271  19.677909248*                       AIXSNA Allocate - output parameters:
                                                rid = A1DEC00
271  19.677939968    0.030720            AIXSNA Allocate - session parameters:
                                                cgid     = 18
                                                session ID = F04B55CA 83F0A657
271  19.677939968*                       AIXSNA  local LU name   = USIBMSC.SC02131I
271  19.677939968*                       AIXSNA  partner LU name = USIBMSC.SCLUDB41
271  19.677939968*                       AIXSNA  mode name       = IBMRDB   2
                                   ...
                                   ...
                                   ...
                                        Tue Oct 24 11:17:09 1995
```

For this example:

1 The CPI-C allocation is successfully executed.

2 The AIXSNA mode name has been changed to IBMRDB.

Appendix C. Bibliography

The publications listed in this section are considered particularly suitable for a more detailed discussion of the topics covered in this document.

- *DB2 Administration Guide for common servers*, S20H-4580
- *An Implementation Guide for AS/400 Security and Auditing*, GG24-4200
- *DB2 API Reference for common servers*, S20H-4984
- *Application Development on AS/400*, GG24-3806
- *DB2 Application Programming Guide for common servers*, S20H-4643
- *AS/400 APPC Programmer's Guide*, SC41-8189
- *AS/400 Distributed Relational Database Guide*, SC41-0025
- *AS/400 ICF Programmer's Guide*, SC41-9590
- *AS/400 Integrated Language Environment: A Practical Approach*, GG24-4148
- *AS/400 SAA SQL/400 Programmer's Guide*, SC41-9609
- *AS/400 SAA SQL/400 Reference*, SC41-9608
- *AS/400: Security Reference*, SC41-8083
- *Backup and Recovery—Advanced*, SC41-3304
- *Character Data Representation Architecture Level 1 Registry*, SC09-1391
- *DB2 Call Level Interface Guide and Reference for common servers*, S20H-4644
- *CICS/VSE Intercommunication Guide*, SC33-0701
- *DB2 Command Reference for common servers*, S20H-4645
- *Common Cryptographic Architecture Services*, G321-5521
- *Connectivity Guide*, SC26-4783
- *DB2 for AIX Planning Guide*, S20H-4758
- *DB2 for AIX Installation and Operation Guide*, S20H-4757
- *DB2 for MVS Connections with AIX and OS/2*, SG24-4558
- *DB2 for MVS DRDA Server: Security Considerations*, GG24-2500
- *DB2 for MVS/ESA Administration Guide*, SC26-3265
- *DB2 for MVS/ESA Application Programming and SQL Guide*, SC26-3266
- *DB2 for MVS/ESA Command Reference*, SC26-3267

- *DB2 for MVS/ESA Installation Guide*, SC26-3456
- *DB2 for MVS/ESA SQL Reference*, SC26-3270
- *DB2 for OS/2 Installation and Operation Guide*, S20H-4785
- *DB2 for OS/2 Planning Guide*, S20H-4784
- *DB2/400 Advanced Database Functions*, GG24-4249
- *DB2/400 Query Manager and SQL Development Kit*, GC41-3058
- *DB2/400 Query Manager Use*, SC41-3212
- *DB2/400 SQL Programming Version 3*, SC41-3611
- *DB2/400 SQL Reference Version 3*, SC41-3612
- *DDCS for OS/2 Installation and Configuration Guide*, S20H-4795
- *DDCS User's Guide for common servers*, SH20-4793
- *DRDA Architecture Reference*, SC26-4651
- *DRDA Client/Server Application Scenarios for VM and VSE*, GG24-4193
- *DRDA Connectivity Guide*, SC26-4783
- *DRDA Problem Determination Guide*, SC26-4782
- *Formal Register of Extensions and Differences in SQL*, SC26-3316
- *IBM SQL Reference Version 2, Volume 1*, SC26-8416
- *Information and Concepts Guide for common servers*, S20H-4664
- *Integrated Language Environment Concepts*, SC09-1524
- *DB2 Problem Determination Guide for common servers*, S20H-4779
- *SAA SQL/400 Programmer's Guide*, SC41-9609
- *SAA SQL/400 Reference*, SC41-9608
- *Setup and Usage of SQL/DS in a DRDA Environment*, GG24-3733
- *SNA Formats*, GA27-3136
- *Software Developer's Kit/DOS Programming Guide*, SC09-1719
- *DB2 SQL Reference for common servers*, S20H-4665
- *SQL/DS Application Programming for IBM VM Systems*, SH09-8086
- *SQL/DS Database Administration for IBM VM Systems*, GH09-8083
- *SQL/DS Database Administration for VSE*, GH09-8095
- *SQL/DS Database Services Utility for IBM VM Systems*, SH09-8088

- *SQL/DS Installation for IBM VM Systems*, GH09-8078
- *SQL/DS Installation for VSE*, GH09-8090
- *SQL/DS Interactive SQL Guide and Reference for IBM VM Systems*, SH09-8085
- *SQL/DS Messages and Codes for IBM VM Systems*, SH09-8079:
- *SQL/DS Messages and Codes for VSE*, SH09-8091
- *SQL/DS Operation for IBM VM Systems*, SH09-8080
- *SQL/DS Operation for VSE*, SH09-8092
- *SQL/DS Performance Tuning Handbook for IBM VM Systems and VSE*, SH09-8111
- *SQL/DS Reference for IBM VM Systems and VSE*, SH09-8087
- *SQL/DS System Administration for IBM VM Systems*, GH09-8084
- *SQL/DS System Administration for VSE*, GH09-8096
- *SQL/400: A Guide for Implementation OS/400 Version 2 Release 2.0*, GG24-3321
- *VM Connectivity Planning, Administration, and Operation*, SC24-5448

A complete list of International Technical Support Organization publications, known as redbooks, with a brief description of each, may be found in

International Technical Support Organization Bibliography of Redbooks, GG24-3070.

Index

Special Characters

Numerics

A

APL   329
APPC
   ALLOCATE verb   182, 276
   APPCLLU environment variable   106
   applications   93
   APPN differences   59
   authentication process   145
   AVS   77, 266
   CFGNAME.NDF file   87
   CICS   277
   client   129, 201, 208
   COMDIR   259
   common DRDA network problems   233
   communications between Germany and the
      United States   69
   configuring APPC APIs through token
      ring   88
   configuring server workstation   208
   CONNECT statement   123
   controller description   219
   conversation   348
   CRTCTLAPPC   219
   database definitions and relation with SNA
      profiles   164
   DB2 for AIX as an AS   190
   DB2 for AIX AS security   198
   DB2 for AIX connectivity options   158
   DB2 for OS/400   218
   DB2COMM environment variable   136,
      202, 214
   DDCS for AIX—client security   196
   DDCS for OS/2 security   144
   device description   221
   DRDA   56, 116
   incoming request   130
   Intel-based servers and clients   15
   LEN   108
   LU6.2 side information profile   181
   mode description AS/400   223
   MVS conversations   35
   node directory   116, 143
   OS/2 connectivity option   82
   OS/2 gateway support   47
   partner LU   99, 130

APPC (continued)
   SECURELOC parameter   237
   security on DB2 for OS/400   228
   SQL/DS AS   276
   token-ring support   73, 78
   TPN   520
   trigger   42
APPC verb   182
APPC/VM VTAM support
   See AVS
APPCLLU environment variable   106
APPCPASS statement   258, 273
APPL statement
   DB2 for MVS/ESA   295, 299
   LU name   184
   VERIFY parameter   152
application
   adopt authority   444
   AS/400 requirements   442
   C considerations   330
   COBOL considerations   332
   development   41, 319
   development language   329
   enhancements for DB2 for OS/400   452
   environment for DB2 for OS/400   242
   execution DB2 for OS/400   230, 449
   function   351
   independence   40
   integration with advanced technology   40
   maintenance   41
   porting   338
   program preparation for DB2 for
      OS/400   441
   recompiling   453
   source code   354
   table definitions   351
   tables   245
   terminating   339
application requester
   See AR
application server
   See AS
APPLID   280, 289

DUW *(continued)*
    TM_DATABASE   82, 158
dynamic calling link station   161
dynamic definition   59, 520, 522
dynamic independent LU definition   107,
  172
dynamic partitions   290
dynamic SQL statement
    authorization checking   35, 151
    CLI   16
    packages   317
    portability   338
    privileges   151, 274, 294
    SPUFI   308
    stored procedure   33
    stored procedures   29
DYNAMICRULES option   29, 35, 317

E

EBCDIC   344
embedded SQL   209, 330, 343, 451, 476
ENCINA   53, 319, 323, 384
encryption
    CAE/DOS   211
    DB2 for MVS/ESA   313
    password   211
ENCRYPTPSWDS column   313
END DECLARE SECTION   358
ENGLISH character set   499
ENQUEUE services   36
environment variable
    DB2 for AIX connectivity options   158
ERROR ALLOWED option   211
error conditions   275, 294
errors
    BIND PACKAGE command   485
    CRTSQLPKG command   458
    for VM AR   260
    for VM AS   275
    for VSE   294
    handling   342
    logging for VSE   281

Ethernet   171
EXCI   35
executable module   405
EXECUTE privilege   151
EXECUTE statement   151
EXPLAIN   22, 466
explicit authorization   151
export   125
extended interface   161
EXTRACT_FMH5   194

F

fencing   38
FETCH statement   20, 22, 24, 236, 335, 338,
  348
FFDC   231, 527
FFST/2   528
file extension   399
file server   159
file server addressing   82, 206, 207, 208
FILESERVER   82, 159
FileTek, Inc.   8
First Failure Data Capture
    See FFDC
First Failure Support Technology
    See FFST/2
flagger   17
FLOAT   37, 336
folding   144, 197, 198, 499
FOR BIT DATA   516
FOR FETCH ONLY cursor   349
FOR FETCH ONLY option   422
FORCE command   291
FORCEIN option   515
Fortran   17, 38, 329, 341, 400
FTP TCP/IP   210

G

GCS machine   264
GENERIC column   305
generic LU   170, 302, 305

instance *(continued)*
    DB2INSTANCE environment
      variable   113
    DDCS owner   197
    down-level clients   135
    multiple   113
    owner primary's group   194
    TCP/IP support   214
instrumentation facility interface   27
INTEGER   37, 332, 337
Intel   11, 14, 50
internal calls   531
internal trace data   536
INTERNATIONAL character set   501
internet domain   213
Internet Engineering Task Force
    See IETF
internetwork address   206, 208
Internetwork Packet eXchange/Sequenced
  Packet eXchange
    See IPX/SPX
interrupt   131, 133, 193, 203, 205, 214
interrupt handling   124
invalid TPN   260
invariant characters   442
ioctl call   194
IP address   205, 206, 213
IPX_SOCKET FILESERVER
  OBJECTNAME parameter   82, 158
IPX/SPX
    AIX client   159
    CAE/DOS   210
    client communication setup   201
    client workstation   207
    configuration   206
    DB2COMM environment variable   202
    DDCS gateway support   47
    DOS client   209
    Intel-based servers and clients   15
    OS/2 connectivity option   82
    server workstation   207
    Windows client   73
ISC   276, 280

ISO   6, 498
ISO/ANSI   27
ISOLATION
    BIND PLAN command   481
isolation level
    BIND command   409
    binding DDCS utilities   127
    COMMIT processing   466
    DB2 common server   402, 410
    DB2 for OS/400   22, 235, 444
    DRDA level 2   327
    escalation   347
    integrity and data protection   13
    ISOLATION option   481, 484
    ISOLATION parameter   402
    no commit   22, 235, 347, 402, 410, 485
    read-only operations   481
    supported in IBM products   346
ISOLATION option
    BIND PACKAGE command (DB2 for
      MVS/ESA)   484
ISOLATION parameter
    DB2 PREP command   402
ISQL   245, 253, 463, 470
IUCV *IDENT   265, 266
IUCV *IDENT S34VMDB0 GLOBAL   265
IUCV ALLOW   266

J

joblog   230, 231, 233, 247, 248
join   12, 50
journaling   235

L

LAN Adapter and Protocol Support
    See LAPS
LAN Server 3.0   202
language   329
LANGUAGE column   34
LAPS   92
large object support   13, 17

M

N

OWNER parameter *(continued)*
    binding from DB2 for MVS/ESA to DB2
      common server 491
    binding from DB2 for MVS/ESA to DB2
      for OS/400 493, 494
    binding to DB2 for OS/2 151
    DB2 for MVS/ESA 306
    DB2 PREP command 402

P

pacing 181, 297, 518
PACKADM authority 35, 316
package
    ACTION option 400
    BIND command 405
    BIND PACKAGE command (DB2 for
      MVS/ESA) 482
    binding from DB2 for MVS/ESA 306
    binding from DB2 for MVS/ESA to DB2
      common server 489
    binding from DB2 for MVS/ESA to DB2
      for OS/400 491
    binding from DB2 for MVS/ESA to
      SQL/DS 493
    binding in DB2 common server 422
    binding in DB2 for MVS/ESA 416
    binding in DB2 for OS/400 418
    binding in SQL/DS for VM and
      VSE 420
    CAE/DOS 211
    collection considerations 411
    compatibility with DB2 for
      MVS/ESA 13
    considerations for DB2 for
      MVS/ESA 486
    CONTROL privilege 151
    creating from SDK for Windows 425
    DB2 for MVS/ESA plan 477, 478
    DB2 PREP command 401
    DSNESM68 305
    dynamic change of the collection 411
    dynamic SQL statement 317
    information 454

package *(continued)*
    local authorization to bind or execute
      remote 149
    management DB2 for OS/400 453
    security 316
    SPUFI 305
    version 401, 409, 484
PACKAGE option 405
parallel data access 23
PARMLIST column 34
PARSESS parameter 279
partitioned table spaces 465
partitioning 12
partner location profile 177
partner LU
    CM/2 107
    configuring for APPC 99
    CPIC side information 111
    DB2 for AIX as an AS 190
    DDCS for OS/2 security 144
    profile 130, 174
    security for DB2 for OS/2 AS 150
    session level security 200
    SNA connectivity parameters 520
PASSWORD column 311
PC/IXF format 515
performance
    block fetch 348
    character conversion 498
    DB2 for OS/400 22, 231
    DB2 Parallel Edition 52
    DRDA level 2 319, 323, 360
    enhancements 12
    JOBLOG 248
    MAXDATA/MAXBFRU 519
    monitor 18
    network 177
    pragma link statements 447
    RDS 53
    SNMP 529
    statistics 464
    stored procedures 19, 39
    SVA 277
    system management 5

programmer authority on DB2 for OS/400
  AS 241
programming language support 17, 329, 467
programming languages 27, 329
Progress Software Corporation 8
project management 4
protected conversation 325
protocol
  APPC 116, 123, 144
  AVS 266
  CHARNAME 499
  commit 82, 412
  commitment control 328
  communication 196, 201, 210
  DB2COMM environment variable 136, 213
  dependent LU 176
  devices 519
  DLC 167
  DRDA 45, 123
  errors 233
  exchange 92
  IPX/SPX 206
  LOGMODE 518
  LU 6.2 56
  migrate DRDA level 1 to DRDA level 2 360
  NetBIOS 203
  network 81, 157
  performance 360
  private xxii, 29, 53, 201, 386
  PTFs 56
  server client combination 14
  SQL/DS 253, 275
  SQLINIT 252
  TCP/IP 131, 424
  token ring 73, 78
  two-phase commit 53, 320, 383, 403
PROTOCOL option 498
PROTOCOL parameter 253, 271, 468
PRTSQLINF command 451, 467
ps command 526
PU
  control point profile 171

PU *(continued)*
  establish a conversation 60
  SNA connectivity parameters 517
  VTAM definition 521

Q

QAPPNLCL 223
QAPPNRMT 223
QSYS2.SYSPACKAGES 419, 491
QUALIFIER parameter
  BIND command 410
  BIND PACKAGE command (DB2 for MVS/ESA) 484
  BIND plan command 480
  binding from DB2 for MVS/ESA to DB2 common server 491
  binding from DB2 for MVS/ESA to DB2 for OS/400 493, 494
  binding in DB2 common server 423
  binding to DB2 for OS/2 151
  DB2 for MVS/ESA 306
  DB2 PREP command 402
query governor 23
QueRY parameter 499
query rewrite 12

R

RACF
  DB2 for MVS/ESA AS 312, 313, 315
  DDCS for AIX clients 197
  encryption 313
  session-level security 258, 273
  stored procedures 35
RDB directory
  ADDRDBDIRE command 234
  DB2 for OS/400 224
  LU 6.2 TPN profile 193
RDB_NAME
  DB2 for MVS/ESA 298, 303
  DCS directory 119, 124
  platform mapping 522

SNA *(continued)*
    CDRM   518
    CDRS   518
    communication trace parameter   233
    configuring the profiles   165
    connectivity parameters   517
    conversation security   237, 302
    CP   519
    definitions   517
    domain   518
    flow exchanged   535
    local node characteristics   93
    log files   535
    LOGMODE   518
    logon mode table   518
    MODETAB   518
    NAU   517
    NETID.LUNAME   224
    node   517
    OS/2 connections   95
    parameters   519
    parameters cross-reference   522
    profiles relationship   163
    security levels   228
    sense code   539
    start   187
    subarea   517
    supported AS/400 link protocols   218
    testing connection   534
    trace   534, 535
sna command   162, 174, 187
SNA Gateway/6000 V2   161
SNA node profile   191, 194
SNA Server/6000 profiles
    DB2 for AIX as an AS   190
SNA Server/6000 Version 2.1   160
snactl call   194
SNADS   228, 238
SNASVCMG COS   181
SNASVCMG mode   539
SNI mode   267
SNMP   13, 529
software
    AIX configuration   159

software *(continued)*
    configuration   71
sort order   343
SPAS   30, 32, 36
special registers   333
SPM
    commitment coordination   48
    DB2 common server   383
    DRDA level 2   320
    protected conversation   328
    two-phase commit   24, 326
SPUFI   305, 308
SQL
    ATOMIC compound   19
    CALL statement   33
    CONNECT statement   230
    FETCH statement   348
    interface   16, 442, 447
    NOT ATOMIC compound   19
    processing messages   525
    statements to maintain the CDB   300
SQL option
    DB2 for MVS/ESA precompiler   476
SQL processing using file input
    See SPUFI
SQL/DS
    *SQL naming mode   444
    AR for VM   459
    ARISDBMA EXEC   252, 270
    ARISSLKE EXEC   270
    binding from DB2 for MVS/ESA   307
    blocking   347
    catalog requirements   459
    CHARACTER data type   467
    column functions   333
    COMDIRC   473
    CONNECT statement   468
    continuous block fetch   348
    CTOKEN   469
    database definitions for VSE   287
    DBSU   253, 470
    dynamic partitions   290
    embedded   330, 343, 451
    error handling   342